Year	12. Trivia	13. Prices	14. Misc. Prices	15. Car Prices	16. Tuition	17. Recap	18. Firsts	19. Winners	20. Films	21. TV	22. Books	23. Comics	Year
1954	7	247	256	260	263	266	270	281	285	293	308	330	1954
1955	12	to	256	to	to	to	270	to	to	293	to	331	1955
1956	17	255	256	262	265	269	271	284	292	294	329	331	1956
1957	25	(inc.)	256	(inc.)	(inc.)	(inc.)	271	(inc.)	(inc.)	294	(inc.)	331	1957
1958	32		256				272			295		331	1958
1959	39		256				272			295		332	1959
1960	46		257				272			295		332	1960
1961	53		–				273			296		332	1961
1962	60		257				273			296		332	1962
1963	66		257				273			297		332	1963
1964	75		–				274			297		333	1964
1965	86		257				274			298		333	1965
1966	96		257				274			298		333	1966
1967	107		257				275			299		334	1967
1968	116		–				275			299		334	1968
1969	127		257				275			300		334	1969
1970	138		257				276			300		334	1970
1971	146		258				276			301		335	1971
1972	154		258				276			301		335	1972
1973	162		258				277			302		336	1973
1974	170		258				277			302		–	1974
1975	178		258				277			303		336	1975
1976	185		–				277			303		336	1976
1977	193		258				277			303		336	1977
1978	202		258				278			304		336	1978
1979	214		259				278			304		336	1979
1980	227		259				279			305		337	1980
1981	244		259				279			306		337	1981

YEAR BY YEAR
IN THE
ROCK ERA

YEAR BY YEAR IN THE ROCK ERA

Events and Conditions Shaping the Rock Generations That Reshaped America

HERB HENDLER

GREENWOOD PRESS
Westport, Connecticut • London, England

Library of Congress Cataloging in Publication Data

Hendler, Herb.
  Year by year in the Rock Era.

  Bibliography: p.
  Includes index.
  1. Rock music—Miscellanea.   2. Music and society.
3. Music, Influence of.   4. United States—Social life
and customs.   I. Title.
ML3534.H45 1983   784.5'4'00973   82-11722
ISBN 0-313-23456-6 (lib. bdg.)

Library of Congress Catalog Card Number: 82-11722
ISBN: 0-313-23456-6

First published in 1983

Greenwood Press
A division of Congressional Information Service, Inc.
88 Post Road West
Westport, Connecticut 06881

Printed in the United States of America

10 9 8 7 6 5 4 3 2

To my wife, Dot, and Dorothy R. MacLeod, the "backstage" combination that made all of this possible.

Contents

The Rock Era by Category

Preface _____

This is not, as one might expect from its title, a book about rock music. Rather, it is about the history, sociology and economics that influenced and were influenced by the rock generations. Although rock music is the core of this book, the chronological history of rock artists, songs, records and events that left their mark is condensed into about one-tenth of the text. The other nine-tenths is concerned with covering a broad spectrum of factual detail about every possible aspect of American life related to the music—from the beginnings of the Rock Era until what now could be considered its end.

In keeping with this announced purpose, any reader seeking analyses, observations, and subjective opinions about the music and its people will find over three hundred volumes listed year by year under the category heading "American Books about Artists and Music in the Rock Era" as a further reference point. Rock music was the germ of creation for those books. But, to a much larger sociological extent, it had major effects on teen and college living and the alternative life styles of almost three generations. These in turn influenced everything from major news happenings to fashion, films, television, books, modern language, fads, and to an extent, the new emancipation of women.

Equally important are the correlations of accelerating statistical fact and the annual inflation in the price of everything from cars to carrots, as well as chronological data about changes in social dancing, comic strip art, and some of the trivial happenings along the way that so clearly reflect the tastes and moods of a people.

Rock music, which was at the root of the new youth culture, provided a background for its new-found voice. From the start, the expressed purpose of this book was to illustrate the era in minute detail. Therefore each chapter covers as large a variety of related subjects as each major focus allows. Since sociological and historical changes often result from incidental influences, rather than from those that might appear to affect them directly at the time, items that may seem trivial during the year they occur are included for the impact they had on later events.

As a reference tool, the text of this work is totally devoted to extracted fact. It offers every single possible positive and negative aspect in its twenty-eight-year coverage of the Rock Era. To put the factual matter into its proper context, the author devotes some of the Introduction to personal opinion.

Along with the reciprocal influences of events, the major guidelines and criteria for the author's comments about the rise and fall of the Rock Era in the following Introduction fall under four umbrella objectives:

1. What was the extent of excitement for new offerings in the 11 of 23 included categories devoted to new products and customs?

2. What was the quality of the excitement for those new offerings?

3. What was innovative and what wasn't?

4. Was there a positive quality to the freshness of important departures?

The book starts in 1954, which is generally agreed upon as the beginning of the Rock Era. Its end is subject to debate. Some claim it was 1968, or 1970, or 1971, when the youth explosion of the 1960s—partially created by the "war baby" population boom—lost much of its impetus, excitement, and style-setting influence. Others contend that it hasn't ended yet but is still continuing in full force—just going through a new phase. In fact, the reader could easily find a great deal of data in the text to refute the allegation that 1982 was the turning point. Yet the short-lived influences of disco and punk rock—two of the few departures from rock rehash in the 1970s—seemed to signal the end of the Rock Era, or at the very least a change in direction that is still evolving. Each argument has its own validity.

Introduction _____

Early in 1982 radio station WABC in New York City switched from rock music to a mostly-talk format. This was hardly an earthshaking event, but it certainly was a significant one, for it marked the end of what future sociological historians may well look back on as the Rock Era. There is little doubt that rock music will survive for many years to come, but when the leading rock music station in America put the music aside for talk, it had very good reason for doing so.

As audience interest dropped in the Top 40 music they were playing, so did their ratings and their annual billings—in the neighborhood of $9 million four years earlier, these had plunged to half that amount. WABC was the prime example of what was happening all over the nation. According to the show business bible *Variety* on December 16, 1981, Top 40 AM radio stations were becoming an endangered species.

Rock music had crashed its way into the American music scene in 1954 via AM radio, which soon became ruled by tight-format programming. Most top-rated stations began devoting a majority of their airtime to hits—the Top 40, then eventually only the Top 30 or 20. WABC was their undisputed leader.

The switch from rock to talk twenty-eight years later by the nation's top music station is only one illustration of the entire climate of change. From 1954 to the early 1970s, rock music influenced almost every aspect of American life. During the wind down in the 1970s and early 1980s, what rock had wrought in the accelerating 1950s and tumultuous 1960s still affected cultural aspects that were virtually ruled by the music and its youthful following in those decades. But, in almost every aspect of American social life—from fashions and fads to films and television—there was a gradual decline in the rock/youth impact.

Rock music's significant contribution in its initial stages was that it gave American youth a unified voice for the first time in the nation's history. And, as the news influenced youth—from the election of President John F. Kennedy to the pull-out from Vietnam—one of the most powerful influences on the news of that period was youth itself. In the different categories shown year by year from 1954 through 1981, this book shows the striking parallels between that particular style of popular music and both the history and culture of a nation.

This book is the product of its Bibliography, which was derived from sifting through several thousand books and periodicals containing historical, sociological and economic references within its time and subject parameters. Every item is based on documented fact and placed in its proper year by an authentic source. There are no footnotes, but the Bibliography contains the names of many researchers and reporters in its upwards of 350 listings. This volume could actually stand as many separate source books, each of which could be expanded upon from its own particular references.

All of the references offer as much material as possible for the pros and cons on this subject. The author has expressed his opinions only in the front matter and in his selection of the youth-related materials. Some may question the years an artist, dance, slang word or fashion emerged, especially if they have special expertise in the field. Because there is considerable divergent information amongst authorities in the sources consulted, the text is based on totally objective admissible data. Readers are left to draw their own conclusions as they follow the chronological evolvement of the Rock Era.

Rock music is far from dead. In twenty-eight years it was never threatened by replacement. Tomorrow an artist with the magnetism and stature of Presley or the Beatles could emerge and begin an entirely new Rock Era. Rock lasted for nearly three decades, whereas the Swing Era peaked out in ten years. Launched by Benny Goodman in 1935, swing essentially died at the end of World War II when millions of servicemen came home to find the mellow dance bands they remembered bopping and playing a different kind of hard-driving swing. After a brief reappearance in the early 1950s, it faded from the scene. Rhythm & blues and country music—the forerunners of rock music—took over.

The big bands are not about to come back. Long before the wild inflation of the 1970s and 1980s rock had changed the economics of music from a dozen or so musicians plus singers to the three or four self-contained singing musicians of a small group. With the escalation of union scales since the dance band years, it is not likely that bigger will ever be better again.

Since rock has already incorporated the other two major forces in U.S. music—country and rhythm & blues—there is nothing from the past to replace rock as rock did swing. And the fast-dying "hype" items of the 1970s, glitter, disco and punk (new wave), certainly proved that contemporary American youth refuses to be overpowered by efforts of the music-record industry, disc-jockey radio, music press, and others who may try to capitalize on the insubstantial images created by the "trendies." Today's young people won't universally accept what hasn't evolved into mass appeal naturally. Perhaps the historical data in this book will "cast a shadow" as to what might become the prefix word for the next era.

By 1982, America was moving away from rock and into a new home video culture as the nation avidly embraced cable TV, videocassettes, videodiscs and video games. At the same time, the preppies were influencing the youth culture in a manner similar to, if not as all-sweeping as, the hippies. But as the accompanying chart shows, a significant segment of the population—those between twenty and fifty—grew up on rock. The sixteen-year-olds of 1954, who gravitated to rock at its beginning, are now in their early forties and had spent the better part of their life in a rock-oriented society. For them, rock is indeed not dead, for some radio stations still feature the rock of the 1950s and 1960s, and the records and tapes they accumulated are totally compatible with the stereo and hi-fi equipment of the 1980s.

In other words, the chart indicates that there may not be a musical "generation gap" in whatever "era" future historians and sociologists will look back on as having followed the Rock Era.

Age During the Rock Era

Note: If a person's age was 10 in 1954, they were 38 in 1982—as shown below. Those 21 in 1954 were 49 in 1982—and, as the chart shows, 49 is the oldest age of all the 10-21-year-olds between 1954 and 1982—still very much conversant with the Rock Era.

Age   **Years of the Rock Era**

Age	1954	1955	1956	1957	1958	1959	1960	1961	1962	1963	1964	1965	1966	1967	1968
10	38	37	36	35	34	33	32	31	30	29	28	27	26	25	24
11	39	38	37	36	35	34	33	32	31	30	29	28	27	26	25
12	40	39	38	37	36	35	34	33	32	31	30	29	28	27	26
13	41	40	39	38	37	36	35	34	33	32	31	30	29	28	27
14	42	41	40	39	38	37	36	35	34	33	32	31	30	29	28
15	43	42	41	40	39	38	37	36	35	34	33	32	31	30	29
16	44	43	42	41	40	39	38	37	36	35	34	33	32	31	30
17	45	44	43	42	41	40	39	38	37	36	35	34	33	32	31
18	46	45	44	43	42	41	40	39	38	37	36	35	34	33	32
19	47	46	45	44	43	42	41	40	39	38	37	36	35	34	33
20	48	47	46	45	44	43	42	41	40	39	38	37	36	35	34
21	49	48	47	46	45	44	43	42	41	40	39	38	37	36	35

Age	1969	1970	1971	1972	1973	1974	1975	1976	1977	1978	1979	1980	1981	1982
10	23	22	21											
11	24	23	22	21										
12	25	24	23	22	21									
13	26	25	24	23	22	21								
14	27	26	25	24	23	22	21							
15	28	27	26	25	24	23	22	21						
16	29	28	27	26	25	24	23	22	21					
17	30	29	28	27	26	25	24	23	22	21				
18	31	30	29	28	27	26	25	24	23	22	21			
19	32	31	30	29	28	27	26	25	24	23	22	21		
20	33	32	31	30	29	28	27	26	25	24	23	22	21	
21	34	33	32	31	30	29	28	27	26	25	24	23	22	21

THE ROCK ERA BY YEAR

The first part of this book is arranged year by year with the same categories under each year, except in the few cases where no information was applicable to a certain category in a particular year.

ARTISTS

Performing artists who surfaced and/or caught on at the time are listed first for each year, giving the history of Rock & Roll at a glance. Rock groups; rock solo performers; soul, R&B, and funk groups; soul, R&B, and funk solo performers; folk & country; young teen oriented; and middle of the road are listed under many of the years 1954-1981. Comic novelties, bubblegum, disco, and other categories are included for the relatively few years of their popularity.

Artists are listed under the one heading that best describes their popular image. Although Fats Domino and Bo Diddley performed with backing groups, their images were primarily solo. Others, such as Bill Haley and His Comets and Frankie Lymon and The Teenagers, were more widely known as groups. Those listed under "Rock Groups" or "Rock Solo Performers" may have had primarily rock, folk-rock, rock & roll, or heavy metal images. Many mainstream rock artists had pre-1954 rhythm & blues origins but crossed over and had hits on the pop charts early on. Artists who performed R&B, soul, funk, or folk and country hits predominantly are included in these different categories, although they may have had subsequent No. 1 hits on the pop charts as well. Artists who made the pop charts mostly through the support of the very young and subteens were rarely popular with older listeners but sold millions of records nevertheless.

These lists of artists are a synthesis of the many rock histories, encyclopedias, periodicals, and other reference works covered by the author during his research. Few of them included the same artists, categorized them similarly, agreed on the years of emergence, or were anywhere near as substantially in agreement as other types of historical or encyclopedic work.

Inclusion and placement in these lists were determined by a correlation of many factors, including, but not limited to, the arrival of the artist's first hit on the pop charts, since some star performers never had hit single records. Also considered were how high a hit got, whether it merited a gold record, whether there were any followup hits, how other rock historians rated the artist's worth, and whether the artist lasted long enough to make an impression. Selectivity was required since in a typical year, 1970, 5,265 new single records were released (mostly by different artists), of which 242 got into the Top 100. A similarly long list of albums were released that year. Some of the artists could be said to have "emerged" through these releases—alongside of those already "in," as the long list of artists' names in this category so vividly illustrates.

In the year-by-year breakdown, this "Artists" category has an obvious direct relationship with "News of Rock" and "Juke Box Hits" during any given year. But, more important, the type of artist emerging and what she or he represented was often influenced by "Some of the News That Influenced the Rock Era," or "Teen and College Living and Alternative Life Styles," or "The New Woman in the Rock Era." Along with these major parallels, there was an exchange of momentum with just about every other element covered by this book—just as each of these elements will be seen to have acted and reacted with each other.

JUKE BOX HITS

The records listed for each year represent a sampling of the 200-300 annual hit single average for the years of the Rock Era. It is a consensus of gold record award listings correlated with the emerging artist category and a review of different Hot 100 charts. Artists who became successful with albums rather than hit singles do not appear here and singles by hitmakers such as Presley, the Beatles and Motown are limited, since they would dominate the sampling if all of their big records were shown.

Rock & roll, soul, rhythm & blues, folk, novelty, country and young teen oriented hits are all mixed together as they would be on any juke box. Middle of the road and phase making product is generally not included to put the focus on the continuity of rock hits by the mainstream artists of the Rock Era.

The major standard of selection for this random sample was which recorded singles were most familiar to the majority of listeners. Some became top pop hits due to an extra ethnic weight factor, but these were obviously agreeable to the mass public ear. Time was another indication— attention has sifted out many Top 10 hits that are no longer heard or remembered. They went up fast but soon disappeared.

DANCES

Most new rock dances were invented in the earlier years of the Rock Era. Just as the jitterbug and variations of the foxtrot became the basic dances of the Swing Era in its early stages (with fad dances such as the Lindy Hop, the Shag or Big Apple having their brief moments), most of the new invention emerged with the music and happened while the excitement was fresh. The Charleston of the Jazz Age, waltz steps of an earlier era and other music-dance associations followed similar patterns; there was little social dance innovation in the later stages of popularity of a particular musical form.

Although the film *Saturday Night Fever* was an enormous hit, and the soundtrack record album featuring the Bee Gees an all-time bestseller, the many varieties of disco dance steps of the mid and late 1970s (on which the film was based) never caught the general public's fancy. As a result, the disco craze was very short lived, producing few hit records or artists, other than those who had the good sense to quickly cross over into the pop market once they got a foothold with disco.

Just as World War II began the wind down of the Swing Era, the Vietnam War removed a great number of young men from the national scene, and social dancing declined. Whether by choice or circumstances, the artists emerging in the mid and late 1960s were more concert directed than dance oriented.

NEWS OF ROCK

Much of the rock news in music fan publications deals with quasi-biographical items and discography (such as titles of new singles, LP selections and titles, release dates, success on Top 100 charts), as well as personnel changes in rock groups, coming play dates, how performers fared on recent engagements, future plans, and changes in recording affiliations. Although this data would naturally be of interest to rock fans specifically concerned with certain types of music or artists, few of the individual items of reported rock news carry much historical importance.

As a result, the text concentrates more on innovation, overall business aspects, important beginnings and endings, sociological factors, significant statistics, landmarks of cyclical change, indications of turning points, and news about people, places and events that would have an influence on the popular music field in general. Also included are some news-behind-the-news items. These could be considered mere gossip by those who are not close enough to the business to see the subtle influence on the overall picture of something as seemingly trite as a superstar's personal affairs, but such news items are important to the chronicles of rock and rock people.

The format for this section is the run-on approach so successfully used by gossip columnists, who are required to get the most information across in the most readable fashion in the briefest style. No attempt is made to put the material in chronological order within a year, since pinning items down to an actual date would be nearly impossible—and often insignificant. The quick-changing face of the rock scene is highly visible in just a glimpse at this category. Hardly had one type of excitement fallen in place, gaining enormous popular acceptance, than it was replaced by something else—abandoned more by those who created the acceptance (the performers) than by the audience which flocked to idolize them.

SOME OF THE NEWS THAT INFLUENCED THE ROCK ERA AND VICE VERSA

This category is the keystone of the entire work and requires little intro-duction. However, delineating the parameters set for selecting headline news and incidental items may be helpful.

Important world news was only reported if it offered a reason for cross-reference to U.S. youth. National news either had to have a past, present, or future effect on youth, or have been influenced by rock generations. (This obviously eliminated stories of crime, disaster, scandal, international relations, and finance that are included in more general historical works.) Some numerical data was considered pertinent, as were some ecological and sociological items that were essential to the chain of reference. Federal acts and Supreme Court decisions involving youth were included if they had a direct correlation to the surrounding matter.

THE NUMBERS GAME: STATISTICAL INFORMATION SHOWING HOW LIFE IN AMERICA INFLUENCED OR WAS INFLUENCED BY THE ROCK ERA

How life in America was affected by the Rock Era is reflected by statistics on population, income, education, religion, sports, housing, and consumer items such as cars, TVs, and computers. Even figures on food and drink—hamburgers, sweets, colas—as well as on the purveyors of these products are an indicator of youth preferences and tastes.

Every imaginable type of influencing factor was researched to find a set of starting numerical facts, even though comparable ending data was not available. The fact-finding was purposely more heavily researched and recorded for the final years of the era.

The focus here is on acceleration. Both the speed and size of change in some of this data is staggering in comparison to pre-rock history, and it appears to reflect the accelerating tempo of change in music preferences.

TEEN AND COLLEGE LIVING AND ALTERNATIVE LIFE STYLES IN THE ROCK ERA

American youth seemingly moved overnight from Victorian innocence to modern morality during the Rock Era. How much the music had to do with the abrupt change in moral, spiritual and ethical matters—as well as with the increased awareness and diminished hypocrisy of contemporary youth—has been thoroughly discussed in works focused on smaller segments of the Rock Era. This book offers an objective panoramic view of rock-related youth culture with descriptive details of the entire period set in their proper years.

The young displayed their tastes in the fashions and fads they created and in the comics, books, films and TV programs they supported—along with the words and phrases they added to the language. Much of their support was made possible by their families' new affluence, yet they used the fruits of this affluence to attack the very source of what put them in place to rebel.

Rather than consider them as three separate elements, teen and college living and alternative life styles were deliberately put together. Not only were they running parallel during the Rock Era, but since each naturally spilled over into the others, the overall picture gives a better idea of their influence on each other as well as on the other categories.

FASHION: CLOTHES AND THE ROCK ERA ACCENT ON YOUTH

The word "jeans" covers the entire Rock Era. It is difficult for anyone to find one other clearly defined garment in fashion history holding sway over all elements of the population—internationally—for so long a period of time. But jeans are only the bellwether of youth influence on fashion during the Rock Era. Before 1954, what youth wore was for the most part dictated by their elders, and what everyone wore was dictated by adult designers. In most civilizations from the Egyptian, Greek and Roman eras to America's Jazz and Swing eras, adults invented, developed and ruled over the stylings of everything from food and shelter to clothing and music. Here again, the Rock Era fostered a major sociological turnabout. At the same time the young began creating their own songs and music (almost to the exclusion of adults), their rebellion extended to their own physical appearance. Street and school fashion standards were created by the wearers rather than by stylists and manufacturers.

Just as adults picked up on youth-oriented music and dancing, much of what the young selected, improvised or invented as wearing apparel had an enormous influence on changing tastes in clothes, hair styles, footwear, makeup, accessories—in fact, all forms of adornment for all ages. The year-by-year rise in rock generation youth dominance of fashion, followed by a gradual diminishing effect when their musical tastes scattered into many different directions, is all here to be seen—even though it was difficult to pin specific styles to single years.

The return to classic preppy stylings at the end of the era was in perfect keeping with the overall "retread" movement of basic rock music of the 1970s. Instead of a complete reversion to pre-rock adult formality, the fashion world joined the music world in settling for a more conservative form of the "laid back" look. Quickly rejecting disco and punk "hypes" by the merchandisers, both fields began seeking out older, more comfortable modes.

FADS (MOSTLY YOUTH-ORIENTED) RELATED TO THE ROCK ERA

Stunts (cramming as many people as possible into a car), toys (Silly Putty, Davy Crockett clothes and toys), trends (decorating jalopies), and other elements of popular fan-insanity are collected under this umbrella if they were originated or subscribed to by the young of the rock generations. Toward the end of the era much attention was given to fads of the young—the latter-day media darlings of America—but during the splintered 1970s, there wasn't much fad activity. Perhaps this was due to the increase in conservatism that culminated in the 1980 elections.

SOME OF THE MORE WIDELY USED ARGOT,
JARGON AND SLANG IN THE ROCK ERA

The special vocabulary of the Rock Era is as characteristic of the rock generation as its music. The rise and fall of slang, argot and jargon invention and adoption, both in quality and quantity, is closely related to the inventiveness and acceptance of new ideas in music. Although rock generation youth was supposed to be rejecting all that came before, much of their argot had an earlier origin. Variations such as hot rod, surfer, subteen and Vietnam jargon are included both to set them into place in time, for the record, and for a comparison with the more generally accepted use and misuse of the language during the same period in which their idiosyncratic means of verbal communication were established. The sudden surge of vintage preppy language toward the end of the Rock Era followed the pattern of current leanings toward conservatism.

THE NEW WOMAN IN THE ROCK ERA

Coverage of the new woman in the Rock Era begins with 1963. Although many of the seeds were planted and many relevant events took place before that time, when leaders such as Betty Friedan came forward in the sixties, cohesive, dynamic action seemed to move with the rhythm of the Rock Era. The new woman naturally concerns women of all ages, rather than just the young. New freedoms, new thinking—much of what was being said in song lyrics, films, books and periodicals—was substantially influenced by the newly cohesive women's movement.

As college campuses erupted, women began to band together. As inequalities were revealed in other fields, sex discrimination came into brilliant focus. As youth found its collective voice, women found theirs.

While action and excitement in the Rock Era seemed to be tailing off during the late 1970s, the women's movement remained on the constant increase—despite various setbacks. Rock music will outlive the Rock Era for many years to come, and the women's movement is going to be one of the strongest of the other survivors. It, too, may have splintered in passing, but so far there is no decline in freshness of approach or continued progress into new horizons.

MOSTLY FACTUAL TRIVIA CONCURRENT WITH THE ROCK ERA

Originally intended by the author to be a humor-slanted catchall, this area took on more importance during the preparation of this book. Along with showing sidelights which are too lightweight to be included in the major categories (such as whiskey-flavored toothpaste being invented in all seriousness by an enterprising American who probably had the same dreams of success as the inventor of corn flakes, and the fact that a member of the audience of the "American Bandstand" TV show had 301 fan clubs of his own), it suggests the tragedy behind all the jokes about the Edsel car in relating how the loss to Ford was $400 million during its first year. The popularity of trivia itself was an offspring of the Rock Era, but the data included here goes beyond the usual "How many runs did Mickey Mantle score in . . . ?"

This category offers some general indication of the American sense of humor—some of the irrelevant items which came to light in the author's years of research were just too entertaining to omit.

THE ROCK ERA BY CATEGORY

The second part of this book is arranged by category for each year. In approaching these categories, it is essential to realize that they inevitably overlap and that there are many obvious parallels between them. Information given in one sometimes appears in another from a different perspective.

Every bit of available data from a variety of sources was included in these compilations. As reporting methods changed, unfortunately, gaps were created. Rather than eliminate important categories where unbroken chronological sequences were not possible, the author felt that the reader, like him, would appreciate as broad a horizontal picture of parallels as possible even though there are gaps in certain listings.

THE COST OF LIVING: PRICES THROUGH THE YEARS IN THE ROCK ERA

Although there is a wealth of information available concerning price indexes, finding actual annual average retail prices in dollars and cents is difficult. Other than many of the actual costs of foodstuffs shown from figures supplied by the U.S. Department of Labor, Bureau of Labor Statistics, the rest of the data had to be gathered piecemeal. In addition, the bureau changed its method of reporting in 1978, eliminating some of the items previously tabulated. Even though it wasn't possible to continue to update the price of those particular items, they were left in for earlier comparisons, as well as for the record. For these reasons, there are evident gaps in the material.

Was the new affluence of youth, beginning in the mid-1950s (coupled with the enormous growth in the number of young people with additional money to spend) an influence in rising costs—over and above the world-event inflationary factors? Has the runaway inflation during the latter days of the Rock Era (combined with a return to favor of vocal and instrumental stars of the 1960s—or new stars who sound like them) influenced youth's fast-changing splintered musical tastes?   These are open questions. And although the fantastic rise in the price of lamb chops might not have a direct bearing on youth culture—as with so many other items in this text—it is certainly a part of the interrelated whole.

More directly related to youth are the price escalations of records, which cost 35ᶜ to 50ᶜ in the Swing Era; candy, gum, soda pop and cones, which could then be had for the same nickel that bought cups of coffee and transit rides; and movie tickets, which used to go for well under a dollar. Although television did not override the preference of youth for its music, films, concerts and out-of-home life-styles during most of the Rock Era, escalating costs are contributing to the growing interest in home entertainment, which had already been nudged into wide acceptance by rising crime in the street. All of these factors have altered the recreational and social habits of youth today.

There is evidence that too many elements in the American way of life—food staples, gasoline, movies, clothing, appliances, vacations, a college education—are being priced out of middle- (to say nothing of lower-) class affordability. The time may have come to begin equating actual dollar and cent prices, rather than indexes, to social influences. This is the major purpose of this section.

MISCELLANEOUS NEWS ABOUT PRICES IN THE ROCK ERA

This section relates news about prices in a textual format and so includes, as its title suggests, bits and pieces of price information that are not detailed enough for the years of the Rock Era to include in the list of the previous section.

CAR PRICES

Especially important to America's youth, who are so extremely automobile-conscious, is the price of cars. Comparing the cost of the up-market Cadillacs and expensive sports cars with the favorite cars of the young shows how the acceleration of prices in this area could ultimately drastically change life for the young by putting one of their prime wants and needs in the previous four decades—a new automobile—more and more out of financial reach.

TUITION FEES AT COLLEGES AND UNIVERSITIES

Tuition fees, shown year by year at both state and private colleges and universities throughout the country, illustrate how the entire higher education system is approaching a crisis point of affordability.

RECAP AND FLASHBACK OF RELEVANT FACTS

Compiled in this list are miscellaneous statistical facts comparing consumption of goods, numbers of persons in the work force, population, income and many other items for the years 1950, 1960, 1970, and 1980.

THE FAST PACE OF FIRSTS IN THE ROCK ERA

Not only was Rock Era youth faced with staggering price rises, but the number of things a person could possibly want was growing with equal lack of restraint through those same years. For generations most youngsters were content with owning just a few things—toys, books, records, skates, a doll, a baseball glove, a watch, or a bike—and usually had only some and rarely all of these. Suddenly the Rock Era was deluged with dozens of products that were equally appealing to young and old.

This section merely touches on a sampling of new products—a fraction of what was being exposed, advertised and merchandised. To compound the problem of want and need, motivational research tools were developed that increased the desire for these products. A country once known for its frugal, enterprising people became a nation living on credit. And surely not being able to afford all these wonderful new things was a partial cause of the upward zoom in burglaries.

Along with product innovation, a variety of firsts in the area of achievement are offered to supplement the widening chronicle of obsolescence of what had so recently been accepted as a great new advance. Rock Era youth contributed to the success of many of the firsts, and, as each generation ages, they will become increasingly responsible for the continuing popularity and use of what came before versus what comes after. With this in mind, a listing was added under each year showing products celebrating their 50th, 75th, or 100th anniversary that year.

WINNERS RELEVANT TO THE ROCK ERA

Winners were selected for their affinity to youth-oriented interests. Many obvious choices were not included—such as Pulitzer and Nobel prizes and TV Emmys—because they are too distanced from the primary focus of this book. Although directly concerned with popular music, the National Academy of Recording Arts and Sciences' Grammy award winners also are not listed with this grouping because much trade opinion considers the voting structure adult-oriented and the awarding group too far removed from the rock market.

Obviously part of the scene that young America grows up with, retains interest in, and accepts (rarely disagreeing with or showing scorn for the final selections) are sports awards, the Academy Awards, the choice of Miss America, the best-seller list of books, and *Time* magazine's "Man of the Year."

National championship teams in college sports rated inclusion because, even before TV brought them into the viewing range of youngsters who rarely attended sporting events (other than their own high school games), youth often based their evaluation of U.S. educational institutions on who had the winning teams.

The Super Bowl is very much a child of the Rock Era. The enormous interest in professional football has been heavily supported by large elements of the population who grew up with rock music. And even though World Series baseball is not as directly connected with educational years as college sport, it is an annual event implanted in American youth consciousness as much as some of the hit songs that were winners at the time.

IMPORTANT FILMS IN THE ROCK ERA

Motion pictures have a powerful influence on contemporary society, and this section shows how greatly—again without historical precedent—rock generation youth affected the films of their era. As mass market films became freer in approach and subject matter, they reflected the loosening of standards and regulations. Simultaneously youth, who became the major source of income for film producers, didn't confine themselves to youth-oriented films, but crossed over to those intended for adults.

Academy Award films are singled out in this section. (Disney films—which most of the youth of the rock generation grew up on, and which their children are now enjoying—are rarely listed because their importance in adolescent development is usually pre-rock.) Both rock films and films about youth or with youth appeal are included under a separate subheading. Dramatic films with rock scores—of which there were and still are many, ever since rock became entrenched—are not included since the films were not necessarily directed at the rock generation. They appear with the money-makers if youth supported them, otherwise not at all.

Horror as well as science fiction and fantasy films deserved separate listings, not only for their effective buildup of youth audiences during the Rock Era, but also to demonstrate how this group made them into the box office blockbusters they became during the final days of the era.

While Rock Era music, fashion, fads, and slang and teen, college, and alternative life-stylings were bearing such a heavy influence on the films (and the films on them), both mass market youth and the population in general were experiencing an immense fall from the innocence which had prevailed for so many years.

GROWING UP WITH TV IN THE ROCK ERA

Rock and TV grew up together. The areas of comparison are obvious—from TV program content and theme versus that of the music, to the images created by rock stars versus those of TV heroes and heroines as both appeared and disappeared through the years. The young of the Rock Era were even more influenced by television than by movies. Although films such as *The Blackboard Jungle* and the Marlon Brando motorcycle epic *The Wild Ones* preceded the real onslaught of TV violence, the beginning of the Rock Era in 1954 was very close to the switch on the tube from westerns to urban crime. Arguments about TV violence being a prime factor in the increase of youth crime and violence from 1958 through 1981 began very early in the era.

In this section, youth-favored startups are shown side by side with the top six shows of each year. In the years following each startup, data indicates how that show fared. TV news, voluminously covered by most trade publications, is mentioned only when events featured had sociological or historical import.

One of the greatest TV influences on rock music was Dick Clark's "American Bandstand." During its period of popularity, this program is credited with the creation of hit songs and artists, the launching of many different social dances, and the outpouring of middle Atlantic state youth culture on the rest of the nation. The damaging effects of payola hearings on this and other TV rock shows, as well as the supportive acclaim which elevated rock performers to superstar status on variety shows such as Ed Sullivan's, are illustrated in the year-by-year data.

Although youth-favored shows on TV weren't necessarily about young people, the similar attributes of programs in current favor during various periods are significant indicators of changing tastes in other elements of the youth market.

BOOKS AND MAGAZINES RELEVANT TO YOUTH AND THE ROCK ERA

Unlike the youth-favored TV shows relating directly to the top six, books favored among the young only made a brief impression on the best-seller list. Although books ran far behind TV and films as an influence on the young, Tolkien, Bradbury, Kerouac, Heller, Heinlein, Schulz, Hesse, Fleming, and many other authors listed in this chronology watched their ideas spread from small cult audiences to mass youth in a very short time during the Rock Era. Their philosophical and psychological influences were far-reaching.

Beginning in 1958, books directly related to rock artists and their music began to appear. Listed here separately are books published in America about rock music and musicians. For the most part they represent a special book market and are often given a section of their own in bookstores and libraries. The book lists get longer in the 1970s, no doubt due in part to a growing nostalgia for and objective distance from 1950s and 1960s rock, on which these later books concentrate. Many of the books included have gained great popularity in the mass market.

COMICS AND COMIC STRIPS IN THE ROCK ERA

Although their influence was less than that of TV, films, and books, comics were a must as a category. As with TV, there was controversy about violence in comics and its detrimental effect on young minds. The varying fortunes of science fiction and fantasy comics—which often bore a direct relationship to films, but hardly any to TV—could be observed along with the changes in life styles and in the music itself. Underground comics, an offshoot of the psychedelic era, emerged as another element in this market.

The durability of certain pre-Rock Era comic strips and characters was remarkable—unlike offerings from other media, they were not displaced by new tastes and thinking. The fact that there were fewer generation gaps in taste in comics all through the Rock Era indicates that there are certain common meeting grounds, such as fashion and books, where adult and youth tastes can coexist without basic conflict or prejudicial thinking. Humor seems to be another of these common grounds.

Although the young vehemently rejected pre-1954 popular music when they found a desirable replacement in rock, and dropped some of their favorite dancing styles as soon as adults picked them up, they remained interested in pre-1954 comic characters, who still held sway in the 1950s and 1960s—with certain modernizations. Since they threw off so many other facets of pop culture they grew up with, why not this? Perhaps this is another harbinger of the much-touted current return to conservatism after the flamboyant years of the Rock Era.

THE ROCK ERA BY YEAR

1954 _____

ARTISTS

Rock Groups
  Crew Cuts
  Bill Haley & His Comets

Rock Solo Performers
  Bo Diddley
  Fats Domino

Soul, R&B, Funk Groups
  Clovers
  Midnighters (Hank Ballard)

Comic Novelties
  David Seville

JUKE BOX HITS

"Shake, Rattle & Roll"
Bill Haley & His Comets

"Shake, Rattle & Roll"
Joe Turner

"Sh-Boom"
Crew Cuts

"Sh-Boom"
Chords

"Gee"/"I Love You So"
Crows

"Sincerely"
Moonglows

"Sexy Ways"
Midnighters

"Lovey Dovey"
Clovers

NEWS OF ROCK

  "Sh-Boom," a rhythm & blues hit by the Chords, is first to cross over into pop bestselling song chart—and is covered by the Crew Cuts, who reach Top Ten in one week . . . First prerecorded stereo tapes . . .Presley's "That's All Right" on Sun Records hits No. 1 in Memphis, and he starts working local clubs for $10 a night . . . 63-year-old songwriter, Max Freedman, with the expressed purpose of cracking the youth market, composes "Rock Around the Clock" . . . On April 12, at New York City's

Pythian Temple, Bill Haley records "Rock Around the Clock" . . . Johnny Ace loses Russian Roulette game. His posthumous single, "Pledging My Love," becomes top hit in 1955 . . . Alan Freed lured to New York from Cleveland. Paid $75,000 a year, he makes radio station WINS No. 1 in just a few months playing "Rock'n'Roll" (a name he coined for rhythm & blues records years earlier) . . . RCA and Mercury send only 45 r.p.m. records instead of 78s to radio stations . . . After making four top rhythm & blues hits with the Drifters, Clyde McPhatter drafted into the Army . . . Following the release of Presley's first records, Sun owner Sam Phillips turns from recording black blues singers to country and rockabilly— soon launching Carl Perkins, Jerry Lee Lewis, Johnny Cash, Charlie Rich and Roy Orbison as pioneers of rock & roll . . . Fender Stratocaster electric guitar reaches market, and given a big boost by Buddy Holly, it soon becomes long-running favorite with rock groups . . . Record sales grossed $215 million last year . . . Five record companies control industry, with 42 of year's 50 top sellers going to RCA Victor (11), Columbia (8), Capitol (8), Decca (now MCA) (8) and Mercury (7) . . .

SOME OF THE NEWS THAT INFLUENCED
THE ROCK ERA AND VICE VERSA

French garrison at Dien Bien Phu falls to Viet Minh led by Ho Chi Minh. Vice President Nixon urges direct U.S. intervention . . . Secretary of State Dulles and other militants propose military intervention by carrier-based planes using small nuclear bombs—and are opposed by a coalition in Congress led by Senator Lyndon Baines Johnson . . . French withdraw from Indo-China . . . Geneva agreements divide Vietnam along Seventeenth Parallel until elections—to be held in 1956 . . . Votes for 18-year-olds defeated by Senate . . . Racial segregation in public schools declared unconstitutional by Supreme Court . . . First H-bomb explosion in test at Bikini Atoll . . . Army manpower reduced in favor of reliance on "massive retaliation," states Chairman of Joint Chiefs of Staff . . . West Germany admitted to NATO and granted sovereignty . . . Geneva summit marks thaw in Cold War . . . U.S. signs pact with Nationalist China . . . U.S. launches first atom-powered submarine . . . Tobacco industry disputes medical profession claims about causes of lung cancer . . . After a long silence, Eisenhower finally speaks out, criticizing Senator McCarthy as a man trying "to set himself above the laws of our land" . . . Army-McCarthy hearings . . . U.S. and Canada agree to construct a radar distant early warning (DEW) line . . . $4 billion cut in military budget recommended along with cut in manpower recommended by President Eisenhower . . . Dangers of fallout revealed after Marshall Islands A-bomb tests . . . U.S. and Japan sign Mutual Defense Agreement . . . Iran gives right to oil production and sales to eight companies (five American) for

50% of net profits . . . Atomic Energy Act allows peaceful development of nuclear plants by private companies . . . Senator Joseph McCarthy formally condemned by Senate vote of 67 to 22 . . . 2,480,000 school children vaccinated in Salk anti-polio vaccine test . . . Senate ratifies a Mutual Defense Treaty with South Korea . . . President signs Communist Control Act, effectively outlawing Communist Party . . . Eisenhower refuses "hawkish" suggestions by V.P. Nixon, John Foster Dulles and Admiral Radford to send troops or air power to help beseiged French in Vietnam . . . Secretary of State Dulles fails to reinstate cleared State Department officials who had been discharged in response to Senator McCarthy's attacks . . .

THE NUMBERS GAME: STATISTICAL INFORMATION SHOWING HOW LIFE IN AMERICA INFLUENCED OR WAS INFLUENCED BY THE ROCK ERA

75,000 records of Beethoven's Ninth Symphony bought, vs. 500 in 1934 . . . Asked: "How do you feel about the money you have saved up?" in nationwide poll, voting satisfied were 47% of the families with an annual income under $3,000; 34% with incomes $3,000-$6,000; and 51% with incomes $6,000 and over. Overall 42% are satisfied and 53% dissatisfied in the Survey Research Center report . . . Report states that America used more of the world's resources in the past 40 years than all the world used in 4,000 years . . . 52 million U.S. telephones in use, vs. 94 million in entire world . . . Only 154 have incomes of $1 million up, vs. 513 in 1929 . . . 10 million Bibles a year being sold—with yearly distribution up 140% in past four years . . . Gallup poll reports 94% believe in God—also that a family of four can live on $60 a week . . . 1,768 U.S. newspapers publishing 59 million copies daily . . . 29 million U.S. homes have TV . . . With only 6% of the world's population, America owns 60% of all cars, 58% of all telephones, 45% of all radio sets, and runs 34% of all railroads . . . 25 new computers sold . . . For the first time in baseball, the majority of players on one team are Negro—in the game played July 17 by the Brooklyn Dodgers . . . Among U.S. urban families, 74% say they're satisfied with their occupational progress, 68% with their standard of living, and 58% with their income . . .

TEEN AND COLLEGE LIVING AND ALTERNATIVE LIFE STYLES IN THE ROCK ERA

Campbell Soup study shows kids aged 6-14 rate foods: (1) Hamburgers, (2) Orange juice, (3) Spaghetti, (4) Frankfurters, (5) Soup, (6) Cold cereal, (7) Ketchup, (8) Macaroni . . . University of Colorado humor magazine *Flatiron* suspended for publishing pinup of co-eds . . . California Home

Economics Association poll of 10,000 high school students reveals that one-third often eat no breakfast . . . San Francisco City Lights bookshop becomes hangout and mailing address for free-floating "Beat Generation" . . .

FASHION: CLOTHES AND THE
ROCK ERA ACCENT ON YOUTH

Note: Feminine fashion is in italics, male in roman, unisex in parentheses, and news in asterisks.

Duck-tail haircuts . . . *Felt skirts with appliquéd poodles called "poodle cut outs"* . . . Dirty white bucks, blazers, flat-tops, crew-cuts . . . Wide belts, heavy black boots, black leather jackets similar to Marlon "The Wild Ones" Brando . . . **Levi Strauss makes first product departure—introduces faded blue jeans** . . . *College girls: straight skirts and matching pastel sweaters* . . . College boys: Ivy League look or pegged pants, padded shoulders and open-neck Hawaiian shirt big in Midwest . . . Teeshirt sleeves rolled over a pack of smokes . . . Pants and Bermuda shorts with buckles in back . . . *Nylon girdles with garter-top elasticized thread* . . . American Girl, *the Girl Scouts' magazine, says their subscribers using their first lipsticks, nylons and bras sooner than girls ten years ago* . . . *Max Factor's "Erace" for hiding dark circles under the eyes or skin discoloration* . . . **Ten million cakes of Max Factor Pancake makeup sold last year** . . . *Strapless evening gowns worn at proms* . . . *Cornell University study on "psychological effects of clothing" had women students whose personal inventories measured them high on the trait of dominance rating themselves high on feelings of being well dressed; while submissive women rated themselves lower in clothing appearance* . . . *Elizabeth Hawes, much ahead of the times, promotes a bra-less look in her book* It's Still Spinach—*feeling that a whole generation of women have ruined their pectoral muscles by binding their breasts after World War I to conform to the boyish look* . . . Rolled-up blue jeans and white sox . . . *Pop-it necklaces that can be changed from chokers to waist length* . . . Males of the Beat Generation wear khaki trousers and sandals. Most have beards, but their hair is short . . . *"Beat" females wear black leotards with tousled hair, no lipstick, but a great deal of eye makeup (some using so much that they are called "raccoons")* . . .

FADS (MOSTLY YOUTH-ORIENTED)
RELATED TO THE ROCK ERA

By Christmas, Davy Crockett teeshirts reduced from $1.29 to 39¢, and still not moving . . . Colleges start car-stuffing craze . . . Silly Putty hits 32 million sales total in a fifth year . . .

SOME OF THE MORE WIDELY USED ARGOT, JARGON AND SLANG IN THE ROCK ERA

Bananas, Greasers/Greasy grinds, Rocks, Skids, Weenies, Yo-yos (The over-studious and/or social outcasts) . . . Bread (money) . . . Chicks (girls) . . . Cool (acceptable) . . . Crazy (great) . . . Cube (ultimate square) . . . Drags, Nerds, Spastics, Turkeys (obnoxious people) . . . Far out (terrific) . . . Flip (accept enthusiastically) . . . Groovy (most acceptable) . . . Hairy (troublesome) . . . Hip (in tune with what's in) . . . Jobwise, Moneywise, Schoolwise ("-wise" = "regarding," "in respect of," or "in the manner of") . . . Like (all-purpose pause word and modifier) . . . Scaggy (distasteful) . . . The end (the best) . . .

Hot Rod Slang: Jack, Stormer, Screamer, Draggin' Wagon (names used for hot rods) . . . Raking (lowering front end) . . . Skins (tires) . . . Snowballs (white walls) . . . Spooking, Bombing (pleasure driving) . . . Chopping (lowering roof) . . .

Pre-1954 Jazz Vernacular: Balling (having fun) . . . Beat (tired) . . . Cat (musician, man) . . . Chick (girl) . . . Dig (understand) . . . Far out (super) . . . Funky (happy-sad) . . . Groovy (great) . . . Hep, Hip (aware of) . . . Jam (spontaneous swinging) . . . Kicks (thrills) . . . Mad (fine, capable, able, talented) . . . Pad (house, apartment, room) . . .

And in Dan Burley's Original Handbook of Harlem Jive (1944): Cool . . . Gone . . . Man . . .

"Togetherness" coined by *McCalls* . . .

"Camp" originates in Christopher Isherwood's novel *The World in Evening* . . .

MOSTLY FACTUAL TRIVIA CONCURRENT WITH THE ROCK ERA

Playboy makes it through first year—*Woman's Home Companion* ceases publication . . . Gallup poll shows average 1954 female is 5 ft. 4 in. and weighs 132 lbs. Also, 51% of all employees get no coffee breaks; 50% of adults had trouble getting to sleep; 33% said their feet hurt; half of all families use car for pleasure ride after Sunday dinner; only 25% of women prefer a shower to a bath . . . World's largest jigsaw puzzle made with 10,000 pieces to cover 10 ft. by 15 ft. area . . . Public Relations Council and motivational enthusiast E. L. Bernays reported as asserting that the most successful breakfast cereals are building crunch into their appeal to appease hostility by giving outlet to aggressive and other feelings . . . First 3-D movie, *Bwana Devil,* and first 3-D movie in color, *The House of Wax,* fail to make motion picture history . . . Actor Ronald Reagan endorses Van Heusen shirts, while John Wayne lends his name to Whitman's chocolates . . .

1955

ARTISTS

Rock Groups
  Cadillacs
  Moonglows
  Penguins
  Platters

Rock Solo Performers
  Chuck Berry
  Little Richard

Soul, R&B, Funk Groups
  Charms

Soul, R&B, Funk Solo Performers
  LaVern Baker
  B. B. King

Young Teen Oriented
  Fess Parker
  Patience and Prudence

Middle of the Road
  Pat Boone
  Georgia Gibbs

JUKE BOX HITS

"Rock Around the Clock"
Bill Haley & His Comets

"Pledging My Love"
Johnny Ace

"Earth Angel"
Penguins

"Hearts of Stone"
Charms

"Dance with Me Henry"
Georgia Gibbs

"Speedoo"
Cadillacs

"Ain't It a Shame"
Pat Boone

"Ain't It a Shame"
Fats Domino

"Only You"
Platters

"Tweedle Dee"
LaVern Baker

"Black Denim Trousers &
Motorcycle Boots"
Cheers

"Tutti Frutti"   "Bo Diddley"
Little Richard   Bo Diddley

"Maybellene"   "Devil or Angel"
Chuck Berry   Clovers

DANCES

Sock hops, record hops

Minor revival of Lindy and Charleston

NEWS OF ROCK

Haley's "Rock Around the Clock" only rock single in Top Ten of year (No. 1), but 18 out of top 42 songs were rock—many as cover versions of R&B by pop artists . . . Elvis Presley's first TV appearance on Tommy Dorsey Show . . . Arthur Murray says rock dance craze healthy for teenagers . . . New Haven, Connecticut, police chief clamps down on rock 'n' roll parties; other towns follow suit . . . Six of year's top ten jukebox records are rock . . . *Cashbox*, top music trade journal, challenges anyone to find smut in rock songs, accusing critics of finding smut in most innocent songs . . . Movie *Blackboard Jungle* makes Bill Haley's "Rock Around the Clock" a smash hit . . . Chuck Berry student at Ford School of Beauty Culture . . . James Dean killed in Porsche crash . . . Bestselling records now hitting million, vs. 500,000 just a year or two ago . . . New York DJ Alan Freed's first rock 'n' roll dances at St. Nicholas Arena draw 15,000 at $2 each . . . Radio Station WTIX New Orleans introduces Top 40 format . . . Generation of consistent record stars, like Bing Crosby, the Andrews Sisters, Tony Bennett, Doris Day, etc., swept out of hit charts by rock . . . In song lyric magazines this year, 30% of the songs focused on loneliness, 17% break-ups, and 39% traditional courtship . . . Muddy Waters introduces Chuck Berry to Chess brothers. Renamed "Ida Red" becomes "Maybellene" . . . 5,000 teenagers vs. special cops at Washington, D.C., Bill Haley concert make rock riot news . . . Columbia begins mail order record club . . . Cover versions of rhythm & blues hits are bonanza for pop stars, far outselling originals: Georgia Gibbs (covering Etta James and LaVern Baker), Crewcuts (Penguins and Chords,) Perry Como (Gene and Eunice), Gale Storm (Smiley Lewis), McGuire Sisters (Moonglows and Teen Queens), Pat Boone (Fats Domino), Bill Haley (Joe Turner) . . . RCA buys Presley's contract from Sun for $25,000 and releases first record in December . . . Deejays like "Symphony Sid" Torin (Boston), Bob "Wolfman Jack" Smith (South of the Border), George "Hound Dog" Lorenz (Buffalo), "Dr. Jive" Smalls (New York), "John R" (Nashville), Peter Potter (Los Angeles) and Al Benson (Chicago) join Alan Freed in playing original black versions of rock 'n' roll hits covered by white artists . . . Chuck Berry, Fats Domino, the Penguins, Platters and Little Richard lead crossover from rhythm & blues hit charts to join Bill Haley on pop Top 50, and rock is further established by its first year of interracial pop . . . Bill Haley's No. 1 pop record, "Rock Around the Clock," surprises industry by showing up on all-black rhythm & blues charts—reaching as high as No. 4 position . . .

SOME OF THE NEWS THAT INFLUENCED
THE ROCK ERA AND VICE VERSA

Salk perfects polio vaccine . . . Estimated 4,000 A-bombs stocked by U.S., 1,000 by U.S.S.R. . . . South Vietnam declared a republic . . . Wave of UFO sightings . . . Martin Luther King leads Montgomery, Ala., bus boycott . . . Nine prominent scientists warn that H-bomb war will end human race . . . Arco, Idaho (pop. 1,350), first community to receive electricity from nuclear plant . . . Churchill resigns . . . Perón in exile . . . U.S. Air Force Academy opens . . . Polio cases half 1952 total as result of Salk vaccinations . . . U.S. begins giving economic assistance to South Vietnam, Laos and Cambodia . . . Supreme Court relegates school desegregation to District Courts—not stipulating time limit . . . Richard J. Daley becomes mayor of Chicago . . . Minimum wage up to $1 per hour from 75¢ . . . American Federation of Labor (AFL) and Congress of Industrial Organizations (CIO) combine into AFL-CIO . . . President Eisenhower tells nation that the combination of the H-bomb and ICBMs capable of delivering it anywhere in the world means that compromise is the only basis for security . . . Ike meets with leaders of U.S.S.R., France and Great Britain in Geneva—reducing tension, but not producing any final settlements—but the President's clear differences with his Secretary of State reassure both the Russians and America's allies . . . September heart attack incapacitates Eisenhower . . . Vice President Nixon, with views similar to Dulles, doesn't exploit peace openings provided by Geneva talks . . . Stock market loses $14 billion in one day when Ike stricken . . .

THE NUMBERS GAME: STATISTICAL INFORMATION
SHOWING HOW LIFE IN AMERICA INFLUENCED
OR WAS INFLUENCED BY THE ROCK ERA

Survey Research Center reports that intentions to buy a new car within next 12 months reach all-time high . . . After-tax pay of average factory worker with three dependents around $70 a week . . . Over 7 million cars sold—a million over any previous year. Only 52,000 are imported . . . Now 1,800 shopping centers in big population shift to suburbs . . . $9 billion poured into advertising—up $3 billion in five years. Now roughly $53 a person being spent in persuasion to buy products . . . Senate Committee reports that less than 1% of all U.S. families owns 80% of publicly-held stocks in the hands of individuals . . . Now 30,000 motels or motor courts, vs. 10,000 twenty years ago . . . 3.8 million people now playing golf on approximately 5,000 courses encompassing 1.5 million acres . . . 4.4 million cars junked . . . U.S. Department of Agriculture study finds 40% of families deficient in one or more major food nutrient . . . Consumption of low-calorie soft drinks up 300% since 1952; while consumption of confectionery items down 10% since 1950 . . . Payments of more than 30 months (often 36) become the rule for buyers of new cars vs. less than 24 months last year . . . Poll reveals 61% replaced refrigerators in good condition (27% five years or less old, 16% 5-10 years old and 16% over 10) during past 18 months. Of the replaced 38% not in fully satisfactory condtion, 8% were less than 10 years old . . . In survey on worries, only 20% show concern about inflation and high prices, 15% about unemployment and 10% near-future depression or recession . . .

TEEN AND COLLEGE LIVING AND
ALTERNATIVE LIFE STYLES IN THE ROCK ERA

Five hundred University of Tennessee students in panty raid . . . Youth Research Institute survey shows teenagers prefer movies to TV, while pre-teens favor TV . . . New buying power of teenagers has top-selling records hitting a million, vs. 500,000 just a few years ago . . . New York State passes law banning sale of lurid crime and horror books to under-18s. Penalty one year in jail and/or $500 fine . . . Allen Ginsberg reads poem "Howl" at Six Gallery, San Francisco, meeting of young writers—with Jack Kerouac passing the wine—as another event calls attention to the "Beats" (discovered by the media three years ago) . . . Underground newspaper *Village Voice* sets pattern in New York for format of burgeoning alternative press to come in 1960s . . . Business majors now largest college undergraduate student population, vs. only 19.4% in 1949 . . .

FASHION: CLOTHES AND THE
ROCK ERA ACCENT ON YOUTH

Note: Feminine fashion is in italics, male in roman, unisex in parentheses, and news in asterisks.

Bouffant hair stylings (back-brushed and back-combed) . . . Roll-on deodorants . . . Peter Pan collars, sweater sets, tweed and plaid skirts, bobby-sox . . . Black denim trousers . . . *Black leotard tights, tweed jumpers . . . Stretch nylon men's socks . . .* **James Dean wears jeans in *Rebel Without a Cause*** . . . *Spiked heels, pop beads . . .* Pink and black hair for men . . . (Green hair) . . . *Petticoat collecting—wearing seven or eight at a time . . . Peroxide-streaked "ducks" in hair . . . Beat generation uniform of black stockings, short bottom-hugging skirts, duffel* *coats, long uncombed hair, becomes "Chelsea look" in London* . . . Pink men's shirts, ties, robes—even shorts . . . **Teen males clamor for haircuts. In five years, barbershop business up 24%. The up-to-25 year olds asking for Boogies, Butches, Flattops, Burrs, Crews, Mohawks, Flattop Boogies, Forward-combback Boogies, Pachucos, and Ducktails or DA (also used by girls)** . . . *Forty-inch nylon stockings to be fastened to panty-girdle* . . . **Mary Quant opens London boutique. First best-sellers are small white plastic collars to brighten black sweater or dress, selling at equivalent of 30¢ each. Also black stretch stockings** . . . *Black tights reaching to waist* . . . **More than 250 new trade marks issued in toilet preparation field** . . . **Velcro fastening invented** . . . **Revlon introduces a "Lanolite" lipstick, claiming it's the only "no-smear" available** . . .

FADS (MOSTLY YOUTH-ORIENTED) RELATED TO THE ROCK ERA

Pizza challenges hamburgers . . . Decorated jalopies . . . Davy Crockett buying surge peters out at $100 million, after selling estimated 4 million records and 14 million books . . . "Mooning" (flashing bare buttocks—especially through car windows) . . . College students set records packing themselves tightly into cars . . .

SOME OF THE MORE WIDELY USED ARGOT, JARGON AND SLANG IN THE ROCK ERA

Beast (unattractive blind date) . . . Blast off (get lost) . . . DDT ("drop dead twice") . . . Grounded (punishment: not allowed out, or forbidden to use the family car) . . . "Har dee har har" (teen response to a joke) . . . Passion pit (drive-in movie) . . . Wheels (car or motorbike) . . .

MOSTLY FACTUAL TRIVIA CONCURRENT WITH THE ROCK ERA

"Davy Crockett" TV show drives prices of coon skins up to $8 a pound . . . Altman's, New York City department store, has big run on mink-handled openers for beer cans . . . Waldorf-Astoria, New York, head waiter jailed four months with $75,000 fine for not reporting tips averaging $500,000 to $1 million a year . . . American Institute of Men's and Boys' Wear raises $2 million war chest to drive home the slogan "Dress well—you can't afford not to" as per capita ownership of men's shoes falls to a low of 1.9 pairs in 1953 compared to 2-plus pairs twenty years earlier, providing just one indication of the male apparel industry being at a standstill, while at the same time most businesses doubling sales and profits . . . First air-conditioned public elementary school opens in San Angelo, Texas . . .

1956 _____

ARTISTS

Rock Groups
  Diamonds
  Frankie Lymon & The Teenagers

Rock Solo Performers
  Bill Doggett
  Clyde McPhatter
  Roy Orbison
  Carl Perkins
  Elvis Presley
  Gene Vincent

Soul, R&B, Funk Groups
  Dells
  Five Satins
  Shirley & Lee

Soul, R&B, Funk Solo Performers
  James Brown
  Little Willie John

Folk & Country
  Johnny Cash
  Jim Lowe

Young Teen Oriented
  George Hamilton IV

Middle of the Road
  Guy Mitchell

Comic Novelties
  Buchanan & Goodman
  Nervous Norvus

JUKE BOX HITS

"Heartbreak Hotel"
Elvis Presley

"Don't Be Cruel"
Elvis Presley

"My Prayer"
Platters

"Honky Tonk"
Bill Doggett

"Fever"
Little Willie John

"I Almost Lost My Mind"
Pat Boone

"Hound Dog"
Elvis Presley

"The Great Pretender"
Platters

"Love Is Strange"
Mickey & Sylvia

"I'm in Love Again"
Fats Domino

"I Want You, I Need You,
I Love You"
Elvis Presley

"Love Me Tender"
Elvis Presley

"Blue Suede Shoes"
Carl Perkins

"Be-Bop-A-Lula"
Gene Vincent

"Why Do Fools Fall in Love?"
Frankie Lymon & Teenagers

"Blueberry Hill"
Fats Domino

"Treasure of Love"
Clyde McPhatter

"Please, Please, Please"
James Brown

"Oh, What a Night"
Dells

"Ooby Dooby"
Roy Orbison

"Born to Be with You"
Chordettes

"Long Tall Sally"
Little Richard

"Corrine Corrina"
Joe Turner

"In the Still of the Night"
Five Satins

"The Green Door"
Jim Lowe

"Let the Good Times Roll"
Shirley and Lee

"See You Later Alligator"
Bill Haley & His Comets

"I Want You to Be My Girl"
Frankie Lymon & Teenagers

"Roll Over Beethoven"
Chuck Berry

"I Walk the Line"
Johnny Cash

"Eddie My Love"
Teen-Queens

"Ivory Tower"
Otis Williams & His Charms

Novelty

"Transfusion"
Nervous Norvus

"The Flying Saucer"
Buchanan & Goodman

NEWS OF ROCK

Lennon and McCartney perform together for first time in John's group, the Quarrymen, in Liverpool . . . "Heartbreak Hotel," first Presley chart hit, reaches No. 1 in May after Elvis's appearance on Sullivan show . . . Tom Parker becomes Presley's manager . . . Presley TV appearances draw bigger audiences than Eisenhower's acceptance speech . . . Retailers sell over $20 million worth of Presley products . . . Rock concert brawls in Hartford, Washington and Minneapolis have officials seeking ban . . . Winner of Capitol Records' Presley Sing-Alike Contest, Gene Vincent, makes own record, "Be-Bop-A-Lula" . . . Buffalo DJ, Dick Biondi, fired for playing Presley record . . . 175 police needed to handle mob scene as teenagers line up at 4:00 a.m. for Alan Freed rock show at New York Paramount Theater . . . Classical pianist Artur Rubinstein singles out Neil Sedaka as best high school pianist, rewarding him with

Juilliard scholarship . . . Presley signs million dollar film contract with 20th Century-Fox for one picture a year for seven years . . . Harry Belafonte "Jamaica Farewell" starts short-lived calypso explosion. RCA and Columbia Records try to put a dent into rock 'n' roll with it, but teenagers ignore calypso, so it never gets past the adult nightclub circuit . . . Sole record release by Emanons group of "Blue Moon" doesn't register, but five years later Marcels will have huge hit with song in much the same style . . . Dick Clark takes over local TV show "Bandstand" in Philadelphia and earns over $50,000 doing personal appearance "record hops" on top of paltry salary during first year . . . On discharge from Army, Clyde McPhatter establishes precedent—as one of first members of a group to try a solo career . . . Carl Perkins grounded by long period of convalescence from car accident just after "Blue Suede Shoes" takes off . . . *Newsweek* report on Elvis Presley finds: "His bodily movements were embarrassingly specific" . . . As rock takes hold, now 25 different record companies have hits in the year's Top 50, vs. control by the Big 5 just two years ago . . . Boston religious leaders urge that rock 'n' roll be banned there, and Hartford psychiatrist calls rock a "communicable disease" and a "cannibalistic and tribalistic form of music" in predicting early downfall . . . Presley in top five of pop, rhythm & blues and country and western hit charts with "Heartbreak Hotel," then "Don't Be Cruel"/ "Hound Dog" and "Love Me Tender" . . . Pat Boone cuts cover records of Little Richard's "Long Tall Sally" as well as "Tutti-Frutti," the Flamingos' "I'll Be Home," Ivory Joe Hunter's "I Almost Lost My Mind" and Joe Turner's "Chains of Love" . . .

SOME OF THE NEWS THAT INFLUENCED
THE ROCK ERA AND VICE VERSA

JFK fails to obtain Democratic Vice Presidential nomination . . . South Vietnam President Diem refuses to hold elections . . . Soviet troops crush Hungarian revolt—50,000 killed . . . Ike defeats Adlai Stevenson for President. Nixon re-elected Vice President . . . Khrushchev denounces Stalin . . . Israel, Britain and France attack Egypt. Pressure by U.S. and Russia brings about cease-fire . . . Fidel Castro released from Cuban prison after serving sentence for revolutionary activities . . . Terrorist activities in Cyprus . . . Supreme Court rules Alabama Intrastate Bus Segregation Law invalid . . . Agricultural (Soil Bank) Act passed—paying farmers to remove croplands from production, to reduce enormous food surpluses. Measure similar to Roosevelt era Agricultural Adjustment Act . . . Supreme Court rules that public servants can't be fired, simply because they invoke the Fifth Amendment . . . One of the last privately-owned giant companies, Ford Motor Company, goes public—selling over 10 million shares to over 250,000 investors for around $650 million—the most spectacular stock distribution on record . . .

THE NUMBERS GAME: STATISTICAL INFORMATION
SHOWING HOW LIFE IN AMERICA INFLUENCED
OR WAS INFLUENCED BY THE ROCK ERA

Income of average American 50% greater than in 1929, even when allowance is made for increased prices and taxes . . . Airlines pull even with railroads in number of passengers carried . . . About 50% hold that buying on installment is "good," 33% feel it is "bad," and the rest think it has both good and bad aspects . . . People earning $5,000-$7,500 averaging $270 on life insurance premiums for policies that include savings for retirement, education, etc. Those just protecting dependents in case of death averaging $155. People earning $7,500 to $10,000 paying $320 a year for built-in savings policies and $215 for straight insurance . . . Number of drive-in theatres mushrooms to new high of 7,000 . . .

TEEN AND COLLEGE LIVING AND
ALTERNATIVE LIFE STYLES IN THE ROCK ERA

Street games (stickball, skating, etc.) virtually disappear from big cities . . . 500,000 teenagers get married—one-third of U.S. total . . . Pizza moving in on burgers as after-date snack. Rates ahead of milk shakes, malts, ice cream and coffee . . . Panty raid at University of Texas sorority house . . . Two-thirds of U.S. teenagers own cameras—take 600 million photos this year . . . International Association of Police Chiefs and National Safety Council condemn drag racing. Racers name cops "fuzz" . . . College-educated women's median individual income $2,468 a year. Only 17% employed fulltime; 41% part-time. 77% are married . . . 2,500,000 spectators watch 100,000 hot rods in official races at 130 legal quarter-mile strips. Record time 166.97 m.p.h. . . . Average freshman college girl spending $361.60 a year on wearing apparel . . . *Newsweek* survey reports that industrial recruiters are mostly looking for "dynamic conformity" in college graduates . . . Teenager annual purchasing power now $4 billion a year . . . More girls going steady at 15 than any other age . . . John Osborne's play *Look Back in Anger* opens in London—bringing media focus in U.K. and U.S. to the "angry young men" . . . Most of the Beat Generation favor Eisenhower over Adlai Stevenson in Presidential election . . . Rock music inspires teenage night clubs serving 10¢ soft drinks and hot dogs (no booze)—with music from a juke box . . .

FASHION: CLOTHES AND THE
ROCK ERA ACCENT ON YOUTH

Note: Feminine fashion is in italics, male in roman, unisex in parentheses, and news in asterisks.

Elvis popularizes open collar shirt, peg-top pants, oily "duck's tail" haircut, blue suede shoes . . . *Long hair with ponytails for girls* . . . (Dog tags for steadies) . . . *Red, green and blue-footed leotards stretching from neck to toe* . . . (Short shorts with hemlines rolled) . . . **Connecticut schoolgirl banned from school for wearing slacks. Compromise after legal battle has her wearing skirt over slacks.** . . . Presley combines Brando and Dean. Jeans, boots, leather jacket with long sideburns . . . **Tenth anniversary of bikinis** . . . *Dungarees, sweater, paperclip chain ("Dungaree Doll"); ribbons, sequinned scarves, lace trim, rubber-soled shoes ("Lipstick, Candy and Rubber-soled Shoes"); sloppy shirt with photo on sleeve ("Seventeen")* . . . Argyll socks and helmets ("Growing Up"); Teeshirts ("Daddy-O") . . . Saddle shoes . . . **Ivy League look sweeps teens. Wearing unpadded shoulders, blazers, peaked caps with back buckles** . . . *Bobby-sox turned up, not down* . . . Knee socks with Bermudas buckled in back; white buck shoes . . . *Colored sneakers, poplin rain-or-shine car coats* . . . *Aerosol cosmetic containers introduced* . . . *Full dirndl-type skirts* . . . (Levis and saddle shoes) . . .

FADS (MOSTLY YOUTH-ORIENTED)
RELATED TO THE ROCK ERA

Panty raids at U.S. colleges . . . Girls wear their steadies' high school rings on gold neckchains . . . "Captain Midnight" decoders . . . Teens freeze home phones with long calls . . . Steadies exchange I.D. tags with each other's names on them—worn on wrist or around neck . . . Enormous tail fins on cars . . .

SOME OF THE MORE WIDELY USED ARGOT,
JARGON AND SLANG IN THE ROCK ERA

The Absolute End, Bitchin', The Greatest, The Most (fabulous) . . . Cop out (v. evade, n. evasion) . . . Flip (back in fashion from early 1950s —"to flip one's lid") . . . Fuzz (police) . . . Glop (distasteful) . . . Put-on (misrepresentation) . . .

Basic Rock Lyric Argot: Hooby-shoobly . . . ootie-ootie . . . oop-shoop . . . boom boom de-addy boom . . . scoobledy boobledy bump . . .

MOSTLY FACTUAL TRIVIA
CONCURRENT WITH THE ROCK ERA

E. A. Rommel becomes first Major League baseball umpire to wear eyeglasses . . . 150th anniversary of carbon paper . . . Shunning election year controversy, Nixon confides: "I lean to the Dodgers, but my wife is a Yankee fan" . . . Grace Kelly becomes Princess of Monaco—also the first movie actress ever depicted on a postage stamp . . . Last Union Army veteran dies at age 109 . . . 19-year-old male is 1½ inches taller than 1905 predecessor—while girls are menstruating 18 months earlier . . . *The Search for Bridey Murphy* book starts amateur hypnotism craze at parties, as reincarnation believers seek former lives . . . Ten-year-old Leonard Ross youngest TV contestant to win $100,000 . . . Procter & Gamble's discovery that U.S. women change babies' diapers around 25 billion times a year results in disposable "Pampers," with sales spiraling into tens of millions of dollars a year . . . Javier Pereira dies at approximately 168 . . . Miltown tranquilizers capture the public imagination . . . University of Illinois professor tells Oklahoma dentists' convention that the man who enjoys puffing a big cigar is merely engaging in an adult form of thumb-sucking—and, perhaps to a lesser extent, cigarette smokers are doing the same . . . Endorsements, Inc., grossing nearly $1 million a year lining up endorsements of products for 400 ad agencies—all of which, the company insists, are "true" . . . Auto makers stress muted colors after going berserk with hues last year . . . National Father's Day Committee proclaims noncommercial, patriotic motif—with this year's theme: "Liberty stems from the home" . . . Piano tuner O. J. Dodd tells National Piano Tuners Convention delegates that the playing of rock 'n' roll pianists is a threat to nation's keyboards . . . Big Bopper (J. P. Richardson) breaks world record for continuous broadcasting by eight minutes over 122 hours in effort to reinstate his top position in local radio on discharge from Army . . .

1957 _____

ARTISTS

Rock Groups
  Coasters
  Danny & The Juniors
  Dell-Vikings
  Everly Brothers
  Buddy Holly & The Crickets
  Buddy Knox
  Mickey & Sylvia

Rock Solo Performers
  Eddie Cochran
  Ricky Nelson
  Jerry Lee Lewis
  Marty Robbins
  Jimmie Rodgers

Soul, R&B, Funk Solo Performers
  Sam Cooke

Folk & Country
  Bobby Helms
  Jim Reeves

Young Teen Oriented
  Paul Anka
  Tab Hunter
  Steve Lawrence
  Sal Mineo
  Tommy Sands

Middle of the Road
  Johnny Mathis
  Sonny James

Comic Novelties
  Stan Freberg

JUKE BOX HITS

"All Shook Up"
Elvis Presley

"Little Darlin' "
Diamonds

"Bye Bye Love"
Everly Brothers

"Party Doll"
Buddy Knox

"Teddy Bear"/"Loving You"
Elvis Presley

"Whole Lotta Shakin' Goin' On"
Jerry Lee Lewis

"That'll Be the Day"
Crickets

"Rock and Roll Music"
Chuck Berry

"Sittin' in the Balcony"
Eddie Cochran

"Young Love"
Tab Hunter

"Young Love"
Sonny James

"Chances Are"
Johnny Mathis

"Lotta Lovin' "
Gene Vincent

"Jailhouse Rock"
Elvis Presley

"A White Sport Coat and
a Pink Carnation"
Marty Robbins

"Come Go with Me"
Dell-Vikings

"Wake Up Little Susie"
Everly Brothers

"You Send Me"
Sam Cooke

"Teen-Age Crush"
Tommy Sands

"Silhouettes"
Rays

"Lucille"
Little Richard

"Love Letters in the Sand"
Pat Boone

"Raunchy"
Bill Justis

"Keep A-Knockin' "
Little Richard

"Searchin' "
Coasters

"School Days"
Chuck Berry

"Diana"
Paul Anka

"A Teenager's Romance"
Ricky Nelson

"Honeycomb"
Jimmie Rodgers

"At the Hop"
Danny & The Juniors

"I'm Walkin' "
Fats Domino

"C. C. Rider"
Chuck Willis

"Peggy Sue"/"Every Day"
Buddy Holly & The Crickets

"Little Bitty Pretty One"
Thurston Harris with The Sharps

"Bony Moronie"
Larry Williams

"Kisses Sweeter Than Wine"
Jimmie Rodgers

"Summertime Blues"
Eddie Cochran

"Start Movin' "
Sal Mineo

"The Stroll"
Diamonds

DANCES

The Stroll

The Bop

The Chalypso

Dick Clark's "American
Bandstand" starts introducing
new dances

NEWS OF ROCK

Many radio stations switch to Top 40 . . . Audio Fidelity releases first
U.S. stereo record, featuring Dukes of Dixieland backed with railroad
sounds . . . Major record companies try to ignore stereo . . . Youth
Research Institute poll shows parental push of calypso to replace rock fails,
with 83% of teenagers pro rock and only 3% against . . . Everlys' "Wake
Up Little Susie" banned in Boston . . . Price for Jerry Lee Lewis goes from
$12 a night to $300 after he has country hit; then to five figures when
"Whole Lotta Shakin' " makes it . . . Buddy Holly leaps onto stage and
gives impromptu performance during Presley Lubbock, Texas, appearance
—just before starting Crickets . . . Crickets pioneer use of bass, drums,
lead and rhythm guitars . . . Tom and Jerry (in 1964 to become Simon and
Garfunkel) have medium hit, "Hey Schoolgirl" . . . Final year of top ten
hit cover records has only three, vs. four in 1956, 11 in 1955 and nine in
1954 when pop artists began exploiting R&B . . . Cavern Club, a jazz
venue, opens in Liverpool . . . Thirties dance band leader, Kay Kyser,
claims 85% of U.S. public wants music with melody, and doubts whether
many understand rock . . . Buddy Holly introduces "aspirated glottal
stop," pressing vocal bands tightly together to resist air pressure from
lungs, to pop music, with "Wo-uh-ho," etc. . . . Nashville becomes pop hit
source for "rock-a-billy" via Marty Robbins, Gene Vincent, Carl Perkins et
al., as Presley leads way. Texas produces its own form of country rock via
Buddy Knox and Buddy Holly. The sound soon becomes known as "Tex
Mex" . . . Rock-a-billy performers begin to record originals instead of
relying on previous R&B hits . . . Final year of new releases on 78 r.p.m.
(in R&B market) . . . First batch of hastily-produced rock films includes
"The Big Beat," "Rock, Rock, Rock" and "Jamboree" . . . After hitting
the top in 18 months, Little Richard retires to evangelism, religious study
and gospel singing for the next seven years . . . Jerry Lee Lewis and the
Everly Brothers join Presley as leaders in the top five of all three types of
music hit charts: pop, rhythm & blues and country and western; as Buddy
Holly and Fats Domino make the top five in both pop and
R&B . . . Frankie Lymon youngest star ever to top bill at London
Palladium as U.S. rock spreads internationally . . . Paramount Pictures
buys Dot Records as film business seeks alternatives to TV competition . . .

SOME OF THE NEWS THAT INFLUENCED
THE ROCK ERA AND VICE VERSA

Russians launch Sputnik 1—first earth-orbiting satellite . . . Congress
passes Eisenhower-proposed resolution allowing him to commit U.S. power
to stop "overt armed aggression" by Reds in Mideast ("Eisenhower Doctrine") . . . Recession begins . . . Senator Joseph McCarthy dies . . .
Russian ICBM (Intercontinental Ballistic Missile) . . . Volkswagen sells

200,000 Beetles in U.S. as consumers begin turn from big cars . . . Air
Force acknowledges 414 UFO sightings . . . Last battleship mothballed
. . . Having no military of its own, Iceland formally agrees to U.S.
responsibility for its defense . . . Three leading atomic scientists say fallout
from H-bomb explosion reduced 95%, and will soon be negligible . . . For
the first time since 1875, Congress passes a bill seeking to protect black civil
rights—making interference with right to vote in national elections a
Federal offense . . . Ike sends 1,000 paratroopers to Little Rock, Arkansas,
to enforce black enrollment at Central High School . . . U.S. occupation
forces withdrawn from Japan . . . American Cancer Society and Public
Health Service issue warnings linking smoking to lung cancer . . . After
talks between Eisenhower and South Vietnam President, Ngo Dinh Diem,
Washington communiqué emphasizes co-operation against Communism
. . . Emphasis on bigness in new car models as ads stress greater length
than previous year . . . U.S. voids Michigan obscenity law prohibit-
ing sale to adults of anything with potential for "corrupting" children
. . . Supreme Court restricts right of Congressional investigating com-
mittees to questions relating to potential legislation—never to the sole
purpose of "exposing" the person's associations or views . . . Inflation
accelerates when food prices, which had been responsible for stability in the
cost of living in some previous years, join in the upward trend . . .

THE NUMBERS GAME: STATISTICAL INFORMATION
SHOWING HOW LIFE IN AMERICA INFLUENCED
OR WAS INFLUENCED BY THE ROCK ERA

Over $31 billion in currency now in circulation vs. just under $8 billion in
1940 . . . Mother's Day grossing $100 million vs. Father's Day $68 million . . . Retail prices up 60% since 1944—13 years ago . . . Close to 25%
now have more than $2,000 in reserve funds (bank deposits, currency,
securities); 20% have between $500 and $2,000; 30% have less than $500
saved, and 26% have no savings—but prior to World War II most families
had no savings or other liquid reserves . . . Number of one-family homes
owned by their occupants up by 10 million in past 11 years . . . Two-thirds
of all families in debt. Eliminating duplications, 47% had some installment
debt, 35% mortgage debt and 30% other personal debt . . . 36% of all new
cars sold bought by families owning more than one . . . Total installment
debt rise in past two years not out of proportion to income increases, so
price increases in same period not attributed to installment purchases
according to some, but other experts demand Government control over
credit to curtail "excessive" buying . . . Record 4.3 million babies born
. . . 90 million people spend approximately $2.5 billion on summer holi-
days . . . In past ten years (since World War II) the number of professional
and technical workers increased 61%, clerical workers 23%; but factory
operatives only 4.5% and laborers 4% . . . Cadillac responds to Ford's

prestige-motivated $10,000 Mark II Continental by bringing out $12,500 car . . . Over half the population vacations by auto . . . Paper:Mate introduces $50 ballpoint and Kaywoodie a $50 pipe to lift brand name prestige . . . Now one in nine adults owns stock, whereas New York Stock Exchange poll just three years ago found that only 23% of the population knew what a stock was and only 10% would even consider putting a penny in the market . . . By end of year, intentions to buy new cars heard less frequently than at any time since 1953 as a substantial portion of consumers believe a recession has developed . . .

TEEN AND COLLEGE LIVING AND
ALTERNATIVE LIFE STYLES IN THE ROCK ERA

Weekly allowance average ranges from $4.61 for 13-year-old boy to $16.65 for 18-year-old . . . Teenage average weekly income $8.50 . . . High school hops in gym big. Basketball floor covered with sawdust, but dancers required to remove shoes. "Clean-cut" kids on one side and Elvis types on other, with many chaperones, and music by local bands or records, often played by local DJ . . . Sword pins tell teen date status (pointing down means "I'm attached") . . . U.S. Office of Education publishes two-year survey revealing that Soviet scientific and technical education far ahead of U.S. . . . Columbia University psychiatrist compares rock dancing craze to 14th-century St. Vitus dance plague, where victims were unable to stop . . . In some high schools, 65% going steady . . . Remmer Purdue University study of 25,000 high school students reports: 58% see no harm in third degree police methods; 60% would censor books, newspapers and magazines; 83% approve of FBI wire-tapping; 49% believe people incapable of knowing what is good or bad for them; 38% feel nothing worse than being considered "oddball"; 46% don't want women holding public office; 80% like school . . . Steady couples dye hair same color . . . Purdue opinion poll of high school freshmen and sophomores ranks problems of major concern: Want people to like me more (54%); Get stage fright before groups (53%); Want to gain or lose weight (52%); Want to make new friends (50%) . . . University of California student launches rock paper called *Rolling Stone* . . . "No Beatniks Wanted" posted throughout San Francisco North Beach enclave after obscenity trial following publication of Allen Ginsberg's "Howl" . . . Kerouac leaves San Francisco beat scene . . .

FASHION: CLOTHES AND THE
ROCK ERA ACCENT ON YOUTH

Note: Feminine fashion is in italics, male in roman, unisex in parentheses, and news in asterisks.

Heavy sweaters with rolled white socks . . . Deep-vent shirts to expose chest . . . **Sweater girl bra reaches its peak** . . . Jeans with belt loops cut off . . . **Return of raccoon coats** . . . *The sack dress* . . . *Baggy sweaters* . . . **American Institute of Men's and Boys' Wear rejects jeans and sweatshirts as classroom garb** . . . *Straw hats with ribbon tie under chin* . . . *White wool socks (plaid buckle in back)* . . . **Levi Strauss reports rising sales** . . . **Marty Robbins record popularizes "White Sport Coat, Pink Carnation"** . . . *Double pony tail* . . . **75,000 Grand Rapids, Michigan, girls get Presley hairdos** . . . *Identical sweaters, skirts, moccasins, plus Daisy Mae Dogpatch outfits, embroidered aprons and ruffled pinafores for slumber parties* . . . *Mou-mous, loose-fitting cotton Hawaiian dresses, big on campus* . . . *Girls' seamless leotard tights* . . . **Dancers' uniforms now a multi-million dollar teen fashion favorite** . . . **$27 million worth of teeshirts, jeans, nylon scarves, charm bracelets, sneakers, nylon stretch bobby-sox, all with Presley insignia, plus lipsticks called "Hound Dog Orange," "Love You Fuschia" and "Heartbreak Pink" sold in past year** . . . *Boyfriend's high school ring on gold chain around neck worn by girls going steady* . . . **Men spending one-third amount spent by women on scented colognes, shaving lotions, etc. Total $27 million—but figured by the gallon, men using more** . . . *Newer eye makeups include iridescent eye shadow in stick form, cream mascara in a tube, and charcoal pencils instead of black* . . . **Survey of college girls: 99.7% using lipstick, 79.4% face powder, 50% using eyebrow pencil and mascara, but not regularly. Fewer used mascara** . . . **Estimated one in three women patronizing beauty shops** . . . **Journal of Home Economics reports college women want clothes to "be in large quantity" and to "look prosperous and expensive," vs. Archives of Psychology 1934 report that the desire to appear prosperous was unimportant, with the desire for conformity, comfort and economy as the leading fashion factors** . . .

FADS (MOSTLY YOUTH-ORIENTED) RELATED TO THE ROCK ERA

Frisbees . . . Bloody Mary jokes about decapitation, amputation, etc. . . . "Living Droodles": funny-face fad . . .

SOME OF THE MORE WIDELY USED ARGOT, JARGON AND SLANG IN THE ROCK ERA

Beat Generation (influenced by beatnik attitudes and customs) . . . Beatniks (Beats—see 1954; "tnik" from Sputnik) . . . Bird-dog (move in on another male's date) . . . Blast (a ball) . . . B'wana Dad (salutation) . . . Funky (down and dirty) . . . Ronchie (good-looking) . . . Shag (get moving) . . . Shook up (disturbed) . . . Straight gouge (the word) . . . Umgowa (Okay) . . .

Beatnik "hip" includes: Goof (blunder) . . . Put down (criticize) . . . Swing (belong) . . .

MOSTLY FACTUAL TRIVIA
CONCURRENT WITH THE ROCK ERA

Whiskey-flavored toothpaste is marketed . . . Ford introduces Edsel car . . . L.A. woman gets record 16th divorce . . . Sales of webbed feet for skin diving up by 250,000 . . . Mexican team beats U.S. in 11th Little League World Series . . . Replica *Mayflower II* takes 54 days to get to Plymouth Rock . . . WAC lieutenant suggests falsies for less-endowed to remove dip from uniform in front of shoulders . . . 6,270 lbs. lifted by Georgia strong man Paul Anderson, using his back to hoist a lead-filled safe and heavy auto parts . . . *New York Herald Tribune* reports boast of Chevrolet general manager: "We've got the finest door slam this year we've ever had—a big car sound" . . . Ecuador issues first foreign postage stamp to bear the likeness of a U.S. Vice President: Richard M. Nixon . . .

1958 _____

ARTISTS

Rock Groups
  Little Anthony & The Imperials

Rock Solo Performers
  Big Bopper
  Jimmy Clanton
  Bobby Darin
  Duane Eddy
  Conway Twitty
  Ritchie Valens

Soul, R&B, Funk Groups
  Chantels
  Silhouettes

Soul, R&B, Funk Solo Performers
  Jerry Butler
  Johnny Otis
  Jackie Wilson

Folk & Country
  Kingston Trio

Young Teen Oriented
  Frankie Avalon
  Jimmy Clanton
  Royal Teens
  Dodie Stevens

Middle of the Road
  Connie Francis
  Tommy Edwards
  Jerry Wallace

Comic Novelties
  Sheb Wooley
  The Chipmunks

JUKE BOX HITS

"Western Movies"
Olympics

"Don't You Just Know It"
Huey Smith & The Clowns

"All I Have to Do Is Dream"
Everly Brothers

"It's Only Make Believe"
Conway Twitty

"Bird Dog"/"Devoted to You"
Everly Brothers

"Get a Job"
Silhouettes

"Twilight Time"
Platters

"Stood Up"/"Waitin' in School"
Ricky Nelson

"Great Balls of Fire"
Jerry Lee Lewis

"Do You Want to Dance"
Bobby Freeman

"Johnny B. Goode"
Chuck Berry

"Good Golly, Miss Molly"
Little Richard

"Tequila"
Champs

"Little Star"
Elegants

"Ten Commandments of Love"
Harvey & The Moonglows

"Ballad of a Teenage Queen"
Johnny Cash

"Secretly"
Jimmie Rodgers

"At the Hop"
Danny & The Juniors

"Yakety Yak"
Coasters

"Wear My Ring Around Your Neck"
Elvis Presley

"Rockin' Robin"
Bobby Day

"Poor Little Fool"
Ricky Nelson

"Lollipop"
Chordettes

"To Know Him Is to Love Him"
Teddy Bears

"Peggy Sue"
Buddy Holly

"A Lover's Question"
Clyde McPhatter

"Donna"
Ritchie Valens

"Lonely Teardrops"
Jackie Wilson

"Who's Sorry Now"
Connie Francis

"High School Confidential"
Jerry Lee Lewis

"Just a Dream"
Jimmy Clanton

"Tom Dooley"
Kingston Trio

"Sweet Little Sixteen"
Chuck Berry

"Book of Love"
Monotones

"Tears on My Pillow"
Little Anthony & The Imperials

"Short Shorts"
Royal Teens

"Splish Splash"
Bobby Darin

"Rebel 'Rouser"
Duane Eddy

"What Am I Living For"/"Hang Up My Rock & Roll Shoes"
Chuck Willis

"Chantilly Lace"
Big Bopper

"For Your Precious Love"
Jerry Butler and The Impressions

"Try Me (I Need You)"
James Brown

"Rumble"
Link Wray

"Maybe"
Chantels

"Problems"
Everly Brothers

"Whole Lotta Lovin'"
Fats Domino

"Queen of the Hop"
Bobby Darin

"Don't"/"I Beg of You"
Elvis Presley

   Novelty

"Witch Doctor"
David Seville

"Pink Shoelaces"
Dodie Stevens

"The Chipmunk Song"
David Seville & The Chipmunks

"The Purple People Eater"
Sheb Wooley

DANCES

The Twist (early days)

The Walk

The Shake

The Fish

NEWS OF ROCK

Elvis becomes No. 53310761 in U.S. Army . . . Introduction of stereo albums by major companies . . . Alan Freed indicted for rock riot in Boston . . . KWK St. Louis announces intention to break rock records one by one on the air . . . Moscow press deplores rock . . . Bulgaria opens drive against rock . . . Alan Freed shows face cancellation in New Haven and Newark after violence at his Boston show . . . Editorials against Freed in nation's leading papers—but his New York Paramount show opens in peace . . . CBS A&R head Mitch Miller advises parents to tell kids they like rock, "then they'll surely drop it" . . . George Harrison joins Lennon and McCartney in the Quarreymen at Liverpool club run by mother of footballer George Best . . . Kingston Trio's "Tom Dooley" hit starts folk revival—and split between ethnics and popularizers . . . 14,000 at first Newport Folk Festival . . . A French actress playing opposite Pat Boone, Gary Crosby and Tommy Sands in film says they'd like to be wolves but they're too insincere to know how . . . Phil Spector forms Teddy Bears to record song taken from epitaph on his father's tombstone, "To Know Him Is to Love Him" . . . First transistor radios hit the market . . . Mutual network joins NBC in banning rock 'n' roll . . . Yakkety sax sound becomes popular . . . Duane Eddy creates twangy guitar (melody on bottom strings) . . . Muddy Waters tours England, influencing growing generation of British rockers . . . Kingston Trio's "Tom Dooley" sales hit two million as folk craze explodes . . . At peak of fame, Jerry Lee Lewis marries 14-year-old cousin, Myra, and runs into career difficulties . . . Classic doo-wop rock, as spawned by the Clovers, Charms, Frankie Lymon, Penguins, Platters, Coasters and their contemporaries gives way to modifications and alterations after previous vintage year . . . Rock music gets firm foothold in New York City "Tin Pan Alley" as Al Nevins and Don Kirschner establish Aldon Music to compete with the publishers of Cole Porter, Rodgers & Hammerstein, Irving Berlin, the Gershwins and the other professional songwriters who monopolized the pop charts for three decades. Neil Sedaka's "The Diary" by the performer and Howard Greenfield hits No. 14—setting the stage for an almost total takeover of the "Alley" by them, Carole King and Gerry Goffin, Barry Mann and Cynthia Weil, Jeff Barry and Ellie Greenwich, Doc Pomus and Mort Shuman, Leiber and Stoller, Neil Diamond, Bobby Darin, Gene Pitney, Burt Bacharach and Hal David and the others who soon have many professional New York songwriters of the past living off their previous hits . . . As Presley, the Everly Brothers and Jerry Lee Lewis become solidly entrenched in the pop field, their hits (for the most part) no longer appear in the country & western and rhythm & blues charts . . . Record business drops off to estimated $300 million gross from $350 million last year, as rock levels off with a relatively few million-sellers . . . Warner Bros., 20th Century-Fox, Columbia Pictures and United Artists all start record companies, following on Paramount Pictures' successful buyout of Dot Records last year . . . Stereo brings new life to record album business as buyers of stereo hardware begin collecting anew . . . Radio station WHB, Kansas City, becomes first all-rock station in U.S. . . .

SOME OF THE NEWS THAT INFLUENCED
THE ROCK ERA AND VICE VERSA

Democrats score large gains in Congressional midterm elections—reflecting public dissatisfaction with nuclear testing, deepening recession (8% unemployment) and racial tensions . . . Senator John F. Kennedy says U.S. on wrong end of missile gap . . . First U.S. space satellite, Explorer 1, launched . . . Arms deliveries to Batista's Cuba halted as many Americans sympathize with rebel Castro . . . Civil war erupts against Diem in Vietnam . . . "Eisenhower Doctrine" allows him to land 14,000 U.S. troops in Lebanon to aid their president against internal opposition . . . First commercial jet airliners put into service . . . U.S. atomic sub Nautilus makes first undersea crossing of North Pole . . . Edsel car launch disaster costs Ford $400 million . . . American Telephone & Telegraph Company has 100 million phones in service—half the world's total . . . Senate majority leader Lyndon Johnson says, "To get along, go along" . . . Volkswagen, Renault, Fiat and Hillman nab 10% of U.S. car sales . . . Six European nations form Common Market . . . V.P. Nixon on goodwill tour of South America meets with hostile demonstrations in Peru and Venezuela . . . Pioneer moon rocket fails to reach target but goes thirty times higher than any earlier man-made object . . . Senator John F. Kennedy of Massachusetts wins with greatest plurality in state's history . . . U.S. fires Atlas ICBM 6,000 miles in Atlantic Ocean testing zone . . . U.S. churches report largest increases in membership since 1950 . . . Civil Rights Commission begins operation . . . Food Additive Amendment prohibits use of any substance that tests find to induce cancer in man or animals . . . U.S. signs agreement with Russia to expand cultural, educational, technical and sports exchanges . . . National Aeronautics and Space Administration (NASA) created as civilian agency to handle all non-military space exploration . . . Resignation of Sherman Adams, Eisenhower's Chief Presidential Assistant, follows scandal involving gifts to Adams by Boston industrialist who has cases pending before Federal regulatory agencies . . .

THE NUMBERS GAME: STATISTICAL INFORMATION SHOWING HOW LIFE IN AMERICA INFLUENCED OR WAS INFLUENCED BY THE ROCK ERA

Chevrolet cars grew 4 ft. in length, with fivefold increase in horsepower since 1925 . . . 1,000 electric computers in use in U.S.—100 in Europe . . . Daily newspapers down to 357 from 2,600 in 1909, as radio and TV take over . . . Poll shows 85% of current 18-25-year-olds participated in family decisions at age 16, vs. only 48% of those who are now over 60—roughly twice as many . . . *Tide* magazine reports that gasoline mileage has dropped to 15 m.p.g. from 20 m.p.g. just eight years ago, because of larger, more complex cars . . . Unemployment jumps to 6.8%—after remaining steady at about 4% from 1955 through 1957 . . . Motel receipts $850 million vs. 36.7 million in 1939 . . . From zero in 1955, this year sees sale of 463,000 lbs. of tranquilizing drugs—worth $2.2 million . . . Number of operating movie houses down to 12,300 from 14,700 just four years ago . . . Now more than 4,000 outdoor drive-in theaters . . . 15% of U.S. families now own two or more cars, vs. only 2% just ten years ago . . .

TEEN AND COLLEGE LIVING AND ALTERNATIVE LIFE STYLES IN THE ROCK ERA

X-ray tests show stomach ulcers in 41 out of 189 University of Michigan students . . . Teenagers spend $9.5 billion . . . Girls between 15 and 19 half the total of women married . . . Survey of approximately 7,500 representative high school students on what is hardest to take: 54% parents' disapproval; 43% breaking with friend; 3% teacher's disapproval. Also reports 68% of boys and 77% of girls non-smokers, 30% of boys and 13% of girls drink beer, while approximately 19% of boys and 12% of girls drink other alcoholic beverages. Approximately 31% of boys want most to become jet pilots; 37% famous athletes; 26% atomic scientists. Approximately 33% of girls want modeling careers; 27% nursing; 19% acting or art; 20% teaching . . . Teens spend $20 million on lipstick, $25 million on deodorants (one-fifth of total sold), $9 million on home permanents. Male teens own 2 million electric razors . . . 47 out of 60 summa cum laude 1957-58 Harvard graduates are from public schools, although 50% of the students in their freshman class had come from private schools . . . Gainesville, Florida, police prevent panty raids at University of Florida by closing all beer and pizza hangouts—resulting in protest clash . . . National Defense Education Act authorizes long-term low tuition loans to college and grad students, with special encouragements for study of sciences, mathematics and languages . . . Teenage girls spend $837 million on back-to-school clothing . . . Harvard tuition up to $1,250 from $455 ten years ago . . . Survey of students in ten selected high schools, and their parents, reveals: (1) Parental political party preference is the best predictor of adolescent preference—but much more so with girls; (2) Boys more influenced by opinion climate in their high school than girls; but (3) Girls more influenced by social climate there . . . San Francisco police declare Bohemian North Beach "a problem area" and no new liquor license is issued . . .

FASHION: CLOTHES AND THE ROCK ERA ACCENT ON YOUTH

Note: Feminine fashion is in italics, male in roman, unisex in parentheses, and news in asterisks.

Dress-up for teen boys: button-down collars, Bermuda shorts, cashmere sweaters . . . *False eyelashes fast-growing fad with teenagers and co-eds— sold in kits costing $2 in plastic and $4.50 for real hair* . . . **Schoolboys, with shirt tails out, protest sack dresses in "Whack the Sack" movement** . . . ("U.S.A. Drinking Team," etc., sweatshirts) . . . *Striped knit pullovers, straight-leg white duck pants and sneakers* . . . **Stretch tights shown in department store windows under tartan skirts for college girls—considered practical rather than proper—replacing girdles, garter belts and slips** . . . **High school girls buying at specialty shops known as "Young Sophisticates," "Telephone Set Shop," etc., featuring separates, man-tailored shirts, ballet slippers, skin-tight "stem" skirts, and balloon layers of petticoats** . . . **Eye shadow rather than lipstick badge of womanhood for young teens** . . . **In the selection of apparel, most college women attached top importance to being fashionably dressed, survey reports** . . . **"$64,000 Question" TV show quadruples Revlon sales to $125 million** . . . *The sack dress gets mostly negative reception . . . Chemise dresses—variation on the sack* . . .

FADS (MOSTLY YOUTH-ORIENTED)
RELATED TO THE ROCK ERA

Thirty million hula-hoops sold at $1.98. Forty imitators of Wham-O original in first six months . . . Steadies trade bobbie pins for football letters . . . Coca-Cola mixed with ginger ale . . . Hootenanny magazines, books, etc. . . . Scrabble . . .

SOME OF THE MORE WIDELY USED ARGOT, JARGON AND SLANG IN THE ROCK ERA

Angry young man (fiery writer) . . . Bit (characteristic act) . . . Bopping clubs (teen street-fighting gangs) . . . BYOB party (bring your own bottle) . . . Debs (street gangs' ladies' auxiliary) . . . Dig (understand) . . . Flicks (movies) . . . Flaked out (tired) . . . Gross (either best or worst) . . . Heart (courage) . . . Loser (old-fashioned in dress or manners) . . . Pad (dwelling) . . . Rumble (fight—often bloody) . . . Scene (where it's at) . . . Turf (territory) . . .

More Hot Rod Terms: Deuce (a 1932 Ford—ideal stock for converting to "Bomber") . . . Stock (conventional car as it comes from factory) . . . Customizing, Shaving, Stripping (removing chrome, etc., from stock) . . . Dagoing, Diegoing or Raking (lowering front end) . . . Frenching (fitting head and tail lights with metal hood) . . . Channeling or Dropping (lowering car body closer to ground) . . . Flippers, Spinners or Moons (hubcaps) . . . Binders (brakes) . . . Tails (coon or fox tails used decoratively) . . . Gutting (removing upholstery, etc. from interior) . . . Spaghetti (excess chrome) . . . Stacks, Pipes, Duals, or Hollywoods (special exhausts) . . . Full House (engines souped up to extreme) . . . Drag or Dragging (race between two or more cars from standing start) . . . Thingie, Rail Job or Slingshot (hot rod designed solely for dragging) . . .

MOSTLY FACTUAL TRIVIA CONCURRENT WITH THE ROCK ERA

Kenny Rossi, 14-year-old "American Bandstand" regular, has 301 fan clubs . . . Heaviest human of all time, Robert Earl Hughes, weighing 1,069 lbs., dies at age 32. Has to be lowered into grave by crane . . . Edsel car cost Ford $400 million loss in first year of market . . . U.S. population of dogs now 26 million—up 35% in ten years . . .

1959 _____

ARTISTS

Rock Groups
  Crests
  Dion & The Belmonts
  Drifters
  Flamingos
  Jan & Dean
  Johnny & The Hurricanes
  Sandy Nelson

Rock Solo Performers
  Freddy Cannon
  Lloyd Price

Soul, R&B, Funk Groups
  Isley Brothers

Soul, R&B, Funk Solo Performers
  Brook Benton
  Ray Charles
  Dee Clark
  Della Reese
  Nina Simone
  Dinah Washington

Folk & Country
  Johnny Horton

Young Teen Oriented
  Annette
  Ed Byrnes
  Fabian
  Bobby Rydell
  Neil Sedaka
  Connie Stevens

Middle of the Road
  Fleetwoods

JUKE BOX HITS

"Battle of New Orleans"
Johnny Horton

"Venus"
Frankie Avalon

"Come Softly to Me"
Fleetwoods

"Stagger Lee"
Lloyd Price

"Smoke Gets in Your Eyes"
Platters

"Sea of Love"
Phil Phillips

"A Teenager in Love"
Dion & The Belmonts

"There Goes My Baby"
Drifters

"A Fool Such As I"
Elvis Presley

"Tallahassee Lassie"
Freddy Cannon

"Never Be Anyone Else but You'
Ricky Nelson

"Poison Ivy"
Coasters

"Teardrops on Your Letter"
Hank Ballard & Midnighters

"There Goes My Baby"
Drifters

"Running Bear"
Johnny Preston

"Teen Angel"
Mark Dinning

"Back in the U.S.A."
Chuck Berry

"Love Potion No. 9"
Clovers

"Mack the Knife"
Bobby Darin

"Lonely Boy"
Paul Anka

"Kansas City"
Wilbert Harrison

"Charlie Brown"
Coasters

"I'm Gonna Get Married"
Lloyd Price

"16 Candles"
Crests

"A Big Hunk O'Love"
Elvis Presley

"Teen Beat"
Sandy Nelson

"Tiger"
Fabian

"What a Diff'rence a Day Makes"
Dinah Washington

"A Lover's Question"
Clyde McPhatter

"I'm Ready"
Fats Domino

"What'd I Say"
Ray Charles

"The Big Hurt"
Toni Fisher

"It Doesn't Matter Anymore"
Buddy Holly

"So Fine"
Fiestas

"Personality"
Lloyd Price

"Dream Lover"
Bobby Darin

"Mr. Blue"
Fleetwoods

"Put Your Head on My Shoulder"
Paul Anka

"('Til) I Kissed You"
Everly Brothers

"Sorry, I Ran All the Way Home"
Impalas

"It's Just a Matter of Time"
Brook Benton

"Red River Rock"
Johnny & The Hurricanes

"Oh Carol"
Neil Sedaka

"You're So Fine"
Falcons

"I Only Have Eyes for You"
Flamingos

"Kookie, Kookie
(Lend Me Your Comb)"
Ed Byrnes & Connie Stevens

"Shimmy, Shimmy, Ko-Ko Bop"
Little Anthony & The Imperials

"Sea Cruise"
Frankie Ford

"The Happy Organ"
Dave (Baby) Cortez

"Tall Paul"
Annette

"Shout"
Isley Brothers

"Primrose Lane"
Jerry Wallace

DANCES

The Shag

The Alligator and the Dog
banned from "American Bandstand"—
too sexy

NEWS OF ROCK

Buddy Holly, Ritchie Valens and the Big Bopper killed in plane crash . . . Top 40 format radio sweeps in . . . Beatles-to-be, Quarrymen, getting 15 shillings (less than $2) per man per night at Casbah Club, Liverpool . . . Buddy Holly's last records were cut in his New York apartment on same Ampex that he used for most of his hits . . . DJ payola scandal—Alan Freed fired . . . Berry Gordy Jr. borrows $700 to launch Gordy (later Motown) Records . . . Dick Clark and Philadelphia record company develop local stars through his TV shows, like Frankie Avalon . . . Decline of classic rock 'n' roll begins . . . Car names big with groups, such as Impalas, Falcons, Fleetwoods . . . First "oldies but goodies" album features "Earth Angel" and "Dance With Me Henry" . . . Buddy Holly tributes mark him as first to use strings on a rock 'n' roll record as well as first rock singer to double-track his voice and guitar . . . House Legislative Oversight Committee urged to broaden its investigation of rigged TV shows—to include the practice of payola in radio. With many new record labels and music publishers prospering at the expense of the big names, rumors spread about cash, gifts and other benefits padding the paltry salaries of lesser disc jockeys as well as some of the most important rock hit makers . . . Leiber and Stoller pioneer use of strings on a rhythm & blues record (probably the first), "There Goes My Baby" by the Drifters . . . Albums pick up the slack as single record business drops off again. Teenage pop fans doing much of their listening to now widespread music radio on portable popularly-priced transistor radios—and many are recording the hits onto their own tapes from disc jockey play . . .

SOME OF THE NEWS THAT INFLUENCED
THE ROCK ERA AND VICE VERSA

Castro wins Cuba . . . Alaska becomes 49th state . . . Hawaii becomes 50th state . . . Synthetic penicillin developed . . . In U.N., Castro and Khrushchev advocate disarmament within four years . . . First seven U.S. astronauts selected . . . Oklahoma is 47th state to repeal prohibition . . . Cumulative death toll on U.S. highways exceeds casualty figures for all U.S. wars . . . U.S. announces extension of its nuclear test ban. Britain and Soviet Union follow suit; however, all will resume testing two years later . . . Vice President Nixon visits Moscow for U.S. exhibition. Soviet propaganda says $14,000, six-room model ranch house there no more typical of U.S. worker's home than Taj Mahal is typical in India . . . Khrushchev visits U.S., has informal talks with Ike, and withdraws Berlin Ultimatum . . . Former hard-liner, Vice President Nixon, supports Eisenhower's attempts to relax tensions with Russia, explaining how "we" want a thaw, "because we realize that if there is none we will all be eventually frozen in the ice so hard that only a nuclear bomb will break it" . . . U.S. commissions first nuclear sub able to launch missiles . . . TV quiz show rigging scandal and deejay payola revelations shock nation . . . Treaty barring warlike developments in Antarctica signed by twelve nations . . . Ford Falcon first U.S. response to Volkswagen and other foreign compact competition . . . Eisenhower imposes mandatory quotas on oil imports, giving national security as reason, in response to pleas from domestic oil producers. Price rise for gasoline and heating oil follows . . . NASA estimates that it will take ten years to get men to the moon . . . Eisenhower tells key Republican leaders: "Dick (Nixon) just isn't Presidential timber" . . .

THE NUMBERS GAME: STATISTICAL INFORMATION
SHOWING HOW LIFE IN AMERICA INFLUENCED
OR WAS INFLUENCED BY THE ROCK ERA

University of Michigan study shows 20% of U.S. families still live below the "poverty line"—unchanged since 1957 . . . Paid vacations now 78 million weeks a year, vs. 17.5 million in 1929 . . . Volkswagen sells 120,000 cars in U.S., up from 29,000 in 1955. Combined sales of all other foreign cars just equals 120,000 . . . TV brings movie attendance down to 42 million a week, from 60 million in 1950 . . . U.S. using 60% of world oil production . . . 531 competing brands of coffee and 249 brands of washing powder mirror new affluence of U.S. consumer . . . 32 million people went swimming at least once, 18 million went dancing, 32 million bowled, and another 32 million went fishing . . . 32,000 supermarkets—only 11% of all food stores—getting 69% of sales . . . Over 579 tons of tranquilizers prescribed . . . Total auto accident deaths now over 1.25 million—more than have died in all U.S. wars combined . . . Contracts for jails and penitentiaries up to $96 million—almost double 1957 . . . Now 3.7 million farms vs. 4.8 million four years ago—a drop of 23% . . . More important problems facing the country during past six years, according to Gallup poll results, were: 1959: keeping peace; 1958: economic conditions; 1957: keeping out of war; 1956: threat of war; 1955: working out a peace; 1954: threat of war . . .

TEEN AND COLLEGE LIVING AND ALTERNATIVE LIFE STYLES IN THE ROCK ERA

Girls in swimsuits promoting male wrestling matches banned at Oregon State . . . Teens spending $10 billion this year . . . Breck shampoo sales to teenagers up $1 million since 1956 . . . Teens eating 20% more than adults. Now downing 3.5 billion quarts of milk a year—almost four times as much as entire infant population under one . . . Teenagers are 7.2% of drivers, but account for 11.5% of auto accidents . . . More than 600,000 teenagers get married . . . 4,000 Yale students put on probation after battling police —six years before campus riots . . . Teenagers own 10 million phonographs, over a million TV sets, and 13 million cameras. 22% of their money goes on food, 16% for entertainment, 15% for clothing, 9% for sports, and 38% for miscellaneous, including transportation, grooming, reading matter and school supplies. 1.5 million own cars . . . Beatnik-inspired fad for public recitation of verse catches on in college towns . . . Teenagers down 145 million gallons of ice cream . . . Detroit auto stylists follow lead of hot rodders by "bullnosing" the hood and removing most of the chrome from standard cars . . . As teen affluence explodes, many surveys focus on them. Gilbert report shows average teenagers spend $10 weekly on: dating ($1), snacks (90¢), entertainment, movies, records, etc. (90¢), clothes (70¢), savings (70¢), school supplies (60¢), reading matter et al. (50¢), cars and gasoline (40¢), sports ($1.10), hobbies (30¢), grooming (20¢), school lunches ($2.30), miscellaneous (40¢) . . . "Hunkerin' " (from Scottish word for haunches) is name for squatting craze at colleges . . . Survey of magazine readerships shows 84% audience of eighth graders, rising to 92% for high school seniors . . . Journal of Educational Psychology report on student survey reveals that those satisfied and dissatisfied with school experience differed little in intelligence or scholastic achievement as is generally assumed. Psychological discontent proved major element in dissatisfaction . . . San Francisco beatnik community dissolves . . .

FASHION: CLOTHES AND THE
ROCK ERA ACCENT ON YOUTH

Note: Feminine fashion is in italics, male in roman, unisex in parentheses, and news in asterisks.

Stuck-on jewelry: paste stones pinned to flesh-colored plastic bandages . . . **Twenty years before punks—"Lunar Look" promotion features pink, blue, orange and green hair coloring** . . . *Eye liner makeup takes hold* . . . **Bikini swimsuits make big splash** . . . *Leotards worn with button-down sport shirts and ponytails* . . . **Los Angeles high school girls making skirt and blazer sets from blankets** . . . **Tights selling 30% over 1958** . . . *Boots with raccoon trim, corduroy or plaid coverings* . . . **Dungarees, sloppy slacks and baggy sweaters give way to new high school look. Girls now wearing wool poncho capes, hooded sweaters and jackets called "Benchwarmers," and shaggy dog coats** . . . (Man-Tan supplies rub-on suntan) . . . **Michigan State University survey of "Adolescent Orientations to Clothing" reports 25% mentioning a movie, sports or TV figure influencing their pattern of dress, vs. 12% indicating a relative or family member as their inspiration. Less than 4% considered their father's opinions about clothes to be important** . . . **Cosmetics industry now marketing "Bedtime" lipstick, eye makeup and perfume** . . . *New York department store offers wigs in 15 different shades—including ice blue and orange ice—also a mother-daughter look-alike wig combination* . . .

FADS (MOSTLY YOUTH-ORIENTED)
RELATED TO THE ROCK ERA

Telephone box squash craze: 34 boys stuffed into Modesto, California, phone booth claim record. Eight girls cram phone booth under water at Hacienda Motel, Fresno . . . Sick jokes . . . Plastic-coated textbook covers stating "Enbalming Can Be Fun," etc. . . . Hot rod songs for next five years—from "Hot Rod Lincoln" to "GTO" and "Dead Man's Curve" in 1964 . . . Barbie Dolls . . . TV Westerns create $283 million in sales of toy guns, spurs, boots, chaps and lassoes in past four years . . . Hunkerin' (squatting while socializing, watching TV, etc.) . . .

SOME OF THE MORE WIDELY USED ARGOT,
JARGON AND SLANG IN THE ROCK ERA

A Gas (great) . . . A Groove (excellent) . . . Ax (any musical instrument) . . . Bugged (bothered) . . . Busted (apprehended by the "Heat") . . . Chick (girl) . . . Cop out (to renege) . . . Cut out (leave) . . . Diet bit, love bit, etc. ("bit" = act) . . . Far out (see 1954) . . . Get with it (join what's "in") . . . Gig (job, musical engagement) . . . Gung-ho (overly zealous) . . . Head (user of mind-bending substances) . . . Joint (marijuana cigarette) . . . "Like that's your reality, man" . . . Make the scene (arrive) . . . Nowhere (not with it) . . . Payola (bribery—revived usage on youth scene) . . . Relate to (establish contact) . . . Shuck (fraud) . . . Split (leave) . . . Stoned (under influence of drugs) . . . Swinging (liberated) . . . Turn on (arouse someone's interest or curiosity; get high on drugs) . . . With it (in the know) . . . Wig (mind) . . . Wig out (go crazy) . . . Zorch (wrong) . . .

Venice, California, lawyer fighting license denial for beatnik coffee house says they "need scene whose kicks are to be dug where found" . . .

MOSTLY FACTUAL TRIVIA
CONCURRENT WITH THE ROCK ERA

On film set, Pat Boone breaks toe on real rock he thought was papier-mâché . . . Khrushchev refused permission to visit Disneyland . . . Last Confederate vet dies at age 117, beating out Union vet by three years . . . Lincoln head penny redesigned to show Lincoln Memorial—after 50-year reign . . . Now 3,000 sport parachute jumpers—doubled in year . . . $100,000 debutante party for Charlotte Ford has 1,200 guests . . . First movie with scent, *Behind the Great Wall*, presented. As well received as 3-D five years earlier . . .

1960

ARTISTS

Rock Groups
  Bill Black's Combo
  Gary "U.S." Bonds
  Chubby Checker
  Ventures
  Maurice Williams & The Zodiacs

Rock Solo Performers
  Johnny Burnette
  Johnny Preston
  Johnny Tillotson
  Bobby Vee

Soul, R&B, Funk Solo Performers
  Jimmy Jones

Folk & Country
  Joan Baez
  Brothers Four
  Brenda Lee

Young Teen Oriented
  Brian Hyland

Dance Fads
  Bobby Freeman
  Olympics

JUKE BOX HITS

"This Magic Moment"
Drifters

"Kiddio"
Brook Benton

"Stay"
Maurice Williams & The Zodiacs

"Shop Around"
Miracles

"Handy Man"
Jimmy Jones

"I'm Sorry"
Brenda Lee

"Puppy Love"
Paul Anka

"Save the Last Dance for Me"
Drifters

"Let It Be Me"
Everly Brothers

"Way Down Yonder in New Orleans"
Freddy Cannon

"It's Now or Never"
Elvis Presley

"You Talk Too Much"
Joe Jones

"Georgia On My Mind"
Ray Charles

"The Twist"
Hank Ballard & The Midnighters

"Stuck on You"
Elvis Presley

"The Twist"
Chubby Checker

"Why"
Frankie Avalon

"Baby (You've Got
What it Takes)"
Brook Benton & Dinah Washington

"Go, Jimmy, Go"
Jimmy Clanton

"Finger Poppin' Time"
Hank Ballard & The Midnighters

"You're Sixteen"
Johnny Burnette

"Poetry in Motion"
Johnny Tillotson

"Once in a While"
Chimes

"Sweet Sixteen"
B. B. King

"Cathy's Clown"
Everly Brothers

"Only the Lonely"
Roy Orbison

"Where or When"
Dion & The Belmonts

"Sixteen Reasons"
Connie Stevens

"Walk, Don't Run"
Ventures

"Chain Gang"
Sam Cooke

"White Silver Sands"
Bill Black Combo

"Lonely Blue Boy"
Conway Twitty

"Wild One"/"Little Bitty Girl"
Bobby Rydell

"Devil or Angel"
Bobby Vee

"He Will Break Your Heart"
Terry Butler

"Harbor Lights"
Platters

"New Orleans"
Gary "U.S." Bonds

Novelty

"Itsy, Bitsy, Teenie, Weenie
Yellow Polka Dot Bikini"
Brian Hyland

"Mr. Custer"
Larry Verne

"Alley-Oop"
The Hollywood Argyles

Folk

"Greenfields"
Brothers Four

DANCES

The Madison

The Hully Gully

The Twist big with youth

NEWS OF ROCK

Eddie Cochran killed in crash . . . Gene Vincent loses leg . . . Jesse Belvin killed in crash . . . Oren Harris (Senate) Committee identifies $263,245 in payola money to DJs to get records played; and this only a small part of it . . . DJ payola by record companies outlawed by Federal Bribery Act . . . Beatles make first trip to Hamburg with Pete Best on drums . . . "Coffee house circuit" for folk singers spreads to colleges from Greenwich Village beatniks . . . National magazines "discover" folk music . . . Soul music develops on Atlantic Records, updating R&B to present-day life—as Ben E. King's "Spanish Harlem" opens way for flood of soul ballads . . . Johnny Tillotson one of first singer-songwriters with "Poetry in Motion" . . . Record sales down 0.5% per year after increasing 36% each year since rock took off in 1950s . . . Ernest Evans becomes Chubby Checker in pun on name Fats Domino . . . Amateur Night at Gerde's Folk City, New York, tagged "Hootenanny" (a term popularized by Woody Guthrie) in *New York Times* story. Word and idea spread through coffee house circuit . . . Congressional investigation reveals that 50.4% of the records available through companies in which Dick Clark had an interest were played on "American Bandstand"; and that Clark had a personal interest in records representing 27% of the spins over a 28 month period. Of these, 65.4% were played before making the "Billboard" charts . . . Clark's "American Bandstand" annual billing is $12 million . . . Bobby Darin and Sandra Dee marry . . . Newport Jazz Festival wrecked by violence . . . First Broadway musical to feature rock music, "Bye Bye Birdie," becomes unexpected smash hit with hybrid Broadway-Rock score . . . With the exception of a few sides with sensational appeal, most single hits fortunate to hit the 500,000 sales mark—with many hits failing to sell even 200,000. Along with Top 40 radio monopolizing the teen ear, some feel that the price differential between a 98¢ single and a $3.98 album is too small—encouraging LP sales at the expense of singles . . . Led by an unknown Bob Newhart, comedians become new record business phenomena as Shelley Berman, Mort Sahl and Jonathan Winters build cult "new wave" comedy audiences among the young. Prior to this year, "spoken word" records were dormant items, catering mostly to classical buyers of poetry and dramatic recitation . . . Led by Enoch Light's "Persuasive Percussion" album hit, the LP business finds another bonanza in percussive sets being arranged with sound gimmicks to show off stereo's potential—with rock music still being mostly confined to single records . . .

SOME OF THE NEWS THAT INFLUENCED
THE ROCK ERA AND VICE VERSA

Viet Cong organized as Communist-led political front in Vietnam . . . Kennedy defeats Nixon for Presidency . . . U.S. population 179,323,175

. . . U2 piloted by Gary Powers shot down by Russia. Khrushchev then calls off Paris summit and cancels scheduled Eisenhower visit to U.S.S.R. . . . House Sub-Committee reports 207 DJs received $260,000 payola. Alan Freed indicted in New York . . . Federal Drug Administration approves first public sale of the Pill . . .Census shows big population gains in Florida (78.7%), Nevada (78.2%), Alaska (75.8%), Arizona (73.7%), California (48.5%) . . . California enacts first law to reduce auto fumes—the chief source of air pollution . . . U.S. scientists patent laser—acronym for "Light Amplification by Stimulated Emission of Radiation" . . . If Nixon had won only 4,500 more votes in Illinois and 2,800 more in Texas, he would have defeated JFK for Presidency . . . Black sit-in movement born at Woolworth lunch counter in Greensboro, N.C.—sit-in tactic quickly spreads . . . TV in 90% of U.S. homes . . . Albania only Communist country to side with China in widening Sino-Soviet rift . . . World circumnavigated underwater by U.S. atomic sub Triton . . . Cuba-U.S. relations deteriorate . . . Second U.S. reconnaissance plane shot down over Soviet territory . . . First successful underwater launching of Polaris missiles from atomic subs hits targets 1,100 miles away . . . Two elementary schools in New Orleans begin desegregation and riots . . . U.S. warns North Vietnam and Communist China to refrain from military activity in Laos . . . Auto industry begins shift to economy compacts to fight imports . . . "Freedom rides" by Negro and white citizens seek to break down "Jim Crow" restrictions in buses and terminals . . . Eisenhower cuts quota for Cuban sugar exports by 95% because of Castro hostility . . . OPEC meets for the first time in Baghdad—and forces Standard Oil to retract unilateral purchase price decrease to 14¢ a barrel from 18¢ . . .

THE NUMBERS GAME: STATISTICAL INFORMATION SHOWING HOW LIFE IN AMERICA INFLUENCED OR WAS INFLUENCED BY THE ROCK ERA

U.S. population increased 33% in 20 years—now 179,323,175 . . . Housing units lacking tub or shower down to 12% from 39% just 20 years ago . . . Coal now supplying 45% of U.S. energy needs—will head down to 18% by 1975 . . . 15% of U.S. families have more than one car, vs. 7% in 1950 . . . 500,000 declare taxable earnings over $25,000, vs. 42,500 in 1939. 5,333,000 were over $10,000, vs. 200,000 in 1939 . . . Average American child receiving $26 worth of toys a year, as stores ring up $6 million in toy sales an hour during December . . . 2,000 computers sold—beginning debate as to whether they wipe out jobs or create new ones . . . Average 70 times as much time spent in outdoor recreation as in 1900 . . . American families throwing away an average 750 cans and bottles a year . . . Beef consumption is 99 lbs. per capita . . . 75 million private cars owned by Americans . . . U.S., a former metal exporter, is now importing half of those needed . . . 35.4% white collar workers vs. 26.6% in 1940 . . . Average non-agricultural work week is 38 hours, vs. 50.3 fifty years ago. Agricultural work week 44 hours, vs. 65 hours in 1910 . . . 60% of all adults participated in automobile riding for pleasure . . . Americans eating 73% less potatoes than 20 years ago—but 25% more meat, fish and poultry and 50% more citrus and tomatoes . . . Estimated U.S. advertising expenditure $11.9 billion—virtually double total of $5.7 billion of ten years ago . . . JFK's winning election campaign costs Democrats just over $10.5 million, vs. over $11 million for GOP loser Nixon . . . Living-in maids now under 160,000 from 200,000 ten years ago, with living-out household workers up to 1.6 million from 1.2 million in 1950 . . . Marguerite Clark, longtime medicine editor of *Newsweek*, testifies that prior to 1940, medicine reporters felt lucky to find one major medical discovery to write about every six months —but now hearing new ones almost every day . . . Close to 60% of all U.S. families now have at least one charge account. About 90% of those with incomes above $10,000 have one or more . . . Production of synthetic pesticides now over 637 million lb. vs. some 124 million just 13 years ago . . .

TEEN AND COLLEGE LIVING AND ALTERNATIVE LIFE STYLES IN THE ROCK ERA

Now 40.8 million 10-24-year-olds in U.S.—22% over 1950 . . . First Civil Rights "sit-in" at North Carolina college . . . National Education Association poll shows 50% of teachers polled would like to exclude married students from schools . . . New baby's life expectancy now 66 years, vs. 48 years in 1900 . . . 850,000 "war baby" freshmen flood colleges—necessitating emergency living quarters in trailer camps, hotels, dorm lounges, and even basements. Total enrollment now almost 4 million . . . Teens spending over $100 million for Mother's Day gifts and $70 million for Father's Day . . . 690 two-year colleges handling a million students . . . 200 San Francisco college students battle police at City Hall, ending conformity of 1950s . . . 10% of 13-14-year-olds now going steady. Up from one-half of 1% in 1945 . . . Pepsi-Cola recognizes new youth power with "For those who think young" campaign . . . Applications for college entrance next year far exceed places open: Columbia 3,300 applicants (680 places); Harvard 5,500 (1,200); Yale 4,600 (1,000); Syracuse 10,000 (2,100); Michigan 11,000 (3,300); Stanford 7,000 (1,280); Brown 5,000 (625); Duke 5,600 (1,000); Northwestern 6,500 (1,650); Pennsylvania 7,000 (1,350) . . . Survey reports teenage girls more disturbed by deejay payola investigations than boys—indicating that they may be real core of rock emergence . . . National Student Association, founded ten years ago by young war veterans, urges members in 500 colleges and universities to mount protest demonstrations against Woolworth's and any other establishment refusing to serve blacks at lunch counters following Greensboro, N.C., "sit-in" . . . *Datebook's Complete Guide to Dating* lists 15 varieties of dates, including:

First, double, Dutch, meet-the-family, church, study, prom, car, blind, dinner, stay-at-home, spectator sports, active sports, concert and museum dates—as sub-teens join social scene . . . Rising rents, police harassment and tourist throngs in San Francisco's North Beach force beatniks across town to the repository for the unwanted, Haight Ashbury . . .

FASHION: CLOTHES AND THE
ROCK ERA ACCENT ON YOUTH

Note: Feminine fashion is in italics, male in roman, unisex in parentheses, and news in asterisks.

Brief bikini bathing suits . . . Hothead men's hats made of old fur coats . . . *Fake fur fabric big* . . . **Dior and Yves St. Laurent flatten the bust** . . . *Eskimo muk luks and patent leather boots* . . . *Whim trimming: cotton rectangles buttoned to skirt waistband hanging like aprons front and back—decorated according to whim* . . . **New high school girls' craze: 18th-century French bouffant hairdo variations—the French roll, French twist, Mushroom, Flip, Twist and Chemise** . . . **Teens using keychain stick-on initials on girls' chokers, ear muffs, headbands and plaster casts** . . . **False hair pieces sales up, with prices lowered by part-machine-made product replacing previous all hand-made** . . . **Planned obsolescence big reason women's clothing and accessories now $12 billion industry** . . . **Size 28AA bras for 9- and 10-year-olds become important market, as advertising stresses bosoms, and bras as status symbols** . . . **Deodorants and depilatories celebrate 50th anniversary—with manicuring only 45 years old and eye makeup coming into use only 30 years ago, as women tried to achieve eyebrows like Greta Garbo** . . . **Michigan State University study of seventh grade girls reports 41.5% allowed independent choice of play clothes, 23.8% blouses, 18.5% underclothes, and 15.8% school dresses—but only 5% dress-up clothes, and 1% coats—with mothers' opinions the weighty determinant in all categories** . . . **Journal of Home Economics report on college freshman girls' clothing expenditure places annual average at $275** . . . **Teenage girls (14-17 only) spent $773,776,000 on "back to school" clothes and other necessities, according to teen marketing expert, Eugene Gilbert** . . .

FADS (MOSTLY YOUTH-ORIENTED)
RELATED TO THE ROCK ERA

Telephone talkathons . . . Barbie gets boyfriend, Ken . . .

SOME OF THE MORE WIDELY USED ARGOT,
JARGON AND SLANG IN THE ROCK ERA

Bazoongies (large or shapely breasts) . . . Bring down (depress) . . . Gear (excellent) . . . Tuff (superb) . . .

MOSTLY FACTUAL TRIVIA
CONCURRENT WITH THE ROCK ERA

American Medical Association reports that patient who swallowed 258 items including 39 nail files and a 3 lb. piece of metal checked into a hospital for a broken ankle . . . Original Playboy Club opens in Chicago . . . British doctor, Barbara Moore, walks across U.S. in 85 days . . . Hot dog production reaches 1,050 million pounds, from 750,000 in 1950 . . . Potato chips up to 532 million from 320 million . . . John D. Rockefeller dies—leaves $150 million . . . Cat population now 28 million; canaries now 6 million . . .

1961 _____

ARTISTS

Rock Groups
  Belmonts
  Marcels
  Mar-Keys

Rock Solo Performers
  Lee Dorsey
  Del Shannon

Soul, R&B, Funk Groups
  Impressions (Curtis Mayfield)
  Marcels
  Marvelettes
  Miracles
  Shirelles
  Ike & Tina Turner

Soul, R&B, Funk Solo Performers
  Bobby Bland
  Solomon Burke
  Clarence "Frogman" Henry
  Ben E. King
  Bobby Lewis
  Gene McDaniels
  Carla Thomas

Folk & Country
  Highwaymen
  Limelighters
  Smothers Brothers

Young Teen Oriented
  Dick and Deedee

Middle of the Road
  Lettermen

Dance Fads
  Joey Dee & The Starlighters
  Dovells

JUKE BOX HITS

"Surrender"
Elvis Presley

"Crying"
Roy Orbison

"Runaway"
Del Shannon

"Take Good Care of My Baby"
Bobby Vee

47

"Dedicated to the One I Love"
Shirelles

"Last Night"
Mar-Keys

"Will You Love Me Tomorrow"
Shirelles

"Hit the Road Jack"
Ray Charles

"Peppermint Twist"
Joey Dee & The Starlighters

"Boll Weevil Song"
Brook Benton

"Raindrops"
Dee Clark

"Runnin' Scared"
Roy Orbison

"Just Out of Reach"
Solomon Burke

"Unchain My Heart"
Ray Charles

"Turn On Your Lovelight"
Bobby Bland

"Mother-in-Law"
Ernie K-Doe

"Bristol Stomp"
Dovells

"Shop Around"
Miracles

"One Hundred Pounds of Clay"
Gene McDaniels

"The Mountain's High"
Dick & Deedee

"Quarter to Three"
Gary "U.S." Bonds

"Calendar Girl"
Neil Sedaka

"Blue Moon"
Marcels

"Tossin' and Turnin'"
Bobby Lewis

"Let's Twist Again"
Chubby Checker

"This Time"
Troy Shondell

"Big Bad John"
Jimmy Dean

"The Wanderer"
Dion

"I Love How You Love Me"
Paris Sisters

"Runaround Sue"
Dion

"Hello Mary Lou"
Ricky Nelson

"Stand By Me"
Ben E. King

"Ya Ya"
Lee Dorsey

"Please Mr. Postman"
Marvelettes

"Mama Said"
Shirelles

"I Like It Like That"
Chris Kenner

"But I Do"
Clarence "Frogman" Henry

"Moon River"
Jerry Butler

"Walk Right Back"/"Ebony Eyes"
Everly Brothers

"Goodbye Cruel World"
James Darren

"Baby, It's You"
Shirelles

"Spanish Harlem"
Ben E. King

"Gee Whiz (Look at His Eyes)"
Carla Thomas

"Can't Help Falling In Love"
Elvis Presley

"Tower of Strength"
Gene McDaniels

"Little Sister"
Elvis Presley

Novelty

"(I Got a Girl Named)
Rama Lama Ding Dong"
Edsels

Folk

"Michael"
The Highwaymen

DANCES

The Bristol Stomp

The Fish

The Pony

The Fly

The Hucklebuck

NEWS OF ROCK

First Beatles performance at Cavern Club, Liverpool . . . Bob Dylan debuts at Gerde's Folk City, New York City . . . Top 40 format radio launched . . . "Twist" reappears on hit charts after 18-week 1960 ride. Runs up 39-week chart record . . . 100,000 guitars sold in U.S. . . . Brian Epstein discovers the Beatles at Cavern . . . Big year for Fabian, Frankie Avalon and Bobby Darin . . . Le Club, first U.S. disco, opens in New York . . . Federal Communications Commission approves stereo FM . . . Bob Dylan cuts first professional recording as harmonica accompaniment to Caroline Hester. Then signed to Columbia Records without audition . . . First edition of *Mersey Beat* published . . . Bob Dylan plays to friends and empty seats at Carnegie Hall . . . Soul music, brought into the pop market by Ray Charles, Sam Cooke and just a few others, gets a big boost from the emergence of the Miracles, Solomon Burke, Ben E. King, Motown Records, producers Leiber and Stoller, combined with the biggest crossover of rhythm & blues hits into pop yet . . .

SOME OF THE NEWS THAT INFLUENCED
THE ROCK ERA AND VICE VERSA

Eisenhower's farewell address warns nation of "military-industrial complex," saying that combination of immense military establishment and large civilian arms industry has "grave implications for the very structure of our society" . . . Defense budget is $40 billion—three times 1950 total . . . Before leaving office President Eisenhower breaks off diplomatic relations with Cuba . . . In his inaugural address, JFK explains policy with: "Ask not what your country can do for you; ask what you can do for your country" . . . Sit-ins in over 100 cities during past year succeed in desegregating many restaurants, hotels, etc. as over 50,000 participate . . . First U.S. troops arrive in South Vietnam: 4,000 men and 30 helicopters, serving as military advisers, reconnaissance units and special forces . . . Bay of Pigs disaster . . . Berlin Wall built . . . JFK establishes Presidential Commission on the status of women . . . President sends 500 more "special advisers" to Vietnam . . . Four U.S. airliners hijacked . . . JFK asks Congress for $93 million to provide shelter against radioactive fallout; and another $10 million for National Emergency Alarm Repeater for Air Defense Command to activate in homes with plug-in devices (cost: $15-$20 each) when missiles start flying. Civil Defense officials distribute 22 million copies of "Family Fallout Shelter" as JFK encourages construction . . . U.N. Security Council authorizes international police action to terminate Civil War . . . John Birch Society accuses Presidents Roosevelt, Truman and Eisenhower of being "Comsymps." Senate becomes concerned . . . U.S. and Soviet put spacemen into orbit . . . Minimum wage raised from $1 to $1.15 per hour for next two years—then to $1.25 . . . Alabama mobs attack interracial busloads of "Freedom Riders" riding southward to force integration . . . Unsatisfactory JFK-Khrushchev Vienna summit on Berlin, Laos neutrality and disarmament . . . Congress authorizes JFK to call 250,000 reservists to active duty for up to a year . . . JFK orders resumption of limited nuclear testing following resumption by U.S.S.R. . . . Peace Corps created by executive order of JFK . . . China premier Chou En Lai walks out on Moscow Party Congress, heralding break in relations . . . New Haven, Conn., birth control clinic forced to close nine days after opening . . . Defense Department spends more than half of the Federal budget . . .

THE NUMBERS GAME: STATISTICAL INFORMATION SHOWING HOW LIFE IN AMERICA INFLUENCED OR WAS INFLUENCED BY THE ROCK ERA

Canned pet food in top three grocery bestsellers as U.S. feeds 25 million dogs and 20 million cats . . . It took 62 years for electric wiring to reach 34 million homes, 80 years for the telephone, 49 for the auto, and 47 for the electric washer. It only took television 10 years to hit that number of homes . . . Ray Kroc, who built McDonald hamburger franchise to 200 stands since 1952, buys out original owners for $2.7 million and begins expansion to 3,500 outlets . . . In *The Challenge of Abundance*, economist Robert Theobald reports: "Products that used to sell for 25 years now often count on no more than five" . . . Average farm worker making only $881 a year—with extras $1,054. Migrant field hand averaging $677 . . . Over 5 million cars junked—around 4.5 million of them passenger cars . . .

Tuberculosis and syphilis causing one-tenth as many deaths per population as in 1939, while measles, whooping cough, diptheria and typhoid now cause few deaths—with polio virtually extinct . . . In national survey 84% think it right to buy a car on the installment plan, but only 32% approve of buying clothing (and 12% jewelry) on time . . .

TEEN AND COLLEGE LIVING AND
ALTERNATIVE LIFE STYLES IN THE ROCK ERA

President John F. Kennedy sets up the Peace Corps . . . Department of Labor Occupation Outlook Handbook estimates that 26 million young people will enter work force in 1960s, and that 7.5 million will leave high school before graduation, while 2.5 million won't go past eighth grade . . . Folk music flourishing on campus. New performers include 20-year-old Joan Baez, Earl Scruggs and Lester Flatt, and New Lost City Ramblers . . . Non-virginity among teen girls is 20%; boys 50% . . . Gallup poll shows 74% of youth very firmly believe in God; 78% believe in Hereafter; 58% of high schoolers plan to go to college. College boys expect to be earning $12,000 a year at 40, average high school boy $9,000 at that age, and working youth $8,000 . . . Another Gallup poll of 16-21-year-old girls shows: (1) Almost all expect to be married by age 22; (2) Most want four kids; (3) Only 20% expect money to be a marriage problem; (4) Only 22% going steady; (5) 75% use mascara on dates, but only 50% every day . . . Yet another Gallup poll shows 10% of high school sophomores have driven faster than 80 m.p.h.; 26% of seniors over 90 m.p.h.; 15% of college upperclassmen over 100 m.p.h.; and 15% of working young over 110 m.p.h. . . . PTA Magazine reports many nine-year-olds are now dating, and 12-year-olds going steady . . . Another Gallup poll conclusion: Teenage youth want very little because they have so much: "(He) is unwilling to risk what he has"; "He is old before his time; almost middle-aged in his teens." He likes himself the way he is, and he likes things the way they are . . . Police use tear gas as several thousand Harvard students demonstrate over decree that future diplomas will be printed in English instead of Latin . . . Rumbles disappear from New York streets after hitting peak three years ago, in 1958, when some 200 street gangs accounted for more than 11 homicides . . . Anthropologist Margaret Mead, in an article, says: "Instead of letting boys and girls go their separate ways in late childhood and adolescence, we are forcing them to practise, not how to be individuals, but how to be spouses and parents; catapulting them into premature, half-baked adulthood before they have a chance to grow up as individuals" . . . Gallup survey concludes that young people overwhelmingly approve of going steady, because it's socially safer and less nerve-wracking, but only 20% actually do it.

FASHION: CLOTHES AND THE
ROCK ERA ACCENT ON YOUTH

Note: Feminine fashion is in italics, male in roman, unisex in parentheses, and news in asterisks.

Suspenders and low-slung pants . . . (Bell-bottoms) . . . **Mary Travers of Peter, Paul and Mary, trying to conform, couldn't make her long, straight blonde hair curl into bouffant teased fashions of day. As result, college girls begin trading beehives for hairstyles of Sixties** . . . *Teens decorating sneakers with sequins, silver buttons, rick-rack, plaid ribbon, iron-on tape and colored hoops through laces* . . . **Twelve million 15-24-year-old girls spending $5 billion on clothes—averaging $439 each** . . . *Thigh-high skirts in* . . . **Natural look—less makeup returning to fashion** . . . *Uplifted lips: outer corners overpainted with upward tilt* . . . **Purdue University professor invents safer cosmetics—made from food** . . . *Last year's brown lipstick shades replaced by pink and golden tones* . . . **Cornell University study reveals that teenagers give greater weight to clothing as a means of gaining acceptance than adults—with the latter placing a higher value on the effects of physical enhancement** . . . **In his book, *Economics for Consumers,* Leland J. Gordon states that the average life of a style is two years: "The first six months is used for introduction, the second six months the style is in vogue, and the last year its status diminishes"** . . . **Ohio State University study on expenditure for new clothes during the summer and early fall before entering college reports $136 average, with girls averaging $163 and boys $97** . . . (White Levis and pastel jeans introduced by Levi Strauss) . . .

FADS (MOSTLY YOUTH-ORIENTED)
RELATED TO THE ROCK ERA

Bed pushing marathons . . . Skateboarding begins in California: called Sidewalk Surfing . . . Return of the yo-yo: 15 million sold . . . Trampolines . . . One million coloring books sold . . . JFK popularizes rocking chair . . . Topps Bubblegum signs 446 out of 450 Major League baseball players . . . Le Club in New York first U.S. discothèque . . .

SOME OF THE MORE WIDELY USED ARGOT,
JARGON AND SLANG IN THE ROCK ERA

A cool set of threads (proper dress) . . . Backseat Bingo (lovemaking) . . . Fream (a misfit) . . . Go ape (lose control) . . . Grok (experience empathy) . . . Heavy (important, serious) . . . "It's been real" (good or bad) . . . "I was shot down" (defeated and/or rejected) . . . "Let's put it in orbit" (It's worth trying) . . . Like crazy (agreement) . . . Nitty-gritty (heart of the matter) . . . Soul (essence) . . . The Tube (TV) . . . Wazoo (bum) . . . Zonked (intoxicated) . . . Zonked out (very high on drugs) . . .

Surfer Language: Kook (beginner) . . . Ho-Daddy (an intruding wise guy) . . . Going over the falls (being caught in a breaking wave) . . . Pearl (plunge straight down into surf) . . . Hot-doggers (surfers) . . . A good set of heavies (big rideable waves) . . . Toes over (going to board's nose for top speed) . . . Into the soup . . .

MOSTLY FACTUAL TRIVIA
CONCURRENT WITH THE ROCK ERA

U.S.C. Delta Chi team pushes bed (including starlet) on bike wheels 42 miles across Nevada desert in five hours . . . 100,000 view Matisse abstract painting, "Le Bateau," mistakenly hung upside down, before error is discovered 47 days later . . . James Bond defeats Spectre's attempt to blackmail Western nations with nuclear weapons . . .

1962 _____

ARTISTS

Rock Groups
  Beach Boys
  Four Seasons
  Isley Brothers
  Jay & The Americans
  Orlons
Rock Solo Performers
  Gene Pitney
  Tommy Roe
  Ray Stevens
  Bobby Vinton
Soul, R&B, Funk Groups
  Booker T. & The MGs
  Crystals
  Patti LaBelle & The Blue Belles
Soul, R&B, Funk Solo Performers
  Gene Chandler
  Dionne Warwick
  Mary Wells

Folk & Country
  Peter, Paul & Mary
  Rooftop Singers
Young Teen Oriented
  Paul and Paula
Middle of the Road
  Herb Alpert/Tijuana Brass
Comic Novelties
  Bobby (Boris) Pickett
Dance Fads
  Little Eva
  Dee Dee Sharp
Hot Rod & Surf
  Marketts

JUKE BOX HITS

"Town Without Pity"
Gene Pitney

"I Can't Stop Loving You"
Ray Charles

"Mashed Potato Time"
Dee Dee Sharp

"Roses Are Red"
Bobby Vinton

"Loco-Motion"
Little Eva

"Let Me In"
Sensations

"Limbo Rock"
Chubby Checker

"Don't Hang Up"
Orlons

"Bobby's Girl"
Marcie Blaine

"Up on the Roof"
Drifters

"Dream Baby"
Roy Orbison

"Patches"
Dicky Lee

"Big Girls Don't Cry"
Four Seasons

"Soldier Boy"
Shirelles

"Zip-A-Dee Doo Dah"
Bob B. Soxx & The Blue Jeans

"He's Sure the Boy I Love"
Crystals

"Playboy"
Marvelettes

"You Beat Me to the Punch"
Mary Wells

"Duke of Earl"
Gene Chandler

"Palisades Park"
Freddy Cannon

"The One Who Really Loves You"
Mary Wells

"Twistin' the Night Away"
Sam Cooke

"The Wah-Watusi"
Orlons

"Breaking Up Is Hard to Do"
Neil Sedaka

"Venus in Blue Jeans"
Jimmy Clanton

"Having a Party"
Sam Cooke

"He's a Rebel"
Crystals

"Papa-Oom-Mow-Mow"
Rivingtons

"Release Me"
Esther Phillips

"She Cried"
Jay & The Americans

"Love Letters"
Ketty Lester

"Twist and Shout"
Isley Brothers

"The Night Has a Thousand Eyes"
Bobby Vee

"Green Onions"
Booker T. & The MGs

"Sherry"
Four Seasons

"Beechwood 4-5789"
Marvelettes

"The Lion Sleeps Tonight"
Tokens

"Do You Love Me?"
Contours

"Johnny Angel"
Shelly Fabares

"Sealed with a Kiss"
Brian Hyland

"Sheila"
Tommy Roe

"Surfer's Stomp"
Marketts

"I Sold My Heart to the Junkman"
Patti LaBelle & The Blue Belles

"Return to Sender"
Elvis Presley

"Surfin' Safari"
Beach Boys

"Two Lovers"
Mary Wells

Novelty

"Monster Mash"
Bobby (Boris) Pickett

"Ahab the Arab"
Ray Stevens

Folk

"Cottonfields"
Highwaymen

"If I Had a Hammer"
Peter, Paul & Mary

"Where Have All the Flowers Gone"
Kingston Trio

DANCES

Adults take over the Twist

The Watusi

The Mashed Potato

The Locomotion

The Hitch Hike

The Bird

The Gravy

The Strand

The Limbo Rock

The Jam

The Stomp

NEWS OF ROCK

First hit records of protest songs, "If I Had a Hammer" (Peter, Paul and Mary) and "Where Have All the Flowers Gone?" (Kingston Trio) begin major trend . . . Future Rolling Stone Brian Jones places ad in *Jazz News* in hope of forming own group . . . Twist music dies out—but only after 15 new songs recorded with "Twist" in title . . . Hootenannies and folk coffee houses in big . . . ABC network launches folk TV show, "Hootenanny"— Judy Collins and Caroline Hester lead artist boycott when Pete Seeger banned . . . "Love Me Do" is first British chart entry for Beatles, and only lasts there a week . . . Strings, brass and percussion embraced by rock . . . Ringo Starr replaces Pete Best in Beatles . . . Herb Alpert cuts "Lonely Bull." Total recording cost is $200 . . . "Duke of Earl" Gene Chandler brings crazy costuming to rock music . . . Brian Epstein makes Beatles cut hair shorter . . . New code limits radio stations to 18 minutes of commercials per hour . . . Pat Boone's final appearance among Top 20 record hits . . . Ray Charles makes hit country & western album—crediting successful gamble to having listened to "Grand Ole Opry" since he was a child . . . Phil Spector a millionaire at age 21, after starting Philles Records with royalties from his song, "Spanish Harlem" (Ben E. King's hit) . . . Cost of recording Dylan's first album "Bob Dylan" is $402 . . . Fats

Domino switches record companies after selling almost 65 million (fantastic for that era) records for Imperial since 1950—with more than 20 million-sellers . . . *Teen* magazine editor Charles Laufer quoted as claiming: "The music market for the first time in history is completely dominated by the young set" . . . Single records selling for 98¢, with albums $3.98 mono and $4.98 stereo . . . Gold record awards all-time high for music business as five singles and 37 LPs hit the $1 million mark . . . Record industry hits $565 million mark as folk music boosts LP sales . . .

SOME OF THE NEWS THAT INFLUENCED THE ROCK ERA AND VICE VERSA

Unmanned Ranger spacecraft reaches the Moon . . . U.S. establishes a military assistance command in Saigon . . . JFK bans all Cuban trade (except certain foods and medicines) . . . 10,000 U.S. troops sent to Vietnam in past year . . . Cuban missile crisis: eyeball-to-eyeball confrontation . . . Nixon defeated by Brown in California Governor race—bows out of politics forever . . . John Glenn, first American in orbit, circles Earth . . . Telstar communications satellite launched . . . JFK contributes White House salary to charity . . . Boston Brinks robbery sets $1,500,000 record . . . Only 3,500 people asked for F.H.A.-insured home fallout shelter loans . . . Soviet refuses to sign treaty banning all nuclear weapons testing, so U.S. resumes tests . . . Protected by Federal officers, black Air Force veteran, James Meredith, begins classes at University of Mississippi . . . JFK authorizes new series of atmospheric nuclear weapon tests . . . During year, JFK made 300 requests for legislation. Congress approved only 44% . . . Supreme Court rules that reciting of official school prayer written by New York State officials is unconstitutional . . . Atomic Energy Commission approves construction of nuclear generating station 28 miles north of New York City after rejecting Electric Company plans to place it in heart of city . . . Scientists discover that the drug Thalidomide causes deformities in babies . . . JFK signs $3.9 billion foreign aid bill. It forbids aid to 18 Communist countries and any nation shipping arms to Cuba . . .

THE NUMBERS GAME: STATISTICAL INFORMATION SHOWING HOW LIFE IN AMERICA INFLUENCED OR WAS INFLUENCED BY THE ROCK ERA

Median family income now $5,700. College graduates earning $7,260, high school graduates $5,050 and men who only completed elementary school $3,450 . . . 70% of population now living in urban households and 20% in rural non-farm households; 7 out of 10 are living in state of birth

. . . Three in five workers travel to the job in cars (owned or in car pool), one in eight uses public transportation, and one in ten walks to work . . . Over 1.5 million left New York City for suburbs in past decade . . . Labor unions lose almost 500,000 members in past two years; and in past seven years the proportion of the total labor force belonging to unions decreased from 24.4% to 22.2%—despite large increases in U.S. population . . . 90% of U.S. households have at least one TV set and 13% have more than one in the house . . . Estimated twice as much factual knowledge in print as there was in 1945 . . . Total patient days spent in mental hospitals relative to national population 12% lower than 22 years ago . . . Rise in installment credit since 1956 smaller than it would have been if it had corresponded to increase in population and income. Average debt repayment stabilized at about 13% of disposable income . . . Rachel Carson's *Silent Spring* states: (1) Almost 500 new chemicals find their way into use annually—"chemicals totally outside the limits of biologic experience . . . to which the bodies of men and animals are required somehow to adapt"; (2) Since the mid-1940s, over 200 basic chemicals have been created for killing insects, weeds, rodents and other "pests"—with "the power to kill every insect, the 'good' and the 'bad,' to still the song of birds and the leaping of fish in the streams, to coat the leaves with a deadly film, and to linger on in the soil—all this though the target may be only a few weeds or insects." . . .

TEEN AND COLLEGE LIVING AND ALTERNATIVE LIFE STYLES IN THE ROCK ERA

Vassar College President tells 1,450 co-eds to stay chaste or leave school . . . Chevys and Plymouths top cars with teens—Chevrolet taking over from Ford in 1955 with Plymouth joining customizing elite in 1959 . . . Parents pick up on the Twist and start imitating other teen dances . . . Sub-teen girls into high school hairdos, pancake makeup, mascara and going steady . . . Over 53% of female college graduates hold jobs, vs. 36.2% of those with only a high school diploma . . . L.A. Cinnamon Cinder and Peppermint Stick start teenage non-alcoholic night club boom across U.S. Tuesday Weld, claiming to be 18, adjudged over age and refused admission to L.A. Pandora's Box . . . Bed-pushing fad begins in schools . . . Bowling alleys add pool tables for young customers . . . Northwestern University students hold three-day conference on the topic, "Personal Commitment in an Age of Anxiety." Dozens of similar actions taken by other college students—some of them devoted to the reform of university education, others to the reform of the political process . . . Florida State Ph.D. study on "Attitudes of Youth Towards Aged Persons" reports more college women than men favored the aged; and college men from intact families had more favorable attitudes than those from broken homes. High school girls who did not have aged family members at home were more favorably oriented than those who did; and high school boys with positive self concepts were more favorable than those with negative self concepts . . . Interviews with sampling of regular readers of *MAD Magazine* have those not doing well in school citing Alfred E. Neuman as its major feature and identifying with him. Also, that wide readership of *MAD* by other teens and parental opposition had much to do with legitimizing its appeal; with the leisure, media activities and problems of adolescents receiving little coverage . . . Average teen income $500 a year—$778 for boys, $392 for girls . . . High and junior high school sampling of student income (from multiple sources) reports: regular allowance, 49.3%; earned in outside jobs, 47.6%; earned at home, 17.5% and odd amounts from parents, 32.9% . . . Teen boys spending 32% of disposable income on food vs. girls 26%; entertainment, records, 22% vs. 11%; sports, 11% vs. 6%; savings, 7% vs. 9%; clothing, jewelry, 7% boys vs. 19% girls; and grooming, 2% boys vs. 7% girls . . . *Teen* magazine editor Charles Laufer quoted as claiming: "The music market for the first time in history is completely dominated by the young set" . . . Most single records selling for 98¢, with albums at $3.98 mono and $4.98 stereo . . . In "Teen-Age Tyranny," Grace and Fred M. Hechinger report: "Less than a generation ago, a fifteen-year-old boy or girl 'without a date' might be privately unhappy, but she or he was nothing to worry about publicly. Today, the teen-ager who is not dating regularly at that age appears to be everybody's problem" . . . University of California study finds that more of today's 9th graders (14-year-olds) approve of the use of lipstick than 11th graders (17-year-olds) did 20 years ago . . . Sociologist Laurence Wylie warns: "At church and school and home both boys and girls are told that it is wrong to express themselves sexually outside of wedlock. But . . . from newspaper stories . . . movies . . . magazines and TV, they learn ideal standards are false. The American adolescent must choose between observing the standards and feeling frustrated and cheated, or violating the standards, feeling guilt and risking social sanctions" . . . A story in *Time* magazine reports that an eight-year-old girl "needed" a garter belt and nylons for a party because "all other girls" had them, and a nine-year-old girl asked her parents for a "training" bra to wear on a movie date with her eleven-year-old boyfriend . . . Teenage charge accounts have doubled in past three years, and some of them start with 13-year-old shoppers, according to *Seventeen* magazine . . . California jeweler advertising "going steady ring" at $12.95 for "nothing down, payments of 50¢ a week" . . . National Retail Merchants Association reports teenage record of paying up credit is good, and some stores claim they are better credit risks than their elders . . . Bra ad explains: "Whether you're ten or a teen, you are moving into the delicious, delightful stage known as womanhood . . . Teenform understands every girl's secret wish. There is a bra called Littlest Angel—the bra that expands as a girl develops" . . .

FASHION: CLOTHES AND THE
ROCK ERA ACCENT ON YOUTH

Note: Feminine fashion is in italics, male in roman, unisex in parentheses, and news in asterisks.

Leather pants . . . Heavy-textured sweaters . . . Burr haircuts and green-dyed hair . . . *Denim pants and blue denim shirts* . . . ("Brahms, Beethoven and Bach" sweatshirts at $4) . . . **Wind, fog and rain not only enemy of bouffant. Hairdressers claim it won't let scalp breathe—but craze continues** . . . *Black turtleneck sweaters and black tights* . . . **JFK abolishes white tie and tails from the annual White House reception for foreign diplomats** . . . **In 926 advertisements in 50 women's magazines skin, hair and breasts are the categories with the most numerous entries** . . . Early-in-the-game young male protesters still in chino pants and button-down shirts . . . *Twist dance addicts buying anything with fringe, from peppermint-striped fringed dresses to fringed belts and garters* . . . Top New York department store, Gimbel Brothers, President Bruce Gimbel warns: "Men, taking a cue from the boys, now want slimmer pants, trimmer suits, sharp colors, some hot shades and gaucho shirts—all of which started in the boys' business . . . If the trend to sports shirts and blue jeans is not checked, our future generation of fathers may well be dressing in exactly this fashion when they go to their jobs as executives and white collar workers" . . .

FADS (MOSTLY YOUTH-ORIENTED)
RELATED TO THE ROCK ERA

Coloring books . . . Worry beads . . . Glue sniffing . . . Grossinger's first singles-only weekend . . . Pop Art becomes "In Thing" via Andy Warhol's soup can paintings and Roy Lichtenstein's comic strips. Spreads quickly into youth culture and rock by-products . . . JFK and Caroline coloring books . . .

SOME OF THE MORE WIDELY USED ARGOT,
JARGON AND SLANG IN THE ROCK ERA

Boink (stupid) . . . Boss (great) . . . Jazzed (excited) . . . Making out (pre-teen phrase for tentative adolescent necking) . . . Mod (in with trends) . . . Shafted (torpedoed) . . . Twink (out of date) . . . Wig (something that excites) . . .

MOSTLY FACTUAL TRIVIA
CONCURRENT WITH THE ROCK ERA

Van de Kamp's bakes 25,000 lb. cake for Seattle Fair . . . New ice cube tossing record set by two Indianapolis girls standing two feet apart. They tossed cube to and fro 4,477 times before it melted . . . Americans on popcorn binge—average 32 quarts per American . . . Auto tail fins, which became the rage in 1956, disappear from Fords and Chevies . . .

1963 _____

ARTISTS

Rock Groups
  Jimmy Gilmer & The Fireballs
  Kingsmen

Rock Solo Performers
  Lou Christie
  Bob Dylan
  Lesley Gore

Soul, R&B, Funk Groups
  Chiffons
  Essex
  Major Lance
  Martha & The Vandellas
  Ronettes
  Ruby & The Romantics
  Supremes
  Tymes

Soul, R&B, Funk Solo Performers
  Marvin Gaye
  Barbara Lewis
  Garnet Mimms
  Rufus Thomas
  Stevie Wonder

Folk & Country
  New Christy Minstrels

Young Teen Oriented
  Shirley Ellis
  Lesley Gore

Middle of the Road
  Nino Tempo & April Stevens
  Wayne Newton

Hot Rod & Surf
  Rip Chords
  Surfaris

JUKE BOX HITS

"Surfin' U.S.A."
Beach Boys

"He's So Fine"
Chiffons

"Hey Paula"
Paul & Paula

"Fingertips (Part II)"
Little Stevie Wonder

"My Boyfriend's Back"
Angels

"Deep Purple"
Nino Tempo & April Stevens

"Anyone Who Had a Heart"
Dionne Warwick

"Walk Like a Man"
Four Seasons

"If I Had a Hammer"
Trini Lopez

"Devil in Disguise"
Elvis Presley

"Easier Said Than Done"
Essex

"Nitty Gritty"
Shirley Ellis

"Baby, I Love You"
Ronettes

"One Fine Day"
Chiffons

"Surfer Girl"
Beach Boys

"When the Lovelight Starts
Shining Through His Eyes"
Supremes

"Quicksand"
Martha & The Vandellas

"Mockingbird"
Inez Foxx

"Surf City"
Jan & Dean

"It's My Party"
Lesley Gore

"Heat Wave"
Martha & The Vandellas

"Our Day Will Come"
Ruby & The Romantics

"Be My Baby"
Ronettes

"Monkey Time"
Major Lance

"Sugar Shack"
Jimmy Gilmer & The Fireballs

"Take These Chains from
My Heart"
Ray Charles

"Louie Louie"
The Kingsmen

"Wipe Out"
Surfaris

"Cry Baby"
Garnet Mimms & The Enchanters

"Blue Velvet"
Bobby Vinton

"Da Doo Ron Ron"
Crystals

"In Dreams"
Roy Orbison

"You've Really Got
a Hold on Me"
Miracles

"Another Saturday Night"
Sam Cooke

"Mickey's Monkey"
Miracles

"Don't Make Me Over"
Dionne Warwick

"Walking the Dog"
Rufus Thomas

"Walk Right In"
Rooftop Singers

"Then He Kissed Me"
Crystals

"Rhythm of the Rain"
Cascades

"So Much in Love"
Tymes

"Hello Stranger"
Barbara Lewis

"Drag City"
Jan & Dean

"On Broadway"
Drifters

"It's All Right"
Impressions

Folk

"Puff (The Magic Dragon)"
Peter, Paul & Mary

"Blowin' in the Wind"
Peter, Paul & Mary

"Green, Green"
The New Christy Minstrels

DANCES

The Monkey

The Dog

NEWS OF ROCK

Beatles see Rolling Stones at Crawdaddy Club in London and recommend them to ex-publicist Andrew Loog Oldham . . . British Decca, who turned down the Beatles, sign Rolling Stones without hesitation . . . Over six million guitars sold . . . Bobby Darin dies . . . Patsy Cline, Cowboy Copus and Hawkshaw Hawkins killed in plane crash . . . Twelve-year-old Little Stevie Wonder first rock artist to hit No. 1 in singles and album charts simultaneously . . . British media invent new word, "Beatlemania" . . . Big year for girl groups and soloists as Martha and the Vandellas, the Chiffons, Crystals, Angels, Dionne Warwick, Mary Wells, Inez Foxx and others dominate pop charts . . . On first British tour, Rolling Stones just support act for Little Richard, Bo Diddley and the Everlys . . . Folk music joins the Civil Rights struggle . . . Surf music "in"—11 songs with surf in title . . . New low in hit rock 'n' roll artists as folk and soul move in to fill gap until British invasion . . . Coffee house circuit of folk clubs spreads from Greenwich Village to almost every key city and college campus in past five years . . . "Detroit Sound" via Motown impetus for soul explosion . . . First two Beatles singles in U.S. released a year too early, and both are failures: "She Loves You" on Swan and "Please Please Me" on Veejay . . . Dylan and Joan Baez star at Newport Folk Festival, with Peter, Paul and Mary, Pete Seeger and Theodore Bikel joining them on stage for show-stopping "Blowin' in the Wind" . . . New Orleans fades from rock spotlight, when producer of Ernie K-Doe, Chris Kenner and Lee Dorsey (among others), Allen Toussaint, gets draft call . . . Bobby Darin is first rock artist to be nominated for an Oscar—as best supporting actor for his role in the film *Captain Newman, M.D.* . . .

SOME OF THE NEWS THAT INFLUENCED
THE ROCK ERA AND VICE VERSA

John F. Kennedy, 30th President, assassinated . . . Oswald shot by Ruby on TV . . . U.S.-Soviet "hotline" established . . . Schools integrated in all states but Alabama . . . Civil Rights march on Washington by 250,000 . . . Diem brothers assassinated in Vietnam . . . Surgeon-General links smoking with lung cancer . . . Public resents Post Office move into ZIP codes . . . Gallup poll reports Lyndon Johnson "most admired American" . . . Now 17,000 U.S. troops in South Vietnam . . . Anti-Diem Buddhists burn themselves to death in Vietnam . . . Shocked by Berlin Wall, JFK takes pride in words, "Ich bin ein Berliner" . . . U.S., Great Britain and Russia sign bill banning nuclear tests in atmosphere, outer space and underwater . . . Last state to hold out against school integration, Alabama, finally bows to Federal law . . . U.S. joins with Soviets in urging renewed neutrality of Laos . . . Almost 14,000 arrests in 75 Southern cities during summer Civil Rights demonstrations . . . U.S. sends up two satellites equipped to detect violations of Nuclear Test Treaty . . . JFK approves sale of four million metric tons of wheat to Russia . . . Cambodia severs economic and military relations with the U.S. . . . Warren Commission to study all aspects of Kennedy assassination named by LBJ . . . Newsmen heavily criticize government for "management of news" during 1962 Cuban crisis . . . Martin Luther King says, "I have a dream" . . . JFK requests anti-segregation measures and development of a Civil Rights program by Congress . . . Kennedy signs bill forbidding sex discrimination in payment for equal work . . . Thermal pollution kills estimated two billion striped bass at Hudson River, N.Y., nuclear plant before safeguards erected . . . Only one state, Kentucky, meets Federal standard on billboard regulations—although Congress approved a plan offering a .5% bonus on highway funds for compliance . . .

THE NUMBERS GAME: STATISTICAL INFORMATION
SHOWING HOW LIFE IN AMERICA INFLUENCED
OR WAS INFLUENCED BY THE ROCK ERA

U.S. factory workers average over $100 a week for the first time . . . 2.5 million Federal employees, up from 1,130,000 in 1940 . . . Overall height of Chevrolet and Ford cars lowered to approximately 4 ft. 7 in. from approximately 5 ft. 3 in. in 1951 . . . Average U.S. per capita meat consumption reaches 170.6 lbs.—chicken up to 37.8 lbs. from 23.5 in 1945, when it was costlier than beef . . . Estimated 5.7 million foreign weapon imports in past four years . . . California now most populous state. In 1960 New York was still 1 million ahead . . . Now 200 different soaps and detergents, vs. 65 in 1950; 350 frozen foods vs. 121; 200 different baking mixes and flours vs. 84;

and 81 pet foods vs. 58 . . . In mining, production shows dramatic increase during past 15 years, but number of mineworkers declines by 300,000 . . . Manufacturing output shows increase in past five years—but there's a new loss since 1958 of 425,000 jobs . . . Expenditures for private construction reach $5.2 billion, vs. $3.2 billion in 1954 . . . In June, the weekly pay for about 40 hours' work by the average production worker passed $100—four times the Depression pay for the same job . . . 40% of all families now earn over $7,000 a year . . .

TEEN AND COLLEGE LIVING AND
ALTERNATIVE LIFE STYLES IN THE ROCK ERA

Survey of 12-17-year-olds reports 90% of boys using hair dressing and 66% a deodorant. 85% of girls using hair spray; 67% get permanents; 87% use lipstick; 84% nail polish, 59% eye makeup; 93% deodorants . . . *Scholastic* magazine survey reports 58% of boys use mouthwash and 69% something on chapped lips . . . 16-year-old Gregory Potter qualifies to fly twin and single-engined planes and helicopters . . . Adolescents spending $22 billion, twice the gross national product of Austria . . . Girls at Louisiana State University stage "drawers raid" on men's fraternity . . . Two Cornell fraternities play 30-hour touch football game. Final score: 664 to 538 . . . Harvard University Dean states that girls' visits to dorms have "come to be a license . . . for wild parties and sex" . . . Closed circuit TV being used in over 300 educational institutions apart from armed forces training centers, and broadcast TV now a curriculum staple in thousands more . . . Illegitimate births among mothers aged 15 to 19 climb to 101,000 out of 4 million births from 40,000 in 1940 . . . Old *Tarzan* movies popular on college campuses . . . University of California, Berkeley, students ask the dispensary to dispense contraceptives. Request ignored . . .

FASHION: CLOTHES AND THE
ROCK ERA ACCENT ON YOUTH

Note: Feminine fashion is in italics, male in roman, unisex in parentheses, and news in asterisks.

Women now wearing male clothing styles . . . **Stretch tights spread from campuses to acceptance at all levels throughout U.S.** . . . Beards becoming popular . . . *Panty-hose in* . . . **Wigs big** . . . *Boots and jeans* . . . **U.S. males break out of gray suits and white shirts—add color to wardrobes** . . . "Surfer" styles: windswept castaway look, ragged clothes, bare feet or sneakers and long blond (often bleached) hair . . . *Pajama suits* . . . **Jackie Kennedy sets adult styles with pillbox hat, shoes with very pointed toes and very slender heels, hair length just below the ears—softly curled or bouffant—skirts a little below the knee, and waistless sheath** . . . *Blushers (face rouge) popularized* . . . **Mary Quant starts exporting London fashions to U.S.—focusing on "mix-and-match" separates, coats, boots, stockings and accessories, creating harmonized total "look"** . . . **Vidal Sassoon debuts with short, angular hairstyle: "The Bob"** . . . **Drug Trade News* reports that women spent around $339 million keeping clean, $194 million in smelling attractive, $91 million coloring the hair, $613 million keeping hair in condition, $133 million caring for the skin, $116 million on their hands, and $457 million on makeup** . . . Striped surfer shirts . . .

FADS (MOSTLY YOUTH-ORIENTED) RELATED TO THE ROCK ERA

Piano wrecking . . . "Kick a Puppy Today" and other sick bumper stickers . . . Protest sweatshirts . . . "Beep-line" makes phone busy signal teen meeting place . . . First large Pop Art exhibition in New York features Warhol, Robert Rauschenberg, Jasper Johns, etc. . . . Tom Swifties . . . In first two years of Demolition Derbies, 15,000 cars destroyed at 154 jousts. . .

SOME OF THE MORE WIDELY USED ARGOT, JARGON AND SLANG IN THE ROCK ERA

Fab (thrilling, exciting) . . . Fox (sexy girl) . . . Lunchy (not with it) . . . Mellow (in) . . . Mouse (cute girl) . . . Out to lunch (not too bright) . . .
Sub-teen Special Language: Blast (great time) . . . Fake out (dupe) . . . Gasser (the best) . . . Hung up (overboard) . . . The Straight Skinnies (truth) . . . Tough toenails (too bad) . . . Triple ratfink (the worst) . . . Wuzza wuzza (and furthermore) . . .
Alleged drug-oriented song titled: "Puff (The Magic Dragon)" (Peter, Paul and Mary) . . .

THE NEW WOMAN IN THE ROCK ERA

Betty Friedan's *The Feminine Mystique* published. In it, she envisages woman as a vain gull of male exploitation, frittering away her talents in boredom and drudgery . . .

MOSTLY FACTUAL TRIVIA CONCURRENT WITH THE ROCK ERA

Eight-hour Andy Warhol film, *Sleep*, features naked man asleep the full time . . . 25th anniversary of flexible drinking straws . . . People in

Pennsylvania like their pancake syrup thicker than rest of U.S., so Corn Products gives their Karo syrup a different viscosity for that region . . . *New York Times* and other periodicals needle "Ice Cream Congress" for doing little more than repealing the 1921 law that prohibits selling solid milk products in less than half-pint packages in D.C.—thereby taking Dixie Cups and Eskimo Pie off the Washington contraband list . . . American Medical Association reports an estimated 40,000 people try to walk through glass doors, walls and picture windows each year, with almost 6,000 winding up in hospitals . . . 75th anniversary of the first Kodak camera—advertised by the slogan, "You push the button, we do the rest" . . . *Playboy* magazine receiving an average of 50 applications a week from girls aspiring to appear unclothed on its gatefold as "Playmate of the Month" . . .

1964 _____

ARTISTS

Rock Groups
  Animals
  Beatles
  Chad & Jeremy
  Dave Clark Five
  Gerry & The Pacemakers
  Herman's Hermits
  Kinks
  Billy J. Kramer & The Dakotas
  Manfred Mann
  Peter & Gordon
  Righteous Brothers
  Rolling Stones
  Searchers
  Shangri-Las
  Zombies

Rock Solo Performers
  Petula Clark
  Bobby Goldsboro
  Johnny Rivers
  Dusty Springfield

Soul, R&B, Funk Groups
  Dixie Cups
  Four Tops
  Temptations

Folk & Country
  Roger Miller
  Buffy Sainte-Marie

Hot Rod & Surf
  Hondells
  Ronny & The Daytonas

JUKE BOX HITS

"I Want to Hold Your Hand"
Beatles

"Dawn (Go Away)"
Four Seasons

"She Loves You"
Beatles

"Oh, Pretty Woman"
Roy Orbison

"I Get Around"
Beach Boys

"My Guy"
Mary Wells

"Where Did Our Love Go"
Supremes

"A Hard Day's Night"
Beatles

"Love Me Do"
Beatles

"I Only Want to Be with You"
Dusty Springfield

"The Little Old Lady
(From Pasadena)"
Jan & Dean

"Time Is on My Side"
Rolling Stones

"You're a Wonderful One"
Marvin Gaye

"I'm into Something Good"
Herman's Hermits

"Dang Me"
Roger Miller

"Remember (Walkin' in the Sand)"
Shangri-Las

"Needles and Pins"
Searchers

"Leader of the Pack"
Shangri-Las

"Fun, Fun, Fun"
Beach Boys

"Rag Doll"
Frankie Valli & The
Four Seasons

"Do Wah Diddy Diddy"
Manfred Mann

"Please Please Me"
Beatles

"Dancing in the Street"
Martha & The Vandellas

"Little Children"
Billy J. Kramer

"You've Lost That Lovin'
Feelin' "
Righteous Brothers

"She's Not There"
Zombies

"Chapel of Love"
Dixie Cups

"Suspicion"
Terry Stafford

"Glad All Over"
Dave Clark Five

"Bits and Pieces"
Dave Clark Five

"Don't Let the Sun Catch
You Crying"
Gerry & The Pacemakers

"Out of Sight"
James Brown

"(Just Like) Romeo and Juliet"
Reflections

"Hold What You've Got"
Joe Tex

"Love Potion No. 9"
Searchers

"There I've Said It Again"
Bobby Vinton

"This Diamond Ring"
Gary Lewis & The Playboys

"No Particular Place to Go"
Chuck Berry

"Walking in the Rain"
Ronettes

"Summer Song"
Chad & Jeremy

"It Hurts to Be in Love"
Gene Pitney

"Come a Little Bit Closer"
Jay & The Americans

"A World Without Love"
Peter & Gordon

"Baby Love"
Supremes

"Let It Be Me"
Betty Everett/Jerry Butler

"Walk On By"
Dionne Warwick

"The House of the Rising Sun"
Animals

"G.T.O."
Ronny & The Daytonas

"Twist and Shout"
Beatles

"My Boy Lollipop"
Millie Small

"Under the Boardwalk"
Drifters

"The Way You Do the Things
You Do"
Temptations

"Quicksand"
Martha & The Vandellas

"Baby, I Need Your Loving"
Four Tops

"You've Really Got Me"
Kinks

"How Sweet It Is"
Marvin Gaye

"It's Over"
Roy Orbison

"See the Funny Little Clown"
Bobby Goldsboro

"How Do You Do It?"
Gerry & The Pacemakers

"Wishin' and Hopin'"
Dusty Springfield

DANCES

The Bird, the Monkey, and the
Jerk still big, as discos begin
to peak out

The Frug

The Swim

The Hitchhiker & the Surf (Paris)

The Woodpecker (London)

NEWS OF ROCK

The Who submit demos to EMI London and are rejected . . . "I Wanna Hold Your Hand" No. 1 in U.S. charts for seven weeks . . . Beatles play Carnegie Hall . . . Beatles win M.B.E. . . . "Can't Buy Me Love" has biggest advance sale of any record to date: 2,100,000 . . . 56,000 fans at Beatles' Shea Stadium concert . . . Beatles get biggest one-performance fee to date: $150,000 in Kansas City . . . Chicagoans buy sheets and pillow-cases Beatles used at Detroit and Kansas City hotels for $1,150, and cut them into 160,000 one-inch squares to sell for $1 each . . . Dave Clark Five first British group with U.S. hit in wake of Beatles. Followed by the Searchers, Peter and Gordon, Gerry and the Pacemakers, Chad and Jeremy, the Stones and the Animals. By year-end two dozen British groups hit U.S. charts . . . Bob Dylan abandons protest songs at Newport Folk Festival . . . 1959 payola inquiry victim Alan Freed dead . . . Randy Sparks gets $2.5 million from L.A. management firm for his interest in the New Christy Minstrels . . . 18-year-old college student is the founder of first rock fan-zine, *Crawdaddy* . . . Purist folk magazine *Sing Out* circulation rises to

20,000 from 1,000 in 1955 as it wails about commercialism of folk surge . . . Jim Reeves dies in plane crash . . . Sam Cooke shot dead at Los Angeles motel . . . Robert Moog develops synthesizer . . . Joe Tex brings focus to "Muscle Shoals" (Alabama) sound; and famed studio there joins Nashville, Memphis and Miami recording facilities as much-sought-after place to record by top rock artists seeking new sounds from studios, engineers and local musicians . . . Capitol Records spends enormous (for the day) sum of $50,000 to introduce the Beatles to America . . . Ed Sullivan TV show features the Beatles, Rolling Stones, Animals and Dave Clark Five as well as some domestic rockers; but he becomes vexed with the squealing teenagers in the audience enjoying themselves at the expense of home viewers . . . After Surgeon-General's report on health hazards of smoking, radio station WMCA, New York, bans cigarette ads from rock music programs, and other teen programs soon follow suit . . . Adult discothèque vogue, which started in Paris and boomed in London, belatedly catches on in New York and spreads West—with the older generation taking over the Watusi, Swim, Frug and Monkey . . . Beatles' total gross $1 million for U.S. tour . . .

SOME OF THE NEWS THAT INFLUENCED
THE ROCK ERA AND VICE VERSA

U.S. destroyer enters Viet combat zone and Tonkin Gulf incident gives LBJ excuse to have U.S. warplane sink 35 North Vietnamese boats . . . Chinese test atomic bomb . . . Khrushchev out, Brezhnev in . . . Civil Rights Act signed by Johnson . . . Warren Committee reports that Oswald acted alone . . . 400th anniversary of Shakespeare's birth . . . U.S. rejects secret peace talks with North Vietnam . . . LBJ orders 44-foot portrait of himself for 1964 Democratic Convention . . . LBJ says, "We don't want our American boys to do the fighting for Asian boys" . . . U.S. force of 750 ICBMs four times that of Soviets . . . First of long hot summers in black ghettos . . . Goldwater says, "Extremism in the defense of liberty is no vice," and suffers worst defeat in Presidential campaign history . . . LBJ calls for "unconditional war on poverty" and gets Congress to help . . . Surgeon-General's negative reports on smoking and cancer based on random sampling of 1,123,000 men, of whom 37,391 were observed until their deaths . . . LBJ asks Congress to create Job Corps for unemployed youths . . . Congress adopts a joint resolution approving North Viet bombing and authorizing President to do what may be required to bar such attacks in future . . . Mariner 4, an unmanned spacecraft, transmits 21 photos of Mars to Earth . . . Martin Luther King awarded Nobel Peace Prize . . . U.S. warns that it will use every means short of military action to end Laos fighting, and sends light planes to anti-Communist forces there . . . Even stronger bill than that proposed by JFK passed by Congress, banning racial discrimination in public places, employment, voting, education and all Federally-aided programs . . . Hearings by Senate Foreign Relations Committee on Tonkin affair end inconclusively with certain senators charging that LBJ administration "manufactured" the incident . . . Secret memorandum by Assistant Secretary of Defense says U.S. objective in Vietnam is not "to save a friend" but "to avoid humiliation" . . . Amendment (24th) barring use of poll taxes to prevent citizens from voting is ratified . . .

THE NUMBERS GAME: STATISTICAL INFORMATION SHOWING HOW LIFE IN AMERICA INFLUENCED OR WAS INFLUENCED BY THE ROCK ERA

Per capita expenditure on new musical instruments $3.93—up from $1.60 in 1950 . . . 83 million coins being dropped into vending machines every 24 hours, as annual volume hits $3.5 billion . . . Now 1,200 U.S. symphony orchestras, vs. 10 in 1900 . . . U.S. spending almost $40 billion annually on recreation—perhaps 20 times more per capita than 1900 . . . U.S. mail volume now 70 billion pieces a year . . . 20 million now playing the piano, 4 million the guitar, 3 million the violin—and there are 2 million Sunday painters . . . 7,841 arrested for marijuana possession . . . Presidential campaign costs by both parties divided by 70.6 million voters amounts to 41¢ a vote. It was 36¢ in 1960 and 19¢ in 1956—which was just about the same as 1928, before TV . . . Now 16,000 mobile-home parks, with over a thousand new ones being built each year . . . U.S. expenditure on outdoor advertising (mostly billboards) now 350% over 1940 . . . Department of Interior reports 100 million visitors to national parks this year vs. some 16 million in 1940 . . . Nationwide alcoholic beverage drinking total 71%, of whom 89% are college-educated, 87% earn over $10,000—and 100% of the study's sample of physicians, dentists, lawyers and judges imbibe . . . Over 6 million scientific papers have been published over the course of world history, and 500,000 a year are now being produced, Yale professor tells American Association for the Advancement of Science . . . Sale of aspirin and other nonprescription painkillers up some 240% in past 15 years . . . Apparent consumption of distilled spirits hit record 276 million gallons—averaging 1.45 gallons a person . . . About 1,000 new shopping centers opened during past two years . . . American Music Conference estimates that there are 37 million amateur musicians in U.S.—double the 1950 number . . .

TEEN AND COLLEGE LIVING AND ALTERNATIVE LIFE STYLES IN THE ROCK ERA

Record 5,320,294 enrolled in colleges and universities—10.8% over last year's 4,800,332 and 20.3% over 1961 . . . 1,255,000 kids enter college—

four times 1934 total, and 20% over 1963 . . . Teens make half a billion phone calls per week and eat 1½ million tons of ice cream. One-third of 15-24-year-old boys now buying used cars . . . Teens own 20% of all U.S. cars . . . 23 million 13-20-year-olds spend $24.5 billion . . . Free Speech Movement at University of California at Berkeley begins campus revolt pattern . . . 60% of first-time brides will be 13-22 years old . . . Marshall McLuhan compares teenage rebellion against uniform consumer values to European values—saying teen norm mirrors 1920s American expatriates . . . American Tissue Games Association Olympics winner unravels 1,000-sheet bog roll in 1 minute 17 seconds . . . Draftee rejection rate rises from 34% in Korean War to 58% . . . Teens have 7 million drivers' licenses . . . 85% of guitars bought by teens. 230,000 are electric, 35,000 more than 1963 . . . Harvard student panty raid revival has to be broken up by police with dogs . . . Several hundred Brandeis University students stage two-day protest over new rule requiring doors to a dormitory room to be kept open when a boy and girl are inside . . . Survey of 1,365 Missouri high school students reveals they spend an average of $8.46 a month each for clothes . . . 300% increase in school-age musicians since 1950, while the school-age population only increased 71% . . . Kansas junior high school survey discloses that school is the greatest source of school-age youth problems, but assists with only 37% of troubles facing adolescents . . . *American Journal of Sociology* report on study of adolescent drinkers reports positive relationship between teenagers' group affiliation and alcohol consumption. Individuals mutually attractive to each other had tendency to display same drinking habits . . . Universities spend $2 billion on research, about 10% of the total national expenditures on research and development . . . Brand Names Foundation study among *Ingenue* readers asks: "How much money do you spend on yourself a week?" Percentage results for A (under $2.50), B ($2.51 to $4.50) and C ($4.51 and over) were: Ages 9-12: A 82%, B 13%, C 5%; Age 13: A 66%, B 18%, C 16%; Age 14: A 58%, B 24%, C 18%; Age 15: A 51%, B 24%, C 25%; Age 16: A 45%, B 23%, C 32%; Age 17: A 29%, B 20%, C 51%; Age 18: A 15%, B 13%, C 72%; Age 19: A 12%, B 10%, C 78% . . . *Los Angeles Free Press* first big underground paper . . . *Berkeley Barb* overnight underground newspaper success in San Francisco . . . Ken "One Flew Over the Cuckoo's Nest" Kesey and Merry Pranksters buy 1939 school bus, wire it for rock, paint it in primary colors, and cross U.S. to New York World's Fair in historic super "trip" which becomes 40-hour movie . . .

FASHION: CLOTHES AND THE
ROCK ERA ACCENT ON YOUTH

Note: Feminine fashion is in italics, male in roman, unisex in parentheses, and news in asterisks.

Mini-skirts arrive in New York . . . *Long straight hair for girls* . . . Long hair for boys . . . (Unisex fashions big) . . . **Topless bathing suit debuts with sale of 3,000** . . . **Topless dress introduced** . . . *Warner "body stocking"—almost invisible foundation, fashioned like a swimsuit in flesh-colored nylon . . . Textured stockings* . . . **Jeans become uniform of college protest** . . . *Co-eds wearing no makeup, shoulder-strap bags, "jiffy" coats, ponchos, and headbands instead of scarves* . . . *Sheer nylon net "no-bra bra"* . . . *Teen favorites strawberry-flavored lipstick, saucer-sized sunglasses, snow-white Levis, and iridescent eye shadow* . . . **Warner replaces panty-and-bra combinations with body stocking** . . . *High-heeled sneakers* . . . Beatles popularize Prince Valiant hairdos, suits buttoned to the chin, and visored caps . . . *Midi-length dresses and skirts* . . . **Lovable calls "no-bra bra" "Bare Minimum"** . . . *Teen most "in" hairstyle—looking like early Barbra Streisand and Mary Travers, with straight and natural hair. Difficult for curly heads. Teen girls spending $300 million on grooming products. Many own three switches, worn separately or in combination* . . . 191 different fragrances of all sorts marketed for men—40 over previous year . . . **London Times* article entitled, "How To Tell a Boy from a Girl"** . . . *Zip fly in front of femme trousers* . . . **Seventeen* magazine survey shows 90% of girls regularly use mascara vs. 20% just 16 years ago** . . . **Discothèques popularize dresses that are bare on top, providing coolness in crowded rooms, and short skirts to give dancing room** . . . **Levi Strauss removes rivets from hip pockets of jeans** . . . **Cornell University study of high school girls reports senior students are usually first to take up a fashion fad; and that by the time junior girls hopped in, it had already lost its novelty for the seniors, who soon dropped it** . . . **Teenage girls, only 11% of the female population, accounting for 23% of all cosmetic and toilet goods sales ($450 million)** . . . **Femme cosmetics companies launch men's toiletries with big fanfare. Aramis introduced by Estée Lauder, and Brut by Faberge** . . . **Although high-fashion experts prescribe the ideal for school and basketball games to be coats with raccoon collars, car coats and pleated skirts, the garments worn most often are plain-colored coats and straight skirts** . . . **Study of 294 male leaders from 107 high schools reports 82% of the sophomores, 67% of juniors and 50% of seniors shopped for major items of clothing with parents or relatives—but for less expensive items, such as sweaters, shirts and ties, 57% to 79% shopped alone or with a friend** . . .

FADS (MOSTLY YOUTH-ORIENTED)
RELATED TO THE ROCK ERA

Guitars and harmonicas in . . . Beatles books, buttons, teeshirts, posters, scarves and wallets rake in $50 million in one year . . . Girls wearing big dime store rings . . . Glassless eyeglasses for boys . . . Play-Doh. . . . Hair ironing . . . Disco craze fades . . . Long hair for males via Beatles . . .

Humphrey Bogart film festivals spread from Harvard campus Brattle Theatre . . . G.I. Joe doll and equipment gross $10 million first year . . . Little Monster cookies for monster fad ("A fright in every bite") . . .

SOME OF THE MORE WIDELY USED ARGOT, JARGON AND SLANG IN THE ROCK ERA

Blow one's cool (lose composure) . . . Cheese (girls) . . . Disco (short for discothèque) . . . Fat City (excellent condition) . . . Jock (athlete) . . . Jock talk (language of athletes) . . . Pits (extension of armpits: unpleasant) . . . Trip (changing moods and feelings) . . . Tune in (become aware) . . . Underground (counter-conventional) . . . Zot (zero, nothing) . . .

THE NEW WOMAN IN THE ROCK ERA

Clause forbidding sexual discrimination included in Civil Rights Act of 1964 . . . Women's Bureau analysis of 43,000 women college graduates shows 62% as teachers and school workers . . . Women represent 38% of all college seniors . . . Only 5% of women aged 35-44 have never been married, vs. 10% in 1940. Males 8% vs. 14% . . . 27% of 18-19-year-old women now married, vs. 12% in 1940 . . .

MOSTLY FACTUAL TRIVIA CONCURRENT WITH THE ROCK ERA

Allan and Midge join Ken and Barbie dolls . . . Ex-hog cutter convicted for all-time greatest swindle—made $175 million substituting sea water for salad oil . . . 180-foot worm washes ashore in Scotland after storm . . . Bourbon largest-selling whiskey in U.S. (and by virtue of this fact, worldwide). Accounts for 83% of total U.S. whiskey production . . . 65 pockets of alcoholic beverage prohibition eliminated in 14 states by local option . . .

1965 _____

ARTISTS

Rock Groups
  Byrds
  Spencer Davis Group
  Wayne Fontana &
    The Mindbenders
  Fortunes
  Freddie & The Dreamers
  Gary Lewis & The Playboys
  Lovin' Spoonful
  McCoys
  Moody Blues
  Seekers
  Simon & Garfunkel
  Sonny & Cher
  Them
  Turtles
  Vogues
  Walker Brothers
  We Five
  Yardbirds

Rock Solo Performers
  Cher
  Donovan
  Marianne Faithfull
  Tom Jones
  Barry McGuire

Soul, R&B, Funk Groups
  Toys
  Junior Walker & The All Stars

Soul, R&B, Funk Solo Performers
  Fontella Bass
  Dobie Gray
  Wilson Pickett
  Otis Redding
  Joe Tex

Folk & Country
  Butterfield Blues Band
  Rod McKuen
  Tom Rush

Middle of the Road
  Jackie De Shannon
  Ramsey Lewis Trio

Comic Novelties
  Sam the Sham & The
    Pharaohs

JUKE BOX HITS

"As Tears Go By"
Marianne Faithfull

"What the World Needs Now
Is Love"
Jackie De Shannon

"We Can Work It Out"
Beatles

"Help Me Rhonda"
Beach Boys

"Ain't That Peculiar"
Marvin Gaye

"Down in the Boondocks"
Billy Joe Royal

"Goin' Out of My Head"
Little Anthony & The Imperials

"I'll Never Find Another You"
Seekers

"Keep Searchin' "
Del Shannon

"Count Me In"
Gary Lewis & The Playboys

"It Ain't Me Babe"
Turtles

"Papa's Got a Brand New Bag"
James Brown

"Game of Love"
Wayne Fontana & The
Mindbenders

"A Lover's Concerto"
Toys

"Like a Rolling Stone"
Bob Dylan

"I'm Henry VIII, I Am"
Herman's Hermits

"Go Now"
Moody Blues

"Sounds of Silence"
Simon & Garfunkel

"Do You Believe in Magic"
Lovin' Spoonful

"I Can't Help Myself"
Four Tops

"Wooly Bully"
Sam the Sham & The Pharaohs

"You Were on My Mind"
We Five

"(I Can't Get No) Satisfaction"
Rolling Stones

"Downtown"
Petula Clark

"Everyone's Gone to the Moon"
Jonathan King

"Help!"
Beatles

"Can't You Hear My Heartbeat"
Herman's Hermits

"Crying in the Chapel"
Elvis Presley

"My Girl"
Temptations

"King of the Road"
Roger Miller

"I Know a Place"
Petula Clark

"Back in My Arms Again"
Supremes

"Baby I'm Yours"
Barbara Lewis

"I'm Telling You Now"
Freddie & The Dreamers

"For Your Love"
Yardbirds

"You've Got Your Troubles"
Fortunes

"Rescue Me"
Fontella Bass

"In the Midnight Hour"
Wilson Pickett

"Respect"
Otis Redding

"Shotgun"
Junior Walker and the All Stars

"I Got You Babe"
Sonny & Cher

"Let's Hang On"
Four Seasons

"Mrs. Brown You've Got a
Lovely Daughter"
Herman's Hermits

"Stop! In the Name of Love"
Supremes

"Unchained Melody"
Righteous Brothers

"Silhouettes"
Herman's Hermits

"Cara Mia"
Jay & The Americans

"Mr. Tambourine Man"
Byrds

"Yes, I'm Ready"
Barbara Mason

"It's Not Unusual"
Tom Jones

"Eve of Destruction"
Barry McGuire

"Hang on Sloopy"
McCoys

"Ticket to Ride"
Beatles

"Ferry 'Cross the Mersey"
Gerry & The Pacemakers

"California Girls"
Beach Boys

"Get Off My Cloud"
Rolling Stones

"Over and Over"
Dave Clark Five

"1, 2, 3"
Len Barry

"She's About a Mover"
Sir Douglas Quintet

"I Got You (I Feel Good)"
James Brown

"Hold What You've Got"
Joe Tex

"Turn! Turn! Turn!"
Byrds

"Tired of Waiting For You"
Kinks

"The 'In' Crowd"
Ramsey Lewis

"Catch the Wind"
Donovan

"Here Comes the Night"
Them

"Tracks of My Tears"
Miracles

"Yesterday"
Beatles

"You're the One"
Vogues

"Heart Full of Soul"
Yardbirds

"Lightnin' Strikes"
Lou Christie

"Catch Us If You Can"
Dave Clark Five

"All I Really Want to Do"
Cher

"People Get Ready"
Impressions

"Positively 4th Street"
Bob Dylan

"The 'In' Crowd"
Dobie Gray

"We've Got to Get Out of
This Place"
Animals

"Make It Easy on Yourself"
Walker Brothers

Novelty

"The Name Game"
Shirley Ellis

DANCES

The Ski

The Clam

The Surf

The Freddie

The Boogaloo

As youth deserts the discos for live music, adults take over—with partially clad go-go dancers (usually in cages) demonstrating new, short-lived dance crazes

NEWS OF ROCK

Beatles set new record by having No. 1, 2, 3, 4 and 5 places on U.S. Hot 100 singles chart . . . British press resents reverse invasion, and top U.S. group the Byrds flops on U.K. tour . . . Marty Balin launches Jefferson Airplane from his Matrix Club in San Francisco . . . Family Dog gets San Francisco rock ballroom scene going with first psychedelic dance at Longshoreman's Hall in October, featuring Jefferson Airplane—then brings in Lovin' Spoonful two weeks later . . . Lovin' Spoonful first East Coast group to challenge West Coast supremacy . . . Folk revival on wane . . . John Lennon introduces feedback on "I Feel Fine" . . . The word "soul" replaces "rhythm & blues" on hit charts . . . Coffee houses and campuses spawn folk-rock sweep via Dylan, Stephen Stills, John Sebastian, Neil Young, Roger McGuinn, David Crosby, Joni Mitchell et al. . . . Hot rod music in . . . L.A. radio station KHJ "Boss Radio" reduces Top 40 to Top 30, and other stations soon pare playlists as low as 18 . . . Bob Dylan booed off stage at Forest Hills, New York, for playing amplified guitar . . . 5,000 discos in U.S. . . . Bill Graham hires San Francisco Fillmore for $60. First show features Jefferson Airplane and Grateful Dead . . . Top pop poster artist Wes Wilson creates what he says is first psychedelic poster to advertise a San Francisco dance . . . Top three records in hit chart in for average of five weeks, vs. eight weeks in 1950-56 . . . Rolling Stones become No. 2 group in world . . . Byrds' "Mr. Tambourine Man" first major use of rock instruments by a folk group. Several months later Dylan booed at Newport Folk Festival for using amplified guitar . . . Folk-rock spawns first rock protest hit, Barry McGuire's "Eve of Destruction" . . . First single by the Who hits U.K. charts in six weeks . . . Historic meeting between Beatles and Elvis Presley in Bel Air, California . . . 34 records made Top 3 on charts vs. much lower average of 20 during years 1950-56 . . . New York deejay Rhett Evers sets nonstop broadcast record of ten days on air—over a day better than first high mark by Peter Tripp at San Francisco in 1959 . . . Attendance at Newport Folk Festival reaches 80,000, from over 70,000 in 1964 and 40,000 in 1963 . . . Beatles get $180,000 for Shea concert which grossed $300,000—just two years after Ed Sullivan was able to get them for $2,800 for his TV show . . . Group of San Antonio, Texas, musicians, promoted as British group, the Sir Douglas Quintet, get big hit on first try, "She's About a Mover" . . . Rock twelve-string guitar sound that becomes feature of many folk-rock hits gets big sendoff by Roger McGuinn on "Mr. Tambourine Man" by the Byrds . . . Jefferson Airplane first San Francisco group signed by a major record label (RCA) . . . Fuzz box (to create deliberate guitar distortion) used for first time by Jeff Beck on Yardbirds' single "Heart Full of Soul"—setting stage for pedal-operated wah-wah units, popularized by Jimi Hendrix, and the voice boxes that Jeff Beck and Peter Frampton use to get talking sounds from their guitars . . . Sonny and Cher gross around $3 million after an income of $3,000 last year . . . Sales of musical instruments, accessories and sheet music hit $850 million—now doubling every ten years . . . Record million-selling singles return with the British invasion and folk rock . . .

SOME OF THE NEWS THAT INFLUENCED
THE ROCK ERA AND VICE VERSA

LBJ commits ground troops to Vietnam . . . U.S. troops begin first full-scale combat offensive in Vietnam . . . Draft card burning is in vogue despite Federal offense punishment of possible five years in jail or $10,000 fine . . . Both Americans and Russians walk in space . . . President signs legislation requiring every cigarette pack or carton to carry statement: "Caution: Cigarette smoking may be hazardous to your health," beginning next January 1 . . . New York City blackout caused by power failure . . . Continuous bombing of North Vietnam in "Operation Rolling Thunder" . . . Voting Rights Act passed—eliminating need for literacy or character fitness . . . Congress approves LBJ's Higher Education Act, aiding needy students . . . Two anti-war protesters burn themselves to death . . . LBJ asks Congress legislation to help realize a "Great Society" . . . First manned Gemini space flight and four follow-ups . . . U.S. sends troops to Dominican Republic to help control rebellion . . . LBJ proposal for "unconditional discussions" to end war ignored by Hanoi . . . Supreme

Court invalidates 19th century Connecticut law forbidding use of contraceptives, even by married couples, on the grounds that it violates constitutional "right of privacy" guarantee . . . Christmas truce in Vietnam . . . Vietnam casualty figures: 1,350 dead, 5,300 wounded, 150 captured or missing. Estimated Viet Cong dead: 34,600 . . . Congress appropriation of $2 million for National Clearing House for Smoking and Health less than 1% of tobacco industry's advertising expenditure . . . Congress passes "Lady Bird (Johnson) Bill" appropriating funds to remove billboards from U.S. highways and compensate their owners . . . Watts riot in L.A. black ghetto ends with 35 dead, 1,032 injured and about $250 million in property damage . . . Water Quality Act of 1965 requires states to set anti-pollution standards for interstate waters within their jurisdiction . . . Clean Air Act of 1965 allows Federal government to set new car emission standards and set up research for control of power plant emissions . . . By year end, 184,300 U.S. troops in Vietnam—almost an eightfold increase in one year . . . Only one U.S. river running near a major metropolitan area, the St. Croix—between Minnesota and Wisconsin, remains unpolluted . . .

THE NUMBERS GAME: STATISTICAL INFORMATION SHOWING HOW LIFE IN AMERICA INFLUENCED OR WAS INFLUENCED BY THE ROCK ERA

Unemployment down to 4.2%—lowest in 8 years . . . National debt now over $317 billion, vs. about $40 billion in 1939 . . . Business upswing which began in early 1961 continues without interruption . . . Birth rate drops to lowest since 1940—19 per thousand people—same as then, and first time under 20 births per thousand people since then . . . Death rate falls to 943.2 per 100,000, down from 1,719 in 1900 . . . 735,000 General Motors employees in U.S. earn $5,448,343,000—more than double the personal income of all Irish citizens . . . More than 5 million color TVs in U.S. Networks predict all nighttime shows will be in color by late 1966 . . . After just seven years, American Express has 1.2 million credit card holders; and 15-year-old Diners Club has 1.3 million. Major banks as a result are inspired to join the Bank of America in credit bonanza . . . Live births 300,000 less than 1957 peak year . . . Study reports 50% now enjoying "good diets"—up from less than 25% in 1943 . . . Now 700 public birth control clinics—with 33 states offering support . . . Number of symphony orchestras in the U.S. has doubled since 1939. Now 1,401 (more than half the 2,000 in the world) vs. about 600 in 1939 . . . NASA costs now $5 billion, from $340 million six years ago . . . Study by Bechtel Corporation reports atomic power plants could reduce the cost of desalinated water to 25¢ per thousand gallons from $4-$5 15 years ago—while making it cheaper than fresh water in most areas . . . U.S. Mint eliminates coins containing 90% silver and switches to "clad" coins . . . Number of non-foreign employees working more than 48 hours a week almost doubled since 1948, rising to 9.4 million from 4.8 million . . . Ralph Nader's *Unsafe at Any Speed* focuses on 51,000 auto deaths a year . . . 1% of Gross National Product goes to foreign aid . . . Production of soft-top convertible cars peaks at 507,000 . . . 18,815 busted for pot possession—up 150% in year . . . Now 240 million radios in use, vs. 74 million in 1948 . . . $100 billion in private pension funds of all types, vs. only $15 billion 10 years ago and $4 billion in 1940 . . . U.S. highways pass through 17,500 automobile graveyards, junkyards and scrapheaps—one every 14.6 miles of main highway in New York, every 10.1 miles in Texas, every 4.5 miles in North Carolina . . . Now 90,000 millionaires vs. some 27,000 in 1953—with 5,000 newcomers annually, according to the National Bureau of Economic Research and Federal Reserve . . . Attendance at Detroit symphony concerts reaches 700,000 a year—up from 300,000 just 10 years ago . . . Now 50% of families deficient in one or more major food nutrients vs. 40% in 1955. Consumption of fruit and vegetables down 9% and dairy products 8%, while soft drinks up 79% . . . Study reveals lung cancer death rate among women regular smokers 2.08 times higher than non-smokers and 4.43 times higher for those using two or more packs a day . . . *Supermarket News* survey of 3,000 customers in eight cities reports 68% prefer lower prices to stamps, and 55% think stamp-giving markets charge higher prices—with 42% less interested in stamps than when they first began collecting them, vs. 36% more interested . . . Falloff in store loyalty, with only 17% of supermarket shoppers patronizing one store exclusively, vs. 41% in 1954 . . . Since 1950, those who can play musical instruments increased 85% . . .

TEEN AND COLLEGE LIVING AND
ALTERNATIVE LIFE STYLES IN THE ROCK ERA

Teenagers, less than a tenth of the labor force, account for nearly half the increase in employment (which is twice the 1963 increase) as economic expansion booms . . . Trimester system begins at some colleges . . . Average high school junior/senior allowances now $9.45 a week, reports National Education Association . . . Black tie proms fade at college . . . Harris poll shows two-thirds of college students feel parents' sense of values is same as theirs, and 75% express belief in God . . . In September return to school, many long-haired boys forced to get haircuts, and girls in long boots and short skirts or high slashed skirts and shirts sent home . . . Boys' low-slung thong shoes, metal cleats or motorcycle or similarly heavy boots also forced to change to normal . . . First singles community's 248 apartments are all rented while still being built in L.A. . . . First "teach-in" at University of Michigan features anti-war analyses by sympathetic faculty and "names." Only 500 expected, but 3,000 attend all-night marathon of protest, discussion, seminars and debate. Similar events at the University of California, Berkeley, Columbia and Harvard precede May 15 national teach-in at Washington, D.C. . . . San Diego State College survey of fashion consciousness reports 18% highly fashion conscious, 55% moderately, 26% little or not at all—with women more concerned than men. 75% of total said they tried to achieve looks by fashion . . . College magazines on downturn as underground newspapers start moving in . . . *Newsweek* reports college students show most confidence in scientific community (76%), medical profession (73%), banks and financial institutions (66%), Supreme Court (65%). Little confidence shown in advertising (16%), organized labor (13%), TV (13%), the Republican Party (12%) . . . Teen rock combos thrive: 500 in L.A., 350 in Detroit, 160 in St. Louis . . . JFK Council of Physical Fitness tests show 16-year-old girls averaging 28 sit-ups vs. 20 in 1958 . . . Counter-culture mushrooms in colleges . . . Bronx High School Dean of Discipline greets returning boy students with scissors and chops long hair . . . *Vogue* magazine article reports that advertising now finds it possible to couple young girls with men 10, 15 and sometimes 20 years their seniors, as men between 40 and 60 are changing very little and are often being used as romantic movie leads . . . With youth merchandising at a peak, the young are crowned "the Pepsi Generation" . . . *New York Times* reports that 60% of all shoplifters are under 21— up from 40% in 1960 . . . From 1931-1965, football responsible for 642 fatalities. Of these, 348 were high school players, 54 college and 72 pro and semi-pro, according to *Encyclopedia of Sports, Sciences and Medicine* . . . "New math" replacing traditional arithmetic in elementary schools . . . Harris nationwide survey reports over 75% gave general approval to the quality of education received by their children in public schools . . . "Captain High" first continuous comix to appear in underground press . . . First draft card burning by Vietnam war protester . . .

FASHION: CLOTHES AND THE ROCK ERA ACCENT ON YOUTH

Note: Feminine fashion is in italics, male in roman, unisex in parentheses, and news in asterisks.

Beatle-inspired military jackets . . . *Calico and gingham granny dresses, old-fashioned shoes costing around $11—banned in most classrooms, but okay on streets and in teen clubs* . . . (Huge sunspecs) . . . *Colored knees and painted thongs on bare feet* . . . *"Bouffs" out, long loose hair in* . . . (Body painting) . . . *Pierced ears* . . . **Jefferson Airplane makes Levi Strauss radio commercial** . . . *See-through dresses and blouses* . . . Beards in . . . (Navy pea coats and Chief Petty Officer coats from Army-Navy surplus stores big on campus) . . . *Using wash-and-wear or silk setting, ironing hair* . . . (Cut-up ["air-conditioned"] shoes and

sneakers) . . . *Thigh-high boots . . . Lipstick "out" on campus . . .*
"Strangle-britches" (tight pants), sneakers, pointed shoes, exposed shirt-
tails and beards banned at most high schools . . . (Hans Brinker
caps) . . . *Baby doll dresses* . . . (Bell-bottoms in strong) . . . (Kangaroo
shoes [Hus for Hustlers], bangs slashed straight across forehead, metal-
rimmed eyeglasses, corduroys, pea jackets and parkas considered coordi-
nated outfit) . . . Dr. Zhivago *film inspires takeoff on czarist Russian look,
with thigh-high boots, fat fur hats, and greatcoats that sweep streets* . . .
(Sunglasses for day, night and all year round) . . . Influx of teased,
greased, tinted, sprayed and curled male hairdos—plus "moptop" in,
crewcut out . . . *British fashion designers bring "little boy look" to U.S.
girls* . . . **Survey shows 15-year-old girls buying same type of cosmetics
16½-year-olds bought a decade ago** . . . Tucking men's trouser bottoms
into the top of calf-length boots . . . *Pale look ("The Big Fade") reaches
peak as eyebrows bleached, covered with foundation or concealed with
bangs— joining up with the disappearance of color from cheeks and trend
to little or no lipstick (started in 1961)* . . . **Americans buy $60 million
worth of prescription drugs designed to help them lose weight—double the
amount purchased just five years ago** . . . **Time *magazine reports
rollers now worn on streets, in stores, and even in cinemas** . . . **Ads for
men's colognes and face lotions up 800% in past five years in men's
magazines as body-building ads, prominent in the first half-century, are
now disappearing** . . . **In survey of high school freshman girls, the
color of a skirt ranked first in what they noticed first in other girls' apparel,
and second only to the fit in their own** . . . Revlon introduces men's
scents with Braggi, and Faberge follows Brut with Musk for Men . . .
**Commenting on the possible diminishing of maleness and femaleness in
garments, Bernard Rudofsky (in *The Kimono Mind*) hints that the slide
fastener, which often doesn't even require an overlap, leaves us without a
clue as to the sex of the clothing—unlike the age-old custom born from
superstition, where buttoning a garment on the right side made it only suitable for men** . . . *Big and gaudy dime-store rings* . . . *Cole of California
swimsuit—solid black lycra one-piece, inset from shoulder to navel with a
plunging black mesh "V"* . . . **Idea of feminine outer or top garment
being an accessory to the basic undergarment, together with the growing
interest in underwear, new fashion trend** . . . *"Pop" coats and jackets—
mostly in dyed rabbit skin* . . . **California girls begin hand sewing own
granny dresses—probably in imitation of Disneyland's ankle-length frontier
dresses** . . .

FADS (MOSTLY YOUTH-ORIENTED)
RELATED TO THE ROCK ERA

I Ching . . . Macrobiotic foods . . . Computer dating . . . Bogart
movies . . . Body painting . . . Trivia contests spread from Columbia

University and All Ivy League Tournament . . . "Camp" enters language, with feather boas, bubblegum cards, Jean Harlow look, sailor suits, tasseled lamps, etc. . . . Skateboards spread from California . . . Superballs . . . Books and films about monsters . . . James Bond toys, like transistor radio that converts to toy rifle . . . Disposable paper dresses in cans for $1-$2 . . . Gronking (primal screams) . . .

SOME OF THE MORE WIDELY USED ARGOT, JARGON AND SLANG IN THE ROCK ERA

Ax (guitar or bass guitar) . . . Bad (meaning good) . . . Bag (mood, object or way of life) . . . Bread (money—see 1954) . . . Crash (settle in; sleep) . . . Crash pad (hippie home) . . . Cut buddy (close friend) . . . Do your own thing (abolish inhibitions) . . . Dude (unfashionable or too trendy) . . . Freak (one who's into drugs) . . . Freak out (leave one's senses) . . . Groupies (over-ardent female rock fans) . . . Hippies (from "hip" and "hipster" in 1950s Beatnik era) . . . Hustle (pressure) . . . Into (involved) . . . "No way!" (definitely not) . . . Off the wall (wild) . . . Old lady (live-in girl) . . . Old man (live-in male) . . . Rap (v. talk, n. conversation) . . . Ripoff (larceny) . . . Roadie (rock group road manager) . . . Shadow (constant companion) . . . Straight (not with it) . . . Teach-in (marathon campus protest meeting involving teachers and students) . . . Teenybopper (stereotyped rock enthusiast, usually early or pre-teen) . . . Tightened up (unrelaxed) . . . Trip (escape from reality) . . . Turn off (bring down) . . . Unreal (impressive) . . . Vibes (tuned-in feelings—good or bad) . . .

College Argot (see 1970 and 1980): Zilch (total loss) . . . Sams (boys sought by co-eds) . . . Wimp, Scuzz, Dimp, Dipley, Nerdly, Lizard, Gink, Barf, Skag, Jane, Lunchbucket (social misfits) . . . Flagged it, Flushed it or Tubed it (flunked) . . . Stoked (in love) . . . Bugs (attractive girls) . . . Stone fox (a sexy bug) . . . A grades are Aces; B's just B's. But: C's are Hooks, D's Dandies or Dogs, E's Eagles, F's Frongs or Keepers . . . Squid, Cull, Troll or Nerd (fink) . . . Fool (dullard or diligent studier) . . . Moose or Scarf (kiss) . . .

Poet Allen Ginsberg introduces term "Flower Power" at Berkeley Anti-War Rally . . .

Alleged drug-oriented song titles: "Mr. Tambourine Man" (Byrds), "Rainy Day Woman" (Bob Dylan), "Get Off My Cloud" (Rolling Stones), "You Turn Me On" (Ian Whitcomb) . . .

THE NEW WOMAN IN THE ROCK ERA

One married woman in three working, vs. one in six in 1940 . . . Only 12 woman members of Congress . . .

MOSTLY FACTUAL TRIVIA
CONCURRENT WITH THE ROCK ERA

23% of new cars equipped with air conditioning, vs. 7% in 1960 . . . Fiftieth anniversary of first movie nude scene played by Annette Kellerman in *Daughter of the Gods* . . . 20 ft. 5 in. loaf of bread, weighing 50 lbs., sets record for New Zealander . . . French women offered gold underwear to make them "fit for James Bond" . . . Record traffic jam in downtown Boston brings cars to virtual standstill for over five hours . . . U.S. agents seize 7,432 stills producing illicit spirits (585 more than last year), and 3,637,881 gallons of mash . . . Record 300,000 new cars sold in ten days, as new models are shown . . . Power-mower sales hit record 4.5 million . . .

1966

ARTISTS

Rock Groups
  Association
  Buckinghams
  Eric Burdon & The Animals
  Cyrkle
  Happenings
  Hollies
  Tommy James & The
    Shondells
  Left Banke
  Mamas & Papas
  Monkees
  Outsiders
  Paul Revere & The Raiders
  Mitch Ryder & The
    Detroit Wheels
  Sandpipers
  Troggs
  Who
  Young Rascals

Rock Solo Performers
  Neil Diamond
  Bob Lind
  Sandy Posey
  Nancy Sinatra
  B. J. Thomas

Soul, R&B, Funk Groups
  Sam & Dave

Soul, R&B, Funk Solo Performers
  Lou Rawls
  Jimmy Ruffin
  Percy Sledge

Folk & Country
  Statler Brothers

JUKE BOX HITS

"Hold On, I'm Coming"
Sam & Dave

"You Keep Me Hanging On"
Supremes

"19th Nervous Breakdown"
Rolling Stones

"California Dreamin' "
Mamas & Papas

"Last Train to Clarksville"
Monkees

"These Boots Are Made for Walkin' "
Nancy Sinatra

"You Can't Hurry Love"
Supremes

"See You in September"
Happenings

"A Groovy Kind of Love"
Mindbenders

"Monday, Monday"
Mamas & Papas

"B-A-B-Y"
Carla Thomas

"Time Won't Let Me"
Outsiders

"Up Tight"
Stevie Wonder

"Paperback Writer"
Beatles

"Bang Bang"
Cher

"96 Tears"
? & The Mysterians

"Reach Out, I'll Be There"
Four Tops

"Kicks"
Paul Revere & The Raiders

"(You're My) Soul and
Inspiration"
Righteous Brothers

"Red Rubber Ball"
Cyrkle

"You Don't Have to Say You
Love Me"
Dusty Springfield

"Hanky Panky"
Tommy James & Shondells

"Bus Stop"
Hollies

"I'm So Lonesome I Could Cry"
B. J. Thomas & Triumphs

"Tell It Like It Is"
Aaron Neville

"Georgy Girl"
Seekers

"Sunshine Superman"
Donovan

"Five O'Clock World"
Vogues

"What Becomes of the
Brokenhearted"
Jimmy Ruffin

"Cherish"
Association

"Good Lovin'"
Young Rascals

"Sunny"
Bobby Hebb

"Working in a Coal Mine"
Lee Dorsey

"Walk Away Renee"
Left Banke

"When a Man Loves a Woman"
Percy Sledge

"Paint It Black"
Rolling Stones

"Summer in the City"
Lovin' Spoonful

"I Am a Rock"
Simon & Garfunkel

"Did You Ever Have to Make
Up Your Mind?"
Lovin' Spoonful

"Good Vibrations"
Beach Boys

"Yellow Submarine"
Beatles

"Single Girl"
Sandy Posey

"Poor Side of Town"
Johnny Rivers

"My Generation"
The Who

"Just Like a Woman"
Bob Dylan

"Working My Way Back to You"
Frankie Valli & The Four Seasons

"River Deep—Mountain High"
Ike & Tina Turner

"Barbara Ann"
Beach Boys

"Try a Little Tenderness"
Otis Redding

"I've Got You Under My Skin"
Frankie Valli & The Four Seasons

"Daydream"
Lovin' Spoonful

"Wild Thing"
Troggs

"Dirty Water"
Standells

"Eleanor Rigby"
Beatles

"Kind of a Drag"
Buckinghams

"Cherry, Cherry"
Neil Diamond

"Black Is Black"
Los Bravos

"I'm Your Puppet"
James & Bobby Purify

"I'm a Believer"
Monkees

"I Fought the Law"
Bobby Fuller Four

"Rainy Day Women No. 12
and No. 35"
Bob Dylan

"Eight Miles High"
Byrds

"This Old Heart of Mine"
Isley Brothers

"Good Thing"
Paul Revere & The Raiders

"I Want You"
Bob Dylan

"Elusive Butterfly"
Bob Lind

"Hooray for Hazel"
Tommy Roe

"Homeward Bound"
Simon & Garfunkel

"Sloop John B"
Beach Boys

"Gimme Some Lovin' "
Spencer Davis Group

"Mellow Yellow"
Donovan

"Guantanamera"
Sandpipers

"Love Is a Hurtin' Thing"
Lou Rawls

"9 & 6"
Keith

"Devil with a Blue Dress On"
Mitch Ryder & The Detroit Wheels

"The Sun Ain't Gonna Shine Anymore"
Walker Brothers

Novelty

"They're Coming to Take Me
Away, Ha, Ha"
Napoleon XIV

DANCES

The Skate
The Philly Dog

The Boston Monkey

NEWS OF ROCK

Beatles make final concert appearance . . . Bob Dylan hurt in motorcycle crash . . .Janis Joplin joins Big Brother and the Holding Company . . .Now 250 underground papers . . . CBS survey shows record sales grew to $650 million from $250 million in 1956. 10,662 new releases, from 6,157 in 1956. Singles now only 2:1 over albums, vs. 3:1 in 1956 . . . Only seven of the 89 new groups who made it in 1961 are still on charts . . . Only 65% of song hits concerned with "boy wants girl" or vice versa, vs. 85% in 1965 . . . Washington pressure starts rock lyric drug reference censorship by radio stations . . . In past four years hit records by groups climbed from 28% to 72%, while single male vocal hits dropped from 52% to 20% . . . Grateful Dead and Big Brother proclaim entry of new musical genre, "acid rock," at San Francisco Trips Festival. "The Haight Ashbury era was born that weekend," Tom Wolfe declares in his book *The Electric Kool-Aid Acid Test* . . . Tape cartridges, first invented 1954, get big launch . . . Phil Spector spends unheard-of (at time) $22,000 to cut Ike and Tina Turner's "River Deep—Mountain High," and quits business when it doesn't hit . . . L.A. Sheriff's office using armored buses to enforce curfew for kids on Sunset Strip . . . 18 people work first light shows at San Francisco Fillmore Ballroom for payment of $3 . . . Fillmore and Avalon become rock dance meccas in San Francisco, setting stage for teen ballrooms in all key cities. Discotheques out and old dance halls back in, as blends of strobes, liquid color blobs, black light, glow paint, films and slides create "psychedelic" accompaniment to rock music—as a new style of poster art for advertising dances spreads from San Francisco . . . The Grateful Dead, Jefferson Airplane, the Association and many other new and established California groups move in together—starting another spreading trend . . . Jan and Dean quit business as Jan almost killed in car crash . . . Beatles' "Rain" first record to use reverse tapes . . . After Dylan's motorcycle accident his backup group, the Hawks, become his Woodstock neighbors at Big Pink and start recording there as "The Band"—leading the way into Country Rock . . . Beatles and Stones on same bill at London poll-winners' concert . . . Number of new record stars down by over 10% . . . Lyrics become important enough to be included on record albums . . . Survey shows that during the past nine years an average of 65% of the performers with Top 10 records had their first hit the year it made the Top 10 . . . Robert Stigwood forces Atlantic Records to sign a new group called Cream as part of giving them the Bee Gees . . . Fillmore and Avalon Ballrooms, San Francisco, with their light shows, psychedelic posters and large dance floors, become top venues for blues bands such as Paul Butterfield from Chicago, Steve Miller from L.A., Janis Joplin from Texas and John Mayall from London; while becoming the springboard for the Grateful Dead, Jefferson Airplane, Country Joe and the Fish, Big Brother and the Holding Company, Moby Grape and Quicksilver Messenger Service . . . Frank Sinatra breaks rock monopoly with No. 1 hit in U.S. and Britain, "Strangers in the Night," and hits Top 10 in over 20 other countries . . . Non-performing hit songwriters Lamont Dozier and Brian and Eddie Holland get standard-setting 28th Top 20 hit in three years of writing for Motown artists . . . Roots of "heavy metal" rock set by the Who's "My Generation" and in the fuzztone-and-feedback explosions of Eric Clapton, Jeff Beck and Jimmy Page . . . Monkee merchandise, from guitars to comic books and Monkee pants, gross $20 million in first year . . . John Lennon makes solo movie debut in *How I Won the War* . . . Speaking to reporters following annual meeting of Northern Songs, Brian Epstein denies any breakup of Beatles, after a fan demonstration outside his home protesting the lack of a concert tour by them starts rumors flying. The press speculation focuses on their individual activities with Lennon into film acting, McCartney into film scores, George Harrison into Indian music, and Ringo into a variety of outside activities . . . National Association of Broadcasters instructs disc jockeys to screen all records for dirty or hidden meanings (drug allusions) . . . Tape cartridges for car and home loom as next big boom in recorded music, as industry pundits foresee the not-too-distant arrival of audio-video records that will play through television sets . . . The Beatles play their final concert at Candlestick Park, San Francisco . . .

SOME OF THE NEWS THAT INFLUENCED
THE ROCK ERA AND VICE VERSA

U.S. bombs Hanoi first time, escalating war . . . 5,008 U.S. troops killed in Viet war; total 6,700 since 1961 . . . War now costing $1.2 billion a month . . . 50,000 men a month being drafted . . . Six years later, six million U.S. women on the Pill . . . Northeast U.S. power blackout . . . 52,500 Americans killed in traffic accidents; nine million injured . . . New York undercover cop infiltrates conspiracy to blow up Statue of Liberty, Liberty Bell and Washington Monument . . . Medicare begins . . . LBJ big factor in reduction of impoverished—now 15.4% living in poverty vs. 22.1% in 1959 . . . In State of Union message, LBJ says U.S. will remain in Vietnam as long as aggression continues . . . Unmanned Surveyor 1 lands on Moon and transmits 11,348 pictures . . . U.S. forces in Vietnam total 380,000 by late December vs. 180,000 at beginning of year . . . Anti-war sentiment mounts . . . Congress passes Clean Waters Restoration Act to keep river waters clear and appropriates $186 million for three-year program to cut down air pollution . . . LBJ admits increased Viet commitments hindered advancement of "Great Society" in proposing record budget . . . U.S. confirms sale of bombers to Israel because Soviet has sold planes to Arabs . . . South Vietnam premier refuses to negotiate with Viet Cong . . . House Foreign Affairs Committee urges attempt to increase peaceful contacts with Communist China . . . LBJ proposes Truth in Packaging law requiring clear and accurate statements of ingredients and amounts on about 8,000 drug, cosmetic and food products . . . France announces its withdrawal of all troops from NATO integrated command . . . LBJ urges housewives to boycott products whose prices keep rising . . . Sole LSD manufacturer withdraws all supplies from market because of public controversy . . . After being attacked from over the Vietnam-Cambodia border, U.S. forces fire on Cambodian targets for first time . . . Top senators criticize Vietnam war effort . . . Defense Secretary McNamara announces that U.S. military strength in Vietnam will reach 285,000 . . . Mental standards for armed forces lowered from score of 16 to 10 (out of 100) . . . Defense Department announces that 2.4 million draft rejectees will be re-examined . . . Congress passes Traffic Safety Act, as almost direct result of Ralph Nader book, *Unsafe At Any Speed.* Act, setting production safety standards for cars and tires, also requires manufacturers to call back after sale all models in which mechanical defects are discovered . . . Congress authorizes President to call up as many as 789,000 reserve forces without their approval or National Emergency declaration . . . Two-thirds of all new electric generating plants now being built are nuclear . . . LSD, mescaline and peyote declared illegal . . . Supreme Court, in 5-4 "Miranda Decision," rules that the police must warn arrestees of their rights to silence and counsel . . . Largest annual rise in cost of living since 1958 . . . California tries to control smog with new standards to take effect on 1969 cars . . . Cola bottlers and canners get Food & Drug Administration dispensation not to list caffeine (usually 4 mg./oz., vs. 12-16 in coffee) as an ingredient . . . Consumer supermarket boycotts in some key cities protest high prices . . .

THE NUMBERS GAME: STATISTICAL INFORMATION SHOWING HOW LIFE IN AMERICA INFLUENCED OR WAS INFLUENCED BY THE ROCK ERA

Food prices climb by over 5% . . . President's Commission on Food Marketing estimates consumers paying 20% more for nationally advertised brands . . . 48% believe flying saucers real in Gallup poll . . . Now 78 million registered passenger cars and 16 million trucks and buses traveling a total of 910 billion miles a year . . . 47 million radio sets sold. Teenagers boost transistor total . . . 20th century auto deaths three times as great as military deaths in all U.S. wars . . . Infant mortality rate now 24.3 per thousand—down from 29 per thousand in 1951 . . . Texas Tech halfback gets $600,000 for signing Green Bay Packers contract, topping Joe Namath's $400,000 from the New York Jets in 1965 . . . 78 endangered species on first list from Department of Interior . . . Sports participation survey puts cycling first, with 59 million riders, then boating, with 40.3 million, volleyball 40 million, bowling 39 million, camping 37 million, fishing 36.2

million, softball 25.8 million, roller-skating 25 million; vs. golf and tennis with only 1.9 million each . . . Minimum wage raised from $1.25 an hour to $1.40 an hour in 1967 and $1.60 an hour in 1968 . . . Over 7,000 new products on supermarket shelves this year; and 55% of items now sold there didn't exist 10 years ago . . . President of large supermarket chain says that each of their stores carries 8,500 items in the grocery department plus about 6,500 more in the meat, produce, delicatessen, drug, bakery and frozen food departments—while being asked to consider 4,000-5,000 new items each year—of which about 1,000 are stocked . . . Secretary of Agriculture blames part of price rises on Americans paying for enlarged supermarket stocks and buying more expensive food items . . . Snack foods market one of faster growing segments of food industry—12%-13% annually, vs. 4% growth in supermarket volume . . . As low-calorie desserts and salad dressings grow in popularity, it's estimated that 33 million of the 58 million U.S. households used low-calorie beverages last year . . . Unemployment at 5.6%—down from 6.7% peak five years ago . . . Estimated 130 million people spend $7.5 billion at carnivals in U.S. and Canada . . . Only 61% of supermarkets offer trading stamps vs. 69% last year and 78% just four years ago . . . Survey shows that 90% of persons 18 years old up listened to radio during the course of a week where only 87% watched TV . . .

TEEN AND COLLEGE LIVING AND
ALTERNATIVE LIFE STYLES IN THE ROCK ERA

Unisex boys imitating girls. Psychologists say Beatles' and Stones' sexless songs represent common meeting ground . . . Girls taking on dominant role in unisex relationships . . . *Newsweek* survey shows most teen free time spent watching TV . . . Blanket student deferments abolished as draft calls hit 50,000 a month—tenfold rise in one year . . . Pediatricians estimate inactivity, not overeating, has 10-15% of U.S. teenagers too fat . . . Average menstruation age down from 14 in 1900 to 12.8 years . . . Over a dozen college football stars get $100,000-$600,000 bonuses on signing pro contracts . . . Old South Church, Boston, draws 1,100 teens with rock service including Frug . . . 10:00 P.M. curfew causes Sunset Strip riots . . . House Armed Services Committee report recommends that draft should begin with 19 or 20-year-olds instead of 22 or 23—making those deferred for college eligible until age 35 . . . Survey of adolescent female fantasies places daydreaming of marriage at top (76%) . . . Now 53% of the 16-19-year-old age group are smokers—4% more than two years ago when the Surgeon-General's report was issued. In the 13-15-year-old age group, 25% now smoke . . . Dr. Timothy Leary coins psychedelic slogan, "Turn on, tune in, drop out" . . . *San Francisco Oracle* born in Haight Ashbury—reflecting psychedelic life style in newspaper layout . . . Yale psychologist Kennedy Keniston notes eclipse of two once-prevalent collegiate types: the gentleman dilettante and the poor boy working his way through school. New dominant type is product of suburbia aiming at professionalism . . . Teenage crime up over 100%, with corresponding population increase only 45% over last decade. Only 9% of population, the 13-17-year-olds, account for 18% of all arrests . . . *Newsweek*/Louis Harris nationwide survey of 13-17-year-olds finds: (1) 77% say they are the same as others their age; (2) 90% feel they have a lot of friends; (3) 33% feel they are friendly; (4) 56% work to earn money; (5) 76% regard shopping as one of the experiences they most enjoy; (6) 86% feel that their parents mind their own business; (7) 38% say the best part of school is friends, 16% say social life and 16% learning; (8) 64% own their own encyclopedias or reference books . . . World's first psychedelic shop opens in Haight Ashbury on January 1—by two ex-Eagle Scouts and stock investors . . .

FASHION: CLOTHES AND THE
ROCK ERA ACCENT ON YOUTH

Note: Feminine fashion is in italics, male in roman, unisex in parentheses, and news in asterisks.

Levi Strauss sales $152 million—twice that of 1963 . . . (No socks) . . . *Fake furs and pants suits for co-eds* . . . No-collar jackets, stovepipe pants, high-heeled boots . . . *High-waisted dresses, textured stockings and lank hair* . . . *Ben Franklin glasses, plaid and checkered pants, wide hip-hugger belts* . . . Paisley shirts, leather vests and round-toed boots . . . *Little-girl shoes, white stockings, Liverpool caps* . . . **Parents imitating teen styles** . . . *Vinyl bathing suits* . . . *Urban unisex hits teen and college girls: boots and heavy-belted Levis, masculine Vidal Sassoon haircuts, jean jackets, snug white teeshirts, straight-leg pants slung from wide garrison belts, husky workmen's boots, man-size watches, and Army-Navy store look* . . . *Teenage girls using 20% of men's cologne called "Canoe"* . . . Midwest and Southern males still heavily into crewcuts and chinos, while many females still in bobby-sox . . . *Military coats and giant gilt earrings* . . . *Daisy tights* . . . **Psychiatrists claim that males see female clothing use as height of non-conformity—this being reason for trend** . . . *Sassoon's geometric hairdos ending in a point at the nape* . . . (His and hers denim suits—made identical with safari-type casual jackets) . . . Hipster trousers fitted just over the hips . . . (Los Angeles kids wearing paisley, suede and days of Charlie Chaplin outfits) . . . **Seventeen-year-old Twiggy voted woman of the year in London** . . . Now 268 different men's colognes vs. 134 three years ago . . . *Bright red nails and lips return to fashion in London* . . . Trousers flared slightly from the knee . . . *Bare knees decorated with plastic jewels, beauty spots, winking eyes, psychedelics, sunbursts or just rouge* . . . **Men's cosmetic sales reach $500 million—three times that of three years ago** . . . *Leg makeup in cream or powder* . . . **Film *Baby Doll* popularizes nightgowns reduced to baby doll brevity** . . . **Cosmopolitan* article entitled "The Beautiful Phony" satirizes fashion magazines' concentration on the natural look by picturing a girl wearing the following (mostly normal) accoutrements: wig, false eyelashes, tinted contact lenses, false fingernails and toenails, padded bra, fake jewelry (along with an easily purchased new nose and false derrière)** . . . (Sandalwood scents) . . . *Wet-looking vinyl fabrics and accessories . . . In sharp reaction to the angled, helmet-shaped cut launched by Vidal Sassoon in London last year, most teenage and adult women follow a natural line that is feminine, fluid and almost childlike. It falls straight from a smooth top of the head to the shoulders or lower—hiding one eye if parted to one side and partially hiding both if parted in the center . . . Deep, brow-length hair fringes very "in" . . . "Hipster minis" drop waistline to hip-bone—with skirts and pants held by wide, slotted leather belts . . .* **Newsweek* describes kids' dress at San Francisco's "psychedelic" Avalon and Fillmore ballrooms as "ecstatic"—men with shoulder-length locks and one earring, cowboy outfits, frock coats, high hats; women in deliberately tatty evening gowns, rescued from some attic, embellished by a tiara and sneakers. Arab kaftans are worn by both sexes, who also affect bead necklaces** . . . (Prince Valiant bobs) . . . **At top New York discotheque, the Cheetah (where *Hair* played between off-Broadway beginnings and Broadway opening) typical costumes are: red vinyl space-age outfits, aluminum wigs, fluorescent clothing and silver motorcycle jackets with purple crepe pants** . . .

FADS (MOSTLY YOUTH-ORIENTED) RELATED TO THE ROCK ERA

Bat pens, Bat guns, Bat guitars, Bat masks, Bat pencils featured among 1,000 licensed Batman items. Almost five million mask and cape sets sold . . . Psychedelics . . . Communes . . . Underground papers . . . Astrology . . . Ouija board sales hit all-time high of 2.3 million—again a wartime staple . . . *Newsweek* reports that teenage fads are carefully calculated to scandalize the adult world, and nothing can kill a fad faster than its being picked up by the wrong people (translation: adults) . . . Tarot card fortune telling . . . Winnie the Pooh buttons . . . Incense and musk. . .

SOME OF THE MORE WIDELY USED ARGOT, JARGON AND SLANG IN THE ROCK ERA

Acid rock (music with effect of drug experience) . . . Baggies (denims or chinos cut off for use as shorts or swim trunks) . . . Beach bunny (bikini wearer who never gets wet) . . . Black (replaces word Negro) . . . Blow the mind (departure from norm) . . . Bogart (fail) . . . Commune (group home) . . . Cope (relate to norm) . . . Cosmic consciousness (mystical introspection) . . . Diggers (hippie benefactors) . . . Drop out (depart from norm) . . . Dropout (nonconformist) . . . Flake off (depart) . . . Flower children (current love generation) . . . Flower power (deep belief in love and peace) . . . Go-go (modish, faddish) . . . Go-go dancer (disco performer) . . . Grass (marijuana) . . . Group grope (multiple lovemaking) . . . Hack it (cope or deal with) . . . Happening (music or art-oriented special event) . . . Hashbury (Haight Ashbury) . . . "It's what's happening baby" . . . Key (2.2 lbs. of marijuana—kilo) . . . Lid (one ounce of marijuana) . . . Love-in (brotherhood celebration) . . . LSD (psychedelic drug lysergic acid diethylamide) . . . Mary Jane (marijuana) . . . Mindbender (something shocking or overwhelming) . . . Mind trippers (drugs) . . . Plastic (grossly artificial) . . . Pot (marijuana) . . . Psychedelic (hallucinogenic) . . . Rip off (v: steal) . . . Ripoff (n: a cheat) . . . Score (obtain, purchase) . . . "Sorry about that, Chief" . . . Spaced or Spaced out (out of communication) . . . Spiffy (good) . . . Strung out (disturbed) . . . Toke (puff) . . . Tribe (hippie group) . . . Uncool (not laid back) . . . Vietnik (pro-war writers and speakers' derogatory name for student anti-war protesters) . . . "You really know how to hurt a guy" . . . Zap (confront, defeat) . . .

Alleged drug-oriented song titles: "Along Comes Mary" (Association), "Good Vibrations" (Beach Boys), "Eight Miles High" (Byrds), "Rainy Day Woman" (Bob Dylan), "Mellow Yellow" (Donovan), "Sunshine Superman" (Donovan), "Kicks" (Raiders), "Mother's Little Helper" (Rolling Stones), "Over, Under, Sideways, Down" (Yardbirds), "Shapes of Things" (Yardbirds) . . .

THE NEW WOMAN IN THE ROCK ERA

NOW (National Organization of Women) founded in Washington, D.C., in Betty Friedan's room at National Conference of Commissions on the Status of Women . . . All ten top officers of Kelly Girl are male . . . Of 72 non-Catholic women's colleges, only one in eight headed by a woman . . . Food and Drug Administration report says "no adequate scientific data" proves the Pill unsafe—but most women reluctant to use it . . .

MOSTLY FACTUAL TRIVIA
CONCURRENT WITH THE ROCK ERA

Topless Batgirl dancer featured at San Francisco nightspot . . . Biologist states no healthy wild North American wolf would ever attack a human being like Red Riding Hood . . . Wrigleys granted patent for chewing gum that won't stick to false teeth . . . English butcher constructs 3,124-foot sausage . . . Scientists at Smithsonian say a boatload of Japanese fishermen discovered the U.S. in 3000 B.C., long before Columbus and Leif

Eriksson . . . Batman Bat tuxedos selling well at $50 each . . . New male cosmetics include false eyelashes called "Executive Eyelash" and an aftershave powder puff named "Brass Knuckles." Both sink without a trace . . . Mississippi, the last dry state, repeals its 58-year-old prohibition law . . . Main food-buying trend toward prepackaged complete meal—whether frozen, dehydrated or canned . . . Instant Nesselrode pie mix introduced . . . Survey of New York company cafeterias reveals that Sukiyaki, Arroz con Pollo and other foreign foods are featured regularly on the menu—even though fried chicken and pot roast are still favored . . .

1967 _____

ARTISTS

Rock Groups
  Bee Gees
  Box Tops
  Buffalo Springfield
  Cream
  Doors
  Fifth Dimension
  Grass Roots
  Grateful Dead
  Jefferson Airplane
  Lemon Pipers
  John Mayall's Bluesbreakers
  Moby Grape
  Procol Harum
  Gary Puckett & The Union Gap
  Linda Ronstadt & The
    Stone Poneys
  Spanky & Our Gang
  Strawberry Alarm Clock
  Frank Zappa & The
    Mothers of Invention

Rock Solo Performers
  Glen Campbell
  Jimi Hendrix
  Scott McKenzie
  Van Morrison
  Frankie Valli

Soul, R&B, Funk Groups
  Gladys Knight & The Pips
  Intruders
  Peaches & Herb
  Smokey Robinson &
    The Miracles
  Soul Survivors

Soul, R&B, Funk Solo Performers
  Arthur Conley
  Aretha Franklin

Folk & Country
  Arlo Guthrie
  Tim Hardin
  John Hartford
  Janis Ian

Middle of the Road
  Cowsills
  Bobbie Gentry
  Engelbert Humperdinck
  Lulu

Cult Groups/Punk/New Wave/
Drone Rock
  Velvet Underground

JUKE BOX HITS

"People Are Strange"
Doors

"Heroes and Villains"
Beach Boys

"Dedicated to the One I Love"
Mamas & Papas

"Windy"
Association

"Happy Together"
Turtles

"I Think We're Alone Now"
Tommy James & Shondells

"Soul Man"
Sam and Dave

"Ruby Tuesday"
Rolling Stones

"Brown-Eyed Girl"
Van Morrison

"A Whiter Shade of Pale"
Procol Harum

"On a Carousel"
Hollies

"Up, Up and Away"
Fifth Dimension

"I Can See For Miles"
Who

"Can't Take My Eyes Off You"
Frankie Valli

"Green Tambourine"
Lemon Pipers

"Funky Broadway"
Wilson Pickett

"The Beat Goes On"
Sonny & Cher

"I Heard It Through the
Grapevine"
Gladys Knight & The Pips

"I Second That Emotion"
Smokey Robinson & Miracles

"Stormy"
Classics IV

"Bend Me, Shape Me"
American Breed

"(Your Love Keeps Lifting Me)
Higher and Higher"
Jackie Wilson

"How Can I Be Sure?"
Young Rascals

"The Letter"
Box Tops

"Daydream Believer"
Monkees

"Groovin' "
Young Rascals

"Respect"
Aretha Franklin

"Never My Love"
Association

"Penny Lane"
Beatles

"All You Need Is Love"
Beatles

"Jimmy Mack"
Martha & The Vandellas

"Don't You Care"
Buckinghams

"Alfie"
Dionne Warwick

"San Francisco"
Scott McKenzie

"Different Drum"
Linda Ronstadt & The
Stone Poneys

"The Happening"
Supremes

"The Rain, the Park and
Other Things"
Cowsills

"Somethin' Stupid"
Nancy & Frank Sinatra

"Woman Woman"
Gary Puckett & The Union Gap

"To Sir with Love"
Lulu

"Sunday Will Never Be the Same"
Spanky & Our Gang

"Release Me"
Engelbert Humperdinck

"59th Street Bridge Song"
Harper's Bizarre

"Hey Joe"
Jimi Hendrix

"Happy Jack"
The Who

"Ode to Billie Joe"
Bobbie Gentry

"Light My Fire"
Doors

"White Rabbit"
Jefferson Airplane

"Incense and Peppermints"
Strawberry Alarm Clock

"For What It's Worth"
Buffalo Springfield

"Somebody to Love"
Jefferson Airplane

"I Got Rhythm"
Happenings

"Sweet Soul Music"
Arthur Conley

"Silence Is Golden"
Tremeloes

"There's a Kind of Hush"
Herman's Hermits

"Love Is Here and Now
You're Gone"
Supremes

"Hello Hello"
Sopwith Camel

"Massachusetts"
Bee Gees

"Itchycoo Park"
Small Faces

"Gimme Some Lovin' "
Spencer Davis Group

"Friday on My Mind"
Easybeats

"Gimme Little Sign"
Brenton Wood

"Baby I Love You"
Aretha Franklin

"Let's Spend the Night Together"
Rolling Stones

"Cold Sweat"
James Brown

"Gentle on My Mind"
Glen Campbell

DANCES

The Shing-A-Ling

NEWS OF ROCK

Emergence of San Francisco Sound . . . Estimated 500-1,500 psychedelic bands spring up in Bay area . . . Public outcry helps Mick Jagger and Keith Richard win appeals on London drug convictions—even *The Times* sympathetic . . . Brian Epstein dies at 32 . . . "Blue-Eyed Soul" becomes popular via the Righteous Brothers, the Young Rascals, Animals, Stones, Procol Harum, etc. . . . Presley marries Priscilla Ann Beaulieu . . . 20,000 jam first Be-In in Golden Gate Park, San Francisco. Everything free. Music by Grateful Dead, Airplane and Quicksilver. Only two policemen. Hippies clear all debris at the end . . . Fantasy Faire and Magic Mountain Music Festival atop Mt. Tamalpais, San Francisco, in June, is first rock festival. Fifteen thousand peacefully bussed two miles to summit. The Byrds, Fifth Dimension, Doors, Jefferson Airplane, Country Joe and the Fish, Dionne Warwick and others on same day—all for only $2 . . . Second rock festival, Monterey Pop, two weeks later. Artists only paid expenses, and about $200,000 profit earmarked for charity. Springboard for many new stars, including Jimi Hendrix and Janis Joplin, who is signed by Columbia Records for $250,000, to be followed by $500,000 promotion . . . "Sgt. Pepper" album introduces electronic rock . . . Keith Moon throws drum set around, and Pete Townsend destroys guitar, as part of Who act, which continues until around time Jimi Hendrix begins similar demolition . . . In February alone, Bill Graham sells 112,000 reprints of Fillmore psychedelic posters . . . Monkees win four gold discs . . . Otis Redding killed in plane crash before the release date of his biggest record hit "(Sittin' on) the Dock of the Bay" . . . U.S. record sales top $1 billion . . . More rock groups defy AFM (musicians' union) rule by forming cooperative groups and playing free gigs . . . Success of folk-rock spawns experiments with jazz-rock, and fusions of country, Indian ragas, etc., to create wave of new sounds . . . Doors expelled from L.A. Whisky-A-Go-Go for ritual enactment of Oedipal complex in song, "The End" . . . Tom Donahue debuts FM underground radio at KMPX San Francisco. Soon tops AM competitors . . . Procol Harum plus Bach cantata "Sleepers Awake" becomes "A Whiter Shade of Pale" . . . Funeral for "Summer of Love" at Buena Vista, California park as disillusion over media overkill sets in . . . Very few hippies found guilty of housing violations during two-day door-to-door sweep of Haight Ashbury ordered by San Francisco Director of Health . . . "Penny Lane" and "Strawberry Fields" become Beatles' 13th No. 1 hit . . . Cambridge, Massachusetts, mayor and platoon of TV cameramen raid hippie pad but are disappointed . . . First important rock musical, "Hair," opens off-Broadway at New York Shakespeare Festival's Public Theatre . . . Albums begin to outsell single records . . . Brian Epstein tells Murray the K in April interview: "When you have Jimi Hendrix (here), I'm sure you'll like him. Jimi has just broken through in England. He'd been

around the Village for a long time, but nobody took any interest" . . .
While playing free gigs in San Francisco's Golden Gate Park, and trying to
cool the Haight Ashbury scene, the Grateful Dead rarely have enough bread
for week-to-week survival, and pile up $50,000 in debts . . . Jefferson
Airplane play 150 dates in year of heavy touring, as manager Bill Graham
(owner of the Fillmore) capitalizes on their hit singles . . . Engineering
alone on the Beatles' "Sergeant Pepper's Lonely Hearts Club Band" LP
said to cost $50,000 . . . Phasing out of monaural records begun by ABC-
Paramount going 100% stereo . . .

SOME OF THE NEWS THAT INFLUENCED
THE ROCK ERA AND VICE VERSA

9,419 Americans dead in Vietnam . . . Estimated 350,000 in New York
and San Francisco anti-war parades on April 15 . . . Anti-war demonstrators try to storm Pentagon . . . Colorado first state to legalize abortion
. . . Che Guevara killed at age 39 . . . Riots in 30 cities . . . Israel wins Six
Day War . . . Apollo 1 explodes on pad at Cape Kennedy, killing three-
man crew . . . Secretary of Defense McNamara sent off to become World
Bank President after calling Vietnam bombing campaign a failure . . . Over
10,000 people mob Oakland, California, draft induction center during
"Stop the Draft Week" (October 16-20) demonstration . . . Supreme Court
rules that courts must grant same procedural safeguards in juvenile delinquency trials as in adult trials . . . More than 60% of Puerto Ricans voting
in plebiscite favor continued association with U.S. as Commonwealth . . .
By late December U.S. troops in Vietnam total 486,000 . . . Dr. Christiaan
N. Barnard does first successful heart transplant in Capetown . . . North
Vietnam refuses U.N. Peace Plan . . . Communist China explodes hydro-
gen bomb . . . LBJ again urges Congress to pass gun control legislation,
pointing out that criminals can legally buy rifles and shotguns without a
permit, although they are kept from driving or voting by state laws . . .
Thurgood Marshall first black Supreme Court justice . . . Food & Drug
Administration chief, Dr. James L. Goddard, says marijuana is not a more
dangerous drug than alcohol . . . Senate Foreign Relations Committee
votes unanimously to require future approval of Congress for sending any
troops abroad—except to repel an attack on the U.S. or to protect U.S.
citizens. Committee also agrees to re-examine Gulf of Tonkin incident,
feeling that LBJ may have "overreacted" based on too little information
. . . Muhammad Ali stripped of title for refusing draft induction . . .
National Security Adviser Walt W. Rostow says of U.S. involvement in
Vietnam: "It looks very good. The other side is near collapse." . . . In
response to Presidential request to CIA to unearth any ties between anti-war
groups and foreign interests, the agency exceeds statutory authority on
domestic scene with 300,000-name index, communication interceptions,
etc. . . . Worst of 164 urban ghetto riots since April hits Detroit July 23-30,
costing 43 lives, 2,000 injured and 5,000 burned-out homes . . .

THE NUMBERS GAME: STATISTICAL INFORMATION
SHOWING HOW LIFE IN AMERICA INFLUENCED
OR WAS INFLUENCED BY THE ROCK ERA

U.S. population reaches 200 million on November 20. Now increases by one every 14½ seconds. Estimated 500 million by year 2015—barring catastrophe . . . 572.6 billion cigarettes bought—averaging 210 packs per adult . . . Only 8 billion mass transit riders—down from 23 billion in 1945 as cars and suburban shopping centers take over . . . *New York Times* reports that oil-shale lands in Colorado, Utah and Wyoming contain five times the world's known oil reserves—worth $5,000 billion—which would come to $25,000 for each U.S. citizen when the extraction becomes economical enough. The U.S. could not only fill its own needs, but again become an oil exporter . . . Now 35,000 computers, vs. 20 in 1954 . . . U.S. population has doubled in 50 years . . . Pro football attendance 438% over 1948—8.2 million from 1.5 million . . . 2,975 corporate mergers—up from 844 in 1960 . . . Beef consumption up again to 105.5 lbs. per capita from 99 lbs. seven years ago—this on top of 71 lbs. of other red meat . . . Chain and department stores increased from 62,000 to 67,000 in past four years, while apparel and accessory stores declined from 116,000 to 110,000 . . . 12 billion cans of beer and 5.3 billion cans of soft drinks consumed this year . . . Profits for three TV networks and 619 stations reported to be $2,275 million . . . 108 million Americans take 360 million trips involving an overnight stay more than 100 miles from home—accounting for 312 billion passenger miles . . . Federal civilian employment now 2.6 million—up 30% from 2 million 20 years ago . . . Over 175 million, 83% of the civilian population, currently covered by private hospital insurance . . . Survey shows that after 20 years, almost one-third of the women interviewed used the same brand of cosmetics, nail polish, soap or toilet water they had used in high school . . . Average annual U.S. consumption of frozen foods is 63.2 lbs. per capita, vs. 10.3 lbs. in Britain, 8 lbs. in West Germany and half a pound in Italy . . . With supermarkets accounting for 73% of total grocery sales, U.S. now has fewer stores—one for every 113 persons, vs. one for every 110 in 1963 and one for every 97 in 1958 . . . New "truth in packaging" law in effect—covering label information, disclosure of ingredients, cents-off sales and "slack filled" packages . . .

TEEN AND COLLEGE LIVING AND
ALTERNATIVE LIFE STYLES IN THE ROCK ERA

Congress extends draft law to June 30, 1971. President given power to cancel deferments of most graduate students . . . Female and male college students start living in same dorm buildings . . . Teenyboppers flourish . . . Many draft boards refuse to follow General Hershey's order to cancel deferments of college students who interfere with campus military recruitment . . . Eight million young singles spending most of $50 billion earnings on dating . . . CIA and plainclothes police spies surface in colleges . . . *Seventeen* magazine survey shows 29% of 18-29-year-old girls never engaged in petting . . . Higher education enrollment almost doubled since 1960: 6,963,687 vs. 3,570,000 . . . Supreme Court declines to hear two cases involving young men refusing to fight in Vietnam because war is illegal . . . Two-year-old computer dating "Operation Match" claims 130,000 singles (out of their 5 million clients) got married . . . National Student Association reveals that it secretly received more than $3 million from CIA for use in student exchange programs. CIA says this is done to avoid labeling NSA as Government agency . . . D.C. swimming pools insist longhair boys also wear swimcaps . . . Gallup college survey shows 49% in favor of Viet escalation vs. 35% favoring reduction . . . Juicy Brucey, WBZ Boston DJ, tells listeners: "If you can't get rid of pimples, at least have them spell 'Love' on your forehead"—while Cousin Brucie, on top rock station WABC New York, says: "If they ever find the perfect pimple cream, I'll be out of a job" . . . Marshall McLuhan and George B. Leonard say that members of the younger generation are "making it clear in dress, music, deeds and words just how equivocally they reject their elders' sexual world. The young men with the long, flowing hair are really saying, 'We are no longer afraid to display what you may call feminine. We are willing to reveal that we have feelings, weaknesses, tenderness—that we are human' " . . . *Time* magazine breaks precedent as its 1966 "Man of the Year" spotlights a generation rather than an individual. Announced winner is: "Twenty-five and under (on the closing third of the 20th century, that generation looms larger than all the exponential promises of science or technology)" . . . Supreme Court gives juveniles the rights of adults in courts, such as right to legal counsel and notice of specific charges against them . . . 29% of high school drivers own their own cars, vs. 60% of college drivers . . . Teens and sub-teens account for 51% of all fountain drinks sold and for 23% of all beverages . . . Teenagers, only 11% of the population, are now over 50% of the movie audience . . . Teen consumption per capita of foods and beverages is 20% greater than adults . . . President of Macy's, New York, quoted as saying: "Teenagers have been credited with everything from the sports car trend to the finished basement (which allows them to give their own parties). In our generation you had to keep up with the Joneses. Today it's more important to keep up with the Joneses' kids" . . . Tens of thousands converge on Haight Ashbury for "Summer of Love" . . . *Rolling Stone* magazine starts in San Francisco. Free roach-holder given with first issue . . . Now estimated 300,000 hippies in U.S.—predominantly middle-class, educated youths 17-25 years old. By late summer, 50,000 based in San Francisco. New York Senator Robert Kennedy (to hippies, the best of a bad lot) says: "They want to be recognized as individuals, but individuals play a smaller and smaller role in society. This is a formidable and forbidding arrangement" . . . Britannica special report notes significance of almost all hippies being white children of "haves"—rejecting the values and rewards that many blacks are struggling to obtain . . . San Francisco State Sociologist, H. Taylor Buckner, Haight Ashbury hippie in-depth study reveals: Only 14% live alone; 25% share quarters with ten or more people; 69% are employed; 68% have some college education; few try heroin, but 96% smoke pot and 90% have tried LSD; 60% are between 16 and 21 years old, 30% 22-30, and only 2% under 16 or over 30; 60% are from cities and 70% from outside California . . . University of Illinois co-eds forbidden to wear long trench coats when "necking" with dates because one was once caught with nothing on underneath. Also, in dorm lounges, couples are required to keep three of their collective four feet on the floor. Ohio State girls' dorm governing body takes pictures of co-eds whose actions with dates are considered inappropriate; but most colleges around the country are relaxing rules and allowing dating in dorms . . . University of Michigan and Reed building co-ed dorms—with strictly separated living quarters . . . Slogan "Haight Is Love" spreads across U.S. as Woolworth's stocks hippie wigs, Air Force pilots daub hippie slogans on their fighter planes and travel agencies offer tours of hippie locales . . . *Time* magazine estimates 50,000 hippies living in San Francisco Bay area; and *Newsweek* predicts a migration there of 100,000 more by summer's end . . .

FASHION: CLOTHES AND THE ROCK ERA ACCENT ON YOUTH

Note: Feminine fashion is in italics, male in roman, unisex in parentheses, and news in asterisks.

Twiggy eyelashes, perfumes and clothes . . . enormous earrings—some homemade . . . George Raft gangster look—pinstripes . . . *High-rise stretch vinyl or synthetic leather boots that pull on and off like gloves . . . Painted soda pop ring-pulls for pierced ears* . . . (Bush jackets and Air Force jackets) . . . *Colored textured hosiery, panty hose and stocking tights* . . . ("Pig Pen" [Grateful Dead] gaudy sweatshirts) . . . **Youth craze has adult women getting $350 eyelid lifts, $500 belly lifts and $650 thigh lifts along with their face lifts** . . . **In London Lord Snowdon wears a turtle neck with his tuxedo** . . . **Twiggy tours America, and is called a "paper cut-out" by *Women's Wear Daily*** . . . *Outfit consisting of wild stockings, baby doll shoes, pale pouty mouth, busy false eyelashes and jagged boy's hairdo* . . . **TV commercials show New York Yankees catcher Yogi Berra and other baseball stars using their wives' hairsprays** . . . *Patterned teeshirts* . . . **Paper dresses out before they come in** . . . (*Ingenue* magazine says newest thing in teen togetherness is for steady daters to smell alike) . . . More getting away with shirt tails out, blue jeans and bare feet at school . . . **Indiana University survey of female fresh-men discloses those with long, slender shapes and stringy muscles accept their body images significantly more than the rotund in contour with soft body tissue—this being an important dress determinant** . . . Stovepipes and tapered slacks dominate male college student fashion scene . . . Military uniforms out in favor of gangster look, with youths buying double-breasted pin-stripe jackets and far-out ties (with palm trees and the like) . . . Brown and white shoes and taxi-driver hats big at Harvard . . . **Marshall McLuhan, in describing Twiggy as the popular idea of the teenage girl who really doesn't look like the feminine ideal of the past, says, "Her power is incompleteness; any person with a very undefined, casual, spontaneous image requires the viewer to complete it"** . . . **James Laver says in St. Louis, "In a patriarchal society—one in which man is dominant—the clothes of men and women are vastly different. But in a matriarchal society the clothes worn by the two sexes become more and more alike"** . . . **Mary Quant says, "Suddenly every girl with a hope of getting away with it is aiming to look not only under voting age, but under the age of consent"** . . . (Salvation Army band coats and flowered pants like those John Lennon wears) . . . (Beaded headbands) . . . *Mismatched pants suits* . . . **Hippies in San Francisco protecting selves from chill with everything from serapes to old Army and Navy foul weather jackets and sturdy boots, hip-snug military jackets and snap-brimmed hats worn by "Diggers" (Australian soldiers)** . . .

FADS (MOSTLY YOUTH-ORIENTED) RELATED TO THE ROCK ERA

Jogging big at colleges . . . Mickey Mouse watches . . . Protest buttons . . . Psychedelic and personality posters . . . Snoopy . . . Toilet paper stunts at colleges: threading the bushes (Michigan); T-P'ing (covering houses with it—Mississippi); rolling (Washington) . . . Hand-painted cars . . .

SOME OF THE MORE WIDELY USED ARGOT, JARGON AND SLANG IN THE ROCK ERA

Bad trip (unpleasant experience) . . . Ballsy (bold, nervy) . . . Beautiful (super) . . . Bummer (bad experience) . . . Grok (relish the scene) . . . Guru (spiritual leader) . . . Hangup (problem) . . . Head shop (boutique dealing in psychedelic and drug paraphernalia) . . . Horn (telephone) . . . Inner space (the beyond within) . . . Kicky (exciting) . . . Narcs (narcotic agents) . . . One-eye wheels (cycles) . . . Peacenik (see Vietnik, 1966) . . . Plastic hippies (teenyboppers and weekend dropouts) . . . "Right on!" (perfect) . . . Shades (sunglasses) . . . The Man (anyone in authority) . . . Uptight (1. great; 2. tense, frightened) . . . Zit (pimple) . . .

Lynda Bird Johnson Glossary of Campus Slang includes: Bag some zzzs (sleep) . . . Bug out . . . Flake out . . . Catch some rays (sunbathe) . . . Put on . . . Hang a right (make a right turn) . . . Blow your cool . . . Flap . . . Hung up . . . Shot down . . . Boondocks . . . Flak . . . Gross . . . Mover . . . Stay loose . . . Zoo . . .

Alleged drug oriented song titles: "Bend Me, Shape Me" (American Breed), "Strawberry Fields Forever" (Beatles), "Up, Up and Away" (Fifth Dimension), "Purple Haze" (Jimi Hendrix), "White Rabbit" (Jefferson Airplane), "Full Measure" (Lovin' Spoonful), "Buy Me For the Rain" (Nitty Gritty Dirt Band), "That Acapulco Gold" (Rainy Daze), "I Can See For Miles" (The Who), "Yellow Balloon" (Yellow Balloon) . . .

THE NEW WOMAN IN THE ROCK ERA

Ad agency headed by Mary Wells Lawrence dazes New York by hitting $50 million billings first year . . . *Redbook* survey report shows 66% of women would vote for woman presidential candidate against equally qualified male . . . Sue Kaufman's *Diary of a Mad Housewife* published . . . Women's Strike for Peace demonstrates outside Pentagon . . .

MOSTLY FACTUAL TRIVIA
CONCURRENT WITH THE ROCK ERA

Hundredth anniversary of potato chips celebrated . . . Fashion expert estimates the cost of being on the women's "Best Dressed List" to be a minimum of $20,000 annually—with the really clothes-conscious aspirant spending $100,000 a year on dresses alone, in addition to furs and jewelry . . . Calculating all possible combinations of styles, options and colors available on a certain new family sports car, computer expert comes up with 25 million different versions for a buyer . . . High-rated "Gunsmoke" TV show dropped from CBS fall schedule because it attracts too many older people—who buy less. It was later reinstated . . . Fidel Castro boast on TV claims Cuban ice cream industry has 26 flavors and will soon top the U.S. with 42. Baskin-Robbins informs their Minister of Information of their own 290 flavors . . . Coldest football game yet at Green Bay when Packers play Dallas Cowboys in 13 below zero temperature with wind at 18 m.p.h. . . . Rum production down 37% as vodka exceeds gin bottling by 11%, while production of bottled cocktails continues significant rise . . . Finnish saunas now installed in over 20,000 homes . . . *New York Times* military editor, Hanson Baldwin, writes about Marine Corps engineers in Vietnam using coathanger dowsers or divining rods to detect tunnels, mines and booby traps . . .

1968

ARTISTS

Rock Groups
  Jeff Beck Group
  Big Brother & The
    Holding Company
  Blue Cheer
  Canned Heat
  Captain Beefheart &
    His Magic Band
  Classics IV
  Country Joe & The Fish
  Creedence Clearwater
    Revival
  Deep Purple
  Electric Flag
  Iron Butterfly
  Sly & The Family Stone
  Small Faces
  Status Quo
  Steppenwolf
  Traffic
  Vanilla Fudge

Rock Solo Performers
  Mama Cass Elliot
  Richard Harris
  Janis Joplin

Soul, R&B, Funk Groups
  Archie Bell & The Drells
  Delfonics
  Foundations

Soul, R&B, Funk Solo Performers
  Arthur Brown
  Clarence Carter
  Tyrone Davis
  Eddie Floyd
  Johnny Nash
  Johnnie Taylor

Folk & Country
  Leonard Cohen
  Judy Collins
  Mary Hopkin

Middle of the Road
  Jose Feliciano

Bubblegum
  1910 Fruitgum Company
  Ohio Express

Cult Groups/Punk/New Wave/
Drone Rock
  Flamin' Groovies

JUKE BOX HITS

"You Keep Me Hanging On"
Vanilla Fudge

"Words"
Bee Gees

"MacArthur Park"
Richard Harris

"The Mighty Quinn"
Manfred Mann

"Over You"
Gary Puckett & The Union Gap

"White Room"
Cream

"Goin' Out of My Head"/"Can't
Take My Eyes off You"
Lettermen

"Hey Jude"
Beatles

"(Sittin' on) the Dock of
the Bay"
Otis Redding

"Those Were the Days"
Mary Hopkin

"Lady Madonna"
Beatles

"Fire"
Crazy World of Arthur Brown

"Jumpin' Jack Flash"
Rolling Stones

"Since You've Been Gone"
Aretha Franklin

"Honey"
Bobby Goldsboro

"Crimson and Clover"
Tommy James & The Shondells

"This Magic Moment"
Jay & The Americans

"Everyday People"
Sly & The Family Stone

"In-A-Gadda-Da-Vida"
Iron Butterfly

"Can I Change My Mind"
Tyrone Davis

"People Got to Be Free"
Rascals

"Sunshine of Your Love"
Cream

"This Guy's in Love with You"
Herb Alpert

"Mrs. Robinson"
Simon & Garfunkel

"For Once in My Life"
Stevie Wonder

"Hello, I Love You"
Doors

"Young Girl"
Gary Puckett & The Union Gap

"Cry Like a Baby"
Box Tops

"Born to Be Wild"
Steppenwolf

"A Beautiful Morning"
Rascals

"Love Is All Around"
Troggs

"Pictures of Matchstick Men"
Status Quo

"Wichita Lineman"
Glen Campbell

"Abraham, Martin and John"
Dion

"I Heard It Through
the Grapevine"
Marvin Gaye

"Going up the Country"
Canned Heat

"Summertime Blues"
Blue Cheer

"Bring It on Home to Me"
Eddie Floyd

"Stoned Soul Picnic"
Fifth Dimension

"Midnight Confessions"
Grass Roots

"Dance to the Music"
Sly & Family Stone

"Piece of My Heart"
Big Brother & The
Holding Company/Janis Joplin

"Hush"
Deep Purple

"Love Child"
Diana Ross & Supremes

"Angel of the Morning"
Merrilee Rush

"The Ballad of Bonnie
and Clyde"
Georgie Fame

"Slip Away"
Clarence Carter

"Green Tambourine"
Lemon Pipers

"La-La Means I Love You"
Delfonics

"The Worst That Could Happen"
Brooklyn Bridge

"Turn Around Look at Me"
Vogues

"Light My Fire"
Jose Feliciano

"You're All I Need to Get By"
Marvin Gaye & Tammi Terrell

"Dream a Little Dream of Me"
Mama Cass Elliot

"Judy in Disguise (With Glasses)"
John Fred & His Playboy Band

"Eleanore"
Turtles

Folk & Country

"Both Sides Now"
Judy Collins

Bubblegum

"Simon Says"
1910 Fruitgum Company

"Yummy, Yummy, Yummy"
Ohio Express

NEWS OF ROCK

Rock ballrooms boom as success of Fillmores East and West is matched by Electric Factory, Philadelphia; Kinetic Playground, Chicago; Grande Ballroom, Detroit; and Boston Tea Party. Live music and name acts pack them in . . . Discos fade . . . Almost 5,000 new LPs being released every year . . . Bob Dylan resurfaces at Woody Guthrie Memorial Concert, Carnegie Hall, New York . . . John Phillips of the Mamas and Papas, key organizer of the Monterey Pop Festival last year, finally gives up on trying to promote a repeat . . . Only major rock fest, Miami Pop Festival, draws peaceful 40,000 . . . Bubblegum music scores with 8-11-year-olds . . . Songwriter Jimmy Webb, 21, boosts income to $300,000 a year in 18 months with smashes like "Up, Up and Away" and "By the Time I Get to Phoenix" . . . Paul Butterfield, Canned Heat and John Mayall lead blues revival . . . Bob Dylan's "John Wesley Harding," recorded in Nashville with local studio musicians, begins pop star influx of studios there . . . Ralph Nader states that rock is producing a nation with impaired hearing . . . Jefferson

Airplane makes cover of *Life* . . . Cream plays farewell concert at London's Albert Hall . . . Independent record producers and self-producing performers now recording 60% of the hits vs. company A&R men's 40% . . . Stones' "Street Fighting Man" released about same time as Chicago Democratic Convention—banned by some radio stations . . . Smash rock musical *Hair* takes Broadway by surprise after being turned down by all top producers. Goes on to become one of all-time top five moneymakers . . . Folk singers shift from protest to self-analysis . . . John and Yoko nude album cover banned . . . Hard rock takes over from folk-rock— beginning long years of domination . . . Rock musical, *Your Own Thing,* based on Shakespeare's *Twelfth Night,* gets rave reviews from *New York Times* when it opens off-Broadway, and runs on for 933 performances. Named Best Musical (9 votes) over *Hair* (2 votes), but stays off-Broadway . . . Beatles form Apple . . . San Francisco heads U.S. music scene with around 500 local bands regularly playing in the Bay area, along with the dozen big names that got their starts there . . . Bank of America vice president predicts that rock music will be San Francisco's fourth largest industry by the mid-1970s . . . Bob Dylan elected President of the United States in a grass ballot vote by the audience of Bob Prescott's show on San Francisco FM rocker, KMPX. Paul Butterfield was elected Vice President; George Harrison, Ambassador to the U.N., and some of the cabinet members were: Attorney General, Grateful Dead; Transportation, Jefferson Airplane; Agriculture, Pig Pen; Secretary of State, Joan Baez; Labor, the Mothers of Invention; Defense, Country Joe MacDonald . . . Richard Harris's 7½-minute record hit, "MacArthur Park," breaks deejay taboo on long records, which is hit soon again by "Hey Jude" . . . Tin Pan Alley songwriters Laura Nyro and Randy Newman score as performers—setting stage for later popularity of other writer/singers such as Carole King . . . Moody Blues team up with London Festival Orchestra for classically-oriented "Days of Future Passed." Enormous success of album blazes way for successful art-rock efforts by Pink Floyd, Emerson, Lake and Palmer, Electric Light Orchestra and Rick Wakeman, and wide exploration in the next decade . . . Moog Synthesizer reaches rock field via the classics as the Walter Carlos "Switched On Bach" album, realizing some of the composer's best-known works on the Moog, becomes all-time bestseller . . . Following the lead of Bob Dylan (1965) and Peter, Paul and Mary (1967), Simon and Garfunkel switch from soft acoustic guitar backgrounds to electric instruments for "Bookends" album . . . Despite unfavorable press, the Beatles' "Magical Mystery Tour" film, which cost only $90,000 to make, pulls an estimated $3 million from overseas sales (in addition to record royalties) . . . Beatles go to Rishikesh, India, for transcendental meditation course at the Maharishi Mahesh Yogi's academy . . . New all-time high in gold records winners, according to Record Industry Association of America, with 45 singles selling 1 million or more copies, and 75 LPs going over $1 million in sales vs. last year's 34 singles and 61 LPs . . .

Efforts to hype the "Bosstown Sound" as Boston's answer to San Francisco's enormous success fail dismally—as do the three groups involved: Ultimate Spinach, Beacon Street Union and Orpheus . . .

SOME OF THE NEWS THAT INFLUENCED THE ROCK ERA AND VICE VERSA

LBJ quits Presidential race—Nixon beats Humphrey . . . Viet Cong reach Saigon U.S. Embassy in Tet offensive, dimming U.S. hopes for winning war . . . Civil Rights Act bars discrimination in sale or rental of 80% of U.S. housing. Also orders punishment for anyone organizing or inciting riots after having traveled inter-state with intention of doing so . . . Martin Luther King and Bobby Kennedy assassinated . . . Crimes of violence in U.S. up 57% since 1960 . . . USS *Pueblo* seized by North Koreans . . . *Washington Daily News* reports one out of every eight Americans getting Social Security benefits . . . Race riots in Chicago, Washington and other U.S. cities . . . French student revolt erupts into general strike . . . My Lai massacre . . . Nixon's 43.4% of the vote is lowest winning Presidential margin since 1912 . . . 10,000-20,000 demonstrators face 11,500 police, 5,500 National Guard and 7,500 U.S. Army troops at Chicago Democratic Convention . . . Four permanent three-day weekends created by shifting Washington's Birthday, Memorial Day, Columbus Day and Veterans Day to Mondays . . . U.S. and North Vietnam start peace negotiation talks in Paris . . . U.S., Soviet and sixty other nations sign Non-Proliferation of Nuclear Weapons Treaty . . . LBJ announces cessation of North Vietnam bombing to end Paris peace talk stalemate . . . Three astronauts in Apollo 8 orbit Moon ten times and safely return . . . Vietnam war casualties exceed Korean War total . . . Direct airline service between U.S. and Russia established . . . Congress passes watered-down Gun Control Law banning interstate sales of rifles, shotguns and ammunition . . . Soviet and East-bloc allies invade Czechoslovakia to extinguish liberalization program . . . Presidential candidate Nixon refuses to debate Humphrey on TV . . . Federal Trade Commission study shows that filter tip cigarettes now dominating market yield more tars and nicotine because tobacco companies are using higher-content leaf . . . Undersecretary of Commerce quoted as saying: "We spend as much for pet food as on food stamps for the poor—more for tobacco than government at all levels spends on higher education, and as much for hair dye as for grants to urban mass transit" . . .

THE NUMBERS GAME: STATISTICAL INFORMATION SHOWING HOW LIFE IN AMERICA INFLUENCED OR WAS INFLUENCED BY THE ROCK ERA

Conglomerates mushroom, with 4,462 new business mergers—up from 2,975 in 1967 . . . 2,407 manufacturing and mining firms disappear through mergers . . . Handgun imports 1,115,000 vs. 346,000 four years ago . . . Department of Interior estimates 15 million fish killed by pollution. 58% of U.S. fish now imported, vs. 41.4% two years ago. Average American eats 11 lbs. a year—highest since mid-1950s . . . Since 1950, towns and villages within commuting distance of large cities grew more than five times faster than urban areas. Now containing 35% of total population, from 24% in 1950 . . . 5.5 million cars recalled for inspection and possible correction of defects—1,117,408 could cause loss of control without warning, 4,000,620 had defects that could cause control to deteriorate . . . In 1929, 33% of the national income went to 5% of the population. Now they only rake in 15% . . . Adults smoking average 205 packs a year—down from 210 in 1967 . . . 569,202 Volkswagens sold—57% of import market—outselling the Chevelle, Fairlane, Fury, Mustang and many other U.S. makes . . . 99,900,000 cars registered in U.S. 78.6% of families own at least one . . . Air pollution damage costing $16.2 billion—rise to $25 billion by 1977 estimated . . . Average American eating 22 lbs. of candy vs. 16 lbs. in 1958 . . . 9,500 new consumer packaged goods items this year. Only 20% meet sales targets . . . In 12 months preceding this March, 36,600,000 Americans (one year old and up) changed their place of residence . . . In his book *Elections in America*, Gerald M. Pomper finds that almost three-quarters of all policy promises in political party platforms are kept—with the party holding the Presidency succeeding 80% of the time vs. 50% for the out party . . . Most important problems facing America, according to Gallup poll results of past eight years, were: 1968/67/66/65: Vietnam; 1964: integration; 1963: racial problems; 1962: war, peace and international tensions; 1961: prices and inflation . . . Air pollution cases in first half of year top 1967 total . . . Estimated $17-$20 million spent for Nixon political advertising, vs. about $12 million for Humphrey and $6 million for Wallace. The $35-$38 million total for 1968 is $10 million higher than the 1964 campaign and $15 million more than was spent on the 1960 Kennedy-Nixon campaigns . . . As many as 10 million Americans suffering from malnutrition, reports TV documentary "Hunger in America" . . . Drop of 14,170 retail stores in past year, to new total of 1,794,744, continues trend to fewer, larger stores. In past decade, 72,000 outlets—mainly small specialty shops—disappeared . . . Charge cards now offered by 625 banks, vs. 70 three years ago. About 10 million consumers hold cards, with 400,000 merchants honoring one or more . . .

TEEN AND COLLEGE LIVING AND ALTERNATIVE LIFE STYLES IN THE ROCK ERA

Yale admits women . . . Democrat Eugene McCarthy almost wins New Hampshire Primary with help of youth support; and Johnson bows out of race . . . National Security Council abolishes most graduate student and occupational draft deferments . . . Columbia University student riots cause campus to be closed after two days of tumultuous demonstration . . . U.S. Department of Agriculture study shows 1968 girl in her 20s is 5 ft. 4 in. tall, with 25.8 in. waist, 37.5 in. hips, and 34 in. bust, vs. average 1939 girl who was 5 ft. 3 in. high, with 26.6 waist, 37.5 hips. Bust measurements didn't change, but since 1968 girl taller, with slimmer waist, she seems bustier . . . Estimated 10,000 draft eligibles now in Canada . . . In one month from September 15, over 200 protest incidents reported in *New York Times* and *Washington Post* . . . 60,000 graduate and undergraduate students enrolled in 1,500 film courses at 120 colleges . . . Serious riots in Haight Ashbury footnote to earlier departure of Flower People . . . 204 separate campus demonstrations, mostly anti-war—new peak . . . Half of all college applications go to less than 10% of schools . . . 1,000 men serving time for turning in draft cards . . . Five states exporting more college students than importing them are: New Jersey (−98,710), New York (−55,716), Illinois (−32,454), Connecticut (−21,125) and Maryland (−15,327.). Biggest net migration states are: Massachusetts (+37,316), Indiana (+26,495), North Carolina (+23,556), Tennessee (+20,037) and Michigan (+17,316) . . . Cornell University group stages mass draft card burning (150-200) at peace march in New York's Central Park . . . Study of fifth and six graders (11- and 12-year-olds) finds 84% of the girls and 62% of the boys expect eventual marriage; while 74% already have boyfriends or girlfriends . . . Oldsmobile attributes near tripling of sales of its sporty Cutlass "S" Coupe to: "The car's appeal to the young and those buyers influenced by the young" . . . Dr. Joyce Brothers reports on results of questionnaire conducted by psychiatric reporter among 313 psychiatrists: 30% believed that fictional violence portrayed in comic books, TV shows and movies teaches actual violence, but 24% felt it helped dissipate aggression. The rest were undecided . . . Decline in college fraternity membership—with Greek letter chapter houses being closed on some campuses. Phi Delta Chi, at the University of California, Berkeley, sent invitations to 209 prospects and failed to pledge even one . . . Only 68 of Harvard's 1,134-man graduating class go directly into work in a business—as the rest head for the professions, graduate study or helpful endeavors like the Peace Corps . . . Now almost 7 million students in all types of colleges and universities vs. 2.7 million in 1955—and 1.4 million before World War II . . . Questionnaires filled out by hippies at Haight Ashbury, the East (Greenwich) Village, New York, and Sunset Strip/Fairfax Avenue in L.A., as well as Venice, Calif., reveal: (1) Median age is 19 years; (2) 77.6% graduated from high school—50.6% had at least some college; (3) Approximately three males to one female; (4) 35.1% came from families with incomes from $7,501 to $14,999—and another 35.7% from families earning $15,000 up; (5) Dropouts from 2 to 4.9 years numbered 28.2%, 5 years up 21.7% and under 2 years 50.1%; (6) Marijuana had been used by 90.7%, LSD by 68.2%, speed (amphetamines) by 57%, and heroin only by 2.8% . . . *Yellow Dog* is first all-comic underground paper . . . Ten College Exchange founded—with students spending a semester or two at Vassar, Williams, Amherst and other participating campuses . . .

FASHION: CLOTHES AND THE
ROCK ERA ACCENT ON YOUTH

Note: Feminine fashion is in italics, male in roman, unisex in parentheses, and news in asterisks.

"Mousers"(leather panty hose) . . . **Football star Joe Namath buys men's mink coat** . . . (Nehru coats) . . . *Levis cut especially for girls introduced* . . . **Survey shows males over 22 are 4:1 in favor of women's dresses over pants, but all-age preference only 2:1** . . . (Hippie costumes sweep pop fashion world—including ruffled shirt fronts and balloon sleeves, shoulder-length hair often held in place by headband, wide belts with heavy brass buckles, felt hats, cowboy and motorcycle boots, sandals, vests, leather pouches, various forms of costume jewelry, and both pubic level and ankle-length hemlines on females, embroidered butterflies and flowers on jeans, the braless look, peace symbols and unbleached muslin shirts and blouses) . . . **In book, *Collective Dynamics*, authors maintain that when a new style is introduced it is relatively easy to defend one's current tastes, but when fashion leaders adopt a new style, "The woman standing aside appears ridiculous even to herself"** . . . "Two of the most costly skin specialists, Laszlo and Kelsen, now doing big business treating adolescent skins** . . . **First fully allergy-tested fragrance-free line of cosmetics, Clinique, introduced by Estée Lauder** . . . **In *Body Covering*, psychologist Alexander Weatherson states that youthful distrust of permanence in part allows them to wear styles of the past out of context (funky or old attic varieties), in order to disclaim the values of the older generation** . . . **Some 200 University of Missouri students complete four-year study of "Foolish Female Fashions"—fashions that never should have been— including: chemise, overblouse with flared shirt, Bermuda shorts, metallic evening dresses, sheer nylon blouses** . . . (Radical chic: cashmere turtle necks and French-cut jeans) . . . (Unisex fashions finally unveiled at New York's most fashionable department stores—many years after teenage "steadies" began wearing matching sweaters) . . . **Observers comment that teen boys are not interested in highly specialized fashion as *Esquire*'s *GQ Scene* magazine folds after two years of publication** . . .

FADS (MOSTLY YOUTH-ORIENTED)
RELATED TO THE ROCK ERA

Transcendental Meditation . . . Frisbees big again . . . Dell Publishing sells eight million astrology books . . . Maharishi posters . . . "Instant Insanity" puzzle (four cubes with six differently colored sides which must be aligned to show four different colors on each side) . . . Yoga . . .

SOME OF THE MORE WIDELY USED ARGOT, JARGON AND SLANG IN THE ROCK ERA

Boxes (guitars) . . . Bubblegum music (appealing to pre-teens and teeny-boppers) . . . Ding A Ling (dizzy person) . . . Gourd guard (crash helmet) . . . Grossed out (disgusted, bored, tired) . . . "Hang it up, baby" (forget it) . . . Outrageous (great) . . . Rag top (convertible) . . . Twink (awkward boy) . . . Using your clyde (being smart) . . . Vibes (feelings, vibrations) . . . Yippies (hippie-like members of Youth International Party) . . .

"Laugh In" TV show introduces: "Sock it to me" . . . "Here comes the Judge" . . . "Verrry Interrresting" . . .

Alleged drug-oriented song titles: "Journey to the Center of the Mind" (Amboy Dukes), "I Had Too Much to Dream" (Electric Prunes), "Jumpin' Jack Flash" (Rolling Stones), "Lady Jane" (Rolling Stones), "Magic Carpet Ride" (Steppenwolf), "Magic Bus" (The Who) . . .

THE NEW WOMAN IN THE ROCK ERA

In past decade, 83% more women enrolled in college, vs. 57% more men . . . Feminists picket Miss America Pageant—dropping girdles and bras in trash can, giving birth to "bra-burning" label in media . . . Poll shows 55% approve of women earning money in business, vs. 18% in 1937 . . . Colorado leads U.S. in liberalizing abortion laws . . . National Organization of Women (NOW) Bill of Rights calls for: (1) Equal Rights Constitutional Amendment; (2) Enforcement of law banning sex discrimination in employment; (3) Maternity leave rights in employment and in social security benefits; (4) Tax deduction for home and child care expenses for working parents; (5) Child care centers; (6) Equal and unsegregated education; (7) Equal job training activities and allowances for women in poverty; (8) The right of women to control their reproductive lives . . .

MOSTLY FACTUAL TRIVIA CONCURRENT WITH THE ROCK ERA

Houston DJ, Larry Vance, claims world record of 12,265 consecutive revolutions on Ferris wheel in 22 days—breaking 1964 mark of 12,240 set in Knoxville, Tennessee . . . Mickey Mouse celebrates his 40th birthday . . . Florida oil heiress leaves $4.5 million to 150 stray dogs . . . Tiny Tim gets court order to ban album he made in 1952 under name Derry Dover. Now released with title, "With Love and Kisses from Tiny Tim Concert in Fairyland" . . . Roll call of James Bond's girls to date yields: Vesper Lynd, Solitaire, Gala Brand, Tiffany Case, Honey Chile Rider, Pussy Galore, Domino Vitali, Kissy Suzuki and Mary Goodnight . . . Dallas department store, Neiman-Marcus, offers "his and her" Jaguars—his car for $5,559, her jaguar fur coat for $5,975. Other gift suggestions include "Jewel of the Month" for $273,950, which promises delivery in 1969 of four bracelets, four pins, two rings, a watch and a pair of earrings. Sears offers a white mink bathrobe for $4,500, and Tiffany has dessert plates selling for $1,000 a dozen . . . Tendency towards lighter and less pungent spirits hits heavier rums and full-bodied fruit brandies as white rums make further headway. . .

1969

ARTISTS

Rock Groups
  The Band
  Blind Faith
  Blood, Sweat & Tears
  Chicago
  Joe Cocker
  Crosby, Stills & Nash
  Flying Burrito Brothers
  Grand Funk Railroad
  Guess Who
  King Crimson
  Led Zeppelin
  Mountain
  Quicksilver Messenger Service
  Kenny Rogers & The First Edition
  Sha Na Na
  Ten Years After
  Three Dog Night

Rock Solo Performers
  John Lennon
  Joni Mitchell
  Nilsson
  Laura Nyro
  Johnny Winter

Soul, R&B, Funk Groups
  Friends of Distinction
  Jackson Five
  Charles Wright & Watts
    103rd St. Rhythm Band

Soul, R&B, Funk Solo Performers
  Joe Simon
  Edwin Starr

Folk & Country
  Richie Havens
  Joe South

Young Teen Oriented
  Bobby Sherman

Middle of the Road
  Andy Kim

Bubblegum
  Archies

Cult Groups/Punk/New Wave/
Drone Rock
  Iggy & The Stooges
  MC5

JUKE BOX HITS

"I Started a Joke"
Bee Gees

"Lay Lady Lay"
Bob Dylan

"Something"
Beatles

"Aquarius"/"Let the Sunshine In"
Fifth Dimension

"I Can't Get Next to You"
Temptations

"Honky Tonk Woman"
Rolling Stones

"Everyday People"
Sly & Family Stone

"Dizzy"
Tommy Roe

"Build Me Up Buttercup"
Foundations

"Whole Lotta Love"
Led Zeppelin

"One"
Three Dog Night

"Crystal Blue Persuasion"
Tommy James & Shondells

"Hair"
Cowsills

"Too Busy Thinking About
My Baby"
Marvin Gaye

"Touch Me"
Doors

"Do Your Own Thing"
Watts 103rd Street Rhythm Band

"Pinball Wizard"
The Who

"Oh, What a Night"
Dells

"Leaving on a Jet Plane"
Peter, Paul & Mary

"Give Peace a Chance"
John Lennon/Plastic Ono Band

"Raindrops Keep Falling
on My Head"
B. J. Thomas

"Get Together"
Youngbloods

"Grazing in the Grass"
Friends of Distinction

"Suspicious Minds"
Elvis Presley

"Proud Mary"
Creedence Clearwater Revival

"It's Your Thing"
Isley Brothers

"What Does It Take to Win
Your Love"
Junior Walker

"Get Back"
Beatles

"Bad Moon Rising"
Creedence Clearwater Revival

"In the Year 2525"
Zager & Evans

"Spinning Wheel"
Blood, Sweat & Tears

"Baby I Love You"
Andy Kim

"Going in Circles"
Friends of Distinction

"You've Made Me So
Very Happy"
Blood, Sweat & Tears

"More Today Than Yesterday"
Spiral Starecase

"Rainy Night in Georgia"
Brook Benton

"Someday We'll Be Together"
Diana Ross & The Supremes

"Tracy"
Cuff Links

"The Chokin' Kind"
Joe Simon

"My Cherie Amour"
Stevie Wonder

"Ruby, Don't Take Your
Love to Town"
Kenny Rogers & First Edition

"Easy to Be Hard"
Three Dog Night

"Green River"
Creedence Clearwater Revival

"A Boy Named Sue"
Johnny Cash

"Baby, Baby Don't Cry"
Smokey Robinson/Miracles

"Only the Strong Survive"
Jerry Butler

"In the Ghetto"
Elvis Presley

"Time of the Season"
Zombies

"Wedding Bell Blues"
Fifth Dimension

"Good Morning Starshine"
Oliver

"These Eyes"
Guess Who

"Put a Little Love in Your Heart"
Jackie De Shannon

"I'd Wait a Million Years"
Grass Roots

"Traces"
Classics IV

"I Want You Back"
Jackson Five

"Reflections of My Life"
Marmalade

"Everybody's Talkin'"
Nilsson

"The Boxer"
Simon and Garfunkel

"The Weight"
The Band

"Games People Play"
Joe South

Bubblegum

"Sugar Sugar"
Archies

NEWS OF ROCK

Estimated 500,000 at Woodstock. Promoters pay Hendrix $18,000; Blood, Sweat & Tears $15,000; Creedence Clearwater Revival $10,000; Baez $10,000; The Band, Airplane and Joplin $7,500 each; Sly Stone $7,000; Canned Heat $6,500; The Who $6,250; Richie Havens $6,000; Arlo Guthrie $5,000; Crosby, Stills, Nash & Young $5,000; Ravi Shankar $4,500; Ten Years After $3,250; Country Joe $2,500; Grateful Dead $2,500 . . . Detroit DJ Russ Gibbs says Paul McCartney dead for several years, using "Abbey Road" and "Magical Mystery Tour" album covers as proof . . . Altamont Rock Festival disaster . . . Beatles' world disc sales over 330 million units . . . Fifties music big again as Presley, Chuck Berry, the Everly Brothers, Fats Domino, Little Richard and Jerry Lee Lewis play live gigs. Presley's concerts first in nine years . . . Brian Jones drowns . . . The Who create first rock opera, *Tommy* . . . Woodstock ends second golden era of rock as Sixties wind up with young people leaving cities and "freaks," faced with bills and children, settling down . . . Sixteen out of 26 songs in show *Hair* released as single records, setting Broadway mark . . . Estimated 3,000 mimeographed high school underground papers in U.S. . . . CBS, Capitol, Decca, RCA and Mercury-owned labels down from 80% of record hits in 1965 to 37% now, as new labels thrive on rock . . . Doors' Jim Morrison charged with lewd behavior in Miami . . . John Lennon marries Yoko Ono . . . Paul McCartney marries Linda Eastman . . . Sha Na Na cashes in on Fifties rock 'n' roll revival . . . Mick Jagger and Marianne Faithfull "busted" . . . Opinion Research poll of West Coast college musical tastes reports 29% prefer folk and folk-rock, 21% rock, 16% classical, 15% soul, and 10% jazz . . . Guitar sales almost quadruple in past nine years. Now $130 million, from $35 million in 1960 . . . New earthiness in rock music as freaks, ex-freaks and musicians move to rural communities . . . Grand Funk Railroad gives free show for 180,000 in 110° heat in Atlanta . . . John and Yoko record "Give Peace a Chance" in Montreal hotel room after dreaming it up during their "Bed-In" there . . . Blood, Sweat & Tears inject 1940s cool jazz into bluesy rock scene . . . *Rolling Stone* magazine warning on rock festivals, "Be prepared for a bummer this summer," proves valid at Newport '69, in California, as violence mars three-day show. Promoters gross $1 million and end with $150,000 loss after paying $282,000 for talent . . . Grand Funk Railroad debut at Atlanta Pop Festival on heels of Led Zeppelin and smash Iron Butterfly album "In-A-Gadda-Da-Vida," heralding emergence of heavy metal era . . . Along with Blood, Sweat & Tears, Chicago and Mike Bloomfield's short-lived "Electric Flag" plant the roots of jazz-rock . . . Rock music now accounts for 60% of Columbia Records' vastly-increased business, vs. about 15% five years ago . . . Tape cassettes now 40% of record business—grossing over $400 million . . . Atlantic Records pays Led Zeppelin $110,000 contract advance . . . Cream's last concert at the Royal Albert Hall, London, both filmed and recorded for an album . . . James Brown, who spent three years of his teens in a Georgia reform school, featured on the cover of *Look* magazine beside a picture of former Democratic Vice Presidential candidate, Senator Edmund Muskie . . .

SOME OF THE NEWS THAT INFLUENCED
THE ROCK ERA AND VICE VERSA

By April, 12,336 Americans killed in Vietnam—passing Korean toll . . . Moratorium days feature peaceful anti-war demonstrations with Congressmen participating . . . Nixon begins second term . . . U.S. begins secret Cambodian bombing . . . 55% in sympathy with anti-war demonstrations, post-moratorium poll shows . . . Assistant Attorney General Kleindienst calls for repression of students and anti-war "ideological criminals" . . . Chicago Seven trial . . . Chappaquiddick . . . U.S. Air Force reports 12,000 UFO sightings in past 20 years, but no evidence of extra-terrestrial intervention . . . 65 airliners hijacked . . . Neil Armstrong first human to walk on Moon . . . Agnew, then Nixon, appeals to "silent majority" . . . U.S. Court of Appeal reverses Dr. Spock's conviction and two-year prison sentence for opposing draft and Viet war . . . Justice Fortas resigns from Supreme Court in conflict of interests scandal . . . In June, Nixon announces coming withdrawal of 25,000 men from Vietnam—then in October, 85,000 more . . . President states that U.S. never used biological weapons, and that all stocks are being destroyed . . . Offshore oil leakages near Santa Barbara, California, cause massive pollution and wildlife destruction . . . Mariner spacecraft photographs Mars . . . Eisenhower dies . . . Department of Agriculture announces phaseout of DDT use, reducing it approximately 90% by 1971 . . . Antiballistic Missile System Bill passed . . . Ho Chi Minh dies in Hanoi . . . Bikini Atoll, site of 23 nuclear blast tests (1946-58) declared safe for habitation by Atomic Energy Commission . . . Secretary of Health, Education and Welfare studies cyclamate artificial sweeteners after cancer link in animals . . . Preliminary meetings for SALT talks with U.S.S.R. open in Finland . . . Group of American Indians representing over 20 tribes occupy Alcatraz Island . . . Unemployment falls to its lowest level in 15 years . . . Nixon begins intimidation campaign against press and electronic media . . . Oil discovered in Alaska . . . U.S. troops in Vietnam number 475,200 at year end—down from 536,100 last year. Over 40,000 Americans killed there since 1961. War now costing about $30 billion a year . . . For first time, more building permits being issued for apartment construction than for private homes . . . Nixon Supreme Court nominee, Clement F. Haynsworth Jr., charged with racial prejudice and anti-labor bias, and Senate votes 55 to 45 against confirmation. Nixon substitutes G. Harrold Carswell, and he too is blocked by Senate . . . Cyclamates banned as low calorie sweetening agent in foods and beverages by Department of Health, Education and Welfare. Ban later eased somewhat in relation to diet foods, but is big blow to soft drink producers—some of whom depend on low calorie drinks for as much as 25% of their sales . . . Hong Kong flu epidemic . . .

THE NUMBERS GAME: STATISTICAL INFORMATION SHOWING HOW LIFE IN AMERICA INFLUENCED OR WAS INFLUENCED BY THE ROCK ERA

Cost of visit to a doctor up 50% in past decade, vs. 25% rise in cost of living. Blue Cross covers 68 million, up from 37 million in nine years . . . Harris poll shows 17% have assured comfortable retirement. 45% eat steak and roast beef whenever they want it, and 63% vacation at least once a year . . . In four years from 1965, Social Security taxes rose to $374 from $174 per person—the highest proportionate rise of any tax . . . Cost of one day in hospital up 84% since 1965. According to Blue Cross, national coverage now $100 a day for semi-private room . . . Frankfurter's average fat content is now 33%—up from 19% in early 1940 . . . 252 astrology books in print, with estimated 1,200 of 1,750 U.S. newspapers carrying astrology columns . . . Agricultural productivity climbs and average U.S. farm worker produces enough food and fibre for 47 people, vs. 40 the year before . . . By March 13, U.S. lead over U.S.S.R. in manned space flights 19 to 12; in Moon orbital flights 1 to 0; manned hours in space 3,938 to 868; space walks 10 to 3; rendezvous missions 8 to 3; and space linkups 9 to 1 . . . Median age now 27.7 years . . . 15 billion hot dogs being consumed annually . . . Presidential salary increased to $200,000 annually. Travel allowance of $40,000 (untaxable) and official allowance of $50,000 (taxable) remain . . . 1,900 community antennae or cable TV stations in operation . . . Average car owner driving 10,000 miles a year . . . Paved streets and roads added to U.S. landscape at rate of 200 miles a day—every day for past 20 years (75,000 miles of new streets and roads a year—enough to circle world three times) . . . Of the 885,000 listings in the Washington, D.C., phonebook, over half are different from last year . . . Average American adult being exposed to 560 advertising messages a day (newspapers, radio, TV etc.)—only noticing 76 of them . . . 2,248,000,000 Christmas cards now being sold annually . . . Now only 50% of major inventions brought to market in U.S. developed here, vs. over 80% in the 1950s . . . Only 13 giant oil fields (10 million or more barrels) found in U.S. during this decade (excluding Alaska), vs. 25 in the 1950s, 45 in the 1940s, 135 in the 1920s and 1930s, and 53 between 1871 and 1919 . . . Price of domestic crude oil only 3.7% higher than 10 years ago, while industry wages up 40.8%, oil field machinery up 24% and oil well pipe up 17% . . . Over $62 billion spent on medical care—up over 11% from last year and twice the 1960 total. $6 billion went to drug companies, almost $10 billion to companies offering everything from hospital bed linen to electrocardiographs, $3.5 billion on profit-making hospitals and nursing homes, $6 billion on commercial health insurances, and private physicians got most of the remainder. The "health industry" netted $2.5 billion in after-tax profits . . . The top 15 of 700 drug firms now account for 50% of the business . . . 100,000 of 200,000 people now employed by worldwide drug firms are Americans—of which 20,000 are the "detail men" who push prescription pills to private doctors . . . Frozen food consumption up to 70.5 lbs. a year from 63.2 lbs. in just two years . . . Although consumer expenditure for food upwards of $105 billion, a new record, it only averages 17% of the customer's disposable income, vs. 20% in 1960 . . . Estimated 100 lbs. of plastics per car in new models—up 15% from last year . . . More than 100 bills to protect buyers introduced in Congress . . . 11 out of every

100 new car customers purchase an imported car . . . Second homes now owned by 1.7 million . . . More than 20,000 new trademarks a year being registered at U.S. Patent Office—with total now over 370,000 . . . TV special on occult claims that $800 million now being spent on astrology alone . . .

TEEN AND COLLEGE LIVING AND ALTERNATIVE LIFE STYLES IN THE ROCK ERA

Total of 448 universities had strikes or were forced to close down during the year due to campus revolt precipitated by Viet war . . . Courses in religion multiply. At Smith College, 1,400 taking them vs. 692 in 1954 . . . *Psychology Today* survey reports that 17% of students don't feel they're learning too much at college, but 81% disagree . . . Spiro Agnew calls anti-war protesters an "effete corps of impudent snobs" . . . Now 39 universities with more than 20,000 students compared to only two in 1941 . . . "Fun school" image brings 7,000 out-of-staters to University of Arizona, 5,300 (41%) to University of Colorado; and 5,000 students travel over 2,500 miles to University of Hawaii . . . District of Columbia Appeals Court rules that Selective Service head's order to reclassify anti-war and anti-draft demonstrators is illegal . . . Colgate and Bowdoin join Yale in admitting women students . . . NBC poll shows 62% of college students "tired" of campus unrest and 80% feel that lawbreakers in campus battles should be arrested and expelled . . . 130 women at Princeton as it goes co-ed . . . Major national surveys study drug use on college campuses. Roper reports 76% of seniors never tried marijuana. Gallup shows 68%, the College Poll 62% . . . Grosse Point, Michigan, high school bans sideburns below ear lobes and skirts higher than five inches above knee . . . Now 40 million between the ages of 14 and 24—20% of U.S. population—increase of 13 million since 1960 . . . 70% vote environment top problem in Gallup poll . . . From Berkeley student revolt (1964) to Columbia University (1968) to Harvard (1969), campus demands broaden from right to use dirty words and changes in courses, to insistence on sexual and other freedom, revision of admission policies, and reorganization of entire courses . . . 90% of 14-17-year-olds and 50% of 18-19-year-olds now enrolled in schools, vs. 60% and 20% of same age groups in 1910 . . . Announcement made of General Hershey's replacement as Selective Service head in 1970 . . . Portland, Oregon, high school student group learns about 1930s Depression by diet of hot dogs, beans, lettuce sandwiches, potatoes; washing socks and underwear by hand with brown soap; with spending money limited to 25¢ a week—and no TV. Girls deny selves lipstick and hairdryers . . . First lottery drawing for draft since 1942 . . . Harris college poll reports 48% respected a man more for his refusal to be drafted because of Vietnam war opposition—up from 29% previous year . . . Army and Air Force announce that identification serial numbers will be replaced by Social

Security numbers . . . "People's Park" battle between University of California students and National Guard . . . *Life* survey asking if students should participate more in policy-making gets 20% affirmative from teachers, 34% from parents, and 58% from students . . . Yankelovich-CBS survey reveals that 89% of college students feel radical left is more of a threat than radical right . . . Market Research Corp. of America reports 16% of teens skip breakfast, 22% of teen males and 28% of females skip lunch, and 11% skip evening meal . . . *Esquire* feature article reports that average of initial menstruation has dropped from 12½ years old to 11 . . . *Fortune,* the elite magazine of big business, makes January publication a special issue devoted to the 18-24-year-old age group under the title, "American Youth—Its Outlook is Changing the World" . . . The August back-to-school issue of *Seventeen* garners an amazing 357 pages of advertising . . . Georgia study of cheating in high school concludes that educational pressures encourage most of it, and: (1) Girls more pessimistic than boys about the amount of it: (2) Girls claimed they would let others copy their homework more often than boys; (3) More boys admitted taking part in cheating activities such as exam cribs; and (4) Boys felt they were more honest than girls, but displayed a more cynical attitude towards cheating . . . Survey by geographer John F. Rooney reveals that a big city like New York, with its crowded areas and inadequate playing space, produces football talent "at the incredibly low rate of only 13% of the national norm." Its suburbs do 15 times better. And the greatest per capita percentage of players for the professional teams come from Mississippi, Louisiana, Texas, Alabama and Georgia, in that order—where, in less advantaged areas, young people look to professional sports as a way of life, according to author James A. Michener . . . In Rooney's study Pennsylvania produced 1,333 high school footballers, and 78% had to emigrate out-of-state to find a college where they could play; whereas 82% of Texas's 1,290 players were wanted by a home state college . . . *Newsweek* reports two million underground papers in regular circulation. In four years, circulation of *L.A. Free Press* went from 5,000 to 95,000; *Berkeley Barb* from 1,200 to 85,000; *East Village Other* from 5,000 to 65,000. Estimated underground readership now 12 million . . . Two-year-old Underground Press Syndicate claims 125 member papers in continuous publication and 200 others in "erratic appearance" . . . Large billboards appear in New York State, Texas, et al., carrying slogans, "Keep America Clean—Take a Bath" and "Keep America Clean—Get a Haircut" . . . Better Berkeley (California) Council, a hip radical coalition, tries to get hippies and freaks to sign on as cops—but meets with big hitch: Berkeley requires all cops to be clean shaven . . . "The Haight Ashbury looks like East Berlin; and Haight Street is a street under siege," comments President of San Francisco Board of Supervisors, Jack Ertola. Storefronts are boarded over, doorways are blocked by steel grates, sidewalks are covered with broken glass and garbage, and the "flower children" are nowhere to be seen . . . *Time* magazine "Cult of the Occult" cover story points out that sheer weight of numbers in "the most scientifically sophisticated generation of adults in history" has turned the occult arts "from a fad into a phenomenon" . . . Christian underground press born in Los Angeles via the *Hollywood Free Paper* and *Right On* . . . Analysis of content of leading underground newspaper, the *Los Angeles Free Press*, comparing current year to the year before last, 1967, reveals: Stories about Vietnam and the draft down to 1.2% from 6.9%; hippies plus the revolution in life style—slight drop to 5.2% from 5.7%; with Black Power news up to 1.9% from 1.7%; new politics, from White Panthers to Gay Power, up to 5.1% from 1.2%; student unrest up to 2.6% from 1.8%, and drugs down to .3% from .8% . . . Stanford University course in "The Science of Creative Intelligence" (per Maharishi International University) draws over 350 students . . . TWA, Bristol-Myers and 45 other national advertisers buy schedules of commercial time on "underground" FM radio stations in key cities—as underground newspapers also lure national advertisers recognizing their youth "clout" . . . More college students (21%) are majoring in education than in any other field . . .

FASHION: CLOTHES AND THE
ROCK ERA ACCENT ON YOUTH

Note: Feminine fashion is in italics, male in roman, unisex in parentheses, and news in asterisks.

Mini-skirt killed by severe winter . . . **Everybody, young and old, wearing jeans** . . . *Maxi-coats* . . . (Blue jeans with patch on seat) . . . **624 million pairs of panty hose sold vs. 200 million previous year** . . . **$500 million worth of wigs sold vs. $35 million in 1960** . . . **Sunglasses gross almost three times 1960 sales—from $14.5 million to $39 million** . . . *Leather Indian dresses, buckskin, old-fashioned tapestry skirts, wool shawls and ponchos big at high schools* . . . *Tiered gypsy dress of crushed velvet with wide belt, chains and jangling costume jewelry* . . . **With many girls and women investing in falls and hairpieces, Mia Farrow, in a fit of temper, cuts off her long blonde hair** . . . *College campuses and fashion magazines stress heavier-looking heels and broader toes in women's shoes—as the stress on footwear continues, with the emphasized awareness of legs with their coverings that began four years ago, and the increased use of colored footwear which began in the spring of 1966* . . . *Belts and chains popular as femme fashion again features waistlines* . . . **Revlon introduces Etherea to compete with Lauder's Clinique** . . . (Nehru shirts) . . . Male hair styling spreads to every age—down to teens . . . Spray can hairsetting preparations and handheld blow hairdryers now big items with both men and boys . . . *Renewed interest in hats by teenagers and younger women* . . . *Estimated 70% of women and girls using hair coloring, vs. 7% in 1955* . . .

FADS (MOSTLY YOUTH-ORIENTED)
RELATED TO THE ROCK ERA

Spiro Agnew watches . . . Fake fangs for pre-teen creepy-boppers . . . Now 10 million hard-core astrology adherents in U.S. and 40 million dabblers. Twelve hundred out of 1,750 newspapers carry daily horoscopes. Thirty different astrology magazines . . . Monster hobby kits hit 1.7 million sales for Aurora . . . *Eerie* and *Vampirella* magazines reach 2 million readers . . . Dune buggy, latest youth auto fad, sells 70,000 units . . .

SOME OF THE MORE WIDELY USED ARGOT,
JARGON AND SLANG IN THE ROCK ERA

Hunk (handsome man) . . . Now (adj: in with the latest style) . . . Rack attack (sleepiness) . . . Total (v: to completely demolish) . . .

Vietnam argot circa late 1960s includes: Choi oy (Vietnamese for disgust or negation—adopted by U.S. troops) . . . Click (kilometer) . . . Grunt (used by U.S. Marines to infantrymen—picked up by GIs) . . . Hooch (shared quarters with female) . . . Slope, Dink, Slant, Slant-eye, Gook, Zip (derogatory references to Orientals or Asians) . . .

THE NEW WOMAN IN THE ROCK ERA

Women's Liberation consciousness-raising groups founded in forty U.S. cities . . . Former Miss America, Bess Myerson, appointed Commissioner of Consumer Affairs for the City of New York . . . In her book, *Sexual Politics*, Kate Millet depicts the average woman as a hapless victim of history—defining the current problem of negative image mirrored by the media as: Norman Mailer, Henry Miller and D. H. Lawrence; and the solution as Genet . . .

MOSTLY FACTUAL TRIVIA
CONCURRENT WITH THE ROCK ERA

Groucho Marx (73), on hearing the cost of a ticket to the rock musical *Hair*, undresses, looks into his mirror for five minutes, and says, "This isn't worth $11" . . . Record 268 sunny days in St. Petersburg, Florida . . . Journalist reports that Jackie and Aristotle Onassis spent $20 million their first year together—then continued at roughly $384,000 a week . . . Hundredth anniversary of suction-type vacuum cleaner . . . Coca-Cola spending upwards of $12 million on redesign of everything from bottle caps to advertising—while retaining trademarks, red color and bottle shape that research shows consumers identify with the company . . . Federal Trade Commission rules that food stores and gas stations must tell customers more about their win probability in promotional games . . .

1970

ARTISTS

Rock Groups
  Allman Brothers Band
  Badfinger
  Black Sabbath
  Bread
  Eric Burdon & War
  Crosby, Stills, Nash & Young
  Dawn (Tony Orlando)
  Delaney & Bonnie & Friends
  Free
  James Gang
  Marmalade
  Mungo Jerry
  New Seekers
  Santana

Rock Solo Performers
  Harry Chapin
  Eric Clapton
  George Harrison
  Elton John
  Melanie
  John Sebastian
  James Taylor
  Neil Young

Soul, R&B, Funk Groups
  Chairmen of the Board
  Funkadelic
  Buddy Miles Band
  Rare Earth
  Spinners (Detroit)

Soul, R&B, Funk Solo Performers
  Eddie Holman
  Freda Payne
  Diana Ross

Young Teen Oriented
  Osmonds
  The Partridge Family

Middle of the Road
  Carpenters
  Anne Murray

Cult Groups/Punk/New Wave/
Drone Rock
  Lou Reed

JUKE BOX HITS

"After Midnight"
Eric Clapton

"Cinnamon Girl"
Neil Young

"Bridge Over Troubled Water"
Simon & Garfunkel

"Up Around the Bend"
Creedence Clearwater Revival

"War"
Edwin Starr

"Let It Be"
Beatles

"Cracklin' Rosie"
Neil Diamond

"Spill the Wine"
Eric Burdon & War

"Lay Down (Candles in
the Rain)"
Melanie

"Green-Eyed Lady"
Sugarloaf

"Patches"
Clarence Carter

"Love Grows"
Edison Lighthouse

"Something's Burning"
Kenny Rogers & First Edition

"Cecelia"
Simon & Garfunkel

"Fire and Rain"
James Taylor

"Instant Karma"
John Lennon

"The Long and Winding Road"
Beatles

"In the Summertime"
Mungo Jerry

"I Think I Love You"
Partridge Family

"The Wonder of You"
Elvis Presley

"Do the Funky Chicken"
Rufus Thomas

"Close to You"
Carpenters

"Ain't No Mountain High Enough"
Diana Ross

"I'll Be There"
Jackson Five

"Make It with You"
Bread

"Walkin' in the Rain"
Jay & The Americans

"Spirit in the Sky"
Norman Greenbaum

"All Right Now"
Free

"Signed, Sealed, Delivered"
Stevie Wonder

"Lookin' Out My Back Door"/
"Long As I Can See the Light"
Creedence Clearwater Revival

"25 or 6 to 4"
Chicago

"Give Me Just a Little
More Time"
Chairmen of the Board

"Love Land"
Charles Wright & Watts
103rd Street Rhythm Band

"My Sweet Lord"
George Harrison

"Woodstock"
Crosby, Stills, Nash & Young

"Evil Ways"
Santana

"I Just Can't Help Believing"
B. J. Thomas

"Everything Is Beautiful"
Ray Stevens

"Gypsy Woman"
Brian Hyland

"The Thrill Is Gone"
B. B. King

"Your Song"
Elton John

"American Woman"/"No Sugar Tonight"
Guess Who

"Mama Told Me (Not to Come)"
Three Dog Night

"Get Ready"
Rare Earth

"The Love You Save"
Jackson Five

"Thank You"/"Everybody Is a Star"
Sly & Family Stone

"Ball of Confusion"
Temptations

"The Letter"
Joe Cocker

"Ride Captain Ride"
Blues Image

"He Ain't Heavy—He's My Brother"
Hollies

"Come and Get It"
Badfinger

"Tears of a Clown"
Smokey Robinson & The Miracles

"Does Anybody Really Know What Time It Is?"
Chicago

"Another Day"
Paul McCartney

"See Me, Feel Me"
The Who

"Snowbird"
Anne Murray

"Easy Come, Easy Go"
Bobby Sherman

"Black Magic Woman"
Santana

"Lola"
Kinks

"Candida"
Dawn

"Cry Me a River"
Joe Cocker

"Reflections of My Life"
Marmalade

NEWS OF ROCK

Jimi Hendrix offered $75,000 for Randall's Island, N.Y., rock festival, after getting only $500 for Monterey in 1967 and $18,000 for Woodstock . . . Lennon and McCartney each make solo albums—both containing only self-penned originals . . . Paul Simon said to have made $7 million from "Bridge Over Troubled Water" . . . Jimi Hendrix dead at 24 . . . Janis Joplin dead at 25 . . . "Jesus Christ Superstar" begins auspicious career as record album . . . Eric Clapton, Ginger Baker and Ringo Starr among stars on first George Harrison album . . . New York radio listening audience for Top 40 programming down to 15% at night, from 50% during late Sixties . . . Only 18 of 48 major rock festivals get on, as City Councils and police find ways to quash them . . . Santana's second album "Abraxas" defines

Latin rock . . . Religious trend in rock music headlined by "Let It Be," "Spirit in the Sky" and "Jesus Christ Superstar" . . . The Who *Tommy* tour opens at Metropolitan Opera House, New York . . . Presley world record sales over 160 million—"Now or Never" from 1960 biggest, with 20 million sold . . . Beatles' world sales 330 million units. Million-sellers in U.S.: 19 albums and 25 singles . . . Bill Haley record sales now over 60 million—"Rock Around the Clock" accounts for 16 million of these . . . Stones leave Decca to form Rolling Stones Records . . . Rod Stewart records with Faces and as soloist . . . FCC rules Jerry Garcia "obscene" on FM interview and fines station . . . Blood, Sweat & Tears first U.S. group to go behind Iron Curtain on State Department tour . . . Only 26% of single records and 39% of albums released this year manage to return their investment . . . U.S. and foreign *Hair* productions grossing $1 million every ten days. Over 300 different versions of score set Broadway record . . . Colonel Tom Parker claims over 3,000 Presley fan clubs exist . . . Warner Bros. Studio hires 150 freaks to give free rock concerts, bathe nude, etc., for contrived festival film. It flops . . . Out of 5,685 singles, only 242 make *Billboard* Hot 100 chart . . . Second Atlanta Pop Festival draws 40,000 in three days for Allman Brothers, Country Joe, etc. . . . Nearly 8.5 million tape players (of all types) sold this year, whereas in 1957 only 10 million had been sold to date . . . FCC Commissioner tells Vice President Agnew that anti-drug songs now equal those in favor . . . Retail sales of musical instruments, sheet music and instrumental accessories around amazing $1 billion mark, vs. under $400,000 in 1955, when rock just began to roll . . . Allman Brothers Band and year-old Capricorn Records bring focus to Macon, Georgia, as birthplace of Southern rock—opening way for later success of the Marshall Tucker Band, Charlie Daniels Band, Lynyrd Skynyrd and the Atlanta Rhythm Section . . .

SOME OF THE NEWS THAT INFLUENCED
THE ROCK ERA AND VICE VERSA

Nixon orders Cambodian invasion . . . 62% of voting age blacks in eleven Southern states registered to vote, vs. 29% in 1960 . . . White House hires "plumbers" . . . Postal strike . . . Cigarette manufacturers banned from TV advertising . . . "Earth Day" demonstrations against water, air and land pollution . . . U.S. Indian population growing at four times national rate—now 792,000. But life expectancy only 46 years compared to national average of 69 . . . Supreme Court in *Welsh* v. *U.S.* rules by five to three votes that individual may qualify for draft exemption as conscientious objector on moral grounds as well as long-held religious belief . . . Unemployment to 6.2% from 3.5% in one year . . . Supreme Court issues order for integration of all schools in six Southern states by February 1 . . . Strategic Arms Limitation (SALT) talks between U.S. and U.S.S.R.

open in Vienna . . . Organized Crime Control Act signed by Nixon . . .
New Air Pollution Control Act, containing provisions not fully enforceable
before 1977, ratified after 1967 Act proved so indecisive that not one ounce
of air pollution abatement could be directly attributed to it . . . Council of
Environmental Quality reports that about one third of nation's citizens
have no sewage service; and another third inadequate sewage systems . . .
Highest unemployment since 1965 . . . Hunger consultant, Robert Burnett
Choate, Jr., tells Senate Committee that 40 of the top 60 dry cereals have
little nutritional content . . . Voting age reduced to 18 beginning
1971 . . . Law provides for construction of 1.3 million new housing
units . . . Government ship loaded with nerve gas scuttled 280 miles off
Florida . . . Fishery experts tell of possible use of TV satellite Telstar to
spot schools of fish . . . Federal Trade Commission analysis of consumer
complaints in five major cities ranks main offenders: (1) New and used car
dealers; (2) Real estate agents; (3) Mail order houses; (4) Radio and TV
repair shops; (5) Direct selling organizations; (6) Furniture stores. Principal
complaints are: (1) Failure to deliver goods; (2) Truth in lending violations;
(3) Defective work or service; (4) Inferior merchandise; (5) False
advertising; (6) Refusal of refunds without prior notice of a "no refund"
policy . . . President Nixon upgrades President's Committee on Consumer
Interests (established in 1964) to Office of Consumer Affairs . . . Nixon,
on TV, announces he plans to have 150,000 more U.S. troops out of
Vietnam by spring next year . . . Interior Secretary Walter J. Hickel's letter
to the President (leaked to the Press) states that: "Youth in protest must be
heard," and warns that the Administration is "embracing a philosophy
which appears to lack appropriate concern" for youth. He adds that a "vast
segment" of young people feel there is "no opportunity to communicate
with government . . . other than through violent confrontation." Hickel
fired from his job later in the year . . .

THE NUMBERS GAME: STATISTICAL INFORMATION
SHOWING HOW LIFE IN AMERICA INFLUENCED
OR WAS INFLUENCED BY THE ROCK ERA

3,066,000 in military uniforms, vs. 458,365 in 1940 and 22,935,107 in
1945 . . . 68% of the people saw a doctor at least once . . . Amount of
collected urban garbage and rubbish up to 5 lbs. per capita from 2.75 lbs. in
1920 . . . 70% of all autos have radios . . . 13 million gave up smoking in
past four years. Male smokers dropped to 42% from 52%, and females to
31% from 34% . . . Survey reports rail travel 2.5 times as safe as air, 1.5
times as safe as bus, and 23 times as safe as auto travel . . . California poll
shows 50% of those who moved to Los Angeles in past eight years want to
move away . . . Fewer than 30 Americans studying Vietnamese language
. . . White collar workers now outnumber blue collar workers by 5 to 4 . . .

Census reports 143,000 living with partner of opposite sex and not married, vs. 17,000 in 1960—a 700% increase . . . Harris poll shows 75% would rather have 10% more income in an interesting job than 50% more in a boring one . . . 60% of all non-farm wives in families earning over $10,000 are now employed . . . *Life* magazine survey on goals and life styles of a cross-section of Americans reported as the top three preferences: Green grass and trees around me (95%), neighbors with whom comfortable (92%), a kitchen with all the modern conveniences (84%) . . . The ten best-selling drugstore products ranked by dollar volume: (1) Crest toothpaste, (2) Alka-Seltzer, (3) Listerine mouthwash, (4) Colgate dental cream, (5) Tampax, (6) Anacin, (7) Bayer Aspirin, (8) Head & Shoulders shampoo, (9) Contac, (10) Bufferin . . . Census shows smallest number of men (94.8) in ratio to women (100) in U.S. history . . . Federal Government scientific and technical reports now 100,000 a year on top of 450,000 articles, books and papers . . . Barbie Doll world population reaches 12 million—surpassing human population of New York or Los Angeles . . . Now 9,000 stores which sell nothing, but rent almost everything, vs. less than half that number five years ago . . . In each year since 1948 one out of every five Americans changed their address . . . Median time for adults reading newspapers is down to 52 minutes a day . . . From 1956 all-time peak of 16,173 wildcat oil wells drilled in U.S., current total only 7,693 (with only one in 49 considered a "significant" discovery, although one in 11 completed as a producer) . . . U.S. oil reserves decline by one billion barrels as new wells in Middle East and Africa boost their oil reserves by 47 billion barrels . . . Average American this year ate 186.2 lbs. red meat, 50.4 lbs. poultry, 14.8 lbs. fish, 102 lbs. sugar and 319 eggs, while drinking 13.8 lbs. of coffee . . . Rise in Americans identifying with religious denomination brings total to 95% . . . Number of black farmers down to 98,000 from 272,000 in 1959 . . . Census reveals that over 45% of 22-24-year-olds changed their address in current year . . . Billings for advertising retail goods and services up to $20 billion, from $2 billion in 1936 . . . Associated Press poll of 850 manufacturers at Toy Fair finds occult games are the industry's big hope to build sales in the next decade . . .

TEEN AND COLLEGE LIVING AND ALTERNATIVE LIFE STYLES IN THE ROCK ERA

National Guardsmen kill four and wound nine at Kent State student demonstration . . . Cambodia moratorium and 200 college closures are last great student uprisings of era . . . Beginning of the "Me" Decade ("I Will Survive") . . . Over seven million students working for degrees in 2,525 colleges and universities, vs. less than three million in 1950 in 1,851 schools . . . Harris surveys on college student participation in protests report 87% signed petitions in 1970, vs. 72% five years ago. 60% demonstrated, vs. 29% in

1965, and 29% picketed, vs. 18% in 1965 . . . Smoking among teenagers—especially girls—on increase, but 21-year-olds up show drop to 26.3%, from 42.5% in 1964 . . . Carnegie Corporation study reports U.S. public schools for most part "grim," "joyless" and "oppressive," and they fail to educate children properly . . . Teenagers spending $20 billion annually—twice 1969 . . . "Earth Day" teach-ins at approximately 1,000 colleges and 2,500 high schools in all 50 states combat pollution with "Dishonor Rolls," special awards to local polluters, mock funerals for cars, and mass phone-ins to polluters . . . Letter to Nixon from Interior Secretary Walter J. Hickel tells President the Administration is contributing to anarchy and revolt by turning its back on U.S. youth. Hickel also states: "Our young people, or at least a vast segment of them, believe they have no opportunity to communicate with Government." . . . Census statistics indicate average age for man's first marriage is 23 years and 3 months, and woman's is 20 years 9 months; highest since 1940. Average man got married ten months younger in 1960, and women were seven months younger . . . Nixon reported to have said: "Bums, you know, blowing up the campuses," after student protest over Cambodia incursion . . . Census shows over 35 million 15-24-year-olds in U.S. vs. 24 million in 1960 and 23 million in 1950. Also, 44 out of 100 U.S. 18-24-year-olds are in higher education vs. 34% in 1960 and only 28% in 1950 . . . 508 incidents of campus unrest from May 1 to June 30 reported in Presidential Commission survey of 1,569 schools. They only showed 136 incidents at 96 schools during the entire 1967-68 school year . . . 35% of the students 16-21 years old are in part-time jobs—up from 20% in 1960 . . . In college poll, 70% rate FBI "excellent" or "good." Only 10% say "poor" . . . California has three times more college students than France—a nation with three times as many people . . . Gilbert college survey finds one-third of students reporting any experience with marijuana or other drugs. However, 34% of the students guessed that 70% or more had drug experience and 65% guessed at 50% . . . Harris poll reports 80% feel their parents' married life is happy, and only 30% have trouble communicating with them . . . As various polls explore every possible aspect of student thinking, Newsweek reports seven out of ten collegians believe there is too little emphasis on family life . . . After Cambodian incursion, Playboy poll of 7,300 students on close to 200 campuses shows 36% favor "pulling out now" vs. only 6% favoring pull-out in 1965—when 56% of the students favored invading North Vietnam . . . Report shows estimated 200,000 fulltime participating hippies at peak of movement, with most of their detractors under 30 years old and the majority of their supporters over 30 . . . Gallup poll reports one-third of college men and a quarter of women have participated in Sixties demos . . . New York Times survey reports 2,000 communes in U.S. . . . Teenagers 13-17 years old accounting for 81% of all record sales, 55% of all soft drinks, 53% of movie tickets, and 44% of camera purchases . . . Buick offers an entire group of cars (from Skylark to Opel GT) as "The cars to light your fire" . . . Only 32% of 15-19-year-olds now drink coffee, vs. 54% in 1950 . . . Pre-teens and teens averaging 40 lbs. of candy a year . . . Big firms court teens with product-associated blowup posters: General Motors (wild bird for Pontiac Firebird), Esso (humble tiger), Alka-Seltzer and Kelloggs . . . Estimated 870,000 golfers under 17—2½ times more than ten years ago . . . Now total of 40 court cases since 1966 involving longhaired standards in U.S. high schools. Most were mainly decided on the individual's freedom to look as he pleases while undergoing compulsory education . . . College curriculum statistics indicate young males displaying greater social awareness in growing shift from Business Administration and Engineering majors to the humanities—English, History and Political Sciences . . . American newspaper publishers' survey reports 59% of teenagers dislike TV commercials; 48% negative to radio advertising; 40% nixed magazine ads and 27% were down on newspaper ads . . . Controlled Substances Act of 1970 reduces offense of possession of marijuana from a felony to a misdemeanor, thus permitting penalties of fines rather than imprisonment. "Decriminalization" for marijuana possession by adults follows in various states—not legalizing it, but making possession of a small amount (usually about an ounce) subject to a fine (usually about $100) instead of jail . . . Famous women's college, Vassar, goes co-ed. At commencement "occasion of the daisy chain," males wear daisies in their lapels and are called ushers . . . *Rolling Stone* magazine said to be worth $7.5 million three years after it was started with $7,500. Circulation now 400,000 from initial sale of 6,000 . . . First Festival of the Occult Arts at the Fillmore East, New York . . . First B.A. in Magical Studies awarded at University of California, Berkeley . . . Occult equipment now standard items in most "head shops" . . . Ecology as a theme hits the underground press as "a magic new world, all about survival techniques and wilderness and building communes and all that kind of stuff," according to *Other Scenes* editor, John Wilcock . . . Growing number of "Jesus Freaks" in Berkeley, California, focal point of many mid-1960s movements; and according to young Baptist student working there, many of them are former drug users . . .

FASHION: CLOTHES AND THE
ROCK ERA ACCENT ON YOUTH

Note: Feminine fashion is in italics, male in roman, unisex in parentheses, and news in asterisks.

Mongolian fur coats and ethnic dress from Far East . . . J. C. Penney selling wigs for 10-16-year-olds in fifteen different colors from $7 to $19 each . . . **Year and a half old California all-jeans outlet, "Jeans West," expands to 29 stores, with $10 million in sales—60% to women** . . . *Hemlines in skirts finally start lowering, after being on rise for 22 years . . .*

Stripes, checks, psychedelic prints and tapestry . . . **Wrangler doubles business from 1964 to $200 million** . . . *50% increase in sales of pants for women as midi length fails* . . . **Levis for Girls join women's apparel Top 6 in just two years** . . . (Shapes for jeans now: standard taper, bell-bottoms, straight-leg stovepipes) . . . **Man-made fabrics now 56% of textile market—twice that of ten years ago. Cotton down to 40% from 65% in 1960** . . . (Afro fuzz hairdos) . . . **In his bestseller, *The Greening of America*, Charles Reich states that young people's clothes are now "earthy and sensual—the browns, greens and blues are Nature's colors, Earth's colors, and the materials are tactile. The clothes are like architecture that does not clash with its natural surroundings but blends in." He also claims that in rejecting the values of the present society, the "new generation" people's clothes have become "an important symbol which represents a deliberate rejection of the neon colors and artificial plastic-coated look of the affluent society." He adds that they are "not uniform, because they express the body inside them, and each body is unique." Also, while "expensive clothes enforce social constraints," no social points are lost by wearing something that costs $4.99—therefore, the young are wearing their clothes "with pride, as befits a statement of principles and basic values"** . . . **Ohio State University study of junior high school girls reports peer group preferences far more important than parental opinions in clothing choices** . . . **As male college graduates face cutbacks in campus recruiting, many cut off their long hair, and even moustaches, as well as putting on suits and ties** . . . **College student unrest brings tradition-shattering costumes to graduation ceremonies, including peace signs on mortarboards, peace doves, clenched fists or flags on the back of robes, and even ornamented hard hats (with doves or tassels) instead of mortarboards** . . . (Ancient methods of tie-dyeing being used to create homemade psychedelic garments out of cheap teeshirts or old jeans) . . . **Year of Radical Chic** . . . **"Funky Chic," from London, hits fashion pages, with debs wearing blue jeans and blue workshirts open to the sternum, and long pre-Raphaelite hair parted on top of the skull—uncoiffed, but recently washed and blown dry with a continental pro-style dryer** . . . **$7.5 million worth of Mickey Mouse watches and clocks sold in six months; while young and old spending $400,000 a month on Mickey Mouse sweatshirts** . . . (Jeans: Denim joined by twill, corduroy, cotton suede and hopsacking, in variety of solid colors, plaids, stripes, checks, psychedelic prints and tapestry) . . . *Girls' floppy-brimmed hats* . . . **Only 12% of the population, teenage girls account for 23% of all cosmetic expenditures and 22% of all women's apparel sales** . . . Average male teenager buying $25 worth of cosmetics a year . . . *Bobbie Brooks president says: "Teenage girls like action clothes in brighter, bolder colors. They shop in packs and want to look alike until they're 19"* . . . *Bright wool ponchos* . . . **Survey of beauty and toilet products reveals that 85% of women use lipstick and 80% use smooth-on fragrance in some form—beginning in the 12-13 age group and continuing up to 60-70-year-olds** . . .

FADS (MOSTLY YOUTH-ORIENTED) RELATED TO THE ROCK ERA

"Fuzzyfoot" earns $15 million . . . Co-ed dorms in at colleges . . . Health food sales top $3 billion . . . Buck Rogers guns (for a box top and a dime in 1930) selling for as much as $30 in nostalgia boom . . . Real tattoos . . . Barbie doll now has 153 changes of wardrobe, from a $5 wedding gown to a $50 mink stole, a boyfriend, girlfriend and little sister . . .

SOME OF THE MORE WIDELY USED ARGOT, JARGON AND SLANG IN THE ROCK ERA

Dynamite (super) . . . Flash (sudden comprehension) . . . Get it on (pull yourself together) . . . Hassle (bother) . . . Heavy (see 1961) . . . Hype (n: con, v: inflate) . . . Jesus Freaks/Jesus People (young evangelists) . . . Preppy, Preppie (prep school student or graduate—popularized by *Love Story*) . . . Put down (downgrade) . . . Trash (vandalize) . . . Untogether (not functioning or co-ordinating well) . . .

Some course names in college slang: Bladder Jabber (Public Speaking) . . . Cuts & Guts (Biology) . . . Gabs & Blabs (Oral Communication) . . . Mumble Jumble (Public Speaking) . . . Nuts & Sluts (Abnormal Psychology) . . . Places & Spaces (Geography) . . . Rocks for Jocks (Geology) . . . Show & Tell (Public Speaking) . . . Slums & Bums (Urban Local Governments) . . . Socks & Jocks (Physical Education) . . .

THE NEW WOMAN IN THE ROCK ERA

Senate holds first Equal Rights Amendment hearings since 1956 . . . House holds first subcommittee hearings on Sex Discrimination in Education . . . Nationwide, women strike for equality on 50th anniversary of women's suffrage. Betty Friedan called the strike . . . 66% of both sexes would now vote for a woman as president, vs. 31% in 1937, says Gallup report . . . Secretary of Labor announces that Federal contracts will now mandate the employment of a certain quota of women . . . Federal lawsuits initiated to end job discrimination against women in such large corporations as Libby, Corning Glass and American Telephone & Telegraph . . . Nixon administration requires 2,000 colleges and universities to turn over personnel files to determine whether females are victims of prejudice in hiring and wages . . . 200,000 women a year receiving abortions—a 1,000% increase over two years ago . . . Number of 3 and 4-year-olds in nursery schools doubled . . .

FDA warns doctors that the Pill could produce blood clots, and urges 300,000 physicians to acquaint patients with risks . . . First women generals commissioned . . . In the past decade, the number of children under five born to 24-year-old women college graduates dropped by 55% . . .

MOSTLY FACTUAL TRIVIA
CONCURRENT WITH THE ROCK ERA

Massachusetts Congressman's survey reveals that males wore long hair and beards 90% of past 2,000 years . . . Of 450,000 words in English language today, perhaps 250,000 would be comprehensible to William Shakespeare . . . Washington, D.C., store now offering such delicacies as hippopotamus steak, alligator meat and wild snow hare . . . Ex-soldier, New York cab driver boasts 700 surgical stitches in his body—all gained through his chief recreation: rodeo riding . . . *Dairy and Ice Cream Field* reports that vanilla accounts for 51% of all ice cream sold and chocolate gets 13.5%, strawberry 6%, butter pecan 2.4%, and coffee 1%. Other flavors now 5.7%, up from 2.2% last year. Orange (40%) dominates sherbet field . . .

1971 _____

ARTISTS

Rock Groups
  Black Oak Arkansas
  Derek & The Dominoes
  Emerson, Lake & Palmer
  Fleetwood Mac
  Hot Tuna
  Humble Pie
  Jethro Tull
  Nitty Gritty Dirt Band
  Poco
  T Rex

Rock Solo Performers
  Carole King
  Lobo
  Paul McCartney
  Don McLean
  Todd Rundgren
  Carly Simon
  Ringo Starr
  Cat Stevens
  Rod Stewart
  Stephen Stills

Soul, R&B, Funk Groups
  Chi-Lites
  Honey Cone
  Staples Singers
  Stylistics

Soul, R&B, Funk Solo Performers
  Al Green
  Isaac Hayes
  Michael Jackson
  Bill Withers
  Betty Wright

Folk & Country
  John Denver
  Kris Kristofferson
  Gordon Lightfoot
  Jerry Reed

Young Teen Oriented
  David Cassidy
  Donny Osmond

Middle of the Road
  Osmonds
  Helen Reddy

JUKE BOX HITS

"Joy to the World"
Three Dog Night

"Maggie May"/"Reason to Believe"
Rod Stewart

"Go Away Little Girl"
Donny Osmond

"Take Me Home Country Roads"
John Denver & Fat City

139

"Want Ads"
Honey Cone

"If"
Bread

"Uncle Albert/Admiral Halsey"
Paul & Linda McCartney

"Amos Moses"
Jerry Reed

"Superstar"
Carpenters

"American Pie"
Don McLean

"Cherish"
David Cassidy

"Beginnings"/"Color My World"
Chicago

"Precious and Few"
Climax

"Theme from 'Shaft' "
Isaac Hayes

"Another Day"
Paul McCartney

"Got to Be There"
Michael Jackson

"Rose Garden"
Lynn Anderson

"Wild Horses"
Rolling Stones

"Behind Blue Eyes"
The Who

"One Bad Apple"
Osmonds

"It's Too Late"/"I Feel
the Earth Move"
Carole King

"Just My Imagination"
Temptations

"Me and Bobby McGee"
Janis Joplin

"Brown Sugar"
Rolling Stones

"The Night They Drove Old
Dixie Down"
Joan Baez

"Ain't No Sunshine"
Bill Withers

"Temptation Eyes"
Grass Roots

"Have You Ever Seen the Rain"
Creedence Clearwater Revival

"Gypsies, Tramps & Thieves"
Cher

"It Don't Come Easy"
Ringo Starr

"Baby I'm-A Want You"
Bread

"Have You Seen Her"
Chi-Lites

"Spanish Harlem"
Aretha Franklin

"You Are Everything"
Stylistics

"Brand New Key"
Melanie

"Respect Yourself"
Staples Singers

"Indian Reservation"
Raiders

"How Can You Mend A
Broken Heart"
Bee Gees

"Knock Three Times"
Dawn

"Tired of Being Alone"
Al Green

"You've Got a Friend"
James Taylor

"What's Going On"
Marvin Gaye

"Me and You and a Dog
Named Boo"
Lobo

"For All We Know"
Carpenters

"Put Your Hand in the Hand"
Ocean

"Never Say Goodbye"
Jackson Five

"Mr. Bojangles"
Nitty Gritty Dirt Band

"If You Really Love Me"
Stevie Wonder

"Wild World"
Cat Stevens

"All I Ever Need Is You"
Sonny & Cher

"It's a Family Affair"
Sly & The Family Stone

"Proud Mary"
Ike & Tina Turner

"Love the One You're With"
Stephen Stills

"Imagine"
John Lennon

"When You're Hot You're Hot"
Jerry Reed

"What Is Life"
George Harrison

    Folk

"If You Could Read My Mind"
Gordon Lightfoot

NEWS OF ROCK

As the new heavy metal bands, Southern rock bands, jazz-rock, progressive rock, Latin rock and art-rock bands all build their own big followings, rock & roll splinters into many different directions . . . Beatles break up . . . Jim Morrison dies at 28 . . . Recorded rock operas big following smash success of *Jesus Christ Superstar* and *Tommy* . . . Rock ballroom boom over. Most of them can't afford top act prices and close. Big concerts take over . . . Marc Bolan and T Rex popularize "glam" (or camp) rock, beginning with British TV's "Top of the Pops" . . . Mick and Bianca Jagger marry and become parents . . . Beatles' aggregate income from June 1962 to December 1970 over $37 million . . . Duane Allman killed in cycle accident . . . Bubblegum music trend cools . . . FCC directive calls for at least one official at each radio station to be responsible for knowing the content and meaning of record lyrics . . . Record and tape sales $1.7 billion. 60% of buyers under 30 . . . McCartney forms Wings . . . Creedence Clearwater Revival getting $30,000-$40,000 a night, vs. $500 for three nights three years ago . . . Phil Spector comes out of semi-retirement to produce Bangla Desh concert with George Harrison at Madison Square Garden, New York. It grosses $243,418 . . . Bill Graham closes both Fillmores . . . Rock musical hit *Godspell* and George Harrison's "My Sweet Lord" further rock religious trend . . . Hits by James Taylor and John Denver open way for new solo male singers . . . Patti Smith debuts reading poetry with guitarist . . . After record and concert tour hits, *Jesus Christ Superstar* opens on Broadway for 711-performance run . . . *God-*

spell, rock musical based upon the Gospel according to St. Matthew, moves from Carnegie Tech student presentation to off-off-Broadway showcase to off-Broadway for an extended run after getting great reviews . . . Gamble and Huff form Philadelphia International Records under the auspices of CBS, and the "Philly Sound" makes big dent in the rhythm & blues market—providing the major rivalry to the long-established Motown sound in the years to come . . . First "Cheech and Chong" comedy album immediate bestseller and long-lasting hit in pop music album charts . . . *Variety* year-end wrapup story headlined "Where's the New Disc Talent?" With subhead "Sounds Are Old But Biz Booms," story goes on to report: "Revolutionary talents are not easy to come by these days. Where the 'rock renaissance' of the 1960s spawned a brilliant and bold generation of youngsters, the current talent crop for the most part is repeating old sounds" . . .

SOME OF THE NEWS THAT INFLUENCED
THE ROCK ERA AND VICE VERSA

Apollo 14 lands on Moon . . . Eighteen-year-olds get the right to vote . . . Secret tape recording equipment installed in Nixon Oval Office . . . Police arrest 12,000 at Washington anti-war demonstration . . . Pentagon Papers published . . . Harris poll shows 60% against Viet war . . . Khrushchev dies . . . Southern California earthquake kills 62 in Los Angeles area and causes $1 billion worth of damage . . . Bangladesh gains freedom from Pakistan . . . U.S. ping-pong players visit China . . . Dollar no longer convertible to gold . . . Federal marshals end Indian occupation of Alcatraz . . . Treaty banning nuclear weapons from sea bed signed by 63 nations including U.S. and U.S.S.R. . . . Supreme Court rules that bussing may be used to integrate education . . . Nixon accepts invitations to visit Communist China and Moscow in 1972 (election year) . . . Nixon imposes 90-day freeze on prices, wages and rents to combat rising cost of living . . . "Pentagon Papers," giving details of U.S. involvement in Vietnam from the end of World War II to 1968, shows that the Government constantly lied to the people about Vietnam . . . Nixon calls for tax cuts and increased public spending to combat "stagflation" (rising unemployment and cost of living vs. falling productivity) . . . Newly-established Office of Consumer Affairs directly handling some 3,000 complaints a month—with more than 80% disposed of in favor of the consumer . . . Food & Drug Administration's new Bureau of Product Safety begins efforts to reduce the 30,000 deaths and 20 million injuries ascribed annually to accidents involving consumer products . . . Total world fish catch (more than trebled since 1945) shows 2% decrease—first in postwar period. Overfishing and pollution of inshore waters blamed . . . Communist China admitted to United Nations after U.S. resumes limited relations . . . President Nixon revives Subversive Activities Control Board—virtually defunct for 20 years—giving it power to investigate individuals and organizations for subversive traits . . . Attorney General John Mitchell denounces Federal courts for denying him carte blanche wiretapping powers—conceding that innocent people would be hurt, and that couldn't be helped . . .

THE NUMBERS GAME: STATISTICAL INFORMATION SHOWING HOW LIFE IN AMERICA INFLUENCED OR WAS INFLUENCED BY THE ROCK ERA

Hertz reports an increase from 300 to 1,300 cities in one year, where it rents trucks for personal home moving—with a saving of roughly two-thirds . . . Electrical appliance repair vans make 100 million home calls . . . 154 assault crimes per 100,000 population in cities over 250,000 vs. 83 per 100,000 in cities of 100,000-250,000, and only 29 per 100,000 in cities with less than 10,000 population . . . Average taxpayer pays $400 for defense, $125 for Viet war, $40 to build highways, $30 for space exploration, and $315 for health activities . . . Fancy food becomes billion dollar industry as *Gourmet* magazine circulation doubles in four years to 550,000 . . . Gallup survey reports 74% never read even one book in a year—but average national expenditure on books is over $25 . . . Average worker now has 2,750 hours of leisure a year after subtracting 8 hours for sleep, eating and commuting on top of working hours . . . Ralph Nader claims worthless drugs and fraudulent home improvements and repairs each cost Americans $1 billion annually. Of the $25-30 billion spent annually for auto repair, $8-$10 billion is charged for work that is unnecessary, poorly done, or not done at all . . . Short-weighing, according to *Wall Street Journal*, is costing consumers from $1.5 billion to perhaps as much as $10 billion a year . . . 9 out of 10 families now have some kind of life insurance —average amount of protection per family is $25,000 . . . 5 out of 6 are covered by some form of private health insurance—costing around $200 a year . . . Independent oil producers spend less than $1.2 billion for domestic exploration and development vs. $2.5 billion just 15 years ago . . . Now 13 black congressmen, 81 mayors, 198 state legislators and 1,567 black local office holders . . . Average American now only eating 239 lbs. of fresh fruit and vegetables a year vs. 414 lbs. in 1925-29, as consumption of processed fruit and vegetables rises from 84 to 293 lbs. in same time span . . . Combined roster of pro football players now 32% black vs. only 14% in 1957. Pro basketball now 54% black; and by last year the percentage had risen to 25% in pro baseball . . .

TEEN AND COLLEGE LIVING AND ALTERNATIVE LIFE STYLES IN THE ROCK ERA

Campuses quiet as *Playboy* poll finds only 36% of students would protest, "but not violently" . . . Although student revolt cools, Washington, D.C., sees massive peace demonstrations . . . Alternative culture on rise . . . Conventional barbers going out of business or becoming hair stylists . . . 730,000 motorcycles sold vs. 585,000 two years ago. 3.3 million now registered . . . 75% of the moviegoers are under 30 . . . 50 million bicycles in use vs. 25 million in 1960 . . . University bookstore study shows 21% of all occult books sold concern astrology . . . Comparison made between National Safety Council statistics on number of 15-24-year-old Americans killed in traffic accidents vs. Americans killed in Vietnam combat quite revealing: 1970: Accidents 16,500; Vietnam 4,221. 1969: Accidents 17,700; Vietnam 9,415. 1968: Accidents 16,600; Vietnam 14,592. 1967: Accidents 15,646; Vietnam 9,378. 1966: Accidents 15,298; Vietnam 5,008. 1965: Accidents 13,395; Vietnam 1,369. 1961-64: Accidents 42,768; Vietnam 267 . . . Gallup poll shows 59% of 21-29-year-olds consider Viet war a mistake, vs. only 14% in August 1965. In each polling year back to 1967, people 50 years old and over were more against the war than the young—exploding the theory that youth opposed the war and the old supported it . . . 1950s nostalgia sweeps now-quiet college campuses. "Howdy Doody," "Hopalong Cassidy" and "Sergeant Preston" TV kinescopes pack auditoriums, while "sock hops" feature "golden oldies" for ponytailed co-eds and pegged-pantlegged males with greased hair . . . Girls admitted to Boy Scout Explorer program for first time . . . Yankelovich survey of national trends in student values reports 34% believe present institution of marriage is becoming obsolete—up from 28% in 1970 and 24% in 1969. Also, 32% did not look forward to being married or were unsure about it . . . Majority of college and post-college youth living on own now concentrated in "youth ghettos" similar to Haight Ashbury and Greenwich Village in the availability of cheaper housing . . . Harris survey of 15-21-year-olds reveals set of values that the researchers described as "remarkably moderate, even conservative"; that "the majority of youth listens to the rhetoric of dissent, picks what it wants, then slowly weaves it into the dominant social pattern" . . . In technical report of the Commission on Obscenity and Pornography, after experiments with young college males aged 21-23, it was concluded that pornography was "a relatively innocuous stimulus without lasting or detrimental effects on the individual or his behavior." When 194 single male and 183 single female freshmen and sophomore college students were shown two pornographic films, they were found to be "moderately aroused," and people who had more sex guilt tended to see the films as more disgusting and offensive and less enjoyable than did less sex-guilty subjects . . . Underground comix idols Robert Crumb, Victor Moscoso, Rick Griffin and their peers rate an entire floor at Chicago Museum of Contemporary Art for a showing of their work . . . Lowering of voting age to 18 by Congress qualifies 11 million new voters between 18 and 21; while 14 million others between 21 and 25 will be eligible to vote for first time in 1972. In Presidential election next year, 25 million

potential new voters will be added to usual count of about 70 million . . .
Of all current college students, 61% of the whites and 71% of blacks are
from homes where the father never went to college . . . Yale University
contracts with 1,257 students to spread tuition payments over a number of
years after graduation. They are soon followed by Duke and others . . .

FASHION: CLOTHES AND THE
ROCK ERA ACCENT ON YOUTH

Note: Feminine fashion is in italics, male in roman, unisex in parentheses, and news
in asterisks.

Hot pants hot item in winter—cooled by summer . . . (Radical Chic
out) . . . **115 million pairs of jeans sold** . . . (Patched jeans and
appliqué designs, emblems, buttons and embroidery sewn over holes or just
used as decoration) . . . *Girls' caps* . . . *Suede boots reaching above
knees* . . . *Smocks over jeans* . . . *During short life of hot pants (from
satin to denim) and very short shorts worn under short skirts, slitted minis
or on own, they were accompanied by short tops showing bare midriff or
tie-dyed teeshirts, halter-necked tops, skinny sweaters and vests. Leg coverings: tights, knee or thigh-high boots, or open-laced sandals* . . . *Flood of
"back to nature" cosmetics, using wheatgerm, cucumber, papaya, etc.,
with U.S. on big health kick* . . . **Bathing in the nude heats up** . . .
More college men going barefoot to class . . . ***San Francisco Chronicle*
poll results show Sixties backlash in replies. 77% think schools right to
order boys to cut hair, 87% think high schools right in forbidding girls to
wear Bermuda shorts, 70% think schools right to ban even the most modest
fashion such as "granny" dresses if authorities think them ridiculous, and
89% favor bans on any femme clothing school authorities consider
"unladylike"** . . . ***Wall Street Journal* story sees anti-materialistic
philosophy of youth culture contradicted when you check the label and find
the "surplus" jacket off the rack at a hip little boutique. And not only are
jeans bought new, but premiums are paid for faded and tattered ones; with
new teeshirts costing $2 more if the manufacturer has tie-dyed them** . . .
**University of Nevada report discloses that: (1) Men favor nonconformity
in dress more than women, but (2) Both sexes conform more than they think
they do, and (3) College men are significantly more conforming in dress
than women** . . . **Another Colorado State study reports that on reaching senior high school, dressing in a more individual manner and to attract
the opposite sex become the important values** . . . **When Carnaby
Street overtook London's conservative Savile Row, a revolution in men's
finery inspired women's wear designers to fashion men's suits—with
expenditures for men's and boys' clothing doubling in the 1960-1970 decade
to $18.6 billion from $9.7 billion** . . . Flares in college men's trousers
take over from stovepipes—coming from nowhere in just three years.

Tapered trousers virtually disappear from campus . . . (G.I. fatigues and battledress big unisex fashion on beaches) . . . *Eyebrows again being plucked . . . Backcombing disappears and wigs lose popularity* . . . Boom in men's ties . . .

FADS (MOSTLY YOUTH-ORIENTED) RELATED TO THE ROCK ERA

Blue denim telephone books, book covers, tote bags and directors' chairs . . . Cybernetics . . . Jogging hits big cities . . . Ping-pong repopularized by Red Chinese . . . Outdoor graffiti from spray cans . . . Bicycles make strong comeback—especially "chopper" with high handlebars . . .

SOME OF THE MORE WIDELY USED ARGOT, JARGON AND SLANG IN THE ROCK ERA

Trendy (n: close follower of trends) . . .

THE NEW WOMAN IN THE ROCK ERA

Supreme Court rules companies can only deny employment to a woman on grounds that she has young children if they have the same rule for men . . . Only 18% of co-eds at top Eastern college would now retire from workforce on becoming mothers, vs. 50% at same school in 1943 . . . Joan Didion's *Play It As It Lays* published . . . Swiss women win right to vote . . . Billie-Jean King first woman athlete to win $100,000 in one year . . . In the 1950s and early 1960s roughly 16% of TV show women characters worked for wages—now the proportion is up to around 25% . . . In the October *Esquire*, feminist Gloria Steinem is quoted as declaring the average American woman in essence "a prostitute," while Germaine Greer's new book has her a *Female Eunuch*, not even being paid . . . Ellen Peck sees women remorselessly trapped by babies in her book, *The Baby Trap* . . .

MOSTLY FACTUAL TRIVIA CONCURRENT WITH THE ROCK ERA

Putnam Food Awards top prize goes to fabricated onion rings . . . Dr. Bruce Dobbs establishes world record distance of 165 feet for catching thrown grape in mouth . . . Wooden cigar store Indians selling for $4,000 . . . Within moments of Apollo 13 moon landing, Baskin-Robbins launches "Lunar Cheesecake" ice cream in all stores, while Good Humor rushes "Moon Shot" into its trucks . . . Betty Crocker (born in an ad man's brain) reaches age of 50 . . .

1972 _____

ARTISTS

Rock Groups
  America
  Commander Cody & His Lost
    Planet Airmen
  Dr. Hook & The Medicine Show
  Doobie Brothers
  Eagles
  Faces
  Loggins & Messina
  Mott the Hoople
  Raspberries
  Seals & Crofts
  Steely Dan
  Uriah Heep
  Wings
  Yes

Rock Solo Performers
  David Bowie
  Jackson Browne
  Ry Cooder
  Jim Croce
  Gilbert O'Sullivan
  Billy Preston
  Lou Reed
  Leon Russell
  Paul Simon

Soul, R&B, Funk Groups
  Love Unlimited
  Main Ingredient
  Curtis Mayfield
  Harold Melvin & The Blue Notes
  O'Jays
  Tower of Power
  Trammps

Soul, R&B, Funk Solo Performers
  Roberta Flack
  Billy Paul

Middle of the Road
  Johnny Nash
  Randy Newman
  Gilbert O'Sullivan

Glitter/Bizarre
  Alice Cooper
  Gary Glitter

Disco
  Tavares

JUKE BOX HITS

"Burning Love"
Elvis Presley

"Alone Again (Naturally)"
Gilbert O'Sullivan

"Without You"
Nilsson

"I Gotcha"
Joe Tex

"Lean on Me"
Bill Withers

"Let's Stay Together"
Al Green

"Nights in White Satin"
Moody Blues

"Sunshine"
Jonathan Edwards

"Rockin' Robin"
Michael Jackson

"I Can See Clearly Now"
Johnny Nash

"Saturday in the Park"
Chicago

"I'll Be Around"
Spinners

"Listen to the Music"
Doobie Brothers

"Playground in My Mind"
Clint Holmes

"You're So Vain"
Carly Simon

"Black and White"
Three Dog Night

"Layla"
Derek & The Dominoes

"Doctor My Eyes"
Jackson Browne

"Crocodile Rock"
Elton John

"Changes"
David Bowie

"Summer Breeze"
Seals & Crofts

"It Never Rains in Southern
California"
Albert Hammond

"Oh Girl"
Chi-Lites

"Brandy (You're a Fine Girl)"
Looking Glass

"My Ding-A-Ling"
Chuck Berry

"Heart of Gold"
Neil Young

"Betcha By Golly, Wow"
Stylistics

"Outa-Space"
Billy Preston

"Go All the Way"
Raspberries

"Day after Day"
Badfinger

"Morning Has Broken"
Cat Stevens

"You Don't Mess Around
With Jim"
Jim Croce

"Everything I Own"
Bread

"Rock and Roll"
Gary Glitter

"I Am Woman"
Helen Reddy

"Papa Was a Rolling Stone"
Temptations

"Take It Easy"
Eagles

"Mother and Child Reunion"
Paul Simon

"Run to Me"
Bee Gees

"Imagine"
John Lennon

"Slippin' into Darkness"
War

"Long Cool Woman"
Hollies

"A Horse with No Name"
America

"Song Sung Blue"
Neil Diamond

"Ben"
Michael Jackson

"Popcorn"
Hot Butter

"I Saw the Light"
Todd Rundgren

"Everybody Plays the Fool"
Main Ingredient

"Back Stabbers"
O'Jays

"Rocket Man"
Elton John

"Superstition"
Stevie Wonder

"Sylvia's Mother"
Dr. Hook & The
Medicine Show

"Puppy Love"
Donny Osmond

"The First Time Ever I Saw
Your Face"
Roberta Flack

"Me and Mrs. Jones"
Billy Paul

"Hot Rod Lincoln"
Commander Cody

"I'll Take You There"
Staples Singers

"You Wear It Well"
Rod Stewart

DANCES

Fifties dances: Slop, Stomp and
Birdland popular at college sock
hops

NEWS OF ROCK

"Underground" FM radio stations playing album tracks replace Top 40
singles AM stations in creating new hit attractions—and rock music travels
still further afield . . . 750,000 pay $4 million to see Stones in 30-city
concert tour as most Sixties groups fade from sight . . . David Bowie and
Gary Glitter celebrate the end of the musically creative Fifties and Sixties by
dressing up their acts with "glitter rock"—setting the stage for the short-

lived disco and punk trends at the end of the decade . . . Donny Osmond replaces Bobby Sherman as bubblegum idol . . . Reggae in . . . $1,200,000 Bangla Desh concert and record album profits donated to UNICEF . . . Pop Art very "in," so Andy Warhol called in to design Rolling Stones album jacket and Truman Capote covers U.S. tour . . . Simon and Garfunkel split up . . . KHJ, Los Angeles, disc jockey plays Donny Osmond's "Puppy Love" continuously from 6-7 A.M. Jury still out . . . Glitter cosmetics and fancy dress characterize "street rock" beginnings at Mercer Arts Center and Max's Kansas City in Manhattan—with the New York Dolls in the vanguard . . . Only two huge rock festivals allowed in U.S.—with 200,000-400,000 at Pocono, Pennsylvania, and 250,000 at Evansville, Illinois . . . Now estimated 25,000 DJs in U.S., vs. 5,000 in 1957 . . . "Golden Oldies" of Fifties thrive again on DJ radio . . . Pop music grosses $2 billion for records and tapes, topping television's possibly $1 billion, movies' $1.3 billion and Broadway's $36 million . . . Three Dog Night demand $125,000 to appear at Pocono Festival, topping Presley and Hendrix highs . . . Chuck Berry and Rick Nelson of the 1950s back in the hit record charts . . . Rock acts start shift from singles to albums, since singles rarely played . . . Fats Domino and Bill Haley into the $400,000 a year bracket with their Fifties music . . . 5,000 new albums released . . . *Grease* opens off-Broadway, New York, gets great reviews, and moves to Broadway four months later, where it will become an all-time smash . . . Willie Nelson moves back home to Austin, Texas, after his Nashville house burns down. Deciding to stay, he becomes involved with country rock concerts; and soon brings the Lone Star State back into the limelight, when he and then Waylon Jennings cross over into the pop charts . . . Neil Diamond guaranteed $400,000 per album on signing with CBS Records . . .

SOME OF THE NEWS THAT INFLUENCED
THE ROCK ERA AND VICE VERSA

Nixon carries 49 of 50 states as he and Agnew are re-elected . . . Last U.S. ground troops leave Vietnam . . . Senate ratifies Strategic Arms Limitation Treaty (SALT I) with Russia . . . Watergate break-in . . . Okinawa returned to Japan . . . One third of delegates at Democratic Convention under 35 . . . Heavy U.S. wheat purchases by Soviets drive U.S. grain prices from 35¢ to 40¢ a bushel, starting bread price rises . . . J. Edgar Hoover dies . . . George Wallace paralyzed by gunshot . . . Nixon visits Red China . . . Federal Water Pollution Abatement actions involving states, industry, and municipalities started back in 1957 are still pending . . . Federal Election Campaign Act passed requiring that all campaign contributions be reported . . . Woodward and Bernstein of the *Washington Post* begin to crack open Watergate affair, but most other media treat it as a "caper" . . . New Surgeon-General's report warns that non-smokers risk health hazard from smokers' "sidestream" and urges greater controls . . . Congress sends Equal Rights Amendment (ERA), banning discrimination on basis of sex, to states for ratification . . . Supreme Court rules that death penalty as currently applied among states is unconstitutional . . . Federal Water Pollution Act passed over Nixon veto—aiming to eliminate all U.S. water pollution by 1985 and permitting suits by citizens against either polluters or Federal government . . . A month before the Presidential election, pollster George Gallup reports that barely half the voters had heard of the Watergate break-in over three months earlier . . .

THE NUMBERS GAME: STATISTICAL INFORMATION SHOWING HOW LIFE IN AMERICA INFLUENCED OR WAS INFLUENCED BY THE ROCK ERA

Life expectancy at birth now 75.2 for females and 67.4 years for males, vs. average 45 years in 1900 and 35 in 1776 . . . Health food sales up $150 million in past year to $550 million . . . *Playboy* nears 7 million circulation plus multiple readership—from 52,000 in December 1953, when first issue featured Marilyn Monroe calendar pose . . . Now one physician for every 562 residents, vs. one to 767 in 1923 . . . Almost 33% of officers and presidents of corporations are divorced or separated, vs. 5% in 1950s . . . Nine million pleasure boats in use . . . Birth rate down to 15.6 per thousand persons from 23.7 in 1960 . . . Average cost now $140 per citizen for meeting prescribed standards of air, water and noise pollution, plus solid waste disposal . . . Nearly 30% of U.S. oil now imported—up from 20% five years ago . . . One billion pounds of food additives of about 1,800 different substances comes to 5 lbs. per capita per year . . . 55 million tons of packaging and containers for products is 56% paper, 18% glass, 14% metals, 7.5% wood, and 3.5% plastic—now increasing disposable waste at rate of 5% a year . . . Current birth rate is lowest since first report, back in 1917 . . . Average soft drink sale up to 30.3 gallons per person from 16.8 gallons 10 years ago—almost double. At the same time, coffee consumption dropped from 39.2 gallons per person to 35.6 per year . . . Shipment of 1.9 million mobile homes in past four years equals number shipped in previous 20 . . . 15-year study of middle to upper middle class marriages in Chicago area finds about half the wives and just over 40% of husbands expressing dissatisfaction in final interviews; with the striking result that the more successful the man in his career, the less happy the marriage . . . Gallup poll again predicts Presidential election winner with amazing accuracy, with final survey showing Nixon getting 62% of vote (he got 61.8%). In 1968, Gallup final was 43% Nixon (he got 43.5%); 1964 poll showed 64% Johnson (he got 61.3%); 1960 final survey 51% Kennedy (he got 50.1%); 1956 showed 59.5% Eisenhower (he got 57.8%) . . . Now 6,784 fast food eating places in U.S. vs. 3,418 in 1967 and 1,120 in 1958—currently up 505.8% from 1958—whereas all eating places only increased 68.9% in the same 14 years . . .

TEEN AND COLLEGE LIVING AND
ALTERNATIVE LIFE STYLES IN THE ROCK ERA

Jesus people, also known as "Jesus Freaks," become latest youth movement . . . Gilbert teenage survey reports 90% own radios, 86% record players or tape playbacks, 86% cameras, and 22% cars . . . Major vintners estimate that 21-30-year-olds drink five gallons of wine a year, vs. two gallons for older buyers . . . Nixon denounces "Spock-mark" generation . . . Opinion Research survey reports 16-24-year-olds averaging 18.2 movie visits a year . . . 83.6% of 15-17-year-olds are enrolled in schools. . . Fifties nostalgia boom spreads from colleges to both young and old . . . American Council of Education poll of 200,000 college freshmen reports environmental pollution top concern (89.6%) and consumer protection second (76.3%) . . . Three times more women enroll in colleges than in 1960—3.5 million vs. 1.2 million . . . Estimated $1 billion hobby sales, vs. $750 million in 1968 . . . Transcendental Meditation being taught in the U.S. Army Staff College and at three Army bases . . . Ten universities now offer degree courses in Transcendental Meditation. Estimated 250,000 meditators in U.S., including 1% of the student population . . . Pan Am offers a $629 "psychic tour" of Britain including a séance and a day at Stonehenge with the Chief Druid . . . New edition of *Chambers Twentieth Century Dictionary* includes definitions of: acid, Black Power, drop out, flower people, freak, groovy, head, hippy, psychedelic, trip and turn on . . . World Health Organization scientific report points out that the great majority of marijuana users never proceed to the morphine-like drugs, even though most heroin users have taken marijuana . . .

FASHION: CLOTHES AND THE
ROCK ERA ACCENT ON YOUTH

Note: Feminine fashion is in italics, male in roman, unisex in parentheses, and news in asterisks.

Teeshirt dresses . . . (Denim overalls) . . . **Levi Strauss produces trousers guaranteed to shrink, wrinkle and fade** . . . (Fisherman's knit sweaters) . . . *Head-hugging knitted caps and cloches with matching scarves* . . . *The "bare look"* . . . Ethnic costumes like Chinese jackets . . . **Bell-bottoms still fashionable** . . . **Monokini spreads from Europe to a few seasides in California and Florida. Some hostile reactions, but police mostly look the other way rather than make arrests** . . . *Youth fashion favorites: pants suits, jumpsuits, overgrown sweaters, long trailing* *scarves, fringes, beads, floppy hats, tams, knee socks, bright colors, gypsy skirts and headbands, wild patterns, funky colors, chain belts, oversized zippers and panty hose . . . Chinoise and battle jackets from fashion designers . . . "Layered dressing" popular with young girls. New fad, along with adding garment to garment, is to combine and coordinate patterns and prints: stripes for the skirt, flowers for the blouse, and possibly dots for the jacket—with everything permissible—encouraging the young to think out their own "total look" . . . Wartime clogs in shades of green, red, yellow, blue or pink worn with matching skintight pants and very full smocks or loose, short-sleeved white surplices, both with square necklines and with yokes in two-color gingham checks or thick lace . . . Jeans rolled up to show multicolored striped socks . . . Individualizing jeans, not only with studs, but with embroidery and appliqué as well . . .* Bow ties make male comeback . . .

FADS (MOSTLY YOUTH-ORIENTED) RELATED TO THE ROCK ERA

Urethane roller skate wheels replacing steel and clay on skateboards renews action . . . New wave of popularity for pinball machines has *Playboy* article comparing game to making love . . . Coin-operated video games (such as "Pong" table tennis) . . . Video games for home TV sets (Magnavox "Odyssey") . . .

SOME OF THE MORE WIDELY USED ARGOT, JARGON AND SLANG IN THE ROCK ERA

Golden Oldie (past pop hit) . . .

THE NEW WOMAN IN THE ROCK ERA

Congress passes the ERA—first introduced in 1923. Hawaii first state to ratify it . . . *Ms.* magazine published . . . Congress passes "IX," affirming women's right to participate equally in all phases of athletics . . . NOW analysis of 1,200 TV commercials records women almost exclusively portrayed in the home: 43% doing household tasks, 38% as domestic adjuncts to men, and 17% as sex objects . . . One-third of delegates at Democratic National Convention are women . . . Federal survey shows average woman in fulltime job earning only $3 for each $5 paid to a man in similar job . . . New York Congresswoman Shirley Chisholm runs for President . . . Democrat Frances T. Farenthold first woman nominated for Vice President at major convention . . . Jean Westwood first woman to chair Democratic National Committee . . . In *The Erotic Life of the*

American Housewife, Natalie Gittelson finds her in a state of continuous sexual frustration and incipient or active promiscuity . . . In his article, "Making Babies—the New Biology and the 'Old' Morality," Dr. Leon R. Kass points out that since a clone is created by implanting the nucleus of a human cell, from any part of the body, into the enucleated cell of a female egg—and since this process can be repeated as often as eggs and wombs are available, creating genetic copies of the donor of the nucleus (identical in all but age), it has the additional fillip of making possible the elimination of males—since the three required elements can all (and only) be provided by a woman. Successful cloning has already been done with frogs, salamanders and fruit flies . . . Nobel prizewinner James D. Watson, the discoverer of DNA structure, has told Congress his fear that cloning will probably be perfected for humans "within the next 20 to 50 years" if research proceeds at its present rate, according to Dr. Kass in his article . . . John Lennon and Yoko record "Woman Is the Nigger of the World" in their "Sometime in New York City" album . . . Helen Reddy hits number one on the record charts with "I Am Woman" . . .

MOSTLY FACTUAL TRIVIA
CONCURRENT WITH THE ROCK ERA

First pinball tournament: the South Carolina Open Pinball Flipper Machine Championship draws 1,000 people . . . Former Oklahoma Governor, Dewey Bartlett, hurls hand-sized wad of cow dung 138 feet to set world record . . . World's highest-paid model, Evelyn Kuen, earns $150,000 . . . Leo Roberts of Rio, Wisconsin, spits watermelon seed 38 ft. 8¾ in. to set new mark . . . *Sun Signs* author Linda Goodman is quoted as thinking that California Governor Ronald Reagan is "a secret astrology freak" in *The Occult Explosion*, by Nat Freedland. "If not, why did he get sworn in at some strange time like six minutes after midnight?," she asks—believing him to be truly "a humane, liberal Aquarius who will drop his faked conservatism after he becomes President" . . .

1973 _____

ARTISTS

Rock Groups
  Aerosmith
  J. Geils Band
  Pink Floyd
  Queen
  Lynyrd Skynyrd
  Stealers Wheel
  Marshall Tucker Band
  Rick Wakeman
  Edgar Winter Group
  Z Z Topp

Rock Solo Performers
  Art Garfunkel
  Olivia Newton-John
  Linda Ronstadt
  Leo Sayer
  Bruce Springsteen

Soul, R&B, Funk Groups
  Earth, Wind & Fire
  Ohio Players
  Pointer Sisters

Soul, R&B, Funk Solo Performers
  Dr. John
  Eddie Kendricks
  Johnny Taylor
  Barry White

Folk & Country
  Willie Nelson
  Charlie Rich
  Loudon Wainwright III

Young Teen Oriented
  Marie Osmond
  Sweet

Middle of the Road
  Trini Lopez

Cult Groups/Punk/New Wave/
Drone Rock
  New York Dolls

JUKE BOX HITS

"We're an American Band"
Grand Funk Railroad

"Space Oddity"
Davie Bowie

"Tie a Yellow Ribbon"
Tony Orlando & Dawn

"Bad, Bad Leroy Brown"
Jim Croce

"Killing Me Softly with His Song"
Roberta Flack

"Let's Get It On"
Marvin Gaye

"My Love"
Paul McCartney & Wings

"Why Me"
Kris Kristofferson

"Goodbye Yellow Brick Road"
Elton John

"Will It Go Round in Circles"
Billy Preston

"I'm Gonna Love You Just
a Little Bit More, Baby"
Barry White

"Dancing in the Moonlight"
King Harvest

"Diamond Girl"
Seals and Crofts

"If You Want Me to Stay"
Sly & the Family Stone

"The Most Beautiful Girl"
Charlie Rich

"The Joker"
Steve Miller

"Photograph"
Ringo Starr

"Mind Games"
John Lennon

"Cover of Rolling Stone"
Dr. Hook & The Medicine Show

"Let Me Be There"
Olivia Newton-John

"Show and Tell"
Al Wilson

"W.O.L.D."
Harry Chapin

"Touch Me in the Morning"
Diana Ross

"Night the Lights Went Out
in Georgia"
Vicki Lawrence

"Frankenstein"
Edgar Winter Group

"You Are the Sunshine of
My Life"
Stevie Wonder

"That Lady"
Isley Brothers

"Say, Has Anybody Seen
My Sweet Gypsy Rose"
Tony Orlando & Dawn

"Time in a Bottle"
Jim Croce

"Midnight Train to Georgia"
Gladys Knight & the Pips

"Smoke on the Water"
Deep Purple

"Money"
Pink Floyd

"Brother Louie"
Stories

"Ain't No Woman"
Four Tops

"Paper Roses"
Marie Osmond

"Basketball Jones
Featuring Tyrone Shoelaces"
Cheech and Chong

"Reeling in the Years"
Steely Dan

"Right Place, Wrong Time"
Dr. John

"Wildflower"
Skylark

"Stuck in the Middle with You"
Stealers Wheel

"Angie"
Rolling Stones

"Loves Me Like a Rock"
Paul Simon

"Rocky Mountain High"
John Denver

"Shambala"
Three Dog Night

"Love Train"
O'Jays

"Keep on Truckin'" (Part 1)
Eddie Kendricks

"Natural High"
Bloodstone

"Give Me Love (Give Me
Peace on Earth)"
George Harrison

"Cisco Kid"
War

"Long Train Running"
Doobie Brothers

"Drift Away"
Dobie Gray

"The Love I Lost" (Part 1)
Harold Melvin & The Blue Notes

"Half Breed"
Cher

"Call Me"
Al Green

"Walk on the Wild Side"
Lou Reed

"All I Know"
Art Garfunkel

"Jungle Boogie"
Kool and the Gang

"Ramblin' Man"
Allman Brothers Band

"Living in the Past"
Jethro Tull

"Little Willy"
Sweet

"Yes We Can"
Pointer Sisters

NEWS OF ROCK

Progressive rock FM stations no longer "breaking" acts . . . *Rolling Stone* changes format to general interest magazine—adding politics and arts to music as early readership now aged 20-30 and settling down . . . 75% of the new LPs fail to break even . . . White country-rock bands move in like rockabilly did 15 years ago—spawning Allman Brothers, Marshall Tucker Band, Z Z Topp, Lynyrd Skynyrd, etc., and later America, the Eagles—and soloist Dolly Parton . . . Elvis gives Priscilla $750,000 in divorce settlement . . . Top four record companies sell 52.8% of all records and tapes . . . Watkins Glen Festival draws 600,000 after involving $1.5 million in financing. Rumored that the Allman Brothers and the Band got $140,000 each and the Grateful Dead $117,000 . . . Now estimated 400 free-form (underground) radio stations . . . Scarce 1952 Little Richard RCA recordings often selling for over $50 . . . Presley records on Sun label priced from $50 to $100 . . . Jim Croce killed in plane crash . . . Rolling Stones benefit concert in L.A. for Nicaraguan earthquake victims raises $200,000. Mick

Jagger adds another $150,000 . . . All 1973 cars required to have FM as well as AM . . . Fifty rock superstars (15 groups and 35 individuals) earning between $2 million and $6 million a year each . . . 51% of new single records are country & western . . . Survey of top hits of years 1955-72 reports songs about love dropping from 73% of hits (1955-69) to 64% (1970-72). Songs about religion rose from 1% (1964-69) to 17% (1970-72). During 1955-63, dance-oriented songs were 7% of the hits, before dropping to nil from 1964 on . . . Dick Clark grossing over $5 million a year . . . Seven No. 1 record hits by female vocalists are most ever, and more than any other type artist in 1973 . . . Smaller record firms feel squeeze as only 19 get Top 10 hits compared with 42 in 1959. In seven of the ten years of the 1960s, at least 35 different companies had Top 10 hits . . . After ten years of attempting a comeback, the Everly Brothers break up, after Phil walks off stage during Buena Park, California, concert . . . Led Zeppelin gross $4 million on U.S. tour . . .

SOME OF THE NEWS THAT INFLUENCED
THE ROCK ERA AND VICE VERSA

Vietnam peace accord signed . . . Watergate hearings nation's top TV show . . . U.S. prisoners freed by Viet Cong . . . Agnew pleads no contest to tax evasion and kickbacks, then resigns . . . Undaunted by journalists' "Jimmy Who?" tag, Jimmy Carter sets out to win Democratic nomination . . . Gerald Ford made Vice President . . . Mideast war . . . Arab oil embargo and price rises . . . Nixon reveals he paid less than $1,000 in taxes in 1970 and 1971. Declares, "I am not a crook." . . . Judge dismisses Government case against Daniel Ellsberg for publishing Pentagon Papers in 1971 . . . All airline passengers screened to stem hijacking; during six months following Nixon order, 1,300 arrested, many with illegal weapons . . . 200 Indian Movement members and supporters occupy Wounded Knee demanding U.S. honor some 371 broken treaties. One Indian killed in siege. Little accomplished . . . Military Selective Service Act of 1971 ends draft as of June 30 . . . Congress passes over the President's veto of a law limiting Presidential authority to commit U.S. troops to overseas combat . . . Supreme Court rules that women have a constitutional right to abortion during first six months of pregnancy . . . Haldeman, Ehrlichman and John Dean resign . . . Skylab launched to orbit the Earth . . . Nixon signs Appropriations Bill which includes August termination date for U.S. bombing of Cambodia . . . House Judiciary Committee begins deliberations on procedures for Presidential impeachment . . . Oregon first state to decriminalize marijuana . . . U.S. and Cuba sign anti-hijacking pact, with each agreeing to extradite hijackers who land planes on their soil . . .

THE NUMBERS GAME: STATISTICAL INFORMATION
SHOWING HOW LIFE IN AMERICA INFLUENCED
OR WAS INFLUENCED BY THE ROCK ERA

Price rises cause big drop in meat consumption from 189 lbs. per person to 178 lbs. in 1973 . . . 60% of the population now employed in the provision of services, with rise to 70% predicted for the early 1980s . . . Domestic oil output little more than 11 million barrels a day—with demand at 17 million . . . Total personal consumption expenditure for recreation up to $52.3 billion from $11.1 billion in 1950 . . . U.S. public health survey shows 25-45% of U.S. adults more than 20% overweight . . . Mastercharge transactions total $7.87 billion . . . Agricultural productivity up again, as average farm worker now produces enough food and fiber for 50 people . . . San Francisco survey shows 49% know at least a bit about yoga, with 8% having taken part. Awareness of Transcendental Meditation is 32%, with 5% participation; Zen 30% and 3%; Hari Krishna 39% and 2% . . . 500,000 compete in National Hot Rod Association-sanctioned drag racing meets . . . 70,000 to 100,000 major air pollution sources each emitting over 25 tons of any one pollutant a year. Monitoring now a major cost—with measurement and analysis of emissions from one smoke stack costing up to $5,000 . . . 1,200 Baskin-Robbins ice cream outlets have 330 approved flavors on tap (for season changes, etc.). Peak before pruning was 431 in 1972 . . . Fast food outlets take over 10% of food industry $250 billion total. With $28 billion gross, McDonald's does $1.5 billion and Kentucky Fried Chicken $1 billion . . . One in three meals eaten outside the home, vs. one in four in 1965—just eight years ago . . . Now over 1,000 consumer programs conducted by Federal Government, Consumer Fraud Units in 39 states, and Consumer Protection Departments in 23. Over 50 cities now have consumer protection agencies . . . California's Director of Consumer Affairs brought legal action in 2,371 consumer cases in a two-year period . . . Higher proportion of people now married than ever before— almost 70% . . . $3 billion combined annual take of coin-operated machine business, which has been dominated by pinball, gets enormous boost from overnight success of video games. Atari sales hit $1 million a month for "Pong" (video ping-pong) game selling to coin-machine operators for over $1,000 each, as many imitators and manufacturers of other formats flood market . . .

TEEN AND COLLEGE LIVING AND
ALTERNATIVE LIFE STYLES IN THE ROCK ERA

Stripper Tempest Storm tours colleges with James Gang rock group . . . Only 25% of fifth graders don't go on to graduate from high school, vs. 50% in 1950 . . . College student movie attendance drops to around 11 films a year vs. 56 a year in pre-TV 1945, according to results of comparison between University of Iowa and Kent State student polls . . . Surveys still keep colleges in sharp focus. Now seeking comparisons with previous generations, Gallup reports that 70% of 18-24-year-olds agree a school's social prestige influences job opportunities and one's future, while only 33% think higher education improves chances of a good job and marriage . . . Another survey indicates a big four-year change in values from 1969: *Importance of privacy*: 71% in 1973 vs. 61% in 1969. *Less emphasis on money*: 80% in 1973 vs. 63% in 1969. *More sexual freedom*: 61% in 1973 vs. 43% in 1969. *Wanting prestige from a job*: 28% in 1973 vs. 15% in 1969. *Need for security*: 58% in 1973 vs. 33% in 1969. *Desire for challenge*: 77% in 1973 vs. 64% in 1969 . . . Gallup survey of 18-24-year-olds' weekend activities reports 44% go shopping, 37% personally participate in sports, 71% meet with friends, and 60% usually see a film or sports event . . . 57% of McDonald's hamburgers sold to 16-34-year-olds, and another 20% to 15-or-unders—with 165,000 teenagers dominating the company's employee rolls . . . Rutgers University student survey reports 30% of senior men and women feel traditional marriage is becoming obsolete: 25% agreed that traditional family structure of mother, father and children living under one roof no longer works, and 40% of the women were uncertain about whether they would ever marry . . . American Council on Education survey of 188,900 freshmen at 373 schools across country finds 48% describing selves as middle of the road and 16.6% as conservative—up slightly from last year . . . Gilbert survey sample of 3.1 million high school students graduating this year shows big change from 1960s. Although many disagree with parents on marijuana and premarital sex, 85% share their family's values and ideas, vs. 61% four years ago. Only 11% hope to be free of social responsibilities in 15 years, while 44.2% expect to be an average family man or wife, with two or three children, living in suburb or small town . . . University of Washington offering courses on yoga, numerology, hypnotism and extrasensory perception. University of Wisconsin offering witchcraft and astrology, and San Francisco State has a seminar on dreams . . . *Playboy* article based on findings of Research Guild of Chicago (which asked 2,000 of both sexes 1,000 questions each) and Morton Hunt reports of 1970s young people that: (1) The great majority continue to attach deep emotional significance to sex; (2) Liberation hasn't cut sex loose from significant personal relationships or the institution of marriage; (3) Sexual liberalism is the emergent ideal that the great majority of young Americans are trying to live up to; (4) It combines the spontaneous and guilt-free enjoyment of a wide range of sexual acts with a guiding belief in the emotional significance of sexual expression; (5) There has been no chaotic or anarchic dissolution of standards, but rather a major shift toward somewhat different, highly organized standards that remain integrated with existing social values, and with the institutions of love, marriage and the family . . . Close to 400,000 young people (under 25) arrested for offenses under narcotic drug laws . . .

FASHION: CLOTHES AND THE
ROCK ERA ACCENT ON YOUTH

Note: Feminine fashion is in italics, male in roman, unisex in parentheses, and news in asterisks.

Used blue denim Levis recycled into skirts, slacks, jackets, bikinis and swimsuits . . . (Unisex look: short hair, teeshirts worn beneath three-quarter sleeved open blouse top, jeans rolled up from the ankles) . . . **Fashion Foundation of America chooses Burt Reynolds, who appeared nude in *Cosmopolitan* centerfold, for its list of best dressed men** . . . (Twenties look returns) . . . *Mary Quant introduces maxi-skirt* . . . **U.S. textile mills produce 482 million square yards of cotton denim, up from 437 million in 1971 . . . **The Pill bred the mini-skirt just as it bred the topless bathing suit, Dr. Rene König, of Cologne University, says, adding that neither costume was intended, by its original wearer at any rate, to be provocative. In fact, they appositely prove women now in control of choosing whom they wish to mate with—that nakedness is "cocking a snook" at sex** . . . *Baby blue or pink fluffy bed jackets* . . . **Acrylics goad International Wool Secretariat into launching machine-washable pure wool** . . . **Shirt back in fashion** . . . Dropoff in popularity of flared men's trousers on campus . . . **Revlon shoots for $3 million in sales of new perfume, Charlie, during first year—and hits amazing $15 million** . . . **Three-year-old L'eggs panty hose, sold through food and drug outlets, now largest-selling single brand in hosiery industry** . . . *Switch in emphasis on blue jeans from thigh hugging to bottom cupping* . . .

FADS (MOSTLY YOUTH-ORIENTED)
RELATED TO THE ROCK ERA

Major backgammon set manufacturer sells as many sets in this one year as in the previous 20 . . . Light bulb chewing (with granola or salad dressing) . . . Watergate posters featuring Nixon's rogues' gallery . . .CB radio takes off with truckers. Becomes fad, with a million licenses, bumper stickers, jacket patches, records, lighters, jewelry . . . Martial arts. Kung Fu . . . "Trekkies" make Star Trek Enterprises multi-million dollar industry . . . Impeachment teeshirts . . .

SOME OF THE MORE WIDELY USED ARGOT,
JARGON AND SLANG IN THE ROCK ERA

Boogie (relax, kid around) . . . Bop (drink, smoke or otherwise have a good time) . . . Do me a solid (do me a favor) . . . Ego trip (act performed to build or gratify one's ego) . . . "Let it all hang out" (relax) . . . Macho (virile and aggressive) . . . Number (trick, tactic) . . . Orbs (eyes, eyeballs) . . . Up front (top priority) . . . Whipped (drunk) . . .

THE NEW WOMAN IN THE ROCK ERA

Supreme Court legalizes abortion . . . Supreme Court outlaws classified ads specifying gender . . . *Fortune* poll shows only 3% of college women want to go into "women's jobs" such as housewife, secretary or nurse—down 12% from class of 1965—while 400% more women intend to go into law, medicine and other professions . . . American Stock Exchange creates Affirmative Action plan . . . Federal Home Loan Bank Board bars sex bias by Savings & Loan institutions . . . Erica Jong's *Fear of Flying* published . . . Boston Women's Health Collective produces bestselling *Our Bodies, Ourselves* . . . World's largest commercial bank, Bank of America, promises to increase overall proportion of woman officers to 40% by 1979 with 5% at highest management level—in response to class action . . . In his book, *Sexual Suicide*, George Gilder states, "If women could be induced to vote only for their own sex, they could control not just 51%, but all our political offices" . . . Ingrid Bengis, in her book, *Combat in the Erogenous Zone*, finds woman hateful and angry . . .

MOSTLY FACTUAL TRIVIA
CONCURRENT WITH THE ROCK ERA

Vodka outsells whiskey in U.S. for first time . . . Elizabeth Taylor tells *Ladies' Home Journal* she never considered herself beautiful. She thinks Ava Gardner, Audrey Hepburn, Sophia Loren, Brigitte Bardot, Raquel Welch and Madame Tito truly beautiful . . . Hundredth anniversary of invention of artificial ice machine . . .

1974 _____

ARTISTS

Rock Groups
  Atlanta Rhythm Section
  Average White Band
  Bachman Turner Overdrive
  Bad Company
  Elvin Bishop Band
  Blue Oyster Cult
  Charlie Daniels Band
  Genesis
  Jefferson Starship
  Supertramp
  10cc

Rock Solo Performers
  David Essex

Soul, R&B, Funk Groups
  Blue Magic
  B.T. Express
  Commodores
  Hues Corporation
  Kool & The Gang
  LaBelle
  M.F.S.B.
  Parliament
  Rufus, Featuring Chaka Khan
  Three Degrees

Folk & Country
  Maria Muldaur
  Jim Stafford

Young Teen Oriented
  Donny & Marie Osmond

Middle of the Road
  Abba
  Barry Manilow

Disco
  Disco Tex & The
    Sex-O-Lettes
  Gloria Gaynor
  George McCrae

JUKE BOX HITS

"Rikki Don't Lose That Number"
Steely Dan

"Come and Get Your Love"
Redbone

"Dancing Machine"
Jackson Five

"The Loco-Motion"
Grand Funk

"T.S.O.P."
"M.F.S.B.

"The Streak"
Ray Stevens

"Bennie & the Jets"
Elton John

"Do It 'Til You're Satisfied"
B.T. Express

"Lady Marmalade"
LaBelle

"Whatever Gets You Through the Night"
John Lennon

"Midnight at the Oasis"
Maria Muldaur

"You Make Me Feel Brand New"
Stylistics

"Angie Baby"
Helen Reddy

"Spiders and Snakes"
Jim Stafford

"Rock the Boat"
Hues Corporation

"Then Came You"
Dionne Warwick & Spinners

"I Can Help"
Billy Swan

"When Will I See You Again"
Three Degrees

"Looking for a Love"
Bobby Womack

"Kung Fu Fighting"
Carl Douglas

"Tangled Up in Blue"
Bob Dylan

"Rock On"
David Essex

"Sunshine on My Shoulder"
John Denver

"Sideshow"
Blue Magic

"Hooked on a Feeling"
Blue Swede

"Billy, Don't Be a Hero"
Bo Donaldson & Heywoods

"Band On the Run"
Paul McCartney & Wings

"Sweet Home Alabama"
Lynyrd Skynyrd

"Cat's in the Cradle"
Harry Chapin

"Annie's Song"
John Denver

"(You're) Having My Baby"
Paul Anka

"Can't Get Enough"
Bad Company

"Sundown"
Gordon Lightfoot

"Rock Me Gently"
Andy Kim

"Living for the City"
Stevie Wonder

"Waterloo"
Abba

"You're the First, the Last,
My Everything"
Barry White

"I'd Love You to Want Me"
Lobo

"Your Mama Don't Dance"
Loggins & Messina

"I Shot the Sheriff"
Eric Clapton

"Sha La La (Makes Me Happy)"
Al Green

"Lucy in the Sky with Diamonds"
Elton John

"Boogie Down"
Eddie Kendricks

"You're Sixteen"
Ringo Starr

"If You Love Me (Let Me Know)"
Olivia Newton-John

"Dark Lady"
Cher

"Best Thing That Ever Happened
to Me"
Gladys Knight & Pips

"Feel Like Makin' Love"
Roberta Flack

"Just Don't Want to Be Lonely"
Main Ingredient

"Nothing from Nothing"
Billy Preston

"Rock Your Baby"
George McCrae

"Top of the World"
Carpenters

"I Honestly Love You"
Olivia Newton-John

"I've Got to Use My Imagination"
Gladys Knight & Pips

"The Show Must Go On"
Three Dog Night

"Smokin' in the Boys' Room"
Brownsville Station

"The Air That I Breathe"
Hollies

"You Ain't Seen Nothing Yet"
Bachman Turner Overdrive

"Seasons in the Sun"
Terry Jacks

"The Night Chicago Died"
Paper Lace

"You Haven't Done Nothin'"
Stevie Wonder

"Tell Me Something Good"
Rufus, Featuring Chaka Khan

NEWS OF ROCK

CBGB, New York, spawns Blondie, the Ramones, Talking Heads, and many glitter-backlash groups, with jeans, teeshirts and leather jackets the norm . . . U.S.-produced single hits down to 1965 level in British Top 10 charts (29.1%) vs. peak 47.7% in 1970 . . . *Rolling Stone* survey indicates average reader buys six LPs and 27 tapes a year . . . $2 billion-plus record business about as big as movies ($1.6 billion) and professional sports ($600,000) combined . . . Male vocal groups only get 20% of No. 1 single record hits vs. 76% in 1965 (56% in 1966, 67% in 1967, 47% in 1968, 53% in 1969 and 67% in 1970). Male solo vocalists, on the other hand, now 54% of No. 1 hitmakers, vs. 4% in 1965. Female solo vocalists tie males, with

22% of No. 1 singles in 1971. Female vocal groups did not have a No. 1 hit during past three years, vs. 22% in 1964 and 20% in 1955 . . . Cass Elliot dies in London . . . U.K. rock group Animation sets record playing 140 hour, 34 minute marathon in Liverpool . . . Scalpers get $15-$75 for Bob Dylan concert seats in New York, Los Angeles and San Francisco for his first tour since 1966. New York reports 1.2 million ticket requests for shows there . . . Soul records oriented completely to the disco market in rhythm patterns and production techniques capitalize on New York disco (shortened from "discothèque") boom which began in the late Sixties as blacks, and, to a lesser extent, gays, popularize clubs where they can drink, socialize and dance long into the night . . . Three producers from Philadelphia (Thom Bell and Gamble & Huff) dominate *Billboard* magazine year-end awards as their product finds early favor in exploding disco scene . . . Elton John signs $8 million deal with MCA Records . . . Set for David Bowie's "Diamond Dogs" concerts costs reported $250,000 . . . Revival of Bill Haley's "Rock Around the Clock" among bestsellers for 14 weeks (19 years later), having sold estimated 16 million records by 1960 and featured in 14 different films . . . *Variety* reports beginning of decline in pop concert business—with only "name" attractions able to fill large auditoriums and concert halls. Led Zeppelin, the Who, Rolling Stones, Bob Dylan, the Moody Blues, Crosby, Stills, Nash & Young, Elvis Presley, Pink Floyd, Eric Clapton and Jethro Tull of the mid-1960s usually instant sellouts— with only John Denver, Elton John and the Allman Brothers Band among the newer names consistently filling houses . . .

SOME OF THE NEWS THAT INFLUENCED
THE ROCK ERA AND VICE VERSA

Nixon first U.S. President to resign post . . . Ford grants Nixon pardon . . . Supreme Court orders Nixon to surrender 64 tapes to Judge Sirica . . . Over 20,000 murders in U.S. . . . Oil crisis has 5% fewer using cars to get to work in past year, and motor cycle sales up 50% in first quarter to 700,000 . . . Nixon agrees to pay $434,000 in back taxes and $32,000 interest . . . Solzhenitzyn exiled from Russia . . . New car sales off 35%. Housing construction down nearly 40% . . . President Ford offers conditional amnesty to deserters and draft evaders on case-to-case basis . . . Patty Hearst kidnapped . . . Gold sales legalized in U.S. . . . John Mitchell, Haldeman, Ehrlichman and Watergate conspirators indicted, and most of them ultimately jailed . . . Eight members of Ohio National Guard involved in 1970 Kent State student killings acquitted . . . Senate Foreign Relations Committee orders investigation into charges that CIA spent more than $8 million to promote the overthrow of Allende in Chile . . . AT&T, Western Electric and Bell Laboratories charged with Sherman antitrust violation by conspiracy to monopolize telecommunications equipment . . .

CIA Director William E. Colby admits that agency has secret files on thousands of Americans—gathered by electronic eavesdropping, postal inspections and break-ins . . . Georgia Governor Carter says he will seek Presidency in 1976 . . . Marriage rate drops for first time since 1958-64 . . . 96% of all homes with electricity now have at least one TV set . . . In response to shattering rise in gasoline prices, U.S. auto manufacturers add accessories such as manifold pressure gauges, radial tires, stiffer shock absorbers and higher gear ratios to existing models—following European lead to larger investment in engineering for better mileage . . . More home baking, cooking and canning and greater sales of home freezers, garden seeds, glass jars, flour and tomato plants—while beef sales per capita show decrease following sharp rise in food prices . . . Continuing military and economic aid to Vietnam amounts to almost $5.4 billion for past year . . . In *U.S.* v. *Richard Nixon*, Supreme Court rules that President has no constitutional right (based on inherent executive privilege or separation of powers) to withhold evidence in a criminal prosecution . . .

THE NUMBERS GAME: STATISTICAL INFORMATION SHOWING HOW LIFE IN AMERICA INFLUENCED OR WAS INFLUENCED BY THE ROCK ERA

New York City Welfare Agency uses $3.4 billion of the city's $12 billion budget . . . Of estimated 6,558,000 living veterans of Vietnam war, 48,000 are 18-19, 1,139,000 are 20-24, 3,510,000 are 25-29, 1,637,000 30-34, 204,000 35-39, and 20,000 40-44 . . . $2 billion spent feeding pets, with $1.4 billion just for dog food . . . Survey shows 65% get news from TV, 47% from newspapers, 21% from radio, 4% from periodicals, and 4% from other people. If news reports were conflicting, 51% would believe TV, while only 20% would trust the newspapers . . . United Nations reports 10.5 marriages per 1,000 U.S. inhabitants, vs. 4.6 divorces per 1,000 . . . Gallup survey indicates favorite leisure pursuit is watching TV (46%); reading only 14%; and sports participation 5% . . . 113 U.S. Army Generals in Vietnam war reply to questionnaire, with 27.8% stating its results were not worth the effort; 25% that it shouldn't have gone beyond advisory effort. 25% felt the effort should have been greater, and only 13.9% said, "worth the effort" . . . Gambling Revision Commission reports over $180 per person (including children) average spent on gambling each year . . . 105 million cars and 4.2 million motorcycles registered in U.S. . . . Convertible car production drops to 28,000 from 507,000 in 1965, because of air pollution, top-slashing vandalism, and air conditioning . . . U.S. women averaging 1.9 children each—after hitting peak of 3.8 in 1968 (in postwar "baby boom"), up from 2.1 in Depression year of 1936 . . . Over 107 billion bottles and cans of soft drinks sold—or 485 bottles per capita—in the U.S. (including infants). Added to this, Americans are drinking another enormous amount of flavored drinks at soda fountains and in homemade preparations from packaged crystals . . . Some food consumption in pounds per capita up sharply since 1957/59; Red meats 187 lbs. vs. 156.6 lbs.; Poultry 50.4 lbs. vs. 33.5 lbs.; Cheese 14.5 vs. 7.9; Processed vegetables 64.4 vs. 49.9. But eggs down to 285 per person from 356, and fluid milk and cream down to 247 lbs. from 337 . . . Food processers deluge U.S. with 31.5 billion coupons—up from 12.8 billion in 1966—with retailers piling on another 20-40 billion coupons. Only 10% were redeemed. 60-70% were ignored, and 20-30% were misredeemed by shoppers, ripoff gangs, etc. at an estimated retail cost of $300 million—about equal to the cost of the refund . . . Food production now only requires 4.4% of the total labor force vs. 90% in 1790—as automation requires fewer and fewer people for farm maintenance . . . Most important problems facing U.S. during past six years, according to Gallup poll results, were: 1974: energy crisis; 1973: high cost of living; 1972: Vietnam; 1971: inflation; 1970: reducing crime; 1969: Vietnam . . . Re-election rate, this year, for members of Congress was 89% for the House and 83% in the Senate—again returning the incumbents to office with astounding regularity . . .

TEEN AND COLLEGE LIVING AND
ALTERNATIVE LIFE STYLES IN THE ROCK ERA

Meagre media coverage of teens and college students as quiet sets in at all levels—reflecting the static quality of the music scene . . . Texas Tech group of students "streak" for five hours . . . President of Virginia's elegant Sweet Briar college gallantly applauds as 50 co-eds sprint by adorned only by their class years, lipsticked on in approximate license plate position . . . 16 University of Alaska students streak in zero temperatures . . . U.S. Route 1 traffic brought to standstill by 533 University of Maryland students chain dancing au naturel . . . Yale places four streakers on probation . . . Stanford University students aim for record in 18-mile streak from Palo Alto to San Jose . . . Record streaks as of March 18 were: Largest: 1,548 streakers at University of Georgia; Longest: Five hours, by Texas Tech students . . . Singles bars, singles resorts and singles housing complexes now $40 billion a year industry . . . College student definitions for the meaning of love in survey by J. Richard Udry for his book, *The Social Context of Marriage*, ranks: (1) Feeling of attraction (40%), (2) Companionship and compatibility, (10%), (3) Giving (20%), (4) Security (17%) . . . Institute of Life Insurance survey of 14-25-year-olds about which life style they found most appealing found 24% of the males and 17% of the females chose the single life as the most appealing alternative, but only 9% of the men and 5% of the women expect to be single 15 years from now . . . Harvard study of 2,000 transcendental meditation adherents reports that 80% had smoked marijuana before joining and have since stopped . . . Network TV show about high school football makes documented statement that 86 out of each 100 players will sustain at least one injury . . .

FASHION: CLOTHES AND THE
ROCK ERA ACCENT ON YOUTH

Note: Feminine fashion is in italics, male in roman, unisex in parentheses, and news in asterisks.

String bikinis . . . **Teeshirts printed to order—costing $3.25 to $14.95 —hottest fashion trend. Supplier of shirts, heat transfers and equipment, J.B.T. Chroma, sells 1.5 million this year** . . . ***Modern Bride* continues to carry more pages of advertising per issue than any other magazine in the U.S.** . . . *Unlined, rainproof coats in polyurethane-coated cotton or nylon* . . . **"Fringe" fashion continues to flourish, with caftans and Afghan coats being worn by all levels of society—after spreading as a "street" fashion among the young as a low-cost attractive warm garment** . . . **At "heavy metal" rock concerts, dress now ranges from $200 velveteen jackets to scruffy jeans** . . . **California rock concert promoter Steve Wolf tells *Time* magazine, "Since Joni Mitchell started wearing gowns, the girls have started wearing dresses and makeup." At that same time, rock glitter stars like Alice Cooper have kids in the audience parading in white tuxedos, top hats and feather boas** . . . **Levi's jeans rank third on list of internationally smuggled goods, right after alcohol and cigarettes, and just before drugs. Highest black market prices now in Soviet Union— reaching as high as $90 a pair** . . . *Cheesecloth blouses with dairymaid-type drawstring necks* . . .

FADS (MOSTLY YOUTH-ORIENTED)
RELATED TO THE ROCK ERA

Streakers . . . Ten thousand discos in U.S. grossing $4 billion a year . . . Marvel comics produce seven new Monster comics as monstermania spreads . . . Kissathon . . .

SOME OF THE MORE WIDELY USED ARGOT,
JARGON AND SLANG IN THE ROCK ERA

Antsy (restless, jittery) . . . Get it on (get into something) . . . Kick out the jams (let loose) . . . Laid back (low-keyed, relaxed) . . . Streak (run nude) . . .

THE NEW WOMAN IN THE ROCK ERA

Coverage under minimum wage requirements extended to more than 1.5 million domestic workers . . . National Little League agrees to admit women . . . Average female earning under $7,000 a year, vs. males $12,000 . . . More than 25 different oral contraceptives on market, with 10 million U.S. women said to be on the Pill . . . *The Total Woman* by Marabel Morgan is No. 1 nonfiction bestseller of year . . . Supreme Court outlaws forced maternity leave for teachers . . . New Connecticut Governor, Ella Grasso, first woman to be elected in her own right . . . University of Texas gets first woman president of a major university, Lorene Rogers . . . Equal Credit Opportunity Act bans credit discrimination on basis of sex or marital status . . . Enrollment of women in medical schools almost doubled in past three years, from 9.6% to 15.4% . . . *The New Woman's Survival Catalog,* patterned after the *Whole Earth Catalog,* covers everything from home repair to mangling a masher—with 20% of royalties going back into movement . . . Connecticut Supreme Court challenges Mory's (made famous by the Whiffenpoof Song) for refusal to admit women . . . Washington, D.C., Police Federation survey of 86 male and female police officers finds little difference in their ability to deal with situations . . .

MOSTLY FACTUAL TRIVIA
CONCURRENT WITH THE ROCK ERA

Evel Knievel fails to jump Snake River Canyon on motorcycle . . . Tootsie Roll makes 4.5 million lollipops a day—the most in the world . . . U.K.'s Keith Harraway blows record 169 smoke rings from single cigarette puff . . .

1975 _____

ARTISTS

Rock Groups
   Captain & Tennille
   Hall & Oates
   Nazareth
   Roxy Music

Rock Solo Performers
   Peter Frampton

Soul, R&B, Funk Groups
   Hot Chocolate
   Jacksons (formerly Jackson Five)
   K.C. & The Sunshine Band
   Bob Marley & The Wailers
   Silver Convention

Soul, R&B, Funk Solo Performers
   Natalie Cole
   Donna Summer
   Minnie Riperton
   David Ruffin

Folk & Country
   Freddy Fender

Young Teen Oriented
   Bay City Rollers

Cult Groups/Punk/New Wave/
Drone Rock
   Patti Smith
   Television

Disco
   Van McCoy

JUKE BOX HITS

"Love Will Keep Us Together"
Captain & Tennille

"Rhinestone Cowboy"
Glen Campbell

"Philadelphia Freedom"
Elton John Band

"My Eyes Adored You"
Frankie Valli

"Some Kind of Wonderful"
Grand Funk

"Shining Star"
Earth, Wind & Fire

"Fame"
David Bowie

"Laughter in the Rain"
Neil Sedaka

"One of These Nights"
Eagles

"Jive Talkin'"
Bee Gees

"Best of My Love"
Eagles

"Lovin' You"
Minnie Riperton

"Mr. Jaws"
Dickie Brothers

"Black Water"
Doobie Brothers

"Ballroom Blitz"
Sweet

"At Seventeen"
Janis Ian

"Pick Up the Pieces"
Average White Band

"Express"
B.T. Express

"Squeeze Box"
The Who

"Before the Next Teardrop Falls"
Freddy Fender

"Why Can't We Be Friends?"
War

"Thank God I'm a Country Boy"
John Denver

"Love Won't Let Me Wait"
Major Harris

"(Hey Won't You Play) Another
Somebody Done Somebody
Wrong Song"
B. J. Thomas

"Boogie on Reggae Woman"
Stevie Wonder

"He Don't Love You (Like I
Love You)"
Tony Orlando & Dawn

"Angie Baby"
Helen Reddy

"The Hustle"
Van McCoy & The Soul City
Symphony

"Fight the Power"
Isley Brothers

"Wasted Days and Wasted Nights"
Freddy Fender

"Fire"
Ohio Players

"Magic"
Pilot

"Please Mr. Postman"
Carpenters

"Sister Golden Hair"
America

"Out of Time"
Rolling Stones

"Full of Fire"
Al Green

"Mandy"
Barry Manilow

"Island Girl"
Elton John

"Could It Be Magic"
Barry Manilow

"Have You Never Been Mellow"
Olivia Newton-John

"Fly Robin Fly"
Silver Convention

"Wildfire"
Michael Murphey

"I'm Not Lisa"
Jessi Colter

"Listen to What the Man Said"
Paul McCartney & Wings

"I'm Not in Love"
10 cc

"Feelings"
Morris Albert

"Fallin' in Love"
Hamilton, Joe Frank & Reynolds

"When Will I Be Loved"
Linda Ronstadt

"You're No Good"
Linda Ronstadt

"Honey"
Ohio Players

"That's the Way I Like It"
K.C. & The Sunshine Band

"Walk Away from Love"
David Ruffin

"Miracles"
Jefferson Starship

"Born to Run"
Bruce Springsteen

"Calypso"
John Denver

"Get Down Tonight"
K.C. & The Sunshine Band

DANCES

The Hustle becomes mainstay of discos

NEWS OF ROCK

Sex Pistols outrage London as punk rock takes over . . . Telly "Kojak" Savalas has U.K. record hit with Bread's "If" . . . Chuck Berry plays to 40 people at New York concert . . . Discos proliferate . . . Bob Dylan's Rolling Thunder Review opens in Plymouth, Mass. . . . Beatles' 23 No. 1 singles beat Presley by three, but new figures reveal Presley had 68 million-selling units (including seven albums) vs. their 61 (with 22 albums) . . . Rolling Stones' U.S. tour grosses $13 million—costs $10 million . . . Record and tape sales up another $160 million to $2.36 billion . . . Record companies beginning to sign new groups spawned in Greenwich Village, New York, at CBGB, the Mercer Arts Center, Max's Kansas City, etc.—with the Ramones and Patti Smith in the vanguard of punk rock . . . New payola probe focuses on some record companies peddling influence, favors and money in exchange for airplay . . . Record manufacturers start making album-sized (12 inch) single records for disco deejays; some of them soon find limited commercial market . . . Estimated worldwide earnings to date of "Jesus Christ Superstar" albums, film and stage productions about $125 million . . . Bruce Springsteen makes the covers of both *Time* and *Newsweek* magazines, and *Time* also devotes covers to Cher and Elton John . . .

SOME OF THE NEWS THAT INFLUENCED
THE ROCK ERA AND VICE VERSA

U.S. pulls out of Vietnam and Cambodia . . . President Ford escapes assassination . . . Viet war cost U.S. 56,555 lives, 303,654 wounded, and

$191 billion in past 14 years . . . U.S. unemployment 7,900,000—highest in 13 years . . . Alaska Supreme Court legalizes home use of marijuana . . . Data shows decrease in heart disease deaths owning to drop in smoking and better diet . . . Marines rescue cargo ship Mayaguez and crew from Cambodians: 41 Americans killed or missing . . . Supreme Court rules that a criminal case defendant may conduct own defense rather than accept court-appointed attorney . . . Council of Economic Priorities says lack of competition among drug companies costs buyers of antibiotics $180 million a year . . . Franco dies . . . U.S. Bicentennial celebrations . . . Helsinki Agreement recognizing post-war East European borders supposedly ends Cold War and extends détente . . . Cracks in Illinois atomic reactor result in shutdown of 23 counterparts . . . Radioactive water spills into Long Island Sound . . . Six nations selling nuclear equipment meet on ways to control spread of atomic weapons . . . Social Security payments exceed income by $13 billion . . . U.S. and Soviet spaceships link up 150 miles above the Atlantic . . . CIA recovers part of Soviet sub sunk in Pacific in 1968 . . . Presidential Commission on CIA domestic spying reports some unlawful activities, while most undertakings were within its statutory authority . . . Attorney General reveals that late J. Edgar Hoover kept files on Presidents, Congressmen and private individuals . . . Report indicates Government officials were involved in or privy to five assassination attempts on foreign leaders, but that four actual deaths did not stem from these plots . . . Federal Court rules that Nixon tapes are Government property . . . Unemployment up to 8.5% . . . Unconditional surrender of Saigon government to Viet Cong leads to evacuation of all remaining Americans . . . Ford again vetoes controls on strip mining, citing energy needs . . . 14-year Apollo space program ends with first internationally-manned flight . . . Patty Hearst arrested by FBI in San Francisco for involvement with Symbionese Liberation Army violence during her abduction . . . New York City saved from last-minute bankruptcy . . . Major car makers introduce a system of rebates on certain models to stimulate lagging sales . . . California Adult Authority grants parole date to convicted assassin of Robert F. Kennedy: Sirhan Sirhan could now be released in February 1986 . . . Senate votes to cut off support to U.S.-backed rightist faction in Angolan civil war—reflecting public fear of another Vietnam-like involvement . . . U.S. now selling arms to over 130 countries and maintaining military comitments with 40 nations . . . Now 400,000 troops stationed overseas and 805 strategic nuclear weapons in full deployment . . .

**THE NUMBERS GAME: STATISTICAL INFORMATION
SHOWING HOW LIFE IN AMERICA INFLUENCED
OR WAS INFLUENCED BY THE ROCK ERA**

Young marrieds averaging $4,500 on home furnishings during first year. They buy 83% of all stainless flatware, 60% of all sterling flatware and

59% of all fine china . . . 43.4% of national income spent by federal, state and local governments . . . Home-delivered milk down to 15% from 25% in 1965 and over 50% before World War II . . . CB radio applications at FCC in October 289,018, vs. 42,775 a year ago. Continuing. Over a million units imported from Japan in first nine months of year . . . Brewers' Society reports average American downed 151 pints of beer a year, vs. West Germany's 259.4 and Ireland's 230.6. U.S. averages 11.5 pints of wine per person annually, vs. Italy's 189.2—and 9.1 pints of spirits, while people in Britain average only 3.5 pints . . . Now 15 million regular golfers and 19 million tennis players in U.S. . . . Survey shows U.S. tops world on annual per capita consumption of eggs (39 lbs.), while lowest on fresh fruit (82 lbs.) Other annual totals: margarine (27 lbs.) vs. butter (4 lbs.); sugar (92 lbs.). Meat total is 123 lbs., much less than Australia (255), West Germany (220), France and Belgium (198) and Austria (172). U.S. fresh vegetable consumption (179 lbs.) is half of Italy's 341 lbs. . . . Divorce rate makes big leap in past five years. 50% more men and 37.1% more women part this year than in 1950—while 3.1% fewer men and 2.6% fewer women get married . . . Now almost 1,800,000 retail stores of all kinds in U.S. . . . 150 of the largest 500 U.S. corporations still controlled by families . . . Grocery products are 38.6% of supermarket sales—meat is 23.3%; frozen foods 6.4%; produce 7.4%; bakery 4.7%; dairy 9.5%; and ice cream 9% . . . Baskin-Robbins sells enough ice cream to fill 800 million cones, vs. 1962 equivalent of 50 million cones . . . Average family size now 3.42 persons vs. 3.58 (1970); 3.54 (1950); 4.3 (1920) . . . 30 million workers have felt the need to take up additional retirement insurance to supplement their expected social security benefits . . . Current defense budget $104 billion—up $15 billion from years of Vietnam involvement, 1972-74 . . . New York Yankees begin baseball salary race with five-year Catfish Hunter contract totalling $2,892,000 . . . House of Representatives has 34 different bills under consideration during the same period the Senate has seven in the works . . . 158 million barrels of beer produced, vs. over 94 million in 1960 —almost double in 15 years . . .

TEEN AND COLLEGE LIVING AND ALTERNATIVE LIFE STYLES IN THE ROCK ERA

Youth "quiatus" remains on hold . . . Estimated 60 million 10-24-year-olds in U.S. almost double 1950's total . . . Gallup, now polling parents, reports that 45% of them feel young people have too many rights and privileges. Only 10% said "too few" . . . Many more young male singles in every age group: 18- and 19-year-olds = 93.1% vs. 77.7%; 20-24 = 59.9% vs. 40.3%; 25-29 = 22.3% vs. 13.6%; 30-34 = 11.1% vs. 7.5%—but in total population 18 years and over, women outnumber the men—74,760,000 to 67,235,000 . . . Nine out of ten singles between 14 and 24 years old living with relatives . . . Bridal market now worth $8 billion a year to retailers—and is considered the "hot market": more than $2 billion being spent on wedding receptions, $1.6 billion on engagement and wedding rings (40% of the total jewelry business), and over $750 million on honeymoons. 86% of first-time weddings are formal and 96% have receptions . . . Number of college students volunteering for ROTC showing steady increase . . . American Council on Education reports highest percentage of college student moderates (55%) since they began their count—with big increase in those calling themselves conservatives . . . Student survey reveals reasons for growing peace on campuses since Kent State: (1) End of Vietnam war; (2) Termination of draft in 1973; (3) Resigned awareness that "establishment" too strong to fight; (4) Since Mao invited Nixon to Peking, left wing hero symbols diminished or dead (like Che); (5) Murders by Manson "Family" in 1969 on conscience of many who had helped promote climate of hostility and violence; (6) The now highly visible ill effects of drugs on self and others—with all the addictions that ended in overdoses, suicide and insanity; (7) Decline of the economic boom, with increasing joblessness for graduates with good records; (8) The declining interest in political issues that accompanies looking inward to "me"; (9) The new vital, nonviolent interests such as ecology and women's liberation . . . "Turn Inward" groups make big inroads on college campuses with psychic festivals, Personal Exploration Groups (PEG), Institutes for Applied Meditation, Centers for Utopian Psychology, Science of the Mind, Feeling Experience, parapsychology and metaphysics, Transactional Analysis (TA), and many others—especially yoga—almost totally replacing protest gatherings . . . Filmgoing by 12-17-year-olds shows significant drop for the first time since 1969, according to Opinion Research Corp. study comparing this year with 1973. While the teen share dropped from 26% to 19%, the adult share (18 up) rose from 74% to 81%. At college level, frequent attenders reach a 36% peak . . . Poll of junior high school students finds television has most influence on their lives (58%), vs. books (19%), radio (12%), newspapers (6%), and magazines (3%), according to Encyclopaedia Britannica Educational Corporation . . .

FASHION: CLOTHES AND THE ROCK ERA ACCENT ON YOUTH

Note: Feminine fashion is in italics, male in roman, unisex in parentheses, and news in asterisks.

After 100 years, U.S. Navy discontinues bell-bottoms, wide-collared jumpers and knotted neckerchiefs . . . **Women spend $12 billion on clothing** . . . **Brides spending $500 million on lingerie—three and a half times as much as the average woman** . . . (Bell-bottoms disappear as trouser legs become narrower) . . . *Warm, quilted Chinese-style coats and jackets . . . Strapped canvas shoes from Woolworth's with cheap tee-shirts . . . Green army fatigue pants with pockets on the sides . . . House painter's pants . . . Teeshirts pulled super-tight and knotted in front like* *calypso shirt bodice . . . Girls wear extra-large men's teeshirts over bikinis . . .* **London boutique popularizes basic long-sleeved teeshirts for girls with scoop necks, square necks, V-necks, low-cut necks and many softened colors** *. . . Black turtle neck or teeshirt with black pants for jogging or dining out . . . Capezio wraparound skirts dyed to match Danskin leotards . . . Femmes wearing men's (old) shirts tucked in at waist over turtle neck or pulled tight with belt at waist if it has straight bottom . . . Velvet blazers with cowboy boots, jeans and an old vest . . . College girls wearing Weejun loafers or Top-Siders without socks . . .* (Unisex cowboy clothes) *. . . Medical uniforms and chefs' or waiters' jackets in dyed colors like dusky rose or deep violet that take beautifully on white cotton . . . Khaki new "in" color for feminine garments and footwear . . .* (Jaws *teeshirts for beachwear) . . . Wooden and leather clogs still popular . . .*

FADS (MOSTLY YOUTH-ORIENTED) RELATED TO THE ROCK ERA

Pet rocks . . . Dance marathons . . . Skateboarding moves East . . . Mood rings . . . Spiderman takes up where Batman left off . . . Pic-throwing by hit men (costing as much as $300 to aim at VIP targets) . . .

THE NEW WOMAN IN THE ROCK ERA

Congress passes bill admitting women to Annapolis, West Point and Air Force Academy in 1976 . . . Supreme Court strikes down "Unequal Treatment" Utah law making a girl an adult at 21 vs. 18 for a boy . . . Lila Cockrell elected San Antonio Mayor—first woman to head one of nation's largest cities . . . Harvard drops five-man-to-two-woman entry ratio, planning equality of admission . . . 408-year-old English public school, Rugby, will admit co-eds . . . U.S. females outnumber males 109.4 million to 103.8 million—larger increase estimated by year 2000 . . . U.S. Office of Education reports that women lost ground in both salary increases and rank . . . Equal Rights Amendment defeated by legislatures in North Carolina, Indiana, Missouri, Florida, Illinois and South Carolina. In five states ratification failed by extremely narrow margins, so outlook for passage still good . . . Gallup poll reports 58% support ERA vs. 24% opposed . . . Congress outlaws automatic discharge from armed services for pregnancy . . . Federal employees given right to sue for sex discrimination . . . First Women's Bank opens in New York City . . . American Chemical Society finds newly-graduated women chemists and chemical engineers being paid on average 5% more than male graduates . . . Though battle for co-education is pretty much won, vestiges of all-male days remain to irk campus feminists—such as the sexism of Princeton's football cheers and the wording of Penn State's alma mater . . .

MOSTLY FACTUAL TRIVIA
CONCURRENT WITH THE ROCK ERA

Steve Anderson becomes the new world guitar-plucking champ. Goes 114 hours and 17 minutes, beating 200 others in L.A. meet . . . *Penthouse* overtakes *Playboy* in sales . . . Buffalo crossbred with cattle to produce Beefalo . . . Leonard McMahon swallows 501 goldfish in four hours at Oakland, California—beating previous record by 300 . . . High bid at charity auction buys $4,000 dinner for two in Paris—including 31 dishes and nine wines . . .

1976 _____

ARTISTS

Rock Groups
  Boston
  England Dan & John Ford Coley
  Foghat
  Heart
  Manfred Mann's Earth Band
  Bob Seger
  Thin Lizzy

Rock Solo Performers
  Elvin Bishop
  Eric Carmen
  Kiki Dee
  Boz Scaggs
  Al Stewart
  John Travolta
  Gary Wright

Soul, R&B, Funk Groups
  Brothers Johnson
  Marilyn McCoo & Billy Davis, Jr.

Soul, R&B, Funk Solo Performers
  George Benson
  Thelma Houston
  Maxine Nightingale

Folk & Country
  Emmylou Harris
  Waylon Jennings
  Pure Prairie League

Glitter/Bizarre
  Kiss

Cult Groups/Punk/New Wave/
Drone Rock
  Ramones

Disco
  Sylvers
  Village People
  Wild Cherry

JUKE BOX HITS

"Silly Love Songs"
Wings

"December 1963 (Oh, What
A Night)"
Four Seasons

"Get Closer"
Seals & Crofts

"I'd Really Love to See
You Tonight"
England Dan & John Ford Coley

"Love Hurts"
Nazareth

"Shake Your Booty"
K.C. & The Sunshine Band

"You Should Be Dancing"
Bee Gees

"Let Your Love Flow"
Bellamy Brothers

"All By Myself"
Eric Carmen

"Kiss and Say Goodbye"
Manhattans

"Lowdown"
Boz Scaggs

"I Love Music" (Part I)
O'Jays

"Welcome Back"
John Sebastian

"Rock 'n Me"
Steve Miller Band

"Tonight's the Night"
Rod Stewart

"Sorry Seems to Be the
Hardest Word"
Elton John

"You Don't Have to Be a Star"
Marilyn McCoo & Billy Davis, Jr.

"Beth"
Kiss

"Say You Love Me"
Fleetwood Mac

"Don't Go Breaking My Heart"
Elton John & Kiki Dee

"Play That Funky Music"
Wild Cherry

"50 Ways to Leave Your Lover"
Paul Simon

"Bohemian Rhapsody"
Queen

"Get Up and Boogie"
Silver Convention

"Sweet Love"
Commodores

"Golden Years"
David Bowie

"Dream Weaver"
Gary Wright

"Love to Love You Baby"
Donna Summer

"A Little Bit More"
Dr. Hook

"Show Me the Way"
Peter Frampton

"Fooled Around and Fell in Love"
Elvin Bishop

"Evil Woman"
Electric Light Orchestra

"Love Roller Coaster"
Ohio Players

"This Masquerade"
George Benson

"Summer"
War

"I Write the Songs"
Barry Manilow

"Car Wash"
Rose Royce

"Wake Up Everybody" (Part I)
Harold Melvin & The
Blue Notes

"Disco Lady"
Johnny Taylor

"Love Is Alive"
Gary Wright

"A Fifth of Beethoven"
Walter Murphy & Big Apple Band

"You Sexy Thing"
Hot Chocolate

"Take It to the Limit"
Eagles

"Right Back Where We
Started From"
Maxine Nightingale

"Only Sixteen"
Dr. Hook

"Lonely Night"
Captain & Tennille

"Deep Purple"
Donny & Marie Osmond

"If You Leave Me Now"
Chicago

"Dream On"
Aerosmith

"Convoy"
C. W. McCall

"Let Her In"
John Travolta

"Boogie Fever"
Sylvers

"Saturday Night"
Bay City Rollers

"Fox on the Run"
Sweet

"Devil Woman"
Cliff Richard

"Rock and Roll Music"
Beach Boys

"Sweet Thing"
Rufus, Featuring
Chaka Khan

"More Than a Feeling"
Boston

"Sara Smile"
Hall & Oates

"Blinded by the Light"
Manfred Mann's Earth Band

"Let 'em In"
Wings

"Magic Man"
Heart

NEWS OF ROCK

In-debt Liverpool Cavern Club closes. Stage sawn into small sections and sold . . . Beach Boys' Brian Wilson makes first full-length stage appearance in 12 years before 74,000 at Anaheim, California . . . Gary Glitter "retires" . . . First wave of New York underground club bands start getting record contracts—beginning short U.S. punk era that will end with breakup of Sex Pistols in January 1978 . . . Allman Brothers Band campaigns for Jimmy Carter . . . Punk/New Wave firmly established in Britain . . . Sid Vicious of Sex Pistols credited with originating pogo dancing—earning title of "Chubby Checker of the Punk Generation" . . . Cher and Gregg Allman become parents of a son . . . 11,500 different single records made top hit charts during past 30 years . . . Sal Mineo murdered in L.A. . . . Punk/New Wave scene cools in U.S. As disco beat sweeps New York, the home for punk purists, CBGB, becomes a tourist attraction. Mercer Arts building collapses, and Manhattan-bred bands get cool reception on tours and records . . . Linda Ronstadt campaigns for Jerry Brown in California . . . Elvis purchases nine cars for friends and acquaintances in Colorado at cost of $110,000 . . . Record and tape sales up nearly $400 million to $2.74 billion . . . No real enthusiasm for punk rock in U.S., so the Ramones and Patti Smith go to London to find audience . . . Jimmy Carter quotes two lines from Bob Dylan song, "It's Alright Ma (I'm Only Bleeding)" in acceptance speech at Democratic National Convention . . . The Band plays final concert "The Last Waltz" at San Francisco Winterland Ballroom— with *La Traviata* stage set on loan from San Francisco Opera Company and a string orchestra playing waltz music. Some critics feel that the event epitomizes the "obese, bourgeois entity" rock has become . . . A number of radio stations give up hard rock sound as audiences dip and post-teens of 1950s, 60s and 70s seek "softer" music, according to studies by the National Association of Record Merchandisers and others . . . The trend of new artists making it via progressive (album-oriented) radio grows, as many Top 40 stations cut their playlists down to Top 20 and as low as Top 12 . . . John Lennon's application to remain in the U.S. as a permanent resident formally approved after four-year battle . . . The Who introduce lasers to live concert performances on their tour . . . The Band's final concert at Winterland, San Francisco, is filmed by Martin Scorsese and released as *The Last Waltz* . . .

SOME OF THE NEWS THAT INFLUENCED
THE ROCK ERA AND VICE VERSA

Jimmy Carter wins narrow 297-241 electoral college victory over Ford for Presidency . . . Minimum wage now $2.30 an hour . . . Secret Pentagon data shows U.S. has built twice as many large combat ships as Russia in past 15 years . . . Viking I lands on Mars after 11-month voyage . . . Federal, state and city social welfare programs reach $331 billion—327% over 1950 . . . One in seven Americans getting Social Security—tax rate increased . . . U.S.-owned cargo ship disappears in Bermuda Triangle with no S.O.S. . . . Swine flu epidemic . . . IRS reports that five persons earning over $1 million and 239 over $200,000 were able to avoid paying any income tax in 1974 . . . New York State disbars Nixon from practicing law there . . . First skyjacking over U.S. in four years . . . Berrigan jailed for digging hole in White House lawn to protest nuclear proliferation . . . Howard Hughes dies . . . Mao Tse Tung dies . . . Census Bureau reports American adults now slower to marry and quicker to divorce . . . UNESCO estimates 800 million illiterates on planet . . . London institute reports U.S. has deployed 1,054 land-based ICBMs . . . Inflation now running at 5-6% annual rate . . . Spending for leisure activity ($146 billion) far exceeds annual outlays for national defense or for all home building . . . One-third of all U.S. households now own two or more autos . . . U.S. vetoes Vietnam admission to U.N. on grounds that Hanoi has failed to give an accounting of 800 missing-in-action American servicemen . . . Environmental Protection Agency bans almost all pesticides containing mercury . . .

Senate creates permanent 15-member Select Committee to oversee CIA activities . . . Supreme Court rules that death penalty is constitutionally acceptable form of punishment in certain cases . . . America celebrates Bicentennial . . . After several appeals, court martial conviction of Lieutenant Calley upheld. Army announces it will parole him. He served about three years . . .

THE NUMBERS GAME: STATISTICAL INFORMATION SHOWING HOW LIFE IN AMERICA INFLUENCED OR WAS INFLUENCED BY THE ROCK ERA

Forty million Mastercharge card holders run up $18.5 billion in bills . . . 71% of population uses alcoholic beverages, vs. 58% in 1939 . . . Traffic deaths almost half of 1956 total, mainly because of interstate highways. U.S. now has 38,000 miles of freeways . . . Last of the convertible cars, Cadillac Eldorado, phased out . . . Beef consumption hits peak 128.5 lbs. per capita, vs. 85.1 lbs. in 1960. Continuing . . . America now eats more than 50 billion hamburgers a year, and pays more than $25 billion for various forms of beef . . . Record $5.3 billion spent by boaters, $4 billion by golfers, and $2.3 billion by skiers . . . U.S. now eats more than 750 million gallons of ice cream a year, or 15 quarts a person (23 if ice cream is defined as all commercially-produced frozen dairy products) . . . Carbon monoxide emissions from road vehicles down to 67.7 million tons from 87.3 million in 1970—in steady annual diminution . . . An average of 13.5 million used cars sold annually during past nine years—averaging more than $21.3 billion a year . . . In the face of energy pessimism, Hudson Institute estimates that proven reserves of five major fossil fuels (oil, natural gas, coal, shale oil and tar sands) alone could provide the world's total energy requirements for about 100 years, and only one-fifth of the estimated potential resources could provide for more than 200 years of the projected energy needs. With the cost of extracting and processing alternative fuels becoming feasible in the not-too-distant future, U.S. potential fossil energy could be increased from 150 years to possibly 600 or more . . . Gallup poll annual deviation between their final survey and the result of 14 national elections since 1950, including this year, only 1.5 percentage points . . . Frozen food consumption now almost double 1963—11.5 billion pounds vs. 6.1 billion pounds . . . In reply to U.S. Department of Commerce sampling question: "Were there any times yesterday when you wanted to watch television but did not because there were no programs worth watching at that time?," only 12% said they turned off their sets . . .

TEEN AND COLLEGE LIVING AND ALTERNATIVE LIFE STYLES IN THE ROCK ERA

Big return to religion on college campuses . . . 14% of 15-24-year-olds unemployed, vs. 9.8% in 1973 . . . Report indicates continued decline in scores of high school seniors on their college board exams . . . U.S. Government data shows one out of five children living with only one, or neither parent, as there are now three divorces for every five marriages . . . Newspaper survey finds only one apparent hippie (or yippie) out of ten in Haight Ashbury; and reports that: "Some have seen the ecological light and gone into rural communes, some have begged forgiveness and taken up college courses where they left off six or seven years ago, but more than half of them have gone back to their home towns and been reconciled with their families" . . . Youth (age 24 and under) continues domination of cinema audiences, which peaked in 1960s—16-20-year-olds are 31% of all admissions, 21-24 are 15%, and 12-15 are 14%, for a total of 60%, according to Opinion Research survey for Motion Picture Association. In 1969 the 12-24 group was 65% of audience, or 5% higher—but the 25-39-year-old audience was only 22% compared to a 9% higher 31% this year, indicating that the 1960s film buffs are hanging on while today's youth is showing a slight drop in interest . . .

FASHION: CLOTHES AND THE
ROCK ERA ACCENT ON YOUTH

Note: Feminine fashion is in italics, male in roman, unisex in parentheses, and news in asterisks.

Headbands . . . Harem pants that tie at ankles . . . **Writer Alison Lurie says, "Ninety percent of middle-class high school and college students are now attired the same below the waist." According to her son in junior high school: "Freaks wear Lee jeans, greasers wear Wranglers, and all others Levis"** . . . (Brand names in clear view on garments spreads to fashion world from schools and colleges, where customarily shown on jeans and teeshirts) . . . **Cotton denim production almost doubles in three years—820 million square yards vs. 482 million in 1973 as denim jeans and jackets rule fashion roost** . . . *Blazer jackets back in . . . Bomber jackets and painters' pants still fashion headliners as the western look goes commercial . . . Boots with thick crepe soles . . . Overalls and mechanics' jumpsuits . . .*

FADS (MOSTLY YOUTH-ORIENTED)
RELATED TO THE ROCK ERA

Forty-six University of Cincinnati students remain stacked on mattress for 60 seconds . . . Farrah Fawcett-Majors posters . . . Skateboards now $250 million a year business, with 150 manufacturers turning out over 50 models . . .

SOME OF THE MORE WIDELY USED ARGOT,
JARGON AND SLANG IN THE ROCK ERA

Pavement pizzas (skateboard accidents) . . .

THE NEW WOMAN IN THE ROCK ERA

Dr. Spock apologizes for sexist attitudes in third edition of *Baby and Child Care* . . . Equal Rights Amendment defeated in New York and New Jersey elections . . . Women's Tennis Association threatens to boycott Wimbledon if prize money not equalized . . . Yale Women's Varsity crew win locker room showers after protest strip in Phys-Ed director's office, citing equality violation . . . President Ford says in Walter Cronkite TV interview that Supreme Court has "gone too far" in striking down anti-abortion laws . . . Nation's largest brokerage house, Merrill Lynch, agrees to pay $1.9 million to individuals it had wrongfully failed to hire or promote . . . Major New York City law firm settles sex discrimination suit by agreeing that in the next three years, the percentage of women receiving job offers must be at least 20% higher than the percentage of women in law school graduating classes . . . Rhodes Scholarships offered to women for first time . . . *Harvard Law Review*, one of most influential legal journals, elects first woman president . . . Women hold less than 5% of all U.S. elective offices, reports Rutgers University Center for the American Woman and Politics . . . Supreme Court requires Federal agencies to end sex discrimination in industries they regulate . . . NASA announces acceptance of women for astronaut training . . . TV show bottlecappers, Laverne and Shirley, first female factory hands to appear on tube . . . *The Hite Report* published . . . *Redbook* editor Sey Chassler inspires other women's magazines to publish stories explaining ERA . . . Barbara Walters debuts as first anchorwoman on a network news program . . .

MOSTLY FACTUAL TRIVIA
CONCURRENT WITH THE ROCK ERA

Smokey the Bear retires from public service . . . Twiggy named most beautiful woman of modern times in London wax museum poll . . . Army General pays U.S. over $900 because his golf shoes were flown to him on otherwise empty military plane . . .

1977 _____

ARTISTS

Rock Groups
  Blondie
  Climax Blues Band
  Foreigner
  Kansas
  Pablo Cruise
  Styx

Rock Solo Performers
  Elvis Costello
  Billy Joel
  David Soul
  Steve Winwood

Soul, R&B, Funk Groups
  Emotions
  Rose Royce

Soul, R&B, Funk Solo Performers
  Teddy Pendergrass

Folk & Country
  Rita Coolidge
  Emmylou Harris
  Ronnie Milsap
  Dolly Parton
  Bonnie Raitt

Young Teen Oriented
  Andy Gibb
  Shaun Cassidy

Middle of the Road
  Debby Boone

Cult Groups/Punk/New Wave/
Drone Rock
  Dictators
  Modern Lovers
  Talking Heads

Disco
  Grace Jones
  Ritchie Family

JUKE BOX HITS

"How Deep Is Your Love"
Bee Gees

"I Just Want to Be Your
Everything"
Andy Gibb

"Best of My Love"
Emotions

"Rich Girl"
Daryl Hall & John Oates

"Don't Give Up on Us"
David Soul

"Blinded By the Light"
Manfred Mann's Earth Band

"Lucille"
Kenny Rogers

"Handy Man"
James Taylor

"Night Moves"
Bob Seger & The Silver
Bullet Band

"It Was Almost Like a Song"
Ronnie Milsap

"Lido Shuffle"
Boz Scaggs

"Give a Little Bit"
Supertramp

"Ain't Gonna Bump No More
(With No Big Fat Woman)"
Joe Tex

"Higher and Higher"
Rita Coolidge

"When I Need You"
Leo Sayer

"Underground Angel"
Alan O'Day

"Short People"
Randy Newman

"Whatcha Gonna Do?"
Pablo Cruise

"You Make Me Feel Like
Dancing"
Leo Sayer

"Telephone Line"
Electric Light Orchestra

"Hot Line"
Sylvers

"Feels Like the First Time"
Foreigner

"Dreams"
Fleetwood Mac

"The Things We Do for Love"
10 cc

"Just a Song Before I Go"
Crosby, Stills & Nash

"Heard It in a Love Song"
Marshall Tucker Band

"New Kid in Town"/"Victim
of Love"
Eagles

"Year of the Cat"
Al Stewart

"Love So Right"
Bee Gees

"You Light Up My Life"
Debby Boone

"Couldn't Get It Right"
Climax Blues Band

"So In to You"
Atlanta Rhythm Section

"I Hope We Get to Love
in Time"
Marilyn McCoo/Billy Davis, Jr.

"Hotel California"
Eagles

"Southern Nights"
Glen Campbell

"I'm Your Boogie Man"
K.C. & The Sunshine Band

"Easy"
Commodores

"I've Got Love on My Mind"
Natalie Cole

"I'm In You"
Peter Frampton

"Da Doo Ron Ron"
Shaun Cassidy

"I Wish"
Stevie Wonder

"Carry On Wayward Son"
Kansas

"Lost Without Your Love"
Bread

"Don't Worry Baby"
B. J. Thomas

"Nobody Does It Better"
Carly Simon

"Torn Between Two Lovers"
Mary McGregor

"Don't Leave Me This Way"
Thelma Huston

"You Made Me Believe in Magic"
Bay City Rollers

"Don't Stop"
Fleetwood Mac

"You're in My Heart"
Rod Stewart

"Fly Like an Eagle"
Steve Miller Band

NEWS OF ROCK

Disco music making it big on records . . . High water mark of U.S. new wave hype—with everyone ready to believe that punk will take Top 40 by storm before year ends . . . Emerson, Lake and Palmer lose money on U.S. tour with 70-piece orchestra, lasers, a miniature hovercraft . . . Santana fire-bombed at Milan soccer stadium concert . . . RKO Radio survey indicates that average 18-24-year-old male keeps switching dial and listens to 5.2 different radio stations a day . . . Twenty-odd promoters or promotion companies control 90% of the money made in all U.S. rock appearances . . . Dirt Band first U.S. rock group to tour U.S.S.R. . . . Britt Ekland sues Rod Stewart for $15 million in breakup . . . Gregg Allman and Cher split . . . Bob Dylan's wife Sara sues for divorce . . . Governor Carter sends Bob Dylan hand-written invitation to visit him during Atlanta concert appearance . . . Showco, leading U.S. staging and sound operation, requires entire 707 jet freighter to fly stage set to London for Bad Company concert . . . Two million Presley records sold within 24 hours of his death . . . Record and tape sales pass $3 billion and go on to $3.5 billion—up from just over $2 billion four years ago . . . *Rolling Stone* reveals that 400 journalists shared information with, and sometimes helped, the CIA during past 25 years . . . Bee Gees corner four of the top records on the Hot 100 charts . . . *Rolling Stone* album of the year, "Fleetwood Mac," earns close to $400,000 for each of the group's five members . . . Bob Dylan's $2.25 million mansion at Malibu Beach, California, joins Keith Moon's $800,000 house and Linda Ronstadt's $325,000 clapboard as rock stars take over Hollywood opulence from movie stars of past. Alice Cooper, Brian Wilson and Al Kooper all have swimming pools and vast games rooms. Joni

Mitchell, Ringo Starr, Bernie Taupin, Rod Stewart and John Mayall all have airy mansions where hundreds could play . . . Tape sales now 26% of music market . . . Neil Sedaka buys back 116 songs from Don Kirshner for $12 million . . . New Jersey grand jury investigation of record industry payolas produces a number of indictments . . . Quadraphonic sound systems fail to make commercial dent . . .

SOME OF THE NEWS THAT INFLUENCED
THE ROCK ERA AND VICE VERSA

Worst winter of century—65% of North America covered with snow in January . . . Worst summer of century. Big droughts . . . White House science adviser asks NASA to consider reopening UFO investigation . . . New York City blacked out by another power failure . . . New Cabinet-level Energy Department created . . . Carter Budget Director, Bert Lance, resigns due to pressure over disputed financial practices . . . FBI releases 40,000 pages of previously secret JFK assassination investigation files . . . President ends travel restrictions to Vietnam, Cambodia, North Korea and Cuba . . . Carter takes Human Rights campaign to U.N. . . . Food and Drug Administration proposes ban on saccharine . . . Nixon admits he "let the American people down" in David Frost interview . . . Unemployment hits 29-month low as total employment sets new high . . . Supreme Court rules that seniority systems which perpetuate past racial discriminations are not necessarily illegal . . . State Department repeats a previous pledge that it will not offer any economic aid to Hanoi after House votes to prohibit any discussion of assistance . . . 5,000 demonstrators arrested for occupying New Hampshire nuclear power plant construction site—later released . . . U.S. and Cuba exchange diplomats . . . Brezhnev named Soviet President . . . Begin voted Prime Minister of Israel . . . *New York Times* details CIA program to develop mind control techniques . . . U.S. Court of Appeals approves $1 billion 1976 sale of offshore drilling rights on 500,000 acres of Atlantic Ocean 47-90 miles off the coast from Long Island to Maryland. Government estimates between 400 million and 1.4 billion barrels of oil might be buried there . . . Vietnam admitted to U.N. . . . Judge Sirica sharply reduces Mitchell, Haldeman and Ehrlichman sentences after hearing tape-recorded admissions of guilt and sorrow for Watergate misdeeds . . . Carter accuses oil industry of staging "biggest rip-off" in history . . . Congress raises Social Security tax . . . Nation's farmers strike by saying they will refuse to buy equipment and supplies for spring planting unless the Government comes to their aid. Strike has little effect . . . Soviets arrest 20 on Human Rights Day . . . More than half the U.S. supply of 20 important minerals now coming from abroad . . . Oil begins to flow through the Alaska pipeline . . .

THE NUMBERS GAME: STATISTICAL INFORMATION SHOWING HOW LIFE IN AMERICA INFLUENCED OR WAS INFLUENCED BY THE ROCK ERA

Carnegie Council on Children estimates (conservatively) total cost of feeding, clothing and educating one child through high school can reach more than $35,000 for a family earning roughly $10,000 a year . . . 81% of the married men and 47% of the married women are now in U.S. labor force . . . Now 600 localities with 38 million total population have 911 emergency phone systems . . . $39.9 billion spent on pollution control . . . 4,472 man-made objects orbiting around the earth—celebrating 20th anniversary of space age . . . Out of 49 million 15-17-year-olds, 43.7 million enrolled in schools . . . Weight Watchers is said to have helped over 9 million members . . . Harris poll shows 54% would use public transportation or car pooling for necessary trips if gas goes to $1.75 a gallon or more, vs. 38% at $1 a gallon. 78% would cut back on pleasure driving at $1.75 a gallon, vs. 64% at $1 . . . Cost per pupil in average daily attendance at public elementary and secondary day schools highest in New York State ($2,645)—lowest is Arkansas ($1,218), and $1,668 in California . . .12-year-old Hari Krishna sect said to have 10,000 fulltime monks on streets of world, with $16 million annual income . . . Imports filling 41% of all petroleum needs as domestic oil production drops to lowest level in ten years . . . President's Council on Environmental Quality estimates air pollution alone will be causing almost $25 billion in damages to health, residential property, materials and vegetation . . . Environmental Protection Agency reports water pollution costing over $10 billion a year . . . National Academy of Sciences estimates 15,000 people will die, and seven million days will be spent in bed with illnesses, as a result of air pollution . . . Only 6% of men and 4% of women in early fifties never married. Also, 85% of men and 88% of women have been married only once . . .Cost of medical care up 9.6% vs. all consumer prices only rising 6.5%. Physicians' fees were up 9.3%, and dentists' 7.5%. Physicians went up 5% in 1974; 12.8% more in 1975; 11.4% more in 1976 . . . Average per capita personal income is $7,057, and median family income $16,740 . . . 162,072,000 telephones in use—74.4 per hundred population . . . A good 12% of 385 billion "eating occasions" (mealtimes, not snacks) were outside of the home . . . Estimated number of minutes in eight-hour day an average worker spends to pay for selected items in family budget: Federal taxes 1 hour 44 minutes; State and local taxes 58 mins.; Food and tobacco 1:08; Housing, household expenses 1:30; Clothing, jewelry, :25; Medical care :26. In 1930, the average worker paid all his taxes with 57 minutes of work vs. today's 2:42 . . . In the mid-1940s, electrical appliances owned by the average family were a radio, refrigerator, toaster, vacuum cleaner, washer and electric iron. Today, many average families have, in addition, an electric range, clothes dryer, food mixer and blender, color TV, electric blankets, electric can openers, and (often) air conditioning. The 1977 family income averages $14,800 vs. $7,700 in the mid-1940s (with most wives not working), and family size now husband, wife and one or two children vs. two or three children then . . . In the early 1920s a wage earner had to work 52 minutes to buy a dozen eggs—today the time would be less than 15 minutes . . . Median annual income for dentists in general practice about $39,000, vs. roughly $51,000 for office-based M.D.s . . . Today's 25-34-year-olds (students of the 1960s) include 23.8% with four or more years of college, vs. 10.9% in 1960, and 19.8% with 1-3 years' college, vs. 11.3% in 1960 . . . Census Bureau again raises estimate of number of people over age 65 in year 2000 to 31.8 million—from estimates of 30.6 million in 1975 and 28.8 million in 1971—as life expectancy continues dramatic increase . . . McDonald's sells 25 billionth hamburger—with 4,700 outlets around the world. Plans of 23-year-old company call for 450 new openings a year for next 50 years. Burger King up to 2,000 locations . . . Every day there is now an average 467 million local calls and 38.8 million long-distance calls in the U.S. . . .

TEEN AND COLLEGE LIVING AND ALTERNATIVE LIFE STYLES IN THE ROCK ERA

Young people still not making news . . . 75% of 17-year-olds graduate from high school, vs. 60% in 1954 . . . *Ladies' Home Journal* student survey asking question, "If you had the choice, who would you want to be?" resulted in girls picking Farrah Fawcett-Majors, and boys Lee Majors . . . President Carter pardons most Vietnam draft evaders—numbering some 10,000 . . . When Ohio school district rules out boys' beards and mustaches while limiting hair length, federal officials state this is "discrimination" against the male, so school board issues same rules for girls . . . Several educators find aversion to mathematics known as "math anxiety" among many college students—especially women—and three remedial courses developed . . . Two-thirds of the husbands who completed high school but no college are now married to wives with the same amount of education . . . Teens spend nearly $29 billion . . . Girls 16-19 averaging $14.80 in weekly earnings vs. boys averaging less—only $14.10 . . . Teen-age mothers give birth to 600,000 babies, as 300,000 more have abortions . . . Teenage girls confused by boys often pressuring them to take responsibility for birth control, while many other young males disapprove of girls who do use birth control—risking a bad reputation by thinking beforehand about having sex . . . Career Education Incentives Act of 1977 passed—will help schools improve career guidance . . . Film showmen, celebrating 50th anniversary of talking pictures, observe that the youth market, on which both films and music have relied heavily, is aging, indicating that a change of emphasis will be needed to keep abreast of a maturing market . . . National Entertainment Conference reports that college campuses are paying $500 million annually for entertainment on campus circuit . . . Filmgoing by 12-17-year-olds bounces back big—to 26% of total yearly admission from 1975 drop to 19% . . . Over half of all adolescents have tasted alcohol and about a third have had a drink within a month, according to National Center for Health Statistics Analytical Coordination Chief, Mary Grace Kovar; who added that more than 90% of this year's graduating class have tried alcohol, more than 75% have smoked cigarettes, nearly two-thirds have experimented with illicit drugs and nearly a quarter have experimented with stimulants. Almost 30% of the seniors smoke cigarettes daily, 10% use marijuana daily and 6% report daily use of alcohol . . .

FASHION: CLOTHES AND THE
ROCK ERA ACCENT ON YOUTH

Note: Feminine fashion is in italics, male in roman, unisex in parentheses, and news in asterisks.

(Unisex running shoes) . . . **Levi Strauss produces 50 million denim garments, using 100 million yards of heavyweight denim, 8.4 million miles of orange thread, and 200 million rivets** . . . (Punk style features safety pins) . . . (Punks dye hair purple, red and other gaudy colors and chop it to make it really unkempt. Also use bizarre makeup like blue or black lips) . . . (Punks slash black leather jackets and add bicycle chains, razor blades and handcuffs as decorations) . . . *Corduroy makes comeback in trousers and skirts* . . . (Shoe prices hit new peak) . . . *Sweaters stretching from neck over hips* . . . **Khaki denim makes inroads on traditional blue** . . . **Model Margaux Hemingway signed to promote Babe perfume for $1 million a year over five years for Faberge** . . . *Women frizz their hair* . . . **Punk rock paraphernalia becomes major industry in Britain—with exploiters turning out zip-strewn jackets, bondage trousers, razor blade pendants, safety pins for insertion in cheeks and ears, appropriately decorated teeshirts, posters, fanzines and badges** . . . *Long-legged look, with pants worn skin-tight all the way from the waist to boot top—while long johns and leggings are paired with high-heeled boots and puffed blousons* . . . *Gypsy look, with gypsy skirts and bows, slides and combs in acid colors for the hair* . . .

FADS (MOSTLY YOUTH-ORIENTED)
RELATED TO THE ROCK ERA

Citizens Band radio becomes national craze . . . Roller disco spreads from New York Empire Rollerdome . . . Renewed disco popularity breeds special dances, fashions and disco-oriented records . . .

THE NEW WOMAN IN THE ROCK ERA

Reader's Digest agrees to pay $1.5 million to 2,600 current and former women employees in one of biggest settlements of sex discrimination cases . . . West Point women cadets on par with men academically, while rating high in physical tasks . . . The book, *Total Woman*, sells 3 million in four years . . . Only 16% of 25-29-year-old women did not complete high school, vs. 30% in 1966 . . . Women's earnings 62% of men's . . . *Ms.* magazine reaches 500,000 circulation in fifth year . . . 43% of 20-24-year-old women who have ever married are childless, vs. 36% in 1970 . . . Proportion of women never married increased from 36% to 45% during 1970-77 period . . . Supreme Court rules that states are not required to spend Medicaid funds for elective abortions. Prior to ruling, funds had covered abortions for as many as 300,000 women a year . . . Supreme Court invalidates Alabama law requiring prison guards to be at least 5 ft. 2 in. tall and weigh 120 lbs. as discriminatory against women unless employer could prove bona fide relationship to job requirements—saying it would exclude 41% of women from such jobs compared to 1% of men . . . Supreme Court affirms a lower court ruling permitting sex-segregated schools by deadlock of case involving separate college prep schools in Philadelphia . . . NBC makes $2 million settlement in sex bias suit filed by women employees. Network also agrees to "good faith efforts" to promote women to managerial positions . . . Navy assigns women as permanent shipboard crew . . . Protest against growing use of advertising images showing women being gagged, beaten, whipped, chained and otherwise made victims by new organization, WAVAW (Women Against Violence Against Women) . . . The wife's earnings are equal to or greater than the husband's in only one married couple in three where the wife has earnings . . .

MOSTLY FACTUAL TRIVIA
CONCURRENT WITH THE ROCK ERA

Opinion Research poll reports frequent moviegoers 12 and over are 30% male vs. 26% female; while those never attending are 36% male vs. 34% female . . .

1978 _____

ARTISTS

Rock Groups
  Journey
  Little Feat
  Little River Band
  Meatloaf
  Alan Parsons Project
  Tom Petty & The
    Heartbreakers
  REO Speedwagon
  Van Halen

Rock Solo Performers
  Gerry Rafferty
  Warren Zevon

Soul, R&B, Funk Groups
  Raydio

Soul, R&B, Funk Solo Performers
  Evelyn "Champagne" King

Folk & Country
  Crystal Gayle
  Dan Fogelberg
  Eddie Rabbitt

Middle of the Road
  Manhattan Transfer

Cult Groups/Punk/New Wave/
Drone Rock
  Cars
  Devo
  Brian Eno
  Sex Pistols

Disco
  Chic
  Linda Clifford
  Dan Hartman
  A Taste of Honey
  Village People

JUKE BOX HITS

"Shadow Dancing"
Andy Gibb

"Stayin' Alive"
Bee Gees

"Love Is Thicker Than Water"
Andy Gibb

"Just the Way You Are"
Billy Joel

"Hot Child in the City"
Nick Gilder

"We Are the Champions"/
"We Will Rock You"
Queen

"Love Will Find a Way"
Pablo Cruise

"Still the Same"
Bob Seger & Silver
Bullet Band

"Here You Come Again"
Dolly Parton

"Reminiscing"
Little River Band

"What's Your Name"
Lynyrd Skynyrd

"Running on Empty"
Jackson Browne

"MacArthur Park"
Donna Summer

"Beacon Blues"
Steely Dan

"Kiss You All Over"
Exile

"Love Is Like Oxygen"
Sweet

"Who Are You"
The Who

"Night Fever"
Bee Gees

"Three Times A Lady"
Commodores

"Miss You"
Rolling Stones

"Last Dance"
Donna Summer

"Hot Blooded"
Foreigner

"Use Ta Be My Girl"
O'Jays

"Slip Slidin' Away"
Paul Simon

"On Broadway"
George Benson

"Blue Bayou"
Linda Ronstadt

"Count On Me"
Jefferson Starship

"Don't It Make My Brown
Eyes Blue"
Crystal Gayle

"Two Out of Three Ain't Bad"
Meatloaf

"If I Can't Have You"
Yvonne Elliman

"With a Little Luck"
Wings

"Boogie Oogie Oogie"
A Taste of Honey

"Close the Door"
Teddy Pendergrass

"You Light Up My Life"
Debby Boone

"Lay Down Sally"
Eric Clapton

"You're the One That I Want"
John Travolta & Olivia
Newton-John

"Dance, Dance, Dance
(Yowsah, Yowsah, Yowsah)"
Chic

"Baby Come Back"
Player

"Baker Street"
Gerry Rafferty

"The Closer I Get to You"
Roberta Flack with Donny
Hathaway

"Imaginary Lover"
Atlanta Rhythm Section

"Come Sail Away"
Styx

"Peg"
Steely Dan

"Baby Hold On"
Eddie Money

"Serpentine Fire"
Earth, Wind & Fire

"Whenever I Call You
'Friend' "
Kenny Loggins & Stevie Nicks

"Dust in the Wind"
Kansas

"Disco Inferno"
Trammps

"Shame"
Evelyn "Champagne" King

"One Nation Under a Groove"
Funkadelic

"Y.M.C.A."
Village People

DANCES

John Travolta features the Hustle
in *Saturday Night Fever*

NEWS OF ROCK

Blondie fuses disco with punk rock . . . Paul McCartney sets record as songwriter with 43 million units sold of his hits . . . Keith Richard gets suspended sentence in Toronto . . . Big year for femme recording artists, with hits by Linda Ronstadt, Rita Coolidge, Heart, Yvonne Elliman, Olivia Newton-John, Roberta Flack, Crystal Gayle and Dolly Parton . . . Bee Gees' "Saturday Night Fever" becomes top seller of all time—getting into 12 million U.S. homes, while becoming worldwide smash . . . Who drummer, Keith Moon, found dead in London flat . . . Out of $4 billion total record and tape sales, Polygram did $1.6 billion, CBS $1 billion and Warner Communications $600 million. The three companies now represent 50% of global sales . . . Rolling Stones' U.S. tour grosses some $6 million, setting a record—along with the $1,060,000 paid by 80,173 at their New Orleans Superdome concert . . . Warner Communications (Warner Bros., Elektra and Atlantic Records) reports that some LPs are costing as much as $500,000 to produce . . . Printed music sales hit a new high of $228 million . . . Sex Pistols' planned nine-day U.S. tour aborts when Johnny Rotten quits and Sid Vicious winds up in hospital for drug treatment . . . California Jam rock festival grosses $2.7 million after spending $1 million for acts . . . Texas Music Festival at Cotton Bowl draws 100,000 . . .

SOME OF THE NEWS THAT INFLUENCED
THE ROCK ERA AND VICE VERSA

Senate extends Equal Rights Amendment ratification to 1982 . . . U.S. importing 8.4 million barrels of oil vs. 1.5 million in 1970 . . . U.S. prices doubled in past ten years—inflation now 9% vs. 2% in 1960 . . . Senate votes to turn Canal back to Panama by year 2000 . . . U.S. opens formal diplomatic relations with China . . . Hubert Humphrey dead at 66 . . . After 2½-year investigation, House Assassination Committee says conspiracy likely in JFK and Martin Luther King killings . . . Ford orders recall of 1.5 million Pintos . . . Kodak convicted of monopolizing amateur photography in antitrust case . . . Haldeman book says Russia proposed joint nuclear attack on China's atomic facilities in 1969 and Nixon rejected idea . . . U.S. smokes two billion less cigarettes . . . Ten-year-old Consumer Federation of America now represents 30 million in 225 groups . . . Two FBI supervisors dismissed for alleged illegal break-ins and wiretaps in early 70s . . . Twelve-day coal strike . . . Big slash in air fares . . . President Carter's decision to delay production of neutron bomb draws criticism. Resigning Major General calls it "militarily unsound" and "ridiculous" . . . Laetrile, considered by some an effective cancer remedy, approved for use by terminally ill patients by U.S. District Court in Denver, despite attempted ban by Food and Drug Administration . . . Carter's "declaration of war" on energy problems ends with passing of Diluted Energy Act of 1978—including much-debated provision to deregulate natural gas . . . Government recommends that dependents of Americans in Iran should leave country as violence and disorder threaten to topple the Shah—an estimated 400,000 anti-Shah supporters in Tehran protest-march headlining the rioting . . . Shell is first petroleum firm to ration gasoline in December . . . Petroleum demand rose again at slowest rate since recession of 1974-75 . . . Legal retirement age raised from 65 to 70, and mandatory retirement at 70 for most Federal employees abolished . . . Unemployment at 3½-year low . . . California referendum cuts property taxes 57%, forcing state and local budget cutbacks and hiring freezes . . . First "test tube baby" born in England . . . Alistair Cooke reports that the Soviet Cosmos 954 satellite (with its nuclear reactor), which crashed in the wilds of Canada, did so by accident—uncontrolled by human skill or computer—with space scientists admitting a few days later that "if the satellite had managed to hobble once more around the Earth, it would have come down close to New York City between eight and nine in the morning" . . .

THE NUMBERS GAME: STATISTICAL INFORMATION
SHOWING HOW LIFE IN AMERICA INFLUENCED
OR WAS INFLUENCED BY THE ROCK ERA

U.S. importing approximately 10.8 million barrels of oil a day, vs. 8.7 million last year, 7.3 million in 1976, and 6 million in 1975 . . . U.S. oil demand is now 18.7 million barrels a day, up 1.4% from 1977. This was a big drop from the 6.9% increase in 1976 and 5% rise in 1977 . . . Approximately 36.8 million labor hours lost in strikes, vs. 6.6 million in 1970—but twice that of years 1960, 1961, 1962 and 1963 . . . 4,000 deaths and 4 million sick days caused by oil emissions alone . . . 1.1 million households of unmarried adult couples—117% increase since 1970 . . . Now 138.2 million TV sets in use, and 444 million radios . . . 51,500 motor vehicle traffic deaths—up from 49,510 in 1977 . . . FBI reports an estimated 10,271,000 arrests in U.S. for year . . . 5,735,000 handguns, rifles and shotguns manufactured and imported—about same amount as 1977 and 1973 with 1974-76 over 6 million—and total for six years over 30 million . . . Estimated 180 billion miles traveled by plane, vs. 10.75 billion by train (excluding commuters)—with 1,500 billion miles on the road traveled by all vehicles . . . Department of Commerce reports consumers spending $240.7 billion on food vs. $70.1 billion in 1960—over three times as much. Expenditures on clothing, personal care and alcohol also tripled in past 18 years, while transportation and housing quadrupled, and recreation quintupled. Medical care is almost seven times more costly. But, pretty much the same happened during the 20 years prior to 1960, with, of course, variations —as population increase and inflation hiked consumer spending from $70.8 billion in 1940 to $325.2 billion in 1960 to current $1,350.8 billion . . . 358 foreign companies now have investments in U.S. manufacturing companies —27% more than in 1977. In the past 10 years, foreign investment in the U.S. has increased by 344% . . . Consumers Union reports Burger King's Big Whopper (flame broiled) contains 3.2 oz. of meat and 4 oz. of bread, while McDonald's Big Mac (fried) has 2.3 oz. meat and 2.9 oz. bread . . . U.S. Bureau of Engraving and Printing now producing $30 million in bills each day on paper strong enough to be folded 4,000 times without tearing . . . Currently 4,600 machines of various sorts in space, and precisely 939 satellites . . . U.S. imports only 25% of total energy consumed, vs. Japan 95% and Germany 60%—yet U.S. shows $10 billion deficit in manufactures vs. Japan $63 billion and West Germany $49 billion surplus . . . Median price for second visit to doctors who are general practitioners is $12 (after first visit at $16). They are averaging 121 office and 31 hospital appointments a week . . .Total income (salary, bonus and other payments) this year for International Harvester President: $1,907,000; Boeing Chairman: $1,227,000; American Broadcasting President: $1,107,000; Ford Motor Chairman: $1,056,000; General Motors Chairman: $975,000; Mobil Oil Chairman: $935,000; Kraft Chairman: $865,000; Procter & Gamble Chairman: $852,000; United States President: $200,000 plus $50,000 for official expenses (taxable) and $40,000 non-taxable travel allowance; while the salary for the head of the University of California is $78,750; University of Pennsylvania $75,000; Princeton $75,000 . . . Over 47.5 million now aged 22-35, vs. 34 million in 1967, as "baby boom" youngsters mature

. . . "Why It's Called the 'Me' Generation" special in *U.S. News and World Report* includes authoritative explanations claiming: (1) Television says, forget about the future, do things today; (2) "The New Narcissism"— where others are seen only as a means for maintaining one's own well-being; (3) Large numbers of self-oriented parents are reluctant to make sacrifices for their youngsters; (4) Ads tend to focus on the individual rather than on families; (5) Inability to form lasting relationships in this highly mobile society; (6) Vietnam, Watergate and similar events caused '60s activists to give up on social improvement and concentrate on self-improvement; (7) Trying to cope in an insane world makes the "me" idea more a question of survival than self-indulgence . . . Department of Labor estimates of annual average jobs opening up between now and 1990 include: Actors, 850; Computer operating personnel, 12,500; Computer programmers, 9,200; Accountants, 61,000; Lawyers, 37,000; Musicians, 8,900; Newspaper reporters, 2,400; Nurses (registered and practical), 145,000; Radio and TV announcers, 850; Retail trade sales workers, 226,000; Secretaries and stenographers, 305,000; and singers' job openings will average 1,600 a year . . . Public Health Service reports an 11% increase in the death rate of 15-24-year-olds vs. an overall drop of 20% in the past 18 years. Chief causes of 15-24 death increase are auto accidents, suicide, drug abuse and murder . . . Average earnings of inexperienced workers in non-Government jobs, according to U.S. Labor Department, are: Accountants, $15,700-$27,300/ year; Bank tellers, $135-$180/week; Computer operators, $160-$300/week; Computer programmers, $365-$465/week; Lawyers, $50,000/year; Office machine operators, $167/week; Receptionists, $155/week; Secretaries and stenographers, $817-$1,085/month; Barbers, $230-$290/week; Bartenders, $3.34-$6.53/hour; Waiters and waitresses, $1.31-$3.45/hour (excluding tips); Secondary school teacher, $15,474/year; College or university faculty, $18,700/year; Carpenters, $10.05/hour; Construction laborers, $8.45/hour; Construction electricians, $11.25/hour; Painters, $9.38/hour; Plumbers, $10.10/hour; Taxicab drivers, $3.90/hour; Local truck drivers, $9.10/hour; Auto mechanics, $9.32/hour; Shoe repairers, $3-$5/hour; Dentists, $50,000/year; Dental assistants, $7,800-$8,400/year; Registered nurses, $275/week; Social workers, $10,300-$13,300/year; Newspaper reporters, $370/week. . . Average life expectancy at birth again increases—reaching record 73.3 years . . . Columbia Pictures pays $9.5 million for film rights to Broadway stage hit *Annie* . . . Average annual soft drink consumption now 36 gallons per capita vs. 12.3 gallons in 1960. Milk now down to 25 gallons a person, vs. 37.9 gallons (topping the list then). Coffee down to 24 gallons, vs. 35.7 gallons in 1960, while beer is up to 23 gallons a person vs. 15.1; tea up to 12 gallons vs. 5.6; wine up to 2 gallons vs. 0.9; distilled spirits up to 2 gallons vs. 1.3; and juice up to 4 gallons vs. 2.7 a person 18 years ago, according to *Progressive Grocer* . . . Now some 169,000 independent (non-chain) grocery stores, vs. almost three times as many in 1940 . . . 600

new health food stores open . . . One out of four new products in super-markets promoted as health-related . . . Cost of preparing almost $44 billion in U.S. advertising amounts to almost $2.5 billion . . . 95% of all cars have radios (106 million out of 444 million radios in use) . . .

TEEN AND COLLEGE LIVING AND
ALTERNATIVE LIFE STYLES IN THE ROCK ERA

Median income of male college graduates now $20,941, vs. $12,960 in 1969—female, $12,347 vs. $7,396 in 1969. Male with high school diploma median $16,396 vs. $9,100 in 1969—female $9,769 vs. $5,280 in 1969 . . . 10.6% of 18-21-year-olds dropped out of high school before graduation because they chose to work; 7.9% for pregnancy; 8.2% for marriage; 6.3% poor grades; 5.4% home responsibilities . . . Supreme Court rules that University of California Medical School's quota system aimed at repressing racial imbalances unfairly discriminated against nonminority candidate, Bakke . . . College enrollment dropped 400,000 in past year—first significant decline since 1951 . . . 40.9% of teachers are in 25-34 age bracket, vs. 26% in 1968 . . . High costs force ten colleges to close down, bringing total for decade to 129—more than double the number of new colleges that opened . . . 6.3 million heads of households 14-25 years old. 2.2% earning $25,000 up a year; 7.6% $15,000-$24,999; 11.6% $10,000-$14,999; 12.8% $7,000-$9,999; and 20.5% under $7,000 . . . Gallup poll reports a majority of parents and their children would like more sex information taught in schools . . . Houston Ballet audience median age now 29—indicating new heavy concentration on the young side . . . Revival of tea dancing in some big hotels by young adults. Hyatt Regency, San Francisco, now one of most popular gathering spots for cheek-to-cheek, 1930s style of dancing . . . 67% of 13-18-year-olds believe in ESP (extrasensory perception), Gallup poll reports, after nationwide survey also finds teenage belief in angels is 64%; witchcraft 25%; clairvoyance 25%; ghosts 20% . . . Current Scholastic Aptitude Test (SAT) for college-bound seniors has 15% scoring 600-800 in mathematics and 8% scoring 600-800 in verbal test—with a score of 600 representing a level of ability considered adequate for successful performance in studies at even the most highly selective U.S. educational institutions. Average score of all students in math was 468 and verbal 429 . . . National Institute of Students opinion poll of high school pupils reports: (1) Most worrying U.S. issues are inflation (51%), crime (46%), energy (32%), unemployment (31%), peace (25%), environment (19%), defense (15%), equal rights (12%). (2) In answer to the question: "Would you cheat on a test if you knew you would not be caught?," 49% said yes, 51% no. (3) Favorite course in school: Physical Education (27%), Mathematics (16%), Social Studies (11%), Science (11%), Fine Arts/Performing Arts (10%), English (7%). (4) Most helpful course in later life: Mathematics (22%), Business courses (18%), Physical Education (7%) . . . Columbia University psychiatrist Richard A. Gardner says: "Today's young people are less likely than their forebears to view the opposite sex as strangers from other planets" . . . Hundreds of thousands of those with 1960s schooling now returning to classrooms for part-time or fulltime study . . . Although overall death rate for all Americans dropped 20% since 1960, it went up 11% for 15-24-year-olds. During past year it jumped by 30% . . .

FASHION: CLOTHES AND THE
ROCK ERA ACCENT ON YOUTH

Note: Feminine fashion is in italics, male in roman, unisex in parentheses, and news in asterisks.

Disco regulars into shiny satin, plunging necklines and skinny pants . . . **Travolta brings back three-piece suits, black shirts and Cuban heels** . . . (Commercial designers move in on punk fashion, with teeshirts and ripped dresses held together by large safety pins) . . . **Author Prudence Glynn says: "Probably the harshest change for women in the 20th century concerned the switch in the (fashion) community's interest from women to girls—all of a sudden, so it seemed, only teenagers were sexy, desirable, worth writing fashion articles for, worth writing music for, worth listening to. Society demolished the dignity and reward of age at precisely the time when medical science had extended the middle period of active life from a likely twenty to forty years"** . . . *Spandex garments inspired by short-lived disco craze* . . . **Sneakers now account for more than 50% of all shoe sales. Current annual sales are 200 million pairs—averaging almost one pair per capita** . . . (Fruit of the Loom and Mickey Mouse teeshirts [celebrating his 50th anniversary] both leading sellers) . . . (Jogging outfits, including special running shoes and visored caps, worn by many non-runners as sports clothes) . . . *Oversize grandpa full shirts with narrow collarbands* . . . *Tawny amber cheek makeup* . . .

FADS (MOSTLY YOUTH-ORIENTED)
RELATED TO THE ROCK ERA

Number of unmarried couples living together now 1,137,000 vs. 523,000 in 1970 . . . Biorhythm fad now multi-million dollar business, with over a million enthusiasts . . . Toga parties make campus comeback as National Lampoon's *Animal House* film focuses on student antics . . .

THE NEW WOMAN IN THE ROCK ERA

Six women selected as astronaut candidates . . . HEW insists on sex equality in sports in granting Federal funds . . . Commerce Department says hurricanes no longer to get all women's names . . . Air Force trains 15 women for missile cruise . . . Federal judge overrules Baseball Commissioner's ban on women reporters in clubhouses . . . U.S. Department of Labor Statistics official says: (1) 50% of U.S. women are working or looking for work, (2) 67% more 25-34-year-olds are in labor market since 1958—and the majority of them are mothers with dependent children at home, and (3) Women are heads of one out of seven families . . . Senate approves extension of Equal Rights Amendment ratification to June 30, 1982—giving proponents time to change the anti-ERA position of three state legislatures . . . NOW declares itself in state of emergency until ERA is ratified . . . Supreme Court rules that individuals can sue educational institutions for sex discrimination . . . Labor Department orders equal opportunity for women on all federal or federally-assisted construction work . . . Supreme Court rules against employers who require women to contribute a greater percentage of their salaries to pension plans than men (because women live longer on the average and are likely to receive 15% more in benefits) . . . NYC Police reverse a longstanding practice and agree to arrest wife-beaters . . . Air Force Academy decides to allow women to remain in school if they become pregnant—but they must leave if they marry, since this is a "permanent condition" instead of a "temporary disability" . . . Family households maintained by a woman with no husband have increased 46% since 1970 . . . 8.2 million families maintained by women—of which 1.3 million have never been married. In the past eight years the total number of female family households has risen by 2.7 million, and single women have accounted for one quarter of this growth . . . 58% of all wife-husband families have more than one earner . . . Record 57.6% of all wives working or looking for work . . . Females comprise over 20% of fatal motor accidents involving drinking drivers, vs. 80% males—and this is cause of about half the fatal accidents . . . After learning how to play the game just a year ago, Kathy Collard, 25, becomes Wisconsin State Billiards Champion . . .

MOSTLY FACTUAL TRIVIA
CONCURRENT WITH THE ROCK ERA

Tennis star Björn Borg earns $50,000 for wearing headband advertising Tuborg beer; $200,000 for donning Fila shirts, shorts, socks and warming suits; $100,000 for using Bancroft rackets, and $2,000 more for having them strung with VS gut. His Tretow tennis shoes added $50,000 and his shoulder patch advertising Scandinavian Airlines another $25,000 . . . Two Pittsburgh contestants kiss for 130 hours and 2 minutes in charity Smoocha-thon . . . Millionaires in U.S. hit 250,000—half of them women . . . Record $70,000 paid for Paul Revere's second ride expense account at auction . . .

Susan B. Anthony $1 coins begin a dismal career . . . Cat named Tiger travels 250 miles from Wausau, Wisconsin, to find his way home to Iowa . . . Japanese farmer develops odor-free garlic . . . Audubon Society reports Snew seen in Rhode Island. It's a white and black Siberian duck first seen in U.S. two years earlier . . . Ali-Spinks boxing gate receipts of over $4.8 million just beats 51-year-old record gate of $4,658,660 for Dempsey-Tunney fight in 1927 . . .

1979 _____

ARTISTS

Rock Groups
  Cheap Trick
  Charlie Daniels Band
  Dire Straits
  Knack
  Police
  Toto

Rock Solo Performers
  Joe Jackson
  Rickie Lee Jones
  Suzi Quatro
  John Stewart

Soul, R&B, Funk Solo Performers
  Stephanie Mills

Middle of the Road
  Melissa Manchester

Cult Groups/Punk/New Wave/
Drone Rock
  Clash

Disco
  McFadden & Whitehead
  Sister Sledge
  Gino Soccio
  Edwin Starr
  Amii Stewart
  Anita Ward

JUKE BOX HITS

"My Sharona"
The Knack

"Do Ya Think I'm Sexy"
Rod Stewart

"When You're in Love with
a Beautiful Woman"
Dr. Hook

"What a Fool Believes"
Doobie Brothers

"Lead Me On"
Maxine Nightingale

"Just When I Needed You Most"
Randy Vanwarmer

"Mama Can't Buy You Love"
Elton John

"Lotta Love"
Nicolette Larson

"Goodnight Tonight"
Wings

"Every 1's a Winner"
Hot Chocolate

"Renegade"
Styx

"Time Passages"
Al Stewart

"Shake Your Body"
Jacksons

"In the Navy"
Village People

"Lonesome Loser"
Little River Band

"Disco Nights"
G.Q.

"Ain't No Stoppin' Us Now"
McFadden & Whitehead

"Gotta Serve Somebody"
Bob Dylan

"Bad Girls"
Donna Summer

"Reunited"
Peaches & Herb

"Ring My Bell"
Anita Ward

"Fire"
Pointer Sisters

"Knock on Wood"
Amii Stewart

"The Logical Song"
Supertramp

"I'll Never Love This
Way Again"
Dionne Warwick

"After the Love Has Gone"
Earth, Wind & Fire

"Lady"
Little River Band

"We Are Family"
Sister Sledge

"Take Me Home"
Cher

"Love Is the Answer"
England Dan & John
Ford Coley

"Suspicions"
Eddie Rabbitt

"Shake Your Groove Thing"
Peaches & Herb

"Chuck E's In Love"
Rickie Lee Jones

"Promises"
Eric Clapton

"Still"
Commodores

"Le Freak"
Chic

"I Will Survive"
Gloria Gaynor

"Sad Eyes"
Robert John

"Heart of Glass"
Blondie

"Stumblin' In"
Suzie Quatro & Chris Norman

"You Can't Change That"
Raydio

"I Want You to Want Me"
Cheap Trick

"The Gambler"
Kenny Rogers

"Gold"
John Stewart

"Rock 'n' Roll Fantasy"
Bad Company

"Sultans of Swing"
Dire Straits

"Shine a Little Love"
Electric Light Orchestra

"Tragedy"
Bee Gees

"Makin' It"   "Please Don't Go"
David Naughton   K.C. & The Sunshine Band

"A Little More Love"   "Babe"
Olivia Newton-John   Styx

"Hot Stuff"   "Hold the Line"
Donna Summer   Toto

"Don't Stop Till You Get   "The Devil Went Down to Georgia"
Enough"   Charlie Daniels Band
Michael Jackson

NEWS OF ROCK

Platinum albums down to 42 from 112 in 1978. Gold album awards down to 112 from 193 . . . Record business in doldrums . . . Elvis Presley's death investigated . . . Woodstock II festival plans fail to materialize . . . Musicians United for Safe Energy (MUSE) nets over $250,000 at Madison Square Garden concert featuring Bruce Springsteen, Jackson Browne, James Taylor, etc. to help finance anti-nuke groups . . . Disco dies . . . Paul McCartney signs for CBS Records at reported $20 million . . . Eagles reject Ted Kennedy to play Presidential campaign fundraisers for Jerry Brown, as candidates woo rock bands for freebies that sidetrack $1,000 campaign contribution limit . . . Eleven trampled to death in rush for seats at Cincinnati concert by The Who . . . Just before "Damn the Torpedoes," Tom Petty files for bankruptcy, close to $600,000 in debt . . . 54 male and 20 female vocalists had their first No. 1 single record hits between 1970 and 1978 . . . Showaddywaddy first Western group to be televised live by satellite in Cuba . . . Sid Vicious dead in New York . . . Eric Clapton marries George Harrison's ex, Patti Boyd . . . Linda Ronstadt and Jerry Brown ("just good friends") go to Africa for ten days . . . Frank Zappas name fourth child, a girl, Diva, instead of Clint Eastwood, as originally planned. Other three were named Moon Unit, Dweezil and Ahmet . . . Some tickets scalped at $150 on Elton John's Russian tour. Says "audience never got carried away"—just sat politely in seats . . . UNICEF concert at U.N. General Assembly featuring Bee Gees, Rod Stewart, John Denver, Kris Kristofferson, Donna Summer, Earth, Wind & Fire, Olivia Newton-John, Andy Gibb and Abba hopes to raise $100 million from performance and donated copyrights . . . Stones play two Canadian shows in lieu of Keith Richard sentence . . . Anti-nuke concert at Hollywood Bowl features Graham Nash, Peter, Paul and Mary and other stars—as fund-raising concerts for causes spread nationally . . . Retail record prices upped again . . . First digital rock album, Ry Cooder's "Bop Till You Drop," released . . . Chicago deejay Steve Dahl's "Disco Demolition"—burning disco records (brought by fans for discount admission) between games at White

Sox double-header—forces teams to forfeit second game as fans start own fires and mini-riot . . . Dylan's "Slow Train Coming" album confirms his conversion to Christianity . . . Broadway rock musical *Grease* breaks performance record held by *Fiddler on the Roof* at its 3,243d playing. The U.S. production alone is reported to have grossed $70 million—returning $400,000 for every $10,000 invested . . . Manufacturers' shipments of records and prerecorded tapes down 6% from last year. Dollar volume was calculated at $3.7 billion based on suggested retail list price . . . CBS Records fires 120 employees, Elektra/Asylum 20, and RCA, MCA and Casablanca join beginning of big shakeout . . . Industry sources blame slump in record sales on home taping and concentration on superstar product . . . Presley estate, valued at $15 million at time of death, diminished by $7 million in expenditures, including his $47,000 funeral, according to Memphis probate court . . . Bee Gees net around $16 million for 10-week tour . . . Four years ago Kenny Rogers was $65,000 in debt. He's now earning about $13 million a year . . . Billy Joel earned only $7,763 in royalties from his first million-selling album due to the terms of his contract . . . Record albums continue to represent some 90% of the business; with home taping resulting in 14%-29% loss in sales . . . Elvis Presley's estate re-valued at $7.6 million with some $3 million in royalties . . . EMI-Capitol buys United Artists Records and MCA buys out ABC Records . . .Proposed reunion of 1969 Woodstock alumni gets not too good reception at Yaphank, Long Island . . . Many radio stations stop uninterrupted album play in bid to cut down home taping . . . Record Industry Association of America reports sales of $3.676 billion for 1979, vs. $4.131 billion in 1978 . . . Disc and tape sales down 6% in units and 11% in dollar volume . . . ASCAP, performing rights organization, takes in over $100 million for first time to compensate songwriters for public performance of their works on radio, TV, etc. . . . Paul Simon makes $14 million deal for seven albums in switch to Warner Bros. Records from Columbia . . . Now, over half of the highest-rated radio stations in the Top 50 U.S. markets are FM, according to *Broadcasting* magazine . . . "Heroes of Rock 'n' Roll" special on ABC-TV considered "the most ambitious retrospective to date." Among the many featured are Elvis, the Beatles, Rolling Stones and Otis Redding, as well as Buddy Holly, Chuck Berry and Little Richard . . .

SOME OF THE NEWS THAT INFLUENCED
THE ROCK ERA AND VICE VERSA

Iran holds Americans hostage . . . Accident at Three Mile Island nuclear plant . . . Soviet troops move into Afghanistan . . . Pope visits U.S. . . . Anti-nuke rally draws 200,000 in New York City. Jane Fonda and husband Tom Hayden then tour 50 cities in opposition to nuclear power . . . Skylab debris crashes in Indian Ocean and Australia . . . Families of Kent State 1970 shooting victims paid $675,000 by State of Ohio . . . Supreme Court bans husband-only alimony . . . New Surgeon-General report claims 54 million Americans still on cigarettes acquired the habit before they were 21 . . . Supreme Court rules that police cannot stop motorists at random to check licenses and registrations unless there are grounds to believe they are breaking the law . . . Begin and Sadat sign Camp David pact . . . Over 200,000 Chinese invade Vietnam and hold a strip there for nearly a month . . . SALT II treaty between U.S. and Soviet drafted after six years of negotiation; but subsequent discovery of Soviet combat troops in Cuba makes ratification without amendment by Senate doubtful . . . Three Mile Island accident investigating commission reports that owner "did not have sufficient knowledge, expertise and personnel to operate the plant or maintain it adequately." Recommends that reactor operating licenses be subject to periodic renewal after open hearings . . . New cars producing more smog, causing more pollution than expected . . . Cambodia entreats U.N. Security Council to get Vietnamese troops out of country . . . Petroleum demand . . . John Mitchell last Watergate prisoner freed. 25 men served 25 days to 52½ months for Watergate crimes . . . Shah leaves Iran—Khomeini returns . . . Carter asks Congress for power to order gasoline rationing . . . Justice Department investigates Carter family peanut business bank loans . . . Carter orders gradual phasing out of controls on domestic oil prices . . . Carter approves MX missile—which would be deployed along railroad tracks . . . Odd-even day gasoline sale restrictions in New York and Connecticut as shortage spreads . . . Senate rejects proposed amendment to end electoral college and have direct popular vote for President . . . Panama takes control of Canal Zone . . . Congress allows car makers a fourth air pollution cleanup delay—until 1982 . . . Senate passes "Windfall" oil tax which should channel $178 billion in oil industry extra profits resulting from price decontrol over next 11 years . . . Howard Johnson's bought by British company for $630 million. Foreign companies now totally or partially own: Lifebuoy soap, Imperial margarine, Taster's Choice coffee, Ovaltine, Magnavox TV, Scripto pens, Baskin-Robbins ice cream, Wish-Bone Dressing and Libby's canned goods . . . Billy Carter confirms that Libya paid for trips to Rome and Tripoli in 1978 . . . National Cancer Institute official tells Senate committee that if lung cancer deaths related to cigarette smoking are subtracted from recent totals, "total cancer mortality has been declining overall" . . .

THE NUMBERS GAME: STATISTICAL INFORMATION SHOWING HOW LIFE IN AMERICA INFLUENCED OR WAS INFLUENCED BY THE ROCK ERA

U.S. now has 71 operational nuclear reactors generating 19,320,000,000 kilowatt hours of electricity . . . U.S. average inflation for decade is

7.2%—under Britain, Italy, Japan and France, but 2.2% over West Germany . . . EPA reports smog a serious problem in 25% of nation's 32,000 counties; but carbon monoxide pollution has declined at a rate of 6% annually since 1970, and levels of other auto pollutants have also dropped . . . 66% of U.S. cities still dumping partially-treated sewage in adjacent waters every day; but about 36,000 of the major industrial polluters are meeting their cleanup deadlines. This amounts to 90% of all major U.S. factories now complying with 1970 federal air pollution standards, with 7,000 monitoring stations in operation . . . Consumer prices rise 13.3%—largest annual increase in 33 years . . . Chrysler loss for year possibly biggest in U.S. corporate history—$1.1 billion . . . More than twice as many women hold fulltime jobs (45% of all women) as did ten years ago (17%) . . . Birth rate down to 15.8 per thousand from 1947 high of 26.6 per thousand "war babies" . . . U.S. handgun murders total 9,848 vs. France 800; United Kingdom (including Northern Ireland), est. 55; Canada 52; Japan 48; Sweden 21. Now 50-60 million handguns in private hands in the U.S. 1968 Gun Control Act prohibits sale of weapons through the mail and importation of certain cheaper handguns ("Saturday Night Specials") but doesn't ban importation of parts for such guns which can be assembled here . . . Without the machines which brought in this year's $60 billion agricultural crop, the U.S. would have required 30 million farmhands and 60 million mules. $100,000 farm machines can now harvest $100,000 worth of soybeans in a day . . . Baseball star Pete Rose signs with Philadelphia Phillies for four-year minimum guarantee of $2,980,000 and a maximum of $4,035,000 over five years; Rod Carew's five-year California Angels contract calls for $4.5 million and Dave Parker's five-year deal with the Pittsburgh Pirates totals $3,875,000—or $775,000 a year . . . Pro football salaries range from $350,000 high and $102,606 average for quarterbacks and $733,358 high with $66,516 average for running backs, down to $72,600 high and $48,354 average for kickers . . . Home study courses averaging $500 to $700 a course . . . Steve McQueen, Burt Reynolds, Clint Eastwood and Marlon Brando each now earning well over $3 million for each film, vs. early 1930s weekly salaries of Edward G. Robinson, $1,975, Joan Crawford, $1,950 and James Cagney's $1,000—all considered extremely highly paid at the time . . . This year 20% of all doctors made over $100,000 after expenses and half of these made over $125,000. Only 29% of all doctors made $50,000 or less . . . Average daily salt consumption now 6-18 grams, vs. maximum 3 gram recommendation of Food and Nutrition Board of National Academy of Sciences . . . *Consumer Reports* analysis discloses that a fast-food milkshake may contain as much as 8-14 teaspoons of sugar . . . Small cars involved in 55% of all fatal accidents, although they represent only 38% of the number of cars on the road . . . U.S. cars now average 14.29 miles per gallon, vs. 13.79 m.p.g. in 1968 . . . Snack food annual sales hit $3.8 billion—with $1.7 billion for potato chips, $1 billion for nuts, $485 million for corn chips, $170 million for pretzels and

$95 million for prepopped popcorn . . . Coca-Cola tops soft drinks with 26.3% of market; Pepsi-Cola has 17.6%; 7-Up 5.9%; Dr. Pepper 5.4%; Sprite 3.1%; Royal Crown Cola 3%; Tab 2.9%; Mountain Dew 2.4%; Diet Pepsi 2.3%; Diet 7-Up 1.1%, according to *Beverage Industry Magazine* . . . Now only 171,000 service stations, vs. 226,459 just seven years ago . . . 475,000 videocassette recorders sold—18% over last year—with VHS systems 60% to Beta's 40% . . . Average list price (before discounting) of videocassette recorder $1,283—up 9% over last year . . . Estimated 315,000 home (micro) computers sold, vs. 172,000 last year . . . Now 6,600 health food stores with over $1.6 billion in sales, vs. 1,000 stores with $140 million in sales only nine years ago . . . 26% of 1,353 consumers surveyed in national random sample shop in health food stores . . .

TEEN AND COLLEGE LIVING AND
ALTERNATIVE LIFE STYLES IN THE ROCK ERA

National Institute of Student Opinion (NISO) opinion poll shows 26% with money worries regarding college, 54% without, and 20% not intending to go . . . Harvard's new undergraduate curriculum turns from general introductory courses to highly specific ones, emphasizing how one approaches knowledge rather than sets of facts . . . More than 45,000 public school teachers strike for higher wages, affecting 865,000 students . . . Supreme Court decides that individuals have the right to sue schools for sex discrimination . . . Record 94% 14-17-year-olds enrolled in high school, vs. 86.2% at beginning of Rock Era . . . Gap between public and private college tuition has grown from $416 yearly in 1956 to more than $2,000 today . . . Northwestern University lost $1 million last year, Yale's shortfall was $2 million, and SMU is wrestling with a cumulative deficit of $6 million as costs go up and endowments down . . . Inflationary pressures hit colleges, with Stanford's annual energy bill now $3.9 million from $1.6 million three years ago, with similar increases hitting U.S.C., now one of Los Angeles' top ten electric consumers . . . Hazy optimism of 1960s blamed for current problems of college survival, with soaring enrollments causing overbuilding and overstaffing. As Northwestern's Vice President, Lee Ellis, puts it: "We let ourselves get fat" . . . Greater number of girls 17-24 smoking than boys in same age group. 26% of the girls 17-18 smoke, vs. 19% of the boys . . . National Institute of Students opinion poll asked, "Would you hold a job though rich?" 78% voted yes, vs. 22% no . . . More than 100 Connecticut teenagers (13-18) organize registered lobbying group: National Alliance of Teenagers. In aiming to make it a national voice, they initially focus on the Equal Rights Amendment, criminal justice system, state funding of schools and teen representation on state and local school boards . . . FBI reports that between 600,000 and a million young people run away from home each year—and that almost all teenage prostitutes start as runaways . . . Nearly a third of all college freshmen (31.5%) receiving federally-funded "Basic Educational Opportunity Grants" vs. 21.7% last year . . . Killings at or near theaters showing "The Warriors" attributed to youthful assailants who had seen the film . . . Carnegie Foundation study finds widespread "negative behavioral traits" among students, teachers and administrators on college campuses. 47% of the students surveyed believed successful students had to "beat the system" to make the grade . . . Pat Boone pays $5,000 into $175,000 Acne-Statin fund for reimbursement to those who purchased skin preparation that was sold through false advertising, according to the Federal Trade Commission. The ad agency had to ante up another $60,000 . . . Massachusetts sixth state to raise legal drinking age in past 2½ years— from 18 to 20. Iowa, Minnesota and Montana had raised theirs to 19, Maine to 20 and Michigan to 21. Chicago restricts drinking in bars to 21 years up. After 18-year-olds won right to vote in 1971, 18 states lowered the legal age—after which teenage alcoholism and liquor-related accidents showed a sharp rise . . . Major concern in raising drinking age is "trickle-down effect," with high school seniors buying liquor for younger teenagers . . . More 16-17-year-olds now hold jobs—30.6% vs. 23.9% just nine years ago . . . Michigan aims to increase youth votes by deputizing high school principals as voter registrars . . . House of Representatives rejects attempts to require 18-year-old males to register for military draft . . . Teenagers (15-19) have average income of $2,370. The 20-24-year-olds average $7,014 . . . Page one story in *New York Times* entitled "Changes Wrought By the 60s Youth Linger in American Life" gives *New York Times*/CBS poll results: Now 55% of the populace see nothing wrong with premarital sex— well over double the number in a Gallup poll taken in 1969, during the month of the Woodstock Festival. Also, 25% now approve the full legalization of marijuana—vs. 12% in 1969 . . . NISO poll of high school students reports 78% have a hero vs. 22% none. Ratings were: (1) Steve Martin, (2) Erik Estrada, (3) Burt Reynolds, (4) John Wayne, (5) Jerry Lewis, (6) Andy Gibb, (7) Clint Eastwood, (8) Robin Williams, (9) Lou Ferrigno, (10) Cheryl Tiegs. 53% say inflation has altered their family's standard of living; with costs being cut by: lower energy use (41%); eating out less (24%); less new clothing (10%); cheaper food (11%); less use of car (9%) . . . University of California philosopher, John R. Searle, who served on the President's Advisory Commission on Campus Unrest in 1970, says: "What we've got is an interpenetration of the generations; people find they are no longer so far apart . . . I am deeply struck by the fact that we now have a great deal of tolerance for all kinds of life styles. There has been a terrific decline of political activity since the '60s, but an awful lot of the cultural changes are still with us" . . . *The New Narcissism* author Christopher Lasch agrees that young people have brought more social tolerance to American life . . . Harvard sociologist, David Riesman, declaring that "the counterculture has triumphed" also decries "the tyranny of enlightenment," saying: "It is marvelous to have relaxation of the older constraints from which Sinclair Lewis fled, but in many places the newer values have such near-total hegemony that people with older values are persecuted" . . . High school seniors name inflation as the nation's greatest problem—62% vs. 47% last year . . . In Encyclopaedia Britannica poll, asked who they consider the greatest person in the world, 43% name their mothers and/or fathers— with less than 1% naming any U.S. political or government figure. Nearly two-thirds expect the U.S. to be in a major war before the year 2000, and 51% think war will come within the next decade. At the same time, 89% say their high school years have been happy . . .

FASHION: CLOTHES AND THE
ROCK ERA ACCENT ON YOUTH
Note: Feminine fashion is in italics, male in roman, unisex in parentheses, and news in asterisks.

Return of button-down shirts, preppy ties and classic loafers (with tassels) . . . **American jeans manufacturers negotiating with Soviets to set up factories there** . . . *Quilted nylon jackets, previously worn by motorcyclists, sailors and sports people, now brightly colored and worn for non-sports activities . . . Lycra and other stretch fabrics graduate from swimwear and ski trousers to skin-tight "disco" dresses and flared skating skirts . . . Jumpsuits enjoy full range of popularity from common use to metallic evening wear . . . Very small collars on shirts and blouses—worn casually unbuttoned at throat . . .* **Leather, tight denims and cottons, wool and synthetic mixtures, and tough denims greatly in demand as clothes take on appearance of having been designed for long life** . . . **Revlon-owned Balmain introduces one of the world's most expensive perfumes, Ivoire, selling at $125 an ounce** . . . **Men's fragrances bring in $445 million—almost seven times 1963 total—mostly (65%) bought for them by women** . . . *Gloria Vanderbilt jeans* . . . (Unisex jogging uniforms) . . . (Black teeshirts emblazoned with insignia of rock groups) . . . *Body glitter worn to discos* . . . (Rainbow-striped suspenders inspired by TV's Mork) . . . Western-styled suede jackets for city cowboys to wear over jeans . . . *Girls wearing men's bow ties and sleeve garters . . . Decorative chopsticks as hair ornaments* . . . **Producing one out of every three pairs of jeans sold in the U.S., Levi's current annual output is 143 million garments, of which 127 million are pants** . . . (Head & Shoulders, Prell and Suave shampoos in virtual three-way tie as market leaders—selling one third of all U.S. shampoos between them) . . . *Softer type jeans new fashion favorite, but tight-as-tight-can-be pants that cup the rear are still in the lead . . . "Designer" jeans appear, with better tailoring and higher prices, offered by Gloria Vanderbilt and her peers, and gaining instant acceptance . . . Jump shorts worn with a wide elasticized belt for roller skating . . .* (Terry cloth headbands, inspired by tennis star Björn Borg—worn dead straight, Indian fashion) . . .

FADS (MOSTLY YOUTH-ORIENTED)
RELATED TO THE ROCK ERA

"Space Invaders" ignites coin-operated video game craze . . .

SOME OF THE MORE WIDELY USED ARGOT,
JARGON AND SLANG IN THE ROCK ERA

Boom boxes, Ghetto blasters (large portable tape players that serenade not only their owners but everybody else within earshot) . . . Buzzwords (important-sounding words or phrases—used out of context to impress others) . . .

THE NEW WOMAN IN THE ROCK ERA

Chris Evert's tennis earnings, 1973-79 ($2,550,339) almost equal Björn Borg's for same period ($2,620,516). Other top woman all-time career earners are Martina Navratilova ($1,670,767, 1974-79), Billie-Jean King ($1,246,035, 1968-79) and Virginia Wade ($1,205,246, 1968-79) . . . N.L.R.B. rules that unions have right to data from employers on number of women workers . . . Eight women get U.S. Navy sea duty on combat vessels. Now 5,130 women in Navy . . . Woman judge rules against Yale co-eds in their sexual harassment suit against professor . . . Suffragette Susan B. Anthony first woman to appear on U.S. coin . . . Supreme Court rules that individuals can sue educational institutions for sex discrimination . . . D.C. District Court dismisses Sears Roebuck suit against ten Federal agencies, charging that laws and guidelines on equal employment are so confusing, they can't comply (Sears is largest employer of women after AT&T) . . . Los Angeles Superior Court finds no legal basis for either an expressed or an implied contract between Michelle Triola Marvin and actor Lee Marvin, in her suit for half his $3.6 million earnings during their 6½ unmarried years together; but landmark decision ruled that unmarried partners had certain property rights if there was such a contract or "some other tacit understanding" . . . Oregon man first to be prosecuted for raping his wife when they lived together. Oregon, Iowa, Delaware and New Jersey had revised their laws to eliminate rape immunity of spouses . . . Only 16 of 45 women who run for Congress win—two fewer than 1976 . . . Women increase their seats in state legislatures from 706 to 770—10.2% of the national total . . . Jane M. Byrne becomes first woman mayor of Chicago with more than 80% of the vote—largest share since 1901 . . . Amendment to 1964 Civil Rights Act requires employers with medical disability plans to provide equal conditions for pregnancy . . . Air Force assigns women pilots to cargo planes and refueling tankers for tactical aircraft—brings end to combat ban closer . . . Six current astronauts in training are women—the first to be admitted to the program . . . Supreme Court ruling in favor of absolute hiring preferences for veterans in sex discrimination suit considered setback—until consideration that male non-vets have same disadvantage . . . Women's rights leaders believe greatest defeat came when Congress, for third straight year, denied use of Medicaid benefits for most abortions . . . Kansas City, Missouri, District Judge upholds NOW to pursue a convention boycott against any state that hasn't ratified ERA . . . One-third of workers holding second jobs are women—double the proportion of ten years ago . . . First woman editor-in-chief for 101-year-old *Yale Daily News* . . . U.S. proposal that both male and female names be adopted for hurricanes accepted by a committee of the World Meteorological Organization . . .

MOSTLY FACTUAL TRIVIA
CONCURRENT WITH THE ROCK ERA

Lone Ranger ordered to unmask by court as producers hire younger replacement . . . Illinois Congressman charges Honest Abe Lincoln with padding expense account. He put in for a 3,252-mile round trip from Washington to Springfield, Illinois, at 40¢ a mile, whereas it's only an 1,800-mile trip . . . Largest payout in Las Vegas slot machine history, $295,000 from a $3 machine, beats last year's record $275,000 (also from a $3 slot) . . . Kentucky Fried Chicken Original Dinner contains 830 calories, vs. Burger King Big Whopper with 606, McDonald's Big Mac with 541, half a ten-inch Pizza Hut Thin & Crispy Pizza with 450, Arthur Treacher Fish Sandwich with 440, McDonald's Filet-O-Fish 402, Taco Bell Taco 186, McDonald's Chocolate Shake 364, and Burger King French Fries 214 . . . After breaking her "Charlie's Angels" TV contract and seeing her career fade in two past film flops, Farrah Fawcett fires the manager who promoted her in the first place . . . Kellogg's Sugar Frosted Flakes are 56% sugar; Fruit Loops 48%; Post's Sugar Crisps 46%; Chex 32%; Cap'n Crunch 32%; Raisin Bran 29%; vs. Shredded Wheat 1%; Cheerios 3%; Kellogg's Corn Flakes and Special K 5%; Post Grape Nuts 7%; and Wheaties 8%, according to U.S. Department of Agriculture . . . 10 million pounds of gum now chewed annually . . . Bestselling candy bars now: (1) Snickers, (2) Reese Peanut Butter Cups, (3) M&Ms Peanut, (4) M&Ms Plain, (5) Hershey's Chocolate Bar with Almonds, (6) Three Musketeers, (7) Kit Kat, (8) Hershey's Milk Chocolate Bar, (9) Milky Way, (10) Baby Ruth, (11) Butterfinger, (12) Nestlé's Crunch, (13) Almond Joy, (14) Reese Crunchy Peanut Butter Cups, and (15) Mounds . . . Aerosol deodorants now outselling rollons . . . Leading beer brands now: (1) Budweiser, (2) Miller, (3) Pabst, (4) Miller Lite, (5) Coors, (6) Schlitz, (7) Michelob . . . Bestselling spirits in U.S. are now: (1) Bacardi Rum, (2) Smirnoff Vodka, (3) Seagram's 7 Crown Whiskey, (4) Seagram's VO, (5) Canadian Club, (6) Jim Beam Bourbon, (7) Popov Vodka, (8) J&B Scotch, (9) Seagram's Gin, (10) Gordon's Gin . . .

1980

ARTISTS

Rock Groups
  AC/DC
  Air Supply

Rock Solo Performers
  Pat Benatar
  Irene Cara
  Kim Carnes
  Christopher Cross
  Rupert Holmes
  Kenny Loggins

Soul, R&B, Funk Groups
  Cameo
  The Gap Band
  Lipps Inc.
  Ray Parker, Jr., and Raydio
  Ray, Goodman & Brown
  Shalamar

Soul, R&B, Funk Solo Performers
  Stacey Lattislaw
  Prince

Cult Groups/Punk/New Wave/
Drone Rock
  Gary Numan
  Pretenders

JUKE BOX HITS

"Another Brick in the Wall"
Pink Floyd

"Call Me"
Blondie

"Magic"
Olivia Newton-John

"Do That to Me One More Time"
Captain & Tennille

"Crazy Little Thing Called Love"
Queen

"Rock with You"
Michael Jackson

"Coming Up"
Paul McCartney

"It's Still Rock & Roll to Me"
Billy Joel

"Escape (The Piña Colada Song)"
Rupert Holmes

"Funkytown"
Lipps Inc.

"The Rose"
Bette Midler

"Working My Way Back To You"
Spinners

"Ride Like the Wind"
Christopher Cross

"Shining Star"
Manhattans

"Sexy Eyes"
Dr. Hook

"This Is It"
Kenny Loggins

"Sailing"
Christopher Cross

"Coward of the County"
Kenny Rogers

"Lost in Love"
Air Supply

"On the Radio"
Donna Summer

"All Out of Love"
Air Supply

"Emotional Rescue"
Rolling Stones

"Cruisin' "
Smokey Robinson

"Upside Down"
Diana Ross

"Don't Do Me Like That"
Tom Petty & Heartbreakers

"Don't Fall in Love with
A Dreamer"
Kenny Rogers & Kim Carnes

"Steal Away"
Robbie Dupree

"With You I'm Born Again"
Billy Preston & Syreeta

"Little Jeannie"
Elton John

"Let's Get Serious"
Jermaine Jackson

"Ladies Night"
Kool & The Gang

"Cool Change"
Little River Band

"Longer"
Dan Fogelberg

"Let My Love Open the Door"
Pete Townshend

"More Love"
Kim Carnes

"Cupid"/"I've Loved You
for a Long Time"
Spinners

"I Can't Tell You Why"
Eagles

"An American Dream"
Dirt Band

"Special Lady"
Ray, Goodman & Brown

"She's Out of My Life"
Michael Jackson

"Brass in Pocket"
Pretenders

"Fire Lake"
Bob Seger & The Silver
Bullet Band

"Him"
Rupert Holmes

"Against the Wind"
Bob Seger & The Silver
Bullet Band

"Heartache Tonight"
Eagles

"Better Love Next Time"
Dr. Hook

"Send One Your Love"
Stevie Wonder

"How Do I Make You"
Linda Ronstadt

"Dim All the Lights"
Donna Summer

"Pilot of the Airwaves"
Charlie Dore

"We Don't Talk Anymore"
Cliff Richard

"Romeo's Tune"
Steve Forbert

"Stomp"
The Brothers Johnson

"Tired of Toein' the Line"
Rocky Burnette

"Daydream Believer"
Anne Murray

"Let Me Love You Tonight"
Pure Prairie League

"Give Me the Night"
George Benson

"Fame"
Irene Cara

DANCES

Proms an institution again, as
anti-prom sentiments of '60s no
longer seem valid

The Jog—a new seven-step
disco dance

Revived interest in tap dancing
via Gregory Hines

The Pump (punk rock)

NEWS OF ROCK

John Lennon murdered in New York . . . Campaign to make Bruce
Springsteen's "Born to Run" New Jersey state song . . . Born-again
Christian Bob Dylan tours U.S. . . . Capricorn Records, flagship of 1970s
Southern boogie, goes bankrupt . . . Pink Floyd's "Dark Side of the
Moon" sets record 303 weeks on *Billboard* hit chart seven years after its
release . . . McCartney spends ten days in Tokyo jail . . . Rolling Stone
Bill Wyman announces intention to leave group in 1983 with 20th anniver-
sary of his joining . . . Elvis Presley autograph on Las Vegas hotel paper
napkin brings over $1,000 at auction . . . Mint copies of Beatles'
"Yesterday and Today" album with "Butcher Cover" selling for $500.
Less than 1,000 were released before recall, and another 8,000 had the
regular cover pasted over the pop art "horrifier" . . . Presley Sun Records
singles selling for around $200 mint . . . Prerecorded audio tapes account
for 39% of prerecorded music volume—20% over last year—while records

declined to 61% of the pie from 68.8% in 1969. Albums account for 90.7% of disc sales, with singles declining to 9.3% from just 10% last year . . . Disco record sales dropped to 1% of the overall total from last year's 9.2%. In reporting this, the National Association of Record Merchandisers noted just under 3% gains for rock, pop and country, and a 1% gain for M.O.R. . . . Almost 2,500 have lost their music business jobs and are not being replaced . . . First videodisc catalog from MCA DiscoVision includes "Elton John at Edinburgh," "Olivia" and "Abba"—all at $19.95 . . . RCA SelectaVision videodisc division licenses seven Presley films, including *G.I. Blues*, *King Creole* and *Girls, Girls, Girls* . . . Linda Ronstadt stars in Broadway smash hit musical revival of *The Pirates of Penzance* . . . At one point in mid-year, over 75% of the top-selling record albums are by artists who have been cutting records for over ten years . . . Arista Records President, Clive Davis, points out that no modern decade in popular music has begun very auspiciously—in terms of era-defining trends—adding that new ground was not broken, and no one style emerged as a dominant force, and that without one mass sound, "All music is splintering" . . . At his death, John Lennon was worth nearly $235 million. He had been receiving $12 million a year in royalties, and owned 25% of Apple Records . . . Led Zeppelin drummer, John Bonham, dead at 32 . . . Some Top 40 radio stations using more talk while restricting play-lists to fewer records . . . Many discos have to revert to playing live acts to keep their businesses going . . . Juke box business shows signs of fatal decline, with number of boxes now 251,000-388,000, down from 400,000-500,000 in 1973. Operators now buying some 45 million records a year, vs. 75 million seven years ago . . . Fleetwood Mac album, "Tusk," reported to have record $1 million in recording costs . . . Both *Time* and *Newsweek* devote their covers to John Lennon . . . Record Industry Association of America reports a sales drop of 34 million units for the year—even though (because of price increases) the total gross sales of over $3.6 billion were $6 million up from last year . . . Single record shipments drop to 157 million units from 212 million in 1979; 190 million during 1976, 1977 and 1978; 164 million in 1975, and 204 million in 1974, according to RIAA. Albums down to 308 million from 344 million in 1977 and 341 million in 1978; but up from 290 million in 1979 . . . At Canadian Stadium concert, the Who, Heart, J. Geils and others gross over $1 million. At Yale Bowl, the Eagles, Heart and Little River Band also top $1 million for a single concert . . .

SOME OF THE NEWS THAT INFLUENCED
THE ROCK ERA AND VICE VERSA

Reagan defeats Carter in landslide victory, and Republicans take control of Senate for first time in 26 years . . . Iran holds U.S. hostages. April attempt to rescue hostages fails dismally . . . 19 million natives of Puerto

Rico, Cuba and Mexico now in U.S., vs. 3.1 million in 1960 . . . Five atomic power plants ordered to close . . . First race riots since mid-1960s in Miami . . . Mount St. Helens volcano erupts in Washington State, with explosion 2,500 times greater than Hiroshima bomb . . . Windfall Profits Tax Act imposes tax on oil producers to offset increased earnings caused by decontrol of domestic crude oil—allowing it to rise to world petroleum levels . . . U.S. Olympic Committee decides to boycott Moscow Games in response to call by President Carter . . . For second time in week, U.S. nuclear forces begin to move into action following computer error warning of Soviet attack . . . Voyager I sends back first ever closeup pictures of Saturn . . . Government buys 14.5 million tons of wheat, corn and soybeans embargoed from delivery to Soviet Union because of Afghanistan invasion. In defending move, Vice President Mondale mentions possible use of it in producing alcohol for gasohol fuel . . . Surgeon-General reports lung cancer in women increasing to point where it can overtake breast cancer as leading female cancer killer in three years—adding that the first signs of epidemic of smoke-related disease among women are now appearing . . . Abscam bribe scandal involves 31 officials including a U.S. Senator and seven Representatives . . . All 1979 foreign cars and most domestic models subjected to 35 mile-an-hour crash tests fail to protect occupants . . . After auto industry announces sharp drop in sales and a decline of 22% in new home construction is announced, President Carter admits that a "short" recession has probably begun . . . Bert Lance cleared of bank fraud . . . Pennsylvania Health Department Epidemiology Director says Three Mile Island accident had little effect on health . . . National Research Council Food and Nutrition Board reports no evidence to recommend reduction of cholesterol or fat by healthy persons—contradicting advice by 18 major health organizations during past decade . . . First override of a Presidential veto by a Congress controlled by the President's own party in 28 years quashes Carter's proposed oil import fee to discourage energy consumption. $4.62 a barrel levy would have upped consumer cost per gallon by 10¢ . . . Synthetic Fuels Bill signed. Goal is 500,000 barrels of oil a day by 1987 and 2 million by 1992 from alternative sources . . . General Motors reports the first loss since the Depression in a quarter when there has been no strike. Ford and Chrysler also report record losses . . . Senate investigates White House role in Billy Carter receiving Libyan loans and registering as their agent . . . Shah of Iran dies . . . John Anderson runs as third party Presidential candidate . . . Carter refuses to debate Reagan and Anderson . . . Nuclear missile silo explodes—but no leaks in warhead to cause environmental contamination . . . Maine voters defeat referendum to shut down nuclear plant . . . End of recession seems in sight . . . Iraq attacks Iran . . . Justice Department report released by Special Senate Subcommittee investigating Billy Carter's relationship with Libya claims that President Carter had not cooperated fully with the investigation . . .

New report by insurance industry indicates that imported sub-compact cars continue to have worst record in accident claims . . . House approves Senate bill creating $1.6 billion fund to deal with dangerous toxic waste dumps and chemical spills . . . U.S. International Trade Commission bars highest tariff to limit car imports—blaming Detroit's problems on consumer taste for smaller cars and economic downturn . . . Chrysler tells Government it will need $400 million loan guarantee in addition to $800 million already guaranteed to keep producing cars . . .

THE NUMBERS GAME: STATISTICAL INFORMATION SHOWING HOW LIFE IN AMERICA INFLUENCED OR WAS INFLUENCED BY THE ROCK ERA

Top 10 franchise fast food companies now: McDonald's, with 18.2% of U.S. market; Burger King, 6.3%; Kentucky Fried Chicken, 5.2%; Wendy's International, 4.4%; American Dairy Queen, 3.7%; Pizza Hut, 3.4%; Hardee's, 3.3%; Denny's, 2%; Jack in the Box, 1.8%; Sambo's 1.8%. Top 10 saw 15.2% business increase in past year, reports Commerce Department . . . Estimated 5 billion world population by 1990, vs. 1 billion in 1850 . . . Inflation rise of 1.6% in January—largest monthly rise in five years . . . Pennsylvania State Health Department report on effects of Three Mile Island accident notes "surprising" persistence of anxiety among local residents—with sleeping pill users up 11.3% and an 88% increase of users of tranquilizers . . . Now 45% of married mothers with children working outside the home—leaving 7 million children needing care, with only 1.6 million licensed day-care openings . . . Number of one-parent families up 50% in ten years. One child in five lives with one parent—eight out of ten with the mother . . . 100 top national advertisers hike advertising spending to estimated $13 billion—11% over 1980. Ford and Chrysler increase ad budgets as sales and earnings drop . . . Total U.S. expenditure for advertising estimated at $54.6 billion, virtually double total of six years ago, $26.8 billion . . . The ten bestselling drugstore products ranked by dollar volume: (1) Polaroid SX70 film, (2) Kodak Kodacolor film C-110, (3) Tylenol tablets, (4) Pampers disposable diapers, (5) Crest toothpaste, (6) Tylenol Extra-Strength capsules, (7) Dexatrim diet pills, (8) Kodak PR10 instant film, (9) Oil of Olay, (10) Kodak Kodacolor C-135 film . . . The world population reached 4.5 billion at 2:42 P.M. on March 14, according to the Environmental Fund's population clock in Washington . . . Census Bureau reveals number of unmarried couples triples in past ten years to 1.56 million from 523,000. Also, one-person households are 23% of all households (17.8 million), and the median age of first marriage for men rose to 24.6 years from 23.2 in the past ten years—women to 22.1 from 20.8 . . . Agriculture Department estimates that it costs $69,232 to raise a child through age 17 in moderate circumstances; and costs $8,600 more to send she or he to a public university for four years. The average cost of a private law degree is $19,516 . . . Between the early 1960s and late 1970s, American imports of manufactured goods have increased by 2,000%. Now importing almost $12 billion more automobiles and trucks than we export . . . U.S. now last among world's industrial nations in annual rate of productivity growth . . . Patents awarded to Americans peaked in 1971 and the number issued since then has been dropping 7% a year . . . If inflation continues but gradually drops off to about half the present rate, the average annual wage in the year 2025 will be $162,000, according to a Social Security Administration projection . . . Fast food outlets show another sharp rise in past year; sales of hamburgers, hot dogs and roast beef over $14.5 billion, up 14.3%; pizza over $2.3 billion, up 9.9%; chicken over $2.4 billion, up 8.7%—and all fast foods over $24.7 billion, up 11.9%, according to the Commerce Department . . . Labor Department study predicts 66.4 million job openings in the 22 years from 1978 to 1990 . . . Average annual per capita consumption of principal foods shows marked change since 1957-59 (average): Red meats: 151.4 lbs. vs. 131.4 lbs.; Poultry 62.2 lbs. vs. 33.5 lbs.; Cheese 17.9 lbs. vs. 7.9 lbs.; Processed vegetables 58.5 lbs. vs. 49.9 lbs.; while sugar is down to 85.6 lbs. a person vs. 96.1 lbs. in 1957-59; Butter now 4.6 lbs. vs. 8.2 lbs. and fresh fruits now 85.9 lbs. vs. 95.5 lbs. . . . Autos recalled by manufacturers down to 5 million from 9 million last year, and record 12.6 million in 1977 . . . Record low 20 major U.S. airline accidents, with 14 deaths, vs. yearly average of 258 deaths in the 1970s . . . FBI reports serious crimes up 9% over last year . . . U.S. oil imports down to about 5.1 million barrels a day from 10.8 million barrels average in 1978 and 7.3 million in 1976 . . . U.S. produced 4.3% of world's crude oil, vs. USSR 19.7% and Saudi Arabia 16.7% . . . Labor Department reports that during November it took $25.62 to buy goods and services that costs $10 in 1967 . . . Cancer mortality continues decrease for people under 45 and now begins drop for 45-49-year-olds . . . Worst year in U.S. automobile history—with total manufacturers' loss estimated $4.06 billion. General Motors, which sold 45.9% of all cars bought in U.S., has first full year loss since 1921 . . . Justice Department reports that 30% of nation's 80.6 million households were victimized by one or more crimes. Violent crimes were experienced in 6% of all homes; and members of 14% of the households experienced personal larceny away from home . . . It costs $5.47 today to buy what $1 purchased in 1940 . . . Working-order radio sets total 456 million—of which 333 million are home and personal sets and 123 million out-of-home receivers, according to estimates by Radio Advertising Bureau . . . Estimated 7% of all processed food products now labeled "natural," according to *Consumer Reports* . . . The movie business sets a new record, with a $2.8 billion gross from a billion ticket buyers . . .

TEEN AND COLLEGE LIVING AND
ALTERNATIVE LIFE STYLES
IN THE ROCK ERA

46.3% of the unemployed are aged 15-24 . . . New draft plan by President Carter passed by Congress and male-only registration follows in July . . . U.S. Court of Appeals, in Richmond, rules that high school officials could prohibit the distribution of underground newspapers that encourage "actions which endanger the health or safety of students" after student editors file suit on the basis of the First Amendment guarantee of freedom of the press when their paper carrying a full-page "head shop" ad is banned. The court rules that minors aren't protected by the First when a possibly damaging activity is being promoted . . . Teenage unemployment rises to 18.7% in November from 16.3% in January . . . Paying money to play on high school football team is growing trend, according to National Federation of State High School Associations. Started in Minnesota 5-6 years ago, budget cuts spread concept. Californians now paying as high as $50 to play on some school football teams; but qualified students can work off costs if unaffordable . . . Percentage of high school seniors who smoke daily down to 21% from 29% in 1977, reports University of Michigan study of 17,000 students. Heavy smoking (half a pack or more a day) among female students now falling at quickening rate—after continuous climb since 1977 . . . In 2030, it's estimated that two people will be contributing Social Security funds for each of today's teenagers. This year an average 3.2 are contributing, but back in 1960 it was as high as 5 . . . More 13-year-old girls than boys expected to complete four years of high school math, reports Education Commission of the States; and trend could bring more women into traditionally male-dominated fields of science and engineering . . . UCLA and American Council on Education poll shows current class of college freshmen more interested in power, status and making money than at any time in past 14 years—now 62.7% vs. fewer than 50% in late '60s . . . FBI and National Collegiate Athletic Association probes reveal grade fixing and fraudulent credits for athletes—allegedly involving 25 schools. Credits for college entrance for athletes who had never attended the schools listed also under investigation in scandal reminiscent of late 1930s college football cleanup . . . U.S. Department of Agriculture reported to have notified schools that they must adopt new federal rule, barring the sale of "junk food" until after the last lunch period. Specifically banned are carbonated sodas, gum, frozen ice desserts, and some candies providing less than 5% of the recommended daily allowance for eight basic nutrients . . . 20% of total public expenditures ($172 billion) goes to those 21 and under for education, welfare and Social Security . . . *Senior Scholastic* sees potentially poor bets in jobs for youth in the 1980s as: stenographers, farm workers, bus drivers, telephone operators, taxi drivers, laborers, tailors, butchers, bakers, barbers, gas station attendants and the like. As job areas likely to be good bets they list: dental hygienists, environmental science teachers, computer specialists, air traffic controllers, legal and medical secretaries, air conditioning mechanics, flight attendants, bulldozer operators, child care workers, electricians, plumbers, practical nurses and medical lab technicians . . . One million teenage girls getting pregnant each year (30,000 age 14 or under). Two of every three are unmarried . . . For those between the ages of 14 and 24 accidents are leading cause of death and disability—with increase in traffic accidents blamed on greater use of alcohol, as well as drugs, by the young . . . Now 74.9 million Americans aged 0-20 years (33.7% of population), vs. 80.8 million 10 years ago (39.5%). Almost 6% drop as "war babies" age. This estimated to dip another 2.6% by 1990—making the young less than a third by then. Now persons under 21 heading crime rates, with 78.1% auto theft, 73.8% burglary, and 65.2% arson—but only 29.3% murder and 36% aggravated assault . . . *U.S. News and World Report* youth special concludes: "Public protests of years past have largely vanished mainly because of recognition that today's complex problems defy ready answers. Energy shortages, soaring inflation, rampant unemployment and the threat of war have made adult Americans jittery, and that sense of pervasive worry has been passed along to the nation's youth. The result is that young people have turned inward, but they are neither the selfish "me" generation portrayed by some critics, nor retreads of the happy-go-lucky youngsters of the '50s . . . If there is any word that fits this present crop of youngsters, say observers, it might be "anxious" . . . University of Michigan study of 17,000 graduating high school students reports 90% want children, almost 75% say happy marriage and good family life extremely important, and 50% feel regular smoking of marijuana could cause a great health risk, vs. 35% in 1978. Also, nearly 80% of the high school seniors are averaging 16-20 hours a week in paying jobs . . . Now 7.4 million 14-15-year-olds; 8 million 16-17; 8.1 million 18-19; 8.1 million 20-21; 11.9 million 22-24-year-olds . . . While the number of households has increased by 27% in the past ten years, the number of people living in them has increased by only 12% . . . A leading underground newspaper of the 1960s, the *Berkeley Barb*, ends publication with weekly readership down to about 2,500 from a peak 90,000-plus in 1969 . . . Rock papers and magazines have virtually disappeared from the market . . . Attempts to outlaw sale of drug paraphernalia through "head shops" spread nationally, with the shops being outlawed in Alabama, Colorado, Connecticut, Delaware, Florida, Idaho, Indiana, Louisiana, Maryland, New York and Virginia. Similar laws are vetoed in Tennessee and declared constitutionally vague in Georgia and West Virginia . . . The National Center for Educational Statistics finds 25% of all public schools have one or more computers for instructional use . . . Among college undergraduates, the second most common major in 1967, business and management, is now number one choice—displacing education and making up 20% of all majors . . .

FASHION: CLOTHES AND THE
ROCK ERA ACCENT ON YOUTH

Note: Feminine fashion is in italics, male in roman, unisex in parentheses, and news in asterisks.

(Preppy look popularized by bestselling book and new conservatism. Ralph Lauren and other designers update classic styles) . . . **National Hairdressers Foundation President urges members not to deplore the punk style, "which will certainly go down in history along with beehives for women and Mohicans for men"** . . . (Jeans and cowboy fringes big on campuses) . . . *Shorter skirts seen as forerunner of things to come—worn with thick colored and textured tights, giving a totally different and more modest look than the leggy, sexy style that surfaced in the 1960s* . . . **Vidal Sassoon, London's haircutting innovator who set many of the new styles of the "Swinging Sixties," hits $100 million turnover with salons and hair products** . . . **Model of the Year, Cheryl Tiegs, to earn $1.5 million over five years from Cover Girl cosmetics, while Clairol uses her as their convincer for Clairesse hair coloring** . . . **Sales of men's deodorants, aftershave lotion, colognes, talcum powders and skin creams now over $1 billion a year** . . . **Now 75 different items in Aramis line for men—first introduced in 1954 as cologne, aftershave and soap** . . . **Disco audiences wearing everything from vinyl jeans and heavy metal teeshirts to campus casuals, crushed velvet, lace and granny prints** . . . *Newest shoes have low or medium curved heels. Ballerina flats and conical-heeled pumps standard items along with white and black stockings, wooly tights and high socks* . . . **Wrangler jeans found guilty of trademark infringement by Ninth District Circuit Court of Appeals in suit won by Levi Strauss & Co. concerning use of a pocket tab** . . . *Pastel sweatshirts and polos with white denim jeans* . . . *Cameo pins* . . . (Brush cuts for boys and girls) . . . (Surgical pants like those in M*A*S*H and other dyed high-tech clothes like chefs' and waiters' jackets) . . . *Clothes layering beginning with a pair of long johns* . . . *Two-piece thermal suits* . . . *Short-sleeve knit top and leggings* . . . *Homemade earrings created from lacquered candy* . . . (Sweat pants tucked into boots) . . . *Sleep shirts worn as dresses over tights* . . . *Leather belts worn backwards* . . . *Long blouses with rugged, baggy pants* . . . *Oversized colored paperclips as barrettes* . . . (Over-the-knee socks for skateboarders, with special cushioning in the knees) . . . *Scented nail polish* . . . *Scatter pins that fasten to skirts* . . . *Low-heeled pumps with the new shorter length* . . . (Spread of preppy fashions for pre-college youth repopularizes teen boys' button-down shirts, navy blue blazers, khakis sitting low on hips and above ankles, Top-Sider shoes, candy-striped shirts—while pre-college girls favor navy blue cardigans [partly unbuttoned], boys' shirts—preferably white and hand-me-down—tartan skirts, navy blue cable-knit kneesocks, Blucher moccasins, gold-button earrings for pierced ears, and men's Timex watches on ribbon watch bands) . . . (College fashions spreading to all walks from preppy trend including girls' turtlenecks, Lacoste shirts, gold hoop earrings, Oxford cloth shirts, cuffless khaki pants [from men's stores], down vests and short hair, and anything with a duck on it. College men reviving pink Oxford cloth shirts, Lacoste [alligator] shirts, worn with collar up, corduroy pants, deck and tennis shoes, button-down shirts, and moccasins) . . .(Tube socks) . . . **G. H. Bass Co., in Wilton, Maine, reports tripled production of their Weejun loafer (a prep and college favorite) to 6,000 a day** . . . (Country and Western influence repopularizes cowboy and Indian stylings—with wide leather fringe trimmings on hems and yokes; fringed moccasins; and beaded headbands over girl's hair parted in the middle with a plait on either side) . . . *Cornrow hair stylings, popularized by Bo Derek in the film 10—with tiny plaited strands of hair hanging straight down from all over the scalp, decorated with all kinds of finery, such as colored beads or shells . . . Bracelets purchased by the dozen—jingling in equal numbers on both wrists . . .*

FADS (MOSTLY YOUTH-ORIENTED) RELATED TO THE ROCK ERA

Rubik's Cube . . . Pocket-sized stereo cassette players with lightweight earphones (e.g. Sony Walkman) . . . "Who Shot J.R.?" miscellany plus takeoffs on theme of TV's "Dallas" anti-hero . . . "Mooning" returns via Preppies (see 1955) . . . Gatoring has Preppy, or reasonable facsimile thereof, yelling "Gator!," at which all fall to the floor and imitate alligators . . .

SOME OF THE MORE WIDELY USED ARGOT, JARGON AND SLANG IN THE ROCK ERA

Current College Argot (see 1965 and 1970) includes: Blow out (fail a course or upchuck) . . . Booting (losing your lunch) . . . Bucking (cutting classes) . . . Busting G.Q. (dressing in high fashion) . . . Busted (now has meanings other than police arrest—for example, being "busted" in conversation by a snappy rejoinder) . . . Cake course (snap course) . . . Clapping for Credit (Music Appreciation) . . . Easy ace (A—top mark) . . . Flag (F—failing grade) . . . Flaming (terrific) . . . Gorge out (suicide threat) . . . Gomes (from Gomer Pyle—those who carry calculators hooked to a belt or who can be seen in shorts with black socks and loafers off campus) . . . Grub (n: a grind, v: cramming) . . . Gut course (snap course) . . . Hook (C grade) . . . Intense (terrific) . . . Lay-tah (see you later) . . . Mick (for Mickey Mouse) . . . Monday Night at the Movies (Art of Film) . . . Monkeys to Junkies (Anthropology) . . . Nerd (see 1954) . . . Nudes for Dudes (Art) . . . Pencil Geeks, Cerebs, Weenies, Wonks,

Gnurds, Tools, Squid, Ink Squirters (overly diligent students) . . . Pig out (overeat) . . . Plato to NATO (European Civilization) . . . Power tower (administration building) . . . Pulling an all-nighter (cramming) . . . Rents (parents) . . . Stars for Studs (Astronomy) . . . Tza (pronounced Zah) or Za (pizza) . . . Veg out (turn into a vegetable) . . .

As Preppy culture spreads, mid-1950s and 1960s words for diligent students are repopularized, specifically: Cereb, Gome, Grind, Grub, Nerd, Spider, Squid, Tool, Weenie, Wonk . . . And even-older terms for inebriation, including: Bombed, Loaded, Looped, Polluted, Smashed, Tight, Wasted, Wrecked . . . Other revived argot (and it's all in how one says it) includes: Bagging z's (napping) . . . Blow-out (big party) . . . Cute (super) . . . Game (a good sport) . . . Gross (disgusting) . . . Lame (weak) . . . Neat (swell) . . . Out to lunch (confused) . . . Panic (funny person) . . .

THE NEW WOMAN IN THE ROCK ERA

Illinois fails to ratify ERA (by five votes). Still needs three more states to approve by June 30, 1982—on top of 35 now in . . . Another setback for ERA when Republican National Convention's platform committee drops its 40-year endorsement . . . First woman to head motion picture studio, Sherry Lansing, 35, named President of 20th Century-Fox Productions . . . 35 women graduate from Annapolis, 61 from West Point and 97 from the Air Force Academy . . . Congress rejects Carter's plan to register both women and men for the draft. ACLU files suit to halt registration but fails . . . Women earning only 59¢ for every dollar men earn. Same earnings gap as 1939 means women have to work nearly nine full days to earn what a man makes in five . . . Women with four years of college still earn less than men with eighth grade educations . . . 50% of all women have jobs that are 70% female and 25% have jobs that are 95% female. Only 6% are managers, and only 17% belong to unions . . . Thirty women become New Jersey state troopers . . . Jane Cahill Pfeiffer, NBC Chairman, earning $425,000 a year; Rosemary Sena, Senior Vice President at Shearson Hayden Stone, $300,000; Katherine Graham, President of the *Washington Post*, $375,000; Joan Hanley, Chairman of Time-Life Books, $203,000; among nation's top earners . . . 26-year-old Julia Y. Cross first woman secret service agent to die in the line of duty in counterfeit investigation . . . San Jose State University professor fired and University of California assistant professor suspended after allegations by women students of sexual harassment. Both actions come in the wake of increasing vocal protests by women's organizations, alleging widespread sexual harassment on U.S. campuses . . . Kellogg agrees to spend $575,000 to settle female job discrimination charges and to allot 40% of future job openings for laborers and mechanics to women . . . Firestone Tire and Rubber barred from doing business with the Federal Government until it complies with anti-discrimination orders with an Affirmative Action program in Orange, Texas . . . Motorola, Inc., will spend $5 million to provide a new college-level program to train women and minorities in electronics technology . . . Iowa City's first female firefighter, who had been suspended for breast-feeding her baby at the firehouse, awarded $2,000 in damages and $26,400 for lawyer's fees by Iowa Civil Rights Commission . . . Ford Motor Company settles job discrimination case involving women and minorities with $23 million for individuals and special training programs—also undertaking employment goals that will eliminate job inequalities . . . Army conducts investigations at Fort Bragg, N.C., and Fort Meade, Md., to determine the amounts of sexual harassment after complaints from women soldiers . . . Women's unemployment rate 7.4% vs. men's 6.9% . . . Women receive almost 50% of all college bachelor's degrees, vs. 33% in 1960; and one-third of undergraduate business degrees, vs. only 8.1% in 1971. At master's level, 22% of 1980 degrees go to women, vs. 4% in 1971 . . .

MOSTLY FACTUAL TRIVIA
CONCURRENT WITH THE ROCK ERA

Lockheed boasts that their largest aircraft in world, the C5-A, can hold 25,844,746 ping-pong balls or 3,222,857 tortillas . . . Doctor Harry Monsen of Illinois College of Medicine says all the chemicals and minerals in the human body are now worth $7.28, vs. 98¢ in 1969 . . . Hundredth anniversary of patent of George Eastman's first successful roll film . . . Baseball pitcher, Jim Palmer, wins out over other famous male athletes with sexy bodies for massive and highly successful advertising campaign aimed at women in their own magazines . . . When consumer protector, Betty Furness, displays skin lotions ranging in price from 45¢ to $35 on TV, a dermatologist finds the major difference between the lowest and highest price is that the $35 one uses purified water . . . New York auction gets record $210,000 and $230,000 for two 19th-century Hawaiian two-cent missionary stamps. Previous top for U.S. single stamp was $135,000 . . . Mickey Mouse Club celebrates its 25th anniversary as reruns continue . . . Average annual yogurt consumption per person now 41.8 oz., vs. 13.6 oz. in 1970—a 207.4% increase in 10 years . . .

1981 _____

ARTISTS

Rock Groups
  Go-Go's
  Loverboy

Rock Solo Performers
  Marty Balin
  Lindsey Buckingham
  Phil Collins
  Sheena Easton
  Juice Newton
  Stevie Nicks
  Rick Springfield
  Billy Squier
  Steve Winwood

Soul, R&B, Funk Solo Performers
  Jermaine Jackson
  Rick James
  Debra Laws
  Teena Marie
  Lionel Richie, Jr.
  Grover Washington, Jr.
  Deniece Williams

Folk & Country
  Alabama
  Oak Ridge Boys

Young Teen Oriented
  Adam & The Ants

Middle of the Road
  Cliff Richard

Disco
  Fantasy

JUKE BOX HITS

"Endless Love"
Diana Ross/Lionel Richie, Jr.

"Bette Davis Eyes"
Kim Carnes

"(Just Like) Starting Over"
John Lennon

"Physical"
Olivia Newton-John

"Celebration"
Kool & The Gang

"Keep On Loving You"
REO Speedwagon

"9 to 5"
Dolly Parton

"Jessie's Girl"
Rick Springfield

"Arthur's Theme (Best
You Can Do)"
Christopher Cross

"Morning Train (9 to 5)"
Sheena Easton

"Rapture"
Blondie

"Theme from Greatest American
Hero (Believe It or Not)"
Joey Scarbury

"Kiss on My List"
Daryl Hall & John Oates

"Being with You"
Smokey Robinson

"I Love a Rainy Night"
Eddie Rabbitt

"Stars on 45 (Medley)"
Stars on 45

"Queen of Hearts"
Juice Newton

"Just the Two of Us"
Grover Washington, Jr.

"The Tide Is High"
Blondie

"A Woman Needs Love"
Ray Parker, Jr., & Raydio

"Slow Hand"
Pointer Sisters

"Angel of the Morning"
Juice Newton

"Woman"
John Lennon

"The Best of Times"
Styx

"Love on the Rocks"
Neil Diamond

"The One That You Love"
Air Supply

"Sukiyaki"
A Taste of Honey

"Take It on the Run"
REO Speedwagon

"Urgent"
Foreigner

"(There's) No Gettin' Over Me"
Ronnie Milsap

"Hearts"
Marty Balin

"Every Woman in the World"
Air Supply

"Lady"
Kenny Rogers

"I Don't Need You"
Kenny Rogers

"I Love You"
Climax Blues Band

"Hit Me with Your Best Shot"
Pat Benatar

"Start Me Up"
Rolling Stones

"Private Eyes"
Daryl Hall & John Oates

"Waiting for a Girl Like You"
Foreigner

"For Your Eyes Only"
Sheena Easton

"Trouble"
Lindsey Buckingham

"Elvira"
Oak Ridge Boys

"Hungry Heart"
Bruce Springsteen

"Stop Draggin' My Heart
Around"
Stevie Nicks with Tom Petty
& Heartbreakers

"Hooked on Classics"
Royal Philharmonic Orchestra

"Who's Crying Now"
Journey

"All Those Years Ago"
George Harrison

"The Stroke"
Billy Squier

"Let's Groove"
Earth, Wind & Fire

"I Can't Go for That
(No Can Do)"
Daryl Hall & John Oates

"Young Turks"
Rod Stewart

"Leather and Lace"
Stevie Nicks with Don Henley

"Every Little Thing She
Does Is Magic"
Police

"Games People Play"
The Alan Parsons Project

"I Can't Stand It"
Eric Clapton & His Band

"Hey Nineteen"
Steely Dan

"The Beach Boys Medley"
Beach Boys

"Oh No"
Commodores

"Don't Stop Believin'"
Journey

"Passion"
Rod Stewart

"While You See a Chance"
Steve Winwood

"It's My Turn"
Diana Ross

"Feels So Right"
Alabama

"In the Air Tonight"
Phil Collins

"Another One Bites the Dust"
Queen

"This Little Girl"
Gary "U.S." Bonds

NEWS OF ROCK

Estimated 5 million Sony Walkman and similar pocket-size stereo cassette players with lightweight earphones sold as demand soars . . . John Lennon murderer, Mark David Chapman, pleads guilty after being promised that his sentence would not exceed 20 years to life imprisonment . . . Smash hit "Stars on 45" medley of Beatles hits leads to 1960s revival on records, with medleys imitating the Beach Boys, Four Seasons and others leading to compilations of the originals . . . Now that $8.98 LP list price is established industry standard, EP records (mini-LPs) containing four to six tracks at $4.98 or $5.98 list are bringing in some big sellers—especially with new artists . . . Top 40 stations in Chicago losing out in listening ratings to those catering to 25-49-year-old age group—stations with wider rock formats, playing much larger selections of old and new records. WLUP, the station most committed to heavy metal, down to 3.5 from 4.7 a year ago; and WMET, which does things like playing the Doors all one weekend, is tied with them at 3.5—up from 3.2 a year ago . . . *Hair* director, Tom O'Horgan, signed to helm Broadway-styled theatrical revue based on "Stars on 45" medley concept—with song and dance routines covering the last 30 years . . . RCA Selectavision videodiscs into first made-for-video music production with RCA Records—taping ex-Fleetwood Mac member Bob Welch with Stevie Nicks, Mick Fleetwood and Christine McVie in a show titled "Bob Welch and Friends—Live at the Roxy." The 75-90 minute show is also licensed for a cable TV special on the Warner Amex MTV music channel . . . John Denver and opera singer Plácido Domingo make Top 10 album chart with "Perhaps Love" duet at about same time classical music is scoring on the pop charts, with the Royal Philharmonic Orchestra's "Hooked on Classics" LP in Top 10 with their combination of "Stars on 45"-type medleys of Beethoven, Bizet and peers augmented by an electronic rhythm section . . . With Linda Ronstadt heading the cast of the Broadway hit musical adaptation of *The Pirates of Penzance*, producers rush to sign other rock names. Andy Gibb plays in the Los Angeles *Pirates*. Donny Osmond will play the title role in the George M. Cohan musical *Little Johnny Jones* when it comes to Broadway—taking over from David Cassidy, who starred on tour. Debby Boone is set for Broadway's *Seven Brides for Seven Brothers*, and Cher for *Come Back to the Five and Dime, Jimmy Dean, Jimmy Dean*—with David Bowie having already scored there when he took over the leading role in *The Elephant Man* last season . . . Elvis Presley's physician acquitted on all counts of prescribing excessive amounts of narcotics, sedatives and amphetamines to Elvis, Jerry Lee Lewis and seven other patients . . . RCA and Warner/Elektra/Atlantic raise list price for 45 r.p.m. records to $1.99—the third singles price increase from $1.29 just two and a half years ago . . . Reported collector's asking price of $1,200 for rare Presley "Speedway" soundtrack album (monaural) on RCA Records; the Beatles' "Yesterday and Today" with butcher block cover on Capitol quoted at $400, and Buddy Holly's "That'll Be the Day" on Decca (monaural) at $100 . . . Harry Chapin killed in auto crash . . . Bill Haley, who started it all, dies of natural causes at age 56 . . . "Rod Stewart: Tonight He's Yours—Worth Staying Home For! Live from Los Angeles Forum" TV concert is the biggest worldwide rock TV special since the "Elvis From Hawaii" show in 1973. Scheduled in 85% of the U.S., the show is also seen on a one-day delay in Australia, New Zealand, Europe, the Far East and Central and South America . . . Rolling Stones, in setting all-time record on U.S. tour, gross over $1.3 million for one performance at Louisiana Superdome, New Orleans; $1.05 million at San Diego Stadium;

$1.1 million at Rich Stadium, Orchard Park, New York; $1.9 million for two performances at the Tangerine Bowl, Orlando, Florida; and $2.9 million for two in Philadelphia for which the Stones received $500,000. The 40-city tour was expected to gross $25 million—which was easily surpassed. Madison Square Garden received about 1.2 million pieces of mail for their ticket lottery, and the Brendan Byrne Arena in New Jersey, pulling from almost the same area, received another 500,000 . . . Playing regular auditoriums, comparative newcomer, Foreigner, on tour, grossed $147,000 in Buffalo, over $287,000 for two performances in Philadelphia and $149,000 in Hartford, Connecticut . . . Rolling Stones tour statistics exceed all early estimates with gross at about $35 million, as over 2 million people buy tickets. Sales of teeshirts, program, badges and other souvenirs bring in approximately $10 million, and sponsorship by a perfume manufacturer brings in over $3 million more. It is estimated that the tour, which was masterminded in every tiny detail by former London School of Economics student, Mick Jagger, earned almost $4 million for each Stone . . . Epic sweeps CBS Records vaults for a four-record sampler of rockabilly roots (entitled "Rockabilly Stars, Vol. 1 and Vol. 2"), as neo-rockabilly stirs excitement among new generation of record buyers; although it has yet to show overwhelming commercial impact . . . Estimates on value of Presley estate much higher than at time of death. State of Tennessee Department of Revenue puts its worth at $31 million, while the Internal Revenue Service has it pegged at $25 million, asking for $14.6 million in taxes in a case pending in U.S. tax court at Memphis . . . Diana Ross signs contracts with RCA Records and EMI Records, reportedly for a total of $18 million for an unspecified number of albums over a period of years . . . Digital-audio stereo due in late 1982 or early 1983 utilizes laser beams and 5-inch long-playing albums. At outset, albums should cost about $14 and players between $500 and $1,000 . . . Sony Walkman (tiny portable cassette player) sales 1.5 million worldwide in first year—as many competitors also show booming sales figures . . . Record dealers now selling homevideo games along with LPs—as both cartridges for play on home TV (through use of player consoles) and hand-held, battery-operated computer games and puzzles show big sales gains following roaring success of Space Invaders and other coin-operated video games during past two years. Games are retailing for $15 to $40—while the top-selling Atari console sells for $129-$159 and Mattel's Intellivision for $239-$279 . . . Paramount Pictures Home Video Division plans to sell 3 million videodiscs during 1982 . . . RCA Selectavision Vice President, Tom Kuhn, announces introduction of stereo videodiscs in mid-1982; adding that the hot dark horse for future software is music, although movies are selling best at present . . . RCA Selectavision survey discloses that consumers owning videodisc players six months or longer have collected nearly 22 albums . . . Radio station WABC, New York, the nation's leading Top 40 station for the past two decades, switching to largely talk format next year—as Top 40 radio becomes an endangered species in most markets, according to *Variety*. Still a potent force in the market four years ago, with billings of about $9 billion, as Top 40 audience fell off, WABC station income has dipped to perhaps half that amount, per industry estimates . . .

SOME OF THE NEWS THAT INFLUENCED
THE ROCK ERA AND VICE VERSA

President Reagan and Pope John Paul II recover from assassination attempts . . . Reagan wins Congressional approval of $35.1 billion 1982 budget cut and 23% tax reduction through 1983. Reagan administration introduces "supply side economics"—reducing taxes to give people more money in their pockets to buy goods and services (on the "demand side") . . . Crude oil prices actually dropping—with $32 top in some markets— and gasoline approaching $1.20 a gallon in some parts of the U.S. . . . Domestic energy consumption drops by unexpected 6.4%. Conservation is main reason, although depressed economy an influence . . . Dependence on foreign oil drops 20% to 5.4 million barrels a day from 6.8 million last year . . . Iran releases 52 American hostages, held for 444 days, moments after Reagan inauguration . . . Reagan abolishes remaining oil price controls. Estimated 12¢ rise in gasoline prices before year end foreseen . . . Senate votes to increase Federal debt limit by $50 billion to $985 billion . . . Justice Department developing five-point plan to fight violent crime. It includes making murder for hire Federal offense; allowing judges to consider community safety in setting bail; new protection for crime victims and witnesses; a Federal law to provide an increased or mandatory sentence for crimes involving the use of a weapon for unusual violence; a victim compensation fund . . . Reagan proposes significant lowering in the level of nuclear confrontation in Europe . . . Use of coal for energy continues to rise as nuclear industry in stall because of Three Mile Island accident . . . Alaska crude oil production shows increase—with new and expanded oil discoveries in Gulf of Mexico, Michigan, and the West—principally due to Federal decontrol of "new" oil prices . . . In attempts to curb lagging sales, Ford and General Motors institute record rebates running from $500 to $1,700 . . . Space shuttle Columbia completes two successful missions . . . Poland's Communist leader, Wojciech Jaruzelski, declares martial law in violent showdown with the trade union Solidarity and its leader Lech Walesa . . . U.S. Meat Animal Research Center reports that optimum conditions have been worked out for producing methane (the principal ingredient in natural gas) from animal dung . . . Miners get 38% increase in wages and benefits as 72-day-old strike, which cost them more than $50 million a week in wages, ends . . . 13,000 air traffic controllers dismissed by Federal government after calling illegal strike . . . Senate votes 52 to 48 to sell AWACS radar planes to Saudi Arabia, overturning negative vote in House of Representatives, as President Reagan personally enlists support for controversial bill . . . Commerce Department plans to hire 100 new investigators to help other police agencies closely monitor illegal exports of computers, heavy industrial machinery and microelectronic equipment that could help Russia reduce U.S. superiority in technology . . . At year end, scientific, cultural and educational exchanges with Soviets almost at a standstill . . . Plan to bolster NATO with new American Pershing II and Cruise missiles in 1983 inspires big anti-nuke demonstrations in Europe—with London, Rome, Paris and Brussels protests bringing out 500,000 marchers . . . Israel Prime Minister Menachem Begin denounces Saudi peace plan . . . Jordan's King Hussein follows Washington courtship with announcement that he is buying his first Soviet weapons . . . Budget Director David Stockman tells magazine interviewer that Reagan's tax cuts would probably not revive the economy, and that supply side doctrines are no more than "a Trojan horse" for tax relief to the rich . . . Reagan appeals to Russia for mutual reductions on nuclear arsenals . . . National Security Adviser, Richard V. Allen, involved in first major Administration scandal over $1,000 gift from Japanese journalists after Nancy Reagan interview . . . After issuing executive order permitting the CIA, for the first time, to mount covert operations in the U.S. and collect intelligence from U.S. citizens even if they are not suspected of working for a foreign agency, President Reagan says that "No intelligence agency . . . will be given the authority to violate the rights and liberties guaranteed to all Americans . . . but an approach that emphasizes suspicion and mistrust of our intelligence efforts can undermine this nation's ability to confront the increasing challenge of espionage and terrorism" . . . Former Lebanese terrorist claims that Libya's Qadhafi has sent an assassination squad to the U.S. to murder the President . . . No hope for balanced budget as Federal deficit soars, with new estimate $100 billion for 1982 . . . Reagan clamps economic sanctions on Soviet Union for "a heavy and direct responsibility for the repressions in Poland." European allies of U.S. refuse to follow suit . . . Unemployment reaches 8.4% in December, with 9 million out of the 107 million-person work force jobless . . . Predicted inflation rate for year down to 8.9%, compared to 12.4% in 1980 . . . Auto manufacturers report worst sales year in more than two decades . . . First test-tube baby born in U.S. hospital . . . National Academy of Sciences reports that marijuana smoking has some undesirable short-term effects, but finds that reliable evidence is too scanty for conclusions about potential long-range perils . . . Government to advise parents, doctors and druggists against use of aspirin for children in the treatment of chicken pox or flu-like symptoms . . . Also warns against starch-blocker diet aids that have swept country . . . Congress approves $200 billion military compromise measure for current fiscal year . . . Baseball strike lasts 49 days, with 712 games canceled—about 34% of the 1981 season. Fans show little sympathy for either side as 650 Major League players, whose average salary is $173,000 a year, lose an estimated $28 million pay during walkout, while owners lose about $116 million over insurance payoffs . . .

THE NUMBERS GAME: STATISTICAL INFORMATION
SHOWING HOW LIFE IN AMERICA INFLUENCED
OR WAS INFLUENCED BY THE ROCK ERA

Survey estimates overall employment in computer field will rise to 2,140,000 in 1990, from 1,158,000 reported in 1978—an increase of 85% . . . Minimum wage now $3.35 per hour, from $3.10 (1980), $2.90 (1979); $2.65 (1978); $2.30 (1976); $2.10 (1975); $2.00 (1974); $1.60 (1967) . . . Now the ages at which young people marry are very similar to the ages at which they married between 1890 and 1940 . . . The four-person household with a $10,000 gross income in 1970 now needs $22,477 to keep up the same standard of living. The rise in prices over the past decade has cut the purchasing power of the dollar by more than half . . . Now 71 nuclear power reactors in U.S., out of 189 in entire world . . . 10.9% of U.S. electricity produced by nuclear power, vs. 2.4% in 1971. Now 4.5% less from hydro sources and 8.1% less from gas . . . Analysis of 1980 Census reveals: (1) About 90% of the nation's net population growth since 1970 occurred in the South and West; (2) As many blacks moved to the South as left it since 1970—halting many decades of migration North and West; (3) Less than 10% growth in population during past decade vs. 13.3% (1960-70) and 18.5% (1950-60) . . . Now 25.5 million people over 65 years old—an increase of 28% over the 1970 figure. The median age rose from 28 to 30 over the past decade partly because people are living longer and partly because children under 15 dropped from 58 million to 51 million . . . Average American eating 283 eggs a year . . . House Subcommittee releases list of 2,100 places around the country where industrial wastes may be contaminating ground water supplies . . . Environmental Protection Agency reports 80 billion pounds of hazardous chemical wastes being generated annually, but only 10% is being disposed of properly . . . Advertising on commercial television up another 11% to $12.6 billion—and this doesn't include cable . . . All food prices up 9% from last year. Food away from home up 10%; beef up 6%; pork up 11%; poultry up 7%; fish and seafood up 10%; fruits and vegetables up 13%; sugars and sweets up 9%; non-alcoholic beverages up 6% . . . Films take in estimated $2,978,000,000 at U.S. box offices with estimated ticket sales of 1,027,000,000 vs. 1,022,000,000 last year and 1,033,000,000 in 1979 . . . November unemployment 8.4% vs. 7.5% last year. Teenage jobless 21.8% vs. 18.6% in 1980 (minority teenagers 41.3%, vs. 36.6%) . . . Nielsen year-end estimates report 85% of all U.S. TV homes now have color sets; 15% black and white only; 51% have two or more sets; 26.5% cable—and 98% of all U.S. homes own at least one set . . . Spending on recreation up 321% in 16 years from $58 billion to $244 billion. TV, radio, records and musical instruments top purchases with $21.6 million; admission to amusements ranks 6th with $6.4 million annual outlay. Swimming is top participating sport, with 105.4 million annual swimmers, topping 69.8 million bicyclists, 60.3 million campers. Fishing gets 59.3 million annual participants; bowling 43.3 million; boating 37.9 million; jogging/running 35.7 million. Auto racing tops spectator sports with 51 million annual attendance; horse racing is next with 50.1 million; Major League baseball draws 43.7 million; college football 35.5 million; college basketball 30.7 million; harness racing 27.4 million; greyhound racing 20.8 million and NFL football 13.4 million . . . 96,600 "Pac-Man" coin-operated video games produced in U.S. to date. "Asteroids" came second with 70,000 vs. 60,000 "Space Invaders" . . . Color TV sales top 11 million for first time—2.4% over 1980. Projection TV gains 112.9% over last year, with sales of 121,650 units, vs. 57,132. Videocassette recorder sales up 69.1% with total over 1.3 million units . . . Home video games in 8% of U.S. TV homes, vs. 2% a year ago . . . Overall consumer electronics business up 500% in past 15 years . . . Over 2,000 home video software outlets open for business, vs. few previous establishments . . . Since 1979 the official "poverty" population has risen by nearly 6 million; and in the same period "real" family incomes have dropped around 10%, after increasing roughly 80% since 1950 . . . Overseas travel up to 8 million annually from fewer than 700,000 in 1950 . . . Ability of the economy to produce more wealth for time worked vanished in past five years. 1981 productivity no higher than 1977 . . . Theme park industry predicts 170 million attendance in 1982 and expenditure of $800 million in salaries and wages plus utilities and food and beverage services . . . $9.2 billion in retail sales dollars spent on video products. By 1985 that amount expected to jump to $15.4 billion . . . Spectator sports earn $2.3 billion this year vs. $2 million in 1950. Books are up to $4.1 billion from $2 million; but cultural events only boosted their 1950 $2 million figure to $1.3 billion, according to study by CBS Economics and Research Department . . . American Petroleum Institute reports consumer gasoline use down to 6.6 million barrels a day this year (same as 1980), vs. 7 million barrels in 1979 and the 1978 peak of 7.4 million barrels . . . Only 75% of the U.S. population will be white and non-Hispanic in the year 2000, vs. 80% last year, according to report by Center for Continuing Study of the California Economy. They expect the percentage of Asians in the U.S. to increase from 2.5% to 4%; Hispanics from 6.4% to 8.6%, and blacks from 11.5% to 12.4% . . . Black population in 1980 census was 26.5 million. Average age of U.S. blacks was 24.9 years vs. 31.3 for whites; and percentage living in the South down to 53%

from 77% in 1940 and 90% in 1910. In 1940, 49% of blacks lived in urban areas, vs. 85% in 1980. Life expectancy among blacks in 1979 was 68.3 years, more than double the 1900 figure, but still less than the 74.4 year figure for whites. The average black woman now has 2.3 children, vs. 1.8 for the average white . . . Reagan administration estimates budget deficit will climb to record $109 billion in 1982, $152 billion in 1983, and $162 billion in 1984 . . . Down 18% from five years ago, beef still number one meat choice; but average annual consumption now 77.2 lbs. vs. 94.4 lbs. in 1976. Poultry picks up most of the slack with 51.7 lbs. current annual average, almost double the 1956 consumption, while pork is up to 65 lbs. from 56.9 lbs. average over the same period. Price is a big factor, but poultry and pork sandwich products, plus high-powered marketing, also influence change in U.S eating habits . . . After rapid decline, birth rates have increased gradually since 1976 . . . Life expectancy continued to increase through 1979 to 69.9 years for men and 77.6 for women; with decline in deaths from heart disease and strokes helping to account for drop in mortality . . . Ratio of doctors to patients reaches record high of one per 500 population . . . Last year some two dozen firms sold 724,000 personal computers for $1.8 billion. This year sales double to $3 billion for 1,400,000 units, as 20 more companies, including IBM, join the home electronics stampede. Dataquest estimates next year's sales will reach 2.8 million units for $4.9 billion . . . Robotics industry (industrial robot makers) reaches $155 million sales, with revenues rising at an annual rate of at least 50% since 1978. As IBM, General Motors and Westinghouse get set for full commitment to robotics, U.S. sales are expected to reach annual revenues of $2.1 billion by 1992—a fourteen-fold increase . . . Only 22,000 New York City policemen swamped by this year's 157,026 violent crimes, vs. 3,000 less cops in 1951 having just 15,812 similar crimes—one-tenth the 1981 total, while averaging about one crime per officer . . . Coin-operated video game manufacturers sell 486,000 machines—double last year's total. Players pay $7 billion into arcade game machines despite home video competition . . .

TEEN AND COLLEGE LIVING AND ALTERNATIVE LIFE STYLES IN THE ROCK ERA

Survey reports that only 10% of 30 million marijuana users are under 18, while regular pot smoking increases yearly among adults over 30. One-third of the 30 million "smokers" are parents, while the biggest decrease is among high school students . . . Jobless rate for teenagers increased to 19.5% in May—from 17.8% in December 1980 . . . Brooke Shields dropped as the centerpiece of a governmental anti-smoking campaign, after volunteering her services. The American Lung Association, suspecting that the Department of Health and Human Services had given in to pressure from the tobacco industry, is not appeased by a spokesman's explanation that Shields' image is not family-oriented enough . . . President Reagan exempts summer youth jobs from budget cuts. $870 million program provides temporary work for 665,000 young people . . . College Entrance Examination Board votes to start providing students nationwide with copies of their Scholastic Aptitude Tests, their answer sheets and the correct answers. Prior to this a Florida high school student challenged his score, and it was revealed that he had a better answer than the correct one—as did 250,000 others of the 800,000 who took the test . . . Senate Labor and Human Relations Committee studying bill to create a sub-minimum wage for young people. Proposed law S348 would allow teens to be paid 75% of the minimum for the first six months of employment. At the current rate: $2.51 per hour . . . Fewer than 10% of all teenagers exposed to any valid sex education in schools, says Director of Syracuse University Institute for Family Research . . . Rand Corporation estimates that by the year 2020 the largest group of population will be between 60 and 70—with today's teens in their 50s to 60s and the survival of more and more individuals combined with a declining birth rate . . . New Jersey and Tennessee have now raised the drinking age to 19, and New Hampshire to 20, as efforts to combat teen alcohol abuse spread nationally . . . Veterans Administration eight-year study reveals that Vietnam war veterans suffered from "significantly more emotional, social, educational and job-related problems" than veterans of other wars. Only 20% completed work for their college degrees, vs. 70% of the veterans who served elsewhere. Only 50% had white collar jobs, vs. 54% of other vets, and 69% of non-vets. Overall, 24% of those engaged in heavy combat were later arrested for criminal offenses, vs. 10% for those in light combat . . . *Seventeen* magazine poll explodes some popular generalizations about teenagers. In a survey of a scientifically-selected cross-section of over 1,000 13-19-year-old girls, they found 41% would go to their mothers with a problem, vs. only 7% to their fathers. Only 7% describe their folks as old-fashioned, while two-thirds find them fairly or very modern. 78% find nothing wrong with premarital sex, but 35% say it isn't for them. 77% see nothing wrong with living with a man before marriage, but 41% say "but not for me." Nearly three-quarters plan to attend college—but only 10% of them hope to meet their husband there. 87% expect to continue work after marriage; and 59% expect to continue working if they have a child. Only 31% feel abortions should be easily obtainable and inexpensive, vs. 49% the reverse . . . U.S. Department of Education survey of high school seniors reports 68.2% would work for $2.25-$3.00 an hour while still in school, and 11.2% would work for as little as $2.25. Of the 63% who worked the previous week, 9.4% earned less than $2.50 an hour and 24% under $3.10 . . . College administrators and recruiters trying to create a volunteer U.S. army, worried by forecast that by 1995 the number of 18-24-year-olds will decline by 21%. Education standards could decline as schools seek to lure students. But crime could lessen while there's reduced strain on the job market . . . Government expects 19% rise in professional and technical jobs in 1980s; but one in four college graduates will have to take jobs in clerical, sales and blue-collar trades—as only 10.2 million jobs open up in fields traditionally served by the estimated 13.5 million who will graduate by 1990 . . . Preps for Rent in Louisville has 25 high school graduates get $7 an hour (double the $3.35 minimum) tripling their business in July, as customers take fancy to well-scrubbed youths in Lacoste shirts, Top-Siders and khaki pants or shorts—mowing lawns, serving drinks, and/or painting houses . . . Jobs bottleneck increases for 60 million 19-33-year-olds born during "baby boom" years (1948-1962), as too many with education and ambition seek to rise at the same time. Because so many millions crowded on the first steps of management at the same time, many who expected to rise to the top will have to settle for less . . . *World Almanac* poll of 13- and 14-year-old 8th grade students seeking "Heroes of Young America" finds top 30 almost all entertainers—mostly TV, especially comedians. Only three pop stars: Kenny Rogers (No. 21), Olivia Newton-John (No. 26) and Billy Joel (No. 30). Three sport stars and five women make list, with top eight rankings: Burt Reynolds, Richard Pryor, Alan Alda, Brooke Shields, John Ritter, Scott Baio, Bo Derek and George Burns . . . Second draft registration calls about 1.9 million men born in 1962. In previous registration of those born in 1960 and 1961, some 95% of the eligible did register . . . Proposed regulations that would have required public schools to teach foreign-speaking students in their native languages barred by Secretary of Education . . . One-third of U.S. high school students are "problem drinkers" (someone who is drunk six times a year up or has alcohol-related problems while driving or with police, family, etc.), according to study by Research Triangle Institute. 13% more girls than boys are moderate drinkers, but 14% more boys than girls are heavy drinkers . . . One-third of major crimes now committed by people under 20 . . . Video games in arcades and other outlets now grossing double the box office receipts for the entire U.S. film industry, with Pac-Man leading the pack . . . Rand Teenage Economic Poll shows 13-15-year-old males averaging 90¢ a week on vidgames vs. 75¢ in 1980. Same-age girls were up to 40¢ a week from 25¢ the previous year . . . Spending on records and tapes by the same girls dropped from $1.60 a week in 1980 to $1.55, while the males were unchanged from their $1.15 average in 1980 . . . 16-19-year-old males upped vidgame spending to $2.30 per week from $1.50, while the girls in that age group increased spending to 65¢ from 45¢. Total weekly teen spending on vidgames jumped to $4.30 a week from $2.95 in 1980, an increase of over 40% . . . Teens involved in family food shopping now 68%, vs. 49% in 1950 . . . Survey of students in 25 colleges and universities shows 63% listen to less than two hours of radio a day, 78% hear it as background while doing something else; while 36% watch no TV on an average day and 51% watch less than an hour a day. CASS survey also shows that 83% read their college newspapers weekly while only 64% read an issue of a daily city newspaper . . . 86% of the students purchased cheese in previous six months; 82% crackers; 69% canned soups; 66% breakfast cereal; 63% peanut butter; 52% yogurt; 44% instant soups; 39% macaroni and cheese mix; 39% breath mints; 30% frozen pizzas; 18% frozen complete dinners; 14% breakfast snack bars . . . 92% of the women and 85% of the men bought deodorant; 54% of the women and 39% of the men pain relievers, and 81% women and 45% men hair conditioner; 59% had a car, truck or van for their own use at school . . . Teenagers now spending more than $1 billion a year on jewelry, according to *Teen* magazine survey . . . Rand poll shows average student with $2,200 a year disposable income after college expenses are paid . . . 58% of the college students working part or full time during school year, and 30% have summer jobs . . . "You can get a few people on a protest for disarmament or against Reaganomics, but you've really got to sweat at it. . . . That's how much this place has changed," says the vice president of the Associated Students of Universities of California (where it all began), Liz Rivera. "There are flower children still around, but they tend to be the originals who have become teachers." Thus the hippies represent the older generation . . . Number of teenagers has declined to 18.4% of the national total. Since 1960, young families have one less child per family unit. And, according to American Bandstander Dick Clark, now in the world of business, mainly catering to youth, 66% of the teens attend a movie at least once a month, 72% swim, and 93% frequent fast food restaurants. 60% are economy-minded, 60% are style-conscious; while 46% are cautious vs. 47% impulsive . . . Veteran Broadway producer, Lester Osterman, plans to bring Lisa Birnbach's *Official Preppy Handbook* to the Broadway stage as *The Official Preppy Musical* in 1983 . . . Administration formally requires federally funded family planning clinics to notify parents when those under 18 years old receive oral contraceptives or prescription birth control devices . . . Senate votes 61 to 36 to end three-month filibuster attempt to block passage of severe restrictions on busing of pupils as means of achieving racially balanced schools . . . Valley Girls movement starts up in Southern California with language all its own . . . Percentage of blacks aged 18-24 in college nearly doubled, from 10.3% in 1965 to 19.4% this year, vs. 26% of the white 18-24-year olds . . . Highest starting salary for college graduates with bachelor's degree in petroleum engineering is $30,432, followed by chemical engineers at $27,432. As enrollments dropped, salaries increased; but enrollments up again as a 90% job increase in computer science is predicted, even in a slow-growth economy . . . Overall unemployment for college graduates in communications less than 7%, well under national average, according to the Newspaper Fund, with over half of all journalism and mass communications graduates finding jobs in the media. Their starting salaries were about half those of engineers . . . Future of steak seems assured as recent Gallup poll finds that teenagers now prefer it by a much wider margin than adults . . . Now 52,000 computers in U.S. schools— approximately one for every 800 pupils. Expected to double to over 100,000 next year, with installations accelerating over next decade . . . Electronic revolution beginning to alter social life at colleges and universities. Computer centers replacing libraries as focus of much academic and social activity. Students alternate working on assignments with computer games and electronic mail over computer networks . . . Some educators worry about home computers being potentially destructive to campus social life . . . College courses planned for future wherein computers will replace lecturers . . . Death rates have increased among 15-24-year-olds. Violent deaths now account for 75% of young fatalities, vs. 50% in 1950. Auto accidents leading killer, accounting for 40% of all white young adult deaths two years ago . . . At Yale University, 50% of 300 students in "Topics of Human Sexuality" course say they are virgins, vs. only 25% in 1976. Dr. Philip Sarrell, who teaches course, says: "I'd say things peaked in about 1975-76. Since 1976, it's swung in a more conservative direction." . . .

FASHION: CLOTHES AND THE
ROCK ERA ACCENT ON YOUTH

Note: Feminine fashion is in italics, male in roman, unisex in parentheses, and news in asterisks.

Hemlines move up. Lots of leg and knee baring. Easy-wearing lengths . . . Feminized camouflage fabrics for skirts, shirt jackets, vests, shorts, teeshirts and tops, with hot spots of color, teamed with khaki or softened with lace . . . Yoked sweatshirts and fringed-tier skirts . . . Zouave pants, culottes and cropped pants . . . (Tie-dyed teeshirts) *. . . Knee-high ski boots . . . Low-heeled shoes . . . Pastel sandals and espadrilles . . . Metallics: fabrics and leather shot through with lines of gold, sewn-on gold leaves and rickrack . . . Billowing pastel gauze dresses and culottes . . . Ruffled swimsuits . . . Woolworth's "instant sundresses"—completed by sewing up one seam . . . Opalescent makeup: giving a rainbow effect with especially pretty pink and blue lights—unlike frosts, which reflect only one tone—in eye shadow, blush, powder gloss and nail color . . . Mom's old sunglasses as an accessory . . .* **End of last year saw "virtual prepidemic" sweep the country's upscale outfitters, according to *Newsweek*. Everything from blush-pink Shetland sweaters to teak-brown Top-Sider moccasins being replicated by manufacturers, "while merchants scramble to serve youth's sudden craving for classical chic"** . . . **Harris Tweeds, Burberrys, tartans and regimental ties lead the British-oriented elements in the preppy invasion of the fashion world** . . . **Monogramming shirts, dresses, sweaters, handkerchiefs and monogrammed jewelry back in via the preppies** . . . (Crew-neck Shetland sweaters) . . . Madras swim trunks . . . **Valley Girl style spreads from clothes-crazy upper-middle-class San Fernando Valley (Los Angeles suburb) teens to New York, with combinations like Pac-Man sweatshirts over red nylon shorts and Adidas sneakers—or turquoise and red striped miniskirt with a puffy-sleeved cotton top, a conch belt and turquoise satin Chinese-style shoes—or for dressup occasions, a white cotton minidress and white ballet slippers—or a black Norma Kamali with conch and rhinestone decorated ballet slippers. In New York, the more sophisticated and fashion-conscious travel the Bloomingdale's-Fiorucci-Gap circuit in search of designer clothes while their California counterparts haunt the shopping malls and have their toenails done at salons** . . . **White anklets worn with gold ballet slippers and miniskirts join Lacoste shirts, Valley Girl teeshirts and corduroy pants as staples with the spread of Val-Speak (see Argot, Jargon and Slang) and Val ideas among the nation's more affluent teen femmes** . . .

FADS (MOSTLY YOUTH-ORIENTED) RELATED TO THE ROCK ERA

Many auto shops specializing in "convertible conversion." (Ford's last was 1973, General Motors' 1976). Booming business in California . . . Diet fad books pass 3,000 mark . . . Chinese yo-yos . . . J. R. Ewing dolls . . . "No Gators" buttons to combat Preppy trend . . . Primal Scream "events" in colleges to help vent exam anxieties . . . Earmuffs worn in discos . . . Baby-food fruit as snacks . . . The Cube, Preppies and cats account for 11 paperback book bestsellers . . . Monogrammed housewares, linens and accessories for Preppy living . . . Estimated $5 billion poured into coin-operated video games—with addicts spending 75,000 man-years playing the games during this one year . . . Radio-controlled cars, horses, robots, boats and planes appeal to all ages in toy business boom . . . Pac-Man gobbles up video game field . . .

SOME OF THE MORE WIDELY USED ARGOT, JARGON AND SLANG IN THE ROCK ERA

Val-Speak (created or resurrected by Valley Girls): Airhead (totally dumb person) . . . Awesome (indescribable) . . . Beige (boring) . . . Bag your face (remove your rotten looks) . . . Beastie (physically or socially unacceptable person) . . . Fer sure (for sure—rolling the suuurrrrre) . . . Grody (most gross) . . . Joanie (out of date and stupid) . . . Space cadet (acts like someone from another planet) . . . Totally (often used

with "to the max") . . . To the max (Is there anything greater?) . . .
Tubular (awe-inspiring awesomeness) . . . Yucky (same meaning as
always before) . . .

THE NEW WOMAN IN THE ROCK ERA

Directors' Guild of America files sex discrimination charges against three
TV networks, six film studios and 11 independent TV producers, charging
bias against women as directors. Although 11% of its members are women,
only 1.3% of the directing jobs of the top 19 companies went to them. The
Guild also contends that only 14 of the 7,332 movies released by major
studios from 1949 to 1979 had women at the helm . . . National Collegiate
Athletic Association adopts proposal to hold championships for women in
twelve Division I (large university) sports . . . Detroit Federal judge rules
that educational institutions receiving Federal funds do not have to provide
equal athletic programs for men and women under Title IX of the 1974
Higher Education Act—saying this extends only to those educational
programs or activities which receive direct Federal financial assistance, and
the Government rarely finances sports activities in public schools or colleges . . . Republican platform drops 40-year-old endorsement of Equal
Rights Amendment . . . Armed forces plan to include approximately
199,000 women (11.1% of the planned strength of the active forces) by
1983—continuing the expansion of military women's programs which the
Department of Defense began in 1970 . . . First woman to take Senate seat
without benefit of politically prominent male relative, Florida Republican,
Paula Hawkins, was the only female Senatorial candidate elected. She
opposed ERA and favored passage of anti-abortion amendment . . . First
woman Supreme Court Justice, Sandra Day O'Connor, nominated by
President Reagan . . . Although public continues to support ERA by 52%
to 46% in Harris poll, no state has passed amendment since 1977 and five
state legislatures voted to withdraw approval—with three more states
required to approve amendment by June 30, 1982 . . . New memberships in
NOW double to 7,500 a month after 1980 elections . . . Women now hold
19 House seats and two in the Senate . . . During first three months in
office, new administration includes only 18 women among some 400
appointees for Federal positions requiring Senate approval . . . Cabinet-
level rank goes to Jeane J. Kirkpatrick, as she becomes Chief U.S. Delegate
to the U.N. . . . Senators Jesse Helms (North Carolina) and Henry Hyde
(Illinois) introduce a bill declaring that human life "shall be deemed to exist
from conception." President Reagan says: "Once you have determined
this, the constitution already protects the rights of human life . . . there
really isn't any need for an (anti-abortion) amendment" . . . Sarah
Weddington, former Carter assistant, and one of the lawyers who argued

the 1973 case for legalized abortion, is key witness for 75 national organizations with 34 million members opposing the Helms-Hyde Bill . . . Supreme Court upholds constitutionality of all-male draft—based on its deference to the authority of Congress on national defense issues. Feminists find this gender distinction ominous. ACLU's David Landau calls decision "a devastating loss for women's rights and civil rights generally" . . . Midwest Women's Music Distributors, Inc., concentrating on feminist music, adds staff as business shows big increase for the 15-20 record labels they handle . . . As Olivia Newton-John's record "Physical" heads the Top 100 single records hit chart at year end, female acts lead the males in the number one spot for the year with 26½ weeks on top, vs. 25½ . . . U.S. Bureau of Labor Statistics says only 37% of all women today are fulltime homemakers. Ratio of working to non-working women now 60:40, vs. about 50:50 in 1972 . . . Now 58% of all mothers with children under 18 have jobs, vs. only 9% in 1940 . . . Percentage of female engineering graduates up to 10% from 1% in 1970; and 54% of all college undergraduates are now women . . . Observers predict that by 1990 the work force will be 46% female, with another 11-14 million women going to work during the 1980s . . .

MOSTLY FACTUAL TRIVIA
CONCURRENT WITH THE ROCK ERA

National Bubblegum Week celebrated April 27 to May 1 . . . Uncut version of early 1900s novel *Sister Carrie*, by Theodore Dreiser, being published by University of Pennsylvania Press—restoring 36,000 words that were deleted by his wife, editor and publisher as being too sexually explicit . . . Egg Board restaurant survey reports scrambled eggs on 50% of menus, fried eggs on 43%, poached or boiled 39%, omelets 38% and Eggs Benedict 9% . . . Cleveland Indian pitcher Len Barker hurls first perfect baseball game (no hits, runs or walks) in 13 years, vs. Toronto . . . Researchers discover that disco music causes homosexuality in mice and deafness in pigs at Aegean University, Izmir, Turkey. Report adds: "There is a caveat in these studies for human beings as well" . . . Comic Barney Weiss tells jokes nonstop for 27 hours, 28 minutes at the Comedy Factory outlet, Philadelphia, topping previous 24 hours, 5 minutes record . . . Larry ("J.R.") Hagman heads Fifth Annual Great American Smokeout attempt to get 18-20 million Americans to give up the habit for 24 hours . . . *Superman II* film sets new opening weekend record of $14.1 million gross at 1,395 cinemas over a three-day period . . . Arlington Heights, Illinois, 15-year-old plays "Defender" video game for 16 hours and 34 minutes on same 25¢ in amusement arcade, scoring 15,963,100 before losing his last ship . . .

THE ROCK ERA BY CATEGORY

The Cost of Living: Prices through the Years in the Rock Era _____

	White Bread 1 lb.	Flour 5 lb.	Margarine 1 lb.	Butter 1 lb.	Large Eggs Grade A Dozen	Coffee 1 lb.	Instant Coffee 6 oz.
1954	$.172	$.536	$.299	$.724	$.585	$1.108	—
1955	.177	.538	.289	.709	.606	.93	—
1956	.179	.533	.289	.721	.602	1.034	—
1957	.188	.546	.299	.743	.573	1.017	—
1958	.193	.552	.295	.742	.604	.907	—
1959	.197	.545	.280	.753	.530	.780	—
1960	.203	.554	.269	.749	.573	.753	—
1961	.298	.560	.286	.763	.573	.736	—
1962	.212	.570	.284	.752	.540	.708	$.908
1963	.216	.570	.275	.750	.551	.694	.922
1964	.207	.567	.261	.744	.539	.816	1.067
1965	.209	.581	.279	.755	.527	.833	.952
1966	.222	.594	.287	.822	.599	.823	.909
1967	.222	.596	.284	.830	.491	.769	.879
1968	.224	.584	.279	.836	.529	.764	.894
1969	.230	.581	.278	.846	.621	.765	.934
1970	.243	.589	.298	.866	.614	.911	1.047
1971	.250	.599	.327	.876	.529	.934	1.093
1972	.247	.596	.331	.871	.524	.927	1.093
1973	.276	.756	.374	.916	.781	1.04	1.16
1974	.345	1.025	.574	.946	.783	1.229	1.385
1975	.360	.994	.629	1.025	.770	1.334	1.603
1976	.353	.926	.526	1.261	.841	1.873	2.050
1977	.355	.846	.572	1.331	.823	3.472	3.123
1978	.368	.883	.624	1.424	.747	3.229	3.311
1979	.501	1.02	.735	1.802	.879	3.208	—
1980	.511	1.07	.725	1.94	.898	3.159	5.10
1981	.524	1.13	.739	1.997	.915	2.46	4.38

(NOTE: Annual averages for U.S. shown 1954 through 1977. Average shown for 1978 is May; 1979 year end; 1980 and 1981 are both September averages. Dashes indicate unavailable data.)

	Tea Bags 48	Frozen Orange Juice 6 oz.	Milk Quart	Milk ½ Gal.	Sugar 5 lb.	Corn Flakes 12 oz.	Baby Foods 4½ oz.
1954	—	$.186	$.219	—	$.526	$.219	$.098
1955	—	.183	.219	—	.521	.220	.097
1956	$.699	.196	.226	—	.528	.220	.099
1957	.708	.183	.234	—	.552	.232	.100
1958	.720	.270	.239	—	.563	.254	.100
1959	.726	.258	.241	—	.572	.256	.101
1960	.732	.225	.247	—	.582	.258	.102
1961	.735	.246	.246	—	.589	.264	.106
1962	.735	.209	.246	—	.585	.273	.107
1963	.637	.304	.243	—	.679	.283	.109
1964	.622	.310	—	$.477	.640	.286	.106
1965	.612	.237	—	.473	.590	.289	.104
1966	.612	.225	—	.498	.602	.298	.103
1967	.608	.183	—	.517	.605	.314	.103
1968	.607	.211	—	.537	.609	.313	.104
1969	.610	.241	—	.551	.620	.313	.107
1970	.631	.225	—	.574	.648	.322	.109
1971	.645	.234	—	.589	.589	.334	.113
1972	.649	.250	—	.598	.695	.312	.113
1973	.661	.251	—	.654	.755	.322	.117
1974	.720	.258	—	.784	1.617	.415	.141
1975	.875	.282	—	.785	1.862	.519	.164
1976	.903	.287	—	.827	1.198	.515	.172
1977	1.079	.346	—	.839	1.081	.556	.189
1978	1.242	.445	—	.872	1.232	.604	.201
1979	—	.466	—	1.015	1.36	—	.210
1980	—	.600	—	1.062	2.39	—	.230
1981	—	.720	—	1.117	1.73	—	—

	Grape Jelly 12 oz.	Cola Drink 6-Pack 36 oz.	Cola Drink 6-Pack 72 oz.	Size & Common Retail Price Hershey Bars	Ice Cream Pint	Ice Cream ½ Gal.	Cookies Cream Filled 1 lb.
1954	$.255	$.318	—	$.05/⅞ oz.	$.296	—	—
1955	.261	.325	—	.05/1 oz.	.290	—	—
1956	.265	.327	—	—	.289	—	—
1957	.273	—	—	—	.294	—	—
1958	.278	.277	—	.05/⅞ oz.	.297	—	—
1959	.282	.292	—	—	.297	—	—
1960	.288	.298	—	.05/1 oz.	—	$.868	—
1961	.292	.307	—	—	—	.864	$.518
1962	.296	.300	—	—	—	.858	.522
1963	.303	—	$.527	.05/⅞ oz.	—	.850	.521
1964	.311	—	.542	—	—	.804	.510
1965	.312	—	.548	.05/1 oz.	—	.787	.507
1966	.315	—	.566	.05/⅞ oz.	—	.806	.512
1967	.262*	—	.608	—	—	.809	.518
1968	.266	—	.651	.05/¾ oz.	—	.807	.509
1969	.279	—	.689	.10/1½ oz.	—	.813	.499
1970	.299	—	.726	.10/1⅜ oz.	—	.845	.522
1971	.314	—	.758	—	—	.854	.545
1972	.329	—	.833	—	—	.858	.555
1973	.353	—	.861	.10/1.26 oz.	—	.910	.578
1974	.452	—	1.089	.15/1.05 oz.	—	1.076	.735
1975	.612	—	1.328	—	—	1.223	.940
1976	.586	—	1.272	.15/1.2 oz.	—	1.271	.955
1977	.577	—	1.074	.15/1.05 oz.	—	1.352	1.041
1978	.582	—	1.214	.25/1.2 oz.	—	1.443	1.151
1979	—	—	—	—	—	1.775	—
1980	—	—	—	—	—	1.825	—
1981	—	—	—	—	—	2.042	—

*Jar size now 10 oz.

	Pretzels 8 oz.	Movie First-Run Indoor	Gasoline Service Station Average Price (Incl. Taxes)	Sardines 4 oz. Can	Tuna Fish 7 oz. Can	Tuna Fish 6½ oz. Can	Canned Chicken Soup 10½ oz.
1954	—	—	—	—	$.391	—	—
1955	—	—	—	—	.387	—	—
1956	—	—	$.291	—	—	$.327	—
1957	—	—	—	—	—	.321	—
1958	—	—	—	—	—	.331	—
1959	—	—	—	—	—	.331	—
1960	—	$.65	.311	—	—	.325	—
1961	—	—	—	—	—	.324	—
1962	—	—	—	—	—	.347	—
1963	—	—	—	—	—	.336	—
1964	$.315	—	—	$.131	—	.320	$.182
1965	.309	.85	.312	.138	—	.320	.182
1966	.298	—	.321	.142	—	.353	.180
1967	.302	—	.332	.151	—	.346	.174
1968	.312	—	.337	.161	—	.345	.173
1969	.381	1.42	.348	.165	—	.357	.177
1970	.393	1.55	.357	.174	—	.398	.184
1971	.423	—	.364	.204	—	.440	.184
1972	.429	—	.361	.221	—	.454	.182
1973	.442	—	.388	.235	—	.492	.186
1974	.533	1.89	.524	.401*	—	.577	.223
1975	.618	2.05	.572	.498	—	.603	.232
1976	.604	2.13	.595	.530	—	.640	.236
1977	.613	2.23	.657	.562	—	.723	.257
1978	.625	2.34	.660	.600	—	.792	.275
1979	—	—	.945	—	—	—	—
1980	—	2.51	1.269	—	—	—	—
1981	—	3.38	1.305	—	—	—	—

*Can size now 3¾ oz.

	Canned Bean Soup 11½ oz.	Spaghetti 15½ oz. Can	Canned Tomatoes #303 Can	Canned Peas #303 Can	Canned Fruit Cocktail #303 Can	Bacon Sliced 1 lb.	Ham- burger 1 lb.
1954	—	—	—	$.214	—	$.817	$.406
1955	—	—	$.151	.215	$.266	.659	.395
1956	—	—	.152	.215	.262	.573	.385
1957	—	—	.150	.215	.260	.738	.420
1958	—	—	.170	.211	.264	.793	.529
1959	—	—	.155	.204	.276	.665	.549
1960	—	—	.159	.207	.270	.655	.524
1961	—	—	.160	.220	.266	.712	.512
1962	—	—	.157	.225	.258	.703	.521
1963	—	—	.155	.226	.257	.683	.513
1964	$.148	$.151	.160	.227	.273	.667	.495
1965	.146	.151	.161	.237	.261	.813	.508
1966	.145	.158	.177	.243	.269	.954	.542
1967	.149	.164	.195	.249	.261	.837	.546
1968	.151	.168	.204	.249	.283	.814	.561
1969	.158	.175	.197	.249	.278	.878	.624
1970	.168	.185	.213	.253	.283	.949	.662
1971	.170	.191	.226	.263	.307	.800	.681
1972	.173	.194	.228	.264	.316	.962	.744
1973	.178	.202	.247	.270	.338	1.325	.957
1974	.245	.233	.298	.322	.408	1.32	.972
1975	.273	.267	.353	.392	.462	1.756	.878
1976	.308	.267	.351	.386	.460	1.711	.876
1977	.306	.279	.376	.383	.478	1.562	.854
1978	.310	.298	.382	.376	.488	1.896	1.098
1979	—	—	.469	—	—	1.451	1.12
1980	—	—	.437	—	—	1.617	1.157
1981	—	—	.525	—	—	1.753	1.233

	Frank-furters 1 lb.	Frying Chicken 1 lb.	Bologna 8 oz.	Salami 8 oz.	Liver Sausage 8 oz.	American Process Cheese 8 oz.	Sirloin Steak 1 lb.
1954	$.555	$.433	—	—	—	$.288	—
1955	.531	.469	—	—	—	.289	—
1956	.518	.494	—	—	—	.286	—
1957	.565	.469	—	—	—	.288	—
1958	.648	.465	—	—	—	.290	—
1959	.640	.420	—	—	—	.290	—
1960	.623	.427	—	—	—	.343	$1.088
1961	.631	.385	—	—	—	.364	1.070
1962	.633	.407	—	—	—	.362	1.108
1963	.632	.401	—	—	—	.363	1.097
1964	.621	.378	$.408	$.503	—	.367	1.063
1965	.662	.390	.426	.516	—	.377	1.137
1966	.733	.413	.475	.567	—	.422	1.172
1967	.710	.381	.470	.564	—	.436	1.150
1968	.710	.398	.478	.571	$.468	.444	1.195
1969	.772	.422	.522	.603	.499	.470	1.318
1970	.827	.408	.562	.661	.549	.504	1.349
1971	.819	.410	.562	.659	.523	.528	1.423
1972	.888	.414	.616	.715	.566	.543	1.532
1973	1.159	.596	.754	.874	.683	.604	1.749
1974	1.145	.560	.757	.902	.718	.729	1.800
1975	1.193	.633	.798	.893	.733	.768	1.987
1976	1.191	.597	.807	.936	.772	.865	1.930
1977	1.162	.601	.801	.949	.766	.870	1.918
1978	1.414	.656	.939	1.034	.828	.936	2.290
1979	1.678	.699	1.972	—	—	—	2.848
1980	1.865	.791	2.094	—	—	—	3.142
1981	1.771	.728	2.707	—	—	—	3.161

	Lamb Chops 1 lb.	Round Steak 1 lb.	Chuck Roast 1 lb.	Veal Cutlets 1 lb.	Pork Chops 1 lb.	Frozen Ocean Perch 1 lb.	Ham Whole 1 lb.
1954	—	$.907	$.514	$1.098	$.863	$.436	$.700
1955	—	.903	.501	1.099	.793	.428	.605
1956	—	.882	.484	1.112	.782	.420	.611
1957	—	.936	.525	1.178	.866	.429	.631
1958	—	1.042	.633	1.328	.918	.456	.677
1959	—	1.073	.641	1.421	.853	.475	.622
1960	—	1.055	.616	1.416	.858	.474	.604
1961	—	1.036	.594	1.43	.879	.475	.700
1962	—	1.078	.623	1.481	.898	.500	.623
1963	—	1.064	.603	1.515	.882	.526	.607
1964	$1.319	1.039	.568	1.422	.880	.528	.609
1965	1.415	1.084	.595	1.463	.973	.527	.666
1966	1.546	1.107	.622	1.545	1.063	.541	.751
1967	1.557	1.103	.607	1.652	1.004	.541	.689
1968	1.649	1.143	.653	1.756	1.029	.543	.689
1969	1.783	1.267	.704	1.959	1.122	.557	.728
1970	1.853	1.302	.725	2.201	1.162	.641	.786
1971	1.897	1.361	.750	2.409	1.081	.725	.710
1972	1.995	1.477	.821	2.701	1.246	.768	.782
1973	2.266	1.746	1.028	3.145	1.559	.988	1.062
1974	2.206	1.798	1.021	3.430	1.575	1.081	1.054
1975	2.711	1.885	1.028	3.235	1.856	1.126	1.239
1976	2.93	1.783	.969	3.005	1.848	1.408	1.369
1977	3.047	1.761	.920	3.162	1.812	1.679	1.298
1978	3.619	2.075	1.163	3.356	1.951	1.839	1.353
1979	—	2.724	1.779	—	1.962	—	1.247
1980	—	2.832	1.859	—	2.072	—	1.291
1981	—	2.864	1.844	—	2.219	—	1.399

	Canned Ham 1 lb.	Apples 1 lb.	Bananas 1 lb.	Oranges Dozen Size 200	Seedless Grapes 1 lb.	Straw-berries 1 pt.	Water-melon 1 lb.
1954	—	$.153	$.168	$.554	$.240	$.342	$.045
1955	—	.151	.170	.528	.198	.315	.050
1956	—	.151	.168	.583	.227	.369	.049
1957	—	.165	.173	.579	.254	.275	.054
1958	—	.147	.173	.670	.259	.294	.047
1959	—	.142	.170	.644	.256	.316	.053
1960	—	.162	.159	.748	.254	.343	.051
1961	—	.173	.159	.777	.278	.336	.049
1962	—	.163	.163	.793	.273	.346	.054
1963	—	.178	.164	.904	.306	.353	.052
1964	$.931	.178	.165	.881	.320	.353	.061
1965	.984	.178	.160	.778	.294	.388	.054
1966	1.146	.195	.157	.799	.316	.391	.058
1967	1.069	.205	.158	.766	.361	.373	.063
1968	1.054	.238	.155	.966	.373	.402	.066
1969	1.094	.239	.159	.838	.389	.419	.067
1970	1.209	.219	.159	.864	.440	.412	.075
1971	1.150	.235	.149	.943	.501	.460	.085
1972	1.239	.246	.158	.942	.564	.455	.079
1973	1.613	.302	.165	1.053	.573	.527	.093
1974	1.681	.343	.184	1.114	.656	.550	.112
1975	1.937	.340	.232	1.148	—	—	—
1976	2.208	.332	.235	1.142	.741	.622	.112
1977	2.068	.390	.255	1.290	.888	.651	.123
1978	2.319	.503	.319	1.507	—	—	—
1979	—	.554	.319	—	—	—	—
1980	—	.702	.335	—	—	—	—
1981	—	.630	.358	—	—	—	—

	Potatoes 10 lb.	Tomatoes 1 lb.	Carrots 1 lb.	Celery 1 lb.	Onions 1 lb.	Italian Salad Dressing 8 oz.	Dried Beans 1 lb.
1954	$.526	$.264	$.134	$.135	$.073	$.180	$.176
1955	.564	.274	.139	.149	.081	.177	.182
1956	.677	.295	.137	.135	.095	.177	.163
1957	.571	.295	.149	.151	.095	.186	.161
1958	.626	.321	.147	.161	.101	.189	.180
1959	.633	.296	.144	.142	.113	.188	.172
1960	.718	.316	.141	.139	.092	.180	.167
1961	.629	.287	.158	.134	.103	.187	.170
1962	.632	.297	.152	.155	.122	.192	.174
1963	.651	.322	.148	.140	.114	.195	.178
1964	.757	.332	.149	.157	.112	.370	.167
1965	.937	.343	.153	.156	.119	.372	.175
1966	.749	.348	.166	.168	.129	.377	.198
1967	.747	.352	.162	.165	.137	.375	.182
1968	.763	.402	.187	.168	.150	.377	.196
1969	.816	.421	.179	.187	.137	.377	.196
1970	.897	.420	.177	.202	.161	.383	.192
1971	.861	.466	.206	.195	.143	.406	.222
1972	.926	.468	.215	.236	.177	.408	.248
1973	1.369	.482	.220	.240	.252	.416	.312
1974	1.664	.548	.232	.239	.208	.482	.691
1975	1.344	.578	.270	.266	.245	.582	.421
1976	1.460	.578	.255	.304	.232	.570	.492
1977	1.497	.678	.320	.339	.291	.619	.422
1978	—	—	—	—	—	.642	.526
1979	—	—	—	—	—	—	—
1980	2.31	.679	.340	.358	.293	—	—
1981	2.22	.604	.347	.384	.355	—	—

Miscellaneous News about Prices in the Rock Era

1954

Gasoline prices averaging 29¢ a gallon, up from 21¢ in 1944 . . . *MAD* magazine 10¢ . . . *TV Guide* 15¢ . . . *Playboy* 50¢ . . . 45 r.p.m. single records 89¢ . . .

1955

Hamburgers (at stands) 15¢ each, or seven for $1 . . . Coffee 5¢ . . . LP record albums $3.98 . . .

1956

At drive-in movies: ice cream 10¢ and 25¢, popcorn 15¢, buttercorn 25¢, French fries 25¢, pizza 60¢ . . . At drugstores: ice cream cones 10¢ and 20¢, sundaes 30¢ and 40¢ . . . Tums 10¢ a roll . . .

1957

Neighborhood movies: adults 75¢, teenagers 60¢, children 25¢. Popcorn 15¢ a box . . . At food drive-ins: milk shakes 29¢ . . .

1958

Gasoline average price 30.4¢ per gallon, up from 25.9¢ in 1948 . . . Postage went to 4¢ from 3¢ . . . Average newspaper prices 5¢ . . . Hospital room that cost $13.09 a day in 1948 now $28.17 . . . Men's shoes that were $9.95 ten years ago now $11.95 . . .

1959

At restaurant near University of Arkansas, hot dog 15¢, chili dog 20¢, grilled cheese sandwich with potato chips 25¢, chicken salad with chips 40¢, bar-B-Q beef on a bun with cheese 40¢, bowl of chili 40¢, ham on toast 40¢ . . .

1960

"The Pill," at 55¢ each, costing women $11 a month . . . 45 r.p.m. single records still cost 89¢ . . .

1962

45 r.p.m. single records 98¢ . . . LP record albums $3.98 monaural, $4.98 stereo . . .

1963

4¢ stamp went to 5¢ . . .

1965

McDonald's hamburgers still 15¢, but French fries up a nickel to 15¢, and milk shakes up 2¢ to 22¢ . . . Whole pizzas selling for around 75¢ . . . $4.20 motel room in 1925 now $12 . . .

1966

Yo-yos now 29¢, from a dime . . . Regular gasoline (including tax) now 33¢ a gallon, up from 17¢ in 1941 . . . Girls' suede shoes with round toes $15 . . . Short plaid skirts $20 . . .

1967

Postage up to 6¢ . . . In hippie Haight Ashbury, at Tracy's: hamburgers 65¢, hot dogs 50¢ . . .

1969

U.S. Department of Labor reports average consumer price rises over past two years: Tooth filling up 13% to $7.83 from $6.91; Movie ticket up 18% to $1.74 from $1.48; Bus fare up 12% to 29¢ from 26¢; Dry cleaning man's suit to $1.61 from $1.48—up 9%; and auto tire average now $28.76, up 8% from $26.59 in 1967 . . . Rockaways (New York) Playland charging $1 for roller coaster rides on weekends, vs. 35¢ in 1950 . . .

1970

Chiclets and Dentyne gum up from a nickel to 10¢ a pack . . .

1971

Nickel candy up to 6¢ and 7¢ . . . Wrigleys gum now 10¢ for seven sticks —first price change since 1893 introduction of five sticks for 5¢ . . . Postage up from 6¢ to 8¢ . . . Comic book annuals now 25¢ for 52 pages, vs. 96 pages in 1961 . . .

1972

Comic books now 20¢ for 32 pages plus a cover—rising from original 64 page books for 10¢ . . . In two years, median price for new home climbs approximately $4,000 to $27,570 from $23,670 in 1970 . . . U.S. Department of Labor reports average consumer price rises in past year: Parking fees up 8.4%; Legal services up 8.9%; TV replacement tubes up 7.2%; Girl's wool skirt up 11.1%; Operating room charges up 7.9% . . .

1973

Postage to 10¢ from 8¢ . . .

1974

Sugar price up 400% . . . Tootsie Rolls still 1¢, with no change in size . . . Wrigleys gum up to 15¢ for seven sticks . . . Chiclets up to 15¢ . . .

1975

Postage up to 13¢ from 10¢ . . .

1977

Record album prices up to $6.98 from $5.98 . . .

1978

Candy bars up from 10¢ to 20¢ in four years . . . Chiclets up to 20¢. Wrigleys gum up to 20¢ for seven sticks . . . Record album prices up to $7.98-$8.98 . . . Single records list priced at $1.29 . . . Food prices rising 10% a year . . . In Atlanta, where price changes closely parallel the national average, price comparisons with 1967 show the following 11-year rises: Levi straight-leg blue jeans $15.50 (from $14.79); 14-karat gold wedding ring $170 ($35 in 1967); One cavity filled by dentist $15 ($5); Paperback bestseller $2.95 ($1.65); 1 gallon premium Gulf gasoline 76.9¢ (39.9¢); One week in hospital (semi-private) $595 ($238) . . . Survey of generic ("no name") products vs. name brands reports price differentials on: Peanut butter (18 oz.), 75¢ generic vs. $1.05 name brand; Tomato catsup (32 oz.), 65¢ generic vs. 88¢ name brand; Cling peaches (29 oz.) 45¢ vs. 59¢; Cut green beans (16 oz.), 22¢ vs. 34¢; Sweet peas (17 oz.), 21¢ vs. 33¢; Macaroni and cheese (7½ oz.), 20¢ vs. 26¢; Fruit cocktail (34 oz.), 65¢ vs. 85¢; Dry roasted peanuts (16 oz.), $1.05 vs. $1.36 . . .

1979

Gasoline still 15¢ a gallon—in Saudi Arabia . . . Average cost of a new house now $54,000 . . . Buying a two-door sedan and driving it 10,000 miles per year for three years now costs 38¢ per mile, vs. 10.9¢ in 1950; 20.2¢ in 1973; 23.8¢ in 1974; 27.2¢ in 1975; 28.1¢ in 1976; 30.1¢ in 1977; and 33.1¢ in 1978. Between 1973 and 1978, the cost of operating a car jumped 88%—25% more than the general cost of living . . . Single records price on rise again to $1.69 . . . Average prices at franchised outlets for hamburgers now 42¢, vs. 30¢ in 1976; with cheese it's 47¢ vs. 38¢; special hamburgers 90¢ now vs. 65¢ three years ago; with cheese, $1 vs. 75¢. French fries are 41¢ vs. 30¢; soft drinks 39¢ vs. 20¢; fish sandwiches 70¢ vs. 55¢ . . . Average price of mass market paperback fiction books now $2.01, vs. 75¢ 1967-69. Hardcover fiction average price now $11.32, vs. $4.96 1967-69 . . . National composite average price of movie tickets is about $2.52 . . .

1980

Survey of cost of organic foods vs. non-organic supermarket items in Washington metropolitan area reported organic eggs $1.40 a dozen vs. $1.11 non-organic; canned apple juice (quart) $1.92 vs. 83¢; whole wheat bread (lb.) 92¢ vs. 50¢; peanut butter (lb.) $1.92 vs. $1.29; apples (lb.) 64¢ vs. 59¢; honey (lb.) $2.21 vs. $1.55 . . . American Chamber of Commerce Research Association 205-city cost of living survey shows average price rises for past year: private residence telephone from $8.92 to $9.35; doctor (general practitioner) from $14.55 to $16.38; bowling (evening) per line from 89¢ to $1.01; woman's shampoo and set from $6.23 to $6.65; man's haircut from $4.32 to $4.79; dry cleaning man's two-piece suit from $3.17 to $3.65; Seagram's 7 Crown whiskey from $5.70 to $6.23; Giant Tide wash powder (or equivalent 49 oz. size) from $1.55 to $1.91 . . . National composite average film ticket price is just over $2.69 . . .

1981

First class postage up from 18¢ to 20¢ . . . 45 r.p.m. single records up to $1.99 . . . List price for most LP albums $8.98 . . . National composite average film ticket price up nearly 8% from last year to $2.90 . . .

Car Prices _____

These twelve models were selected for their possible interest to the wide spectrum of the rock market. Prices are manufacturers' suggested advertised delivered prices in the Eastern U.S. including standard equipment, but not transportation or local taxes. LE = least expensive model.

	Cadillac (LE)	Chevrolet	Ford	Thunderbird	MG	Plymouth (LE)
	Calais				*Series 1600*	
1954	$3,838	$1,539	$1,548	—	$2,115	$1,618
1955	3,882	1,593	1,606	$2,944	—	1,639
1956	4,201	1,734	1,748	3,151	2,195	1,784
1957	4,677	1,885	1,879	3,408	2,269	1,899
1958	4,784	2,013	1,977	3,630	2,462	2,028
1959	4,892	2,160	2,132	3,696	2,462	2,143
		Corvair	*Falcon*			*Valiant*
1960	4,892	1,984	1,912	3,755	2,444	2,053
1961	4,892	1,920	1,914	4,172	2,440	1,955
1962	5,025	1,992	1,985	4,321	2,449	1,930
					MGB	
1963	5,026	1,992	1,985	4,445	2,658	1,910
1964	5,048	2,000	1,996	4,486	2,658	1,921
		Chevy II				
1965	4,959	1,968	2,060	4,486	2,607	2,004
1966	4,986	2,028	2,060	4,426	2,607	2,025
1967	5,040	2,090	2,118	4,603	2,607	2,117
1968	5,315	2,222	2,252	4,716	2,670	2,254
1969	5,484	2,237	2,283	4,824	2,817	2,094
		Nova	*Maverick*			
1970	5,637	2,176	1,995	4,961	2,875	2,172

	Cadillac (LE)	Chevrolet	Ford	Thunderbird	MG	Plymouth (LE)
		Vega	*Pinto*			*Cricket*
1971	5,899	2,090	1,919	5,295	3,140	1,915
1972	5,771	2,060	1,960	5,293	3,320	2,017
						Valiant
1973	5,866	2,087	2,021	6,437	3,695	2,376
1974	7,371	2,505	2,406	7,330	4,149	2,829
1975	8,184	2,786	2,769	7,701	4,350	3,243
		Chevette				*Arrow*
1976	8,629	2,899	2,895	7,790	4,795	3,175
	De Ville					
1977	9,810	2,999	3,099	5,063	5,150	3,379
						Volare
1978	10,584	3,149	3,139	5,498	5,995	3,771
1979	11,728	3,437	3,434	6,328	6,550	4,387
1980	12,899	4,057	4,117	6,818	7,950	5,033
						Horizon
1981	13,626	4,595	4,595	7,757	discontinued	5,299

	Volkswagen (LE)	Corvette	Volkswagen Karmann Ghia	Triumph (LE)	Porsche	Mustang (LE)
				TR3		
1954	$1,495	$3,523	—	$2,499	$3,445	—
1955	1,495	2,934	—	2,499	2,995	—
1956	1,495	3,149	$2,395	—	3,215	—
1957	1,495	3,465	2,395	2,625	3,215	—
1958	1,545	3,631	2,445	2,675	3,215	—
1959	1,545	3,875	2,445	2,675	3,581	—
1960	1,565	3,872	2,430	2,675	3,580	—
1961	1,565	3,934	2,430	2,675	3,780	—
1962	1,598	4,038	2,295	2,675	3,884	—
				TR4		
1963	1,595	4,037	2,295	2,675	4,178	—
1964	1,595	4,037	2,295	2,849	4,195	—
1965	1,563	4,106	2,295	2,791	4,099	$2,372
1966	1,585	4,084	2,250	2,791	4,690	2,416
1967	1,639	4,141	2,250	2,899	4,790	2,461
1968	1,699	4,320	2,254	2,775	4,950	2,602
				TR6		
1969	1,799	4,438	2,365	2,995	5,095	2,635
1970	1,839	4,849	2,399	3,095	5,999	2,721
1971	1,845	5,296	2,575	3,374	5,999	2,911
1972	1,999	5,246	2,750	3,523	7,250	2,679
1973	2,299	5,399	3,050	3,955	8,199	2,760
1974	2,625	5,846	3,475	4,695	9,950	3,134
				TR7		
1975	2,999	6,337	—	5,100	12,845	3,529
1976	3,499	7,605	—	5,649	10,845	3,525
	Rabbit					
1977	3,599	8,648	—	5,849	9,395	3,702
1978	4,220	9,645	—	6,995	11,995	3,824
1979	4,799	12,313	—	7,695	14,600	4,494
1980	5,215	13,965	—	8,465	16,770	5,338
1981	5,765	15,599	—	10,995	16,770	6,250

Tuition Fees at Colleges and Universities _____

	Univ. of Alabama	Boston College	Brown	New York Univ.	Notre Dame Univ.	Okla- homa State	Penn. State	Stan- ford	Yale
1963	-	-	$1,400	$1,280	$1,200	-	$480- $960	$1,260	-
1964	$260- $610	$1,350	1,600	1,440	1,300	$224- $576	525- 1,050	1,410	$1,550
1965	-	-	1,800	1,600	1,400	224- 576	525- 1,050	1,410	1,800
1966	300- 325	-	1,800	1,600	1,400	224- 576	525- 1,050	1,575	1,800
1967	350- 700	1,400	2,000	1,800	-	224- 648	450- 1,050	1,575	1,950
1968	350- 700	1,600	2,000	1,900	1,600	270- 690	450- 1,050	1,770	1,950
1969	350- 700	1,600	2,150	2,100	1,800	360- 900	450- 1,050	1,920	-
1970	450- 900	-	2,300	2,275	1,900	360- 900	525- 1,200	-	2,350
1971	428- 856	2,100	2,600	2,275	1,950	384- 960	600- 1,350	-	-
1972	510- 1,020	2,500	2,600	-	2,200	448- 1,152	675- 1,500	-	2,900
1973	510- 1,020	2,650	3,250	2,700	2,600	-	855- 1,986	2,850	3,400
1974	510- 1,020	2,690	3,510	2,950	2,616	464- 1,244	900- 2,100	3,375	3,650
1975	595- 1,190	2,950	3,930	3,300	2,782	464- 1,244	960- 2,160	3,810	4,050
1976	618- 1,236	3,580	3,900	3,550	2,982	474- 1,254	1,096- 2,295	4,275	4,400

(Note: Where two figures are given, the lower applies to in-state students and the higher applies to out-of-state students. Dashes indicate unavailable data.)

	Univ. of Alabama	Boston College	Brown	New York Univ.	Notre Dame Univ.	Okla-homa State	Penn. State	Stan-ford	Yale
1977	645-1,275	3,890	4,300	3,850	3,230	600-1,500	2,379	4,695	4,750
1978	688-1,413	3,645	5,050	4,000	3,480	500-1,500	1,452-2,832	4,695	5,150
1979	722-1,543	3,980	5,050	4,150-5,355	3,780	545-1,460	1,368-2,748	5,595	5,550
1980	722-1,543	4,530	6,140	4,150-5,355	4,630	600-1,600	1,368-2,748	6,285	6,210
1981	944-2,119	5,180	7,120	5,516	5,250	600-1,650	1,641-3,297	6,285	7,150
1982	966-1,932	5,180	7,120	6,634	6,000	600-1,650	1,848-3,711	7,140	8,190

	Univ. of Chicago	Dart-mouth	Drake	Duke	George-town	Harvard	Holy Cross	Howard Univ.
1973	$2,850	$3,270	$2,320	$2,600	$2,350	$3,000	$2,730	$1,043
1974	3,000	3,570	2,700	2,800	2,650	3,200	2,900	1,100
1975	3,000	3,570	2,750	2,780	2,900	3,400	3,200	1,350
1976	-	-	-	-	-	-	-	-
1977	3,720	4,530	3,150	3,530	3,500	4,100	3,675	1,350
1978	3,720	6,040	3,150	3,830	3,500	4,850	3,875	-
1979	4,500	6,040	3,680	4,230	3,500	5,300	4,200	1,550
1980	5,100	5,370	4,060	4,740	4,970	5,300	4,600	1,750
1981	5,100	6,075	4,590	5,400	-	6,930	5,400	1,965
1982	5,100	7,050	5,230	6,210	6,830	8,195	5,400	2,000

	Johns Hop-kins	L.I.U. C.W. Post Center	M.I.T.	Univ. of Miami	Mills Coll.	Ober-lin	Ohio State	Univ. of Penn-syl-vania
1973	$3,000	$2,400	$3,100	$2,500	$2,290	$2,850	$750	$3,165
1974	3,000	2,400	3,350	2,500	2,405	3,025	750	3,450
1975	3,300	2,460	3,700	2,900	2,405	3,325	780	3,790
1976	-	-	-	-	-	-	-	-
1977	3,750	2,690	4,350	3,663	3,270	3,675	840	4,125
1978	4,050	3,060	4,700	-	3,270	4,300	915-2,025	-
1979	4,500	3,566	5,300	3,700	4,150	4,925	975-2,160	-
1980	5,075	3,566	6,200	4,530	4,150	4,925	1,005-2,280	6,000
1981	5,850	4,400	7,400	4,530	5,550	6,440	1,155-2,520	6,900
1982	6,700	4,590	8,700	4,530	6,380	6,640	1,380-3,510	6,900

	Prince-ton	Rad-cliffe	Univ. of San Fran-cisco	Sarah Law-rence	Smith Coll.	U.S.C.	Southern Meth-odist	Swarth-more	Syra-cuse
1973	$3,300	$3,200	$1,950	$3,650	$2,670	$1,350	$2,000	$2,650	$2,880
1974	3,500	3,200	2,200	3,900	4,580	2,910	2,200	2,870	-
1975	3,900	3,740	2,200	4,150	3,330	3,400	2,200	3,170	3,030
1976	-	-	-	-	-	-	-	-	-
1977	4,300	4,450	2,860	4,750	-	3,840	-	4,210	3,650
1978	5,100	4,450	-	5,050	4,100	4,200	2,760	4,250	-
1979	5,100	5,300	3,400	5,500	4,700	4,200	3,460	5,040	3,735
1980	5,585	5,300	3,850	6,200	5,900	5,310	3,840	5,200	4,500
1981	7,250	5,300	4,430	7,200	5,900	6,150	4,350	6,250	5,000
1982	8,380	8,195	4,430	8,150	6,800	6,300	5,000	7,130	5,000

	Temple	Texas Chris-tian	Tufts	Tulane	Vander-bilt	Vassar	Villa-nova	William & Mary
1973	$1,050	$1,632	$3,200	$2,500	$2,600	$2,900	$2,250	$756
1974	1,050	2,240	3,300	2,700	2,800	2,900	2,400	914
1975	1,050	-	3,600	3,000	3,100	2,900	2,650	944
1976	-	-	-	-	-	-	-	-
1977	1,300	2,400	4,150	3,300	3,400	3,875	3,050	958
1978	1,450-$2,650	2,816	4,500	3,940	3,950	3,875	3,200	1,074-$2,524
1979	1,610-3,000	2,820	5,050	4,546	4,260	3,875	3,500	1,076-2,658
1980	1,810-3,374	3,200	5,850	5,046	4,700	5,375	3,850	1,184-2,928
1981	2,068-3,854	3,520	5,850	5,056	5,300	6,400	4,290	1,344-3,368
1982	2,832-4,440	3,750	7,650	5,600	6,100	6,400	4,362	1,334-3,368

Recap and Flashback
of Relevant Facts _____

	1950	1960	1970	1980
U.S. Population	150,697,361*	179,323,175*	203,302,031*	226,504,825*
% of Population				
5-19 years old	23.2%*	27.1%*	29.5%*	24.8%*
20-44 years old	37.6%*	32.2%*	31.7%*	37.1%*
Males per 100 Females				
Total	98.6*	97.1*	94.8*	94.5*
5-19 years old	102.5*	102.7*	103.3*	104.0*
20-44 years old	96.2*	95.6*	95.1*	98.1*
Marriages	11.1%	8.5%	10.6%	10.9%
Divorces	2.6%	2.2%	3.5%	5.3%
Ever Married				
Males 15-19 yrs.	2.9%	3.3%	2.6%	2.7%
Females 15-19 yrs.	14.4%	13.5%	9.7%	8.9%
Males 20-24 yrs.	41.0%	46.9%	45.3%	31.4%
Females 20-24 yrs.	67.7%	71.6%	64.2%	49.8%
Males 25-29 yrs.	76.2%	79.2%	80.9%	67.6%
Females 25-29 yrs.	86.6%	89.5%	89.5%	79.2%
Living Alone				
Males 15-24 yrs.	—	1.8%	2.5%	5.2%
Females 15-24 yrs.	—	1.6%	2.6%	4.2%
Males 25-44 yrs.	—	9.7%	8.6%	16.0%
Females 25-44 yrs.	—	7.4%	6.2%	9.9%
Households in U.S.	43,554,000	52,799,000	63,401,000	79,108,000
Average Number of Persons per Household	3.37	3.33	3.14	2.75
Families in U.S.	39,303,000	45,111,000	51,586,000	52,426,000
Average Number of Persons in a Family	3.54	3.67	3.58	3.28

*Data from official U.S. government census.
Note: Dashes indicate unavailable data.

	1950	**1960**	**1970**	**1980**
Families Maintained				
by Women				
Total	—	4,494,000	5,591,000	8,540,000
Under 35 yrs.	—	17.7%	24.4%	34.0%
35-44 yrs.	—	20.9%	19.2%	22.5%
45 and over	—	61.4%	56.3%	43.4%
Births per 1,000				
Population	24.1%	23.7%	18.4%	16.2%
Births to Unmarried				
Women				(1978)
Under 15 yrs.	3,200	4,600	9,500	9,400
				(1978)
15-19 yrs.	56,000	87,100	190,400	239,700
				(1978)
20-24 yrs.	20,900	68,000	126,700	186,500
	(1949)	(1959)	(1969)	(1978)
Motor Vehicle Deaths	31,701	37,910	55,791	51,900
Total Motor Vehicle				
Registrations	49.2 million	73.9 million	108.4 million	154.7 million
Households with				
TV Sets	3,875,000	45,750,000	59,550,000	150,000,000
Households with Radio	40,700,000	50,193,000	62,000,000	—
				(1975)
Books Published	11,022	15,012	36,071	39,372
Telephones per				(1975)
1,000 Population	280.9	407.8	583.4	695
Average Purchasing				
Power of the Dollar	Approx.	Approx	Approx.	Approx.
Worth $1.00 in 1967	$1.38	$1.12	86¢	40¢
(Consumer Prices)				
Currency in				(1981)
Circulation (in billions)	$27.156	$32.064	$54.351	$138.080
U.S. Receipts (in billions,				
to nearest hundred	(1955)			
million)	$60.4	$77.8	$193.8	$520
U.S. Expenditures				
(in billions, to nearest	(1955)			
hundred million)	$64.6	$76.5	$195	$579

	1950	1960	1970	1980
Social Welfare Percentages of all Govt. Expenditures	37.6%	38.0%	47.8%	(1975 est.) 58.4%
Annual Per Capita Personal Income	$,1,501	$2,219	$3,893	$9,458
Gross Personal Income (in billions, to nearest hundred million)	$227.6	$401.0	$808.3	$2,160.2
Disposable Personal Income (in billions for spending and saving)	$206.9	$350.0	$691.7	$1,821.7
Rate of Personal Saving	6.3%	4.9%	8.1%	5.6%
Families Earning				
$25,000 and over	—	1.0%	5.0%	41.6%
$15,000-$24,999	—	3.1%	18.7%	28.3%
$12,500-$14,999	—	3.3%	11.5%	6.8%
$10,000-$12,499	—	7.9%	16.4%	7.1%
$7,500-$9,999	—	16.2%	16.8%	6.0%
$5,000-$7,499	—	29.6%	14.6%	5.3%
$2,500-$4,999	—	23.8%	11.4%	3.3%
Under $2,500	—	15.1%	5.6%	1.6%
Non-Installment Outstanding Consumer Credit (in billions, to nearest hundred million)	$10.1	$20.1	$37.6	$72.2
Personal Consumption Expenditures (in billions, to nearest hundred million)	$192.0	$324.9	$618.8	(1979) $1,510.0
Women in Total Working Population (Age 10 up)	17.3%	19.4%	22.5%	26.9%
Working Women in Female Population (Age 10 up)	33.9%	37.8%	43.4%	51.7%
Women's Earnings as a Percentage of Men's	—	60.7%	59.4%	(1979) 59.7%
Median Age First Marriage: Male	22.8 years	22.8 years	23.2 years	24.6 years
Median Age First Marriage: Female	20.3 years	20.3 years	20.8 years	22.1 years

	1950	1960	1970	1980
U.S. (proved) Crude Oil Reserves (thousands of 42-gallon barrels)	25,268,398	31,613,211	39,001,335	(1979) 27,051,289
Annual Average Per Capita Consumption of (all in pounds unless otherwise noted)				
Meat	—	134.1	151.4	151.1
Fish	—	10.3	11.8	13.2
Eggs	—	42.4	39.5	35.4
Chicken (ready to cook)	—	27.8	40.5	51.2
Turkey (ready to cook)	—	6.2	8.0	10.6
Cheese	—	8.3	11.5	17.6
Condensed & Evaporated Milk	—	13.7	7.1	3.8
Fluid Milk & Cream (product weight)	—	302	277	250
Butter	—	7.5	5.3	4.6
Margarine	—	9.4	11.0	11.2
Fresh Fruits	—	90.0	79.4	84.0
Canned Fruit	—	22.6	23.2	18.0
Canned Juice	—	12.9	14.5	17.3
Frozen Fruit & Juice	—	9.2	9.3	12.6
Fresh Vegetables	—	96.0	91.1	100.2
Frozen Vegetables	—	7.0	9.6	10.7
Coffee	—	11.6	10.4	8.1
Refined Sugar	—	97.3	101.8	85.6
Physicians Per 100,000 Resident Population	(1955) 255,000	275,000	348,000	(1978) 454,000
Dentists Per 100,000 Resident Population (excluding those in Federal service)	(1955) 47,000	47,000	47,000	(1978) 53,000
Population Aged 5-17 Years	30,788,000	43,881,000	52,435,000	(1978) 48,046,000
Pupils Enrolled in Public Schools	25,111,427	36,086,771	45,909,088	(1978) 42,611,000
% of 5-17-year-old Population Enrolled in Public Schools	82%	82%	88%	(1978) 89%
High School Graduates	1,199,700	1,864,000	2,896,000	(1978) 3,147,000
College Graduates	432,058	392,440	827,234	921,000
Total Institutions of Higher Education	1,863	1,959	2,525	(1978) 2,606

The Fast Pace of Firsts in the Rock Era _____

1954

First: Atomic-powered submarine (*Nautilus*) . . . RCA color TV—15-inch set selling for $1,000 . . . Frozen TV dinners marketed . . . Silicon transistors (Texas Instruments) . . . Mass injections of Salk polio vaccine . . . Practical system for recording the complete TV waveform onto magnetic tape (RCA) . . . Transistorized radio receiver . . . Coast-to-coast color telecast ("Tournament of Roses" parade) . . . Tri-X high-speed film from Kodak . . . Appearance of Trix breakfast food (46.6% sugar) . . . Miltown tranquilizer . . . Oral contraceptives tested . . . Under-four-minute mile run by Roger Bannister, in 3 min. 59.4 sec. . . . Vertical takeoff airplane ("Flying Bedstead") developed in Britain . . . Jet transport built . . . Automatic toll collector (on Garden State Parkway) . . . Rocket to exceed 150 mile altitude . . . Electronic business computer . . . Traveling sidewalk (in Jersey City railroad station) . . . Large transistorized computer . . . Dual headlamps on cars introduced by Cadillac . . . Solar batteries . . . Gas-turbine auto exhibited . . . Body tissue bank (at Bethesda Hospital) . . . Regular scheduled round-the-world flights—over North Pole . . . Measles vaccine . . . Instant dry milk which dissolves quickly in water (Carnation) . . . McDonald's hamburger stand outside of California begins national chain . . . Eight-track tape recorder (built by Les Paul) . . .

ANNIVERSARIES OF FIRST PUBLIC OFFERINGS OF NEW PRODUCTS

100th: Perforated postage stamp (Britain) . . .

1955

First: Roll-on deodorant . . . Colonel Sanders' Kentucky Fried Chicken . . . Fluoride toothpaste (Crest) . . . Stereo radio broadcast . . . Electronic kitchen stove for domestic use . . . Ads in *Reader's Digest* . . . Non-stick (Tefal) pans . . . Home stereo tape recorder . . . Coca-Cola Company official use of word "Coke" . . . Appearance of Special K breakfast food (4.4% sugar) . . . "Ann Landers Says" newspaper column . . . Filter cigarettes promoted by a major firm . . . Ford Thunderbird and Volkswagen Karmann-Ghia . . . Sun-powered auto demonstrated . . . Parachute bailout from supersonic plane . . . Atom bomb-resistant Federal building . . . Midas Muffler shops spread nationally . . . Disneyland opens . . . Use of UHF (Ultra High Frequency) waves developed at M.I.T. . . . Atomically-generated power (used in Schenectady, New York) . . . Electronic computers for weather forecasting . . . Nuclear reactor patent issued to Enrico Fermi and Leo Szilard . . . Seatbelts and padded dashboards offered by Ford as optional equipment . . . Pinball game for two players (Gottlieb's Duette) . . . Solar-cooled building . . . Radiation-cooled house . . . Mr. Donut shop—with 40 varieties . . .

ANNIVERSARIES OF FIRST PUBLIC OFFERINGS OF NEW PRODUCTS

50th: Electric toasters . . . Gasoline stations . . . Portable vacuum cleaners . . . *100th:* Potato chips . . . Safety matches . . .

1956

First: Instant coffee . . . Telephones and typewriters in wide range of colors . . . Transatlantic cable telephone transmission . . . Visual telephone devised . . . No-hit, no-run, no-walk World Series game . . . Movie star on postage stamp (Grace Kelly) . . . Video recorder for broadcast industry (taped TV shows) from Ampex . . . Baseball umpire wearing eyeglasses . . . Motorcycle racer exceeds 200 miles an hour . . . Airborne H-bomb exploded . . . Ion microscope magnifying 2¾ million times; individual atoms seen . . . Fabric softeners (Sta-Puf and Nu-Soft) . . .

ANNIVERSARIES OF FIRST PUBLIC OFFERINGS OF NEW PRODUCTS

50th: Animated cartoon films . . . Radio broadcast . . . *100th*: Detective novel (Britain) . . .

1957

First: Nuclear power plant . . . Electric portable typewriter . . . Intercontinental ground-to-air ballistic missile . . . Wankel rotary engine . . . Go-karts . . . Pocket-sized transistor radio (Sony) . . . Nuclear plant to produce commercial electric power (in Pennsylvania) . . . Compact cars from U.S. auto industry . . . Dual headlamps become standard equipment on cars . . . Edsel automobile (Ford) . . . Jet plane round-the-world nonstop flight . . . Pay TV test: Bartlesville, Oklahoma, theatre owner sends movies to home audience for monthly fee . . .

ANNIVERSARIES OF FIRST PUBLIC OFFERINGS OF NEW PRODUCTS

50th: Army Air Force . . . Commercial radio telephone . . . Paper towels (Scott) . . . Photocopiers . . . *75th*: Camera film (Britain) . . . Electric fans . . . Electric signs . . . *100th*: Condensed milk (Borden) . . . Electric street lighting (France) . . . Passenger elevator in department store . . .

1958

First: Stereo records . . . Jet transatlantic passenger service . . . U.S. earth satellite, Explorer I . . . Transistorized FM radio (Sony) . . . Television recording in color . . . Liquid shampoo . . . Solid state electronic computer . . . Guided missile destroyer . . . Bifocal contact lenses . . "Telecopter"—airborne TV unit . . .

ANNIVERSARIES OF FIRST PUBLIC OFFERINGS OF NEW PRODUCTS

50th: Horror film . . . Model T Ford . . . *100th*: Divorce courts (Britain) . . . Steel ship (Britain) . . .

1959

First: Domestic passenger jet service (transcontinental) . . . Polaroid cameras . . . Transistorized TV set from Sony . . . Ballistic missile sub launched . . . Astronauts selected by NASA . . . Anti-missile missile . . . Metrecal—weight-reducing aid . . . Synthetic penicillin marketed . . .Identi-kit (Los Angeles Police) . . . Barbie doll . . . Xerox automatic copier . . . Rocket plane (North American X-15) successful flight under own power . . . Photograph in color of Earth from Outer Space . . . Telecast received from England . . .

ANNIVERSARIES OF FIRST PUBLIC OFFERINGS OF NEW PRODUCTS

50th: Pilots' licenses (France) . . . *75th*: Cash register . . . Commercially successful fountain pens . . . *100th*: Passenger elevators in hotel . . . Railway car lavatories . . . Vaseline . . .

1960

First: Laser built at Hughes Aircraft . . . Nuclear-powered aircraft carrier launched . . . Privately-financed nuclear power plant, just outside Chicago . . . Oral contraceptives (Enovid) marketed . . . Communications satellite—Echo I . . . Aluminum cans for food and beverages—but 90% of soft drinks and 50% of beer still in returnable bottles . . . Weather satellite—Tiros 1—launched. Sends back 23,000 TV pictures of global cloud cover . . . Pentel fibre-tipped pen . . . Marketing of FDA-approved

anti-anxiety Librium . . . Transistorized videotape recorder (Sony) . . .
Heart pacemaker . . . Presidential candidate TV debate (Kennedy-Nixon)
. . . Add-a-Ball pinball flipper—for areas where free games prohibited
although pinball is legal . . . Electronic wristwatch placed on sale . . .

ANNIVERSARIES OF FIRST PUBLIC OFFERINGS OF NEW PRODUCTS

50th: Aeroplane radio transmission . . . Aircraft carrier . . . Crisco
shortening . . . Neon lighting (France) . . . Policewoman . . . Rayon
stocking . . . *75th*: Bottled fresh milk (Borden) . . . Motor boats . . .

1961

First: Successful manned space flight by an American (Virgil I. Grissom)
. . . Seawater conversion plant opened . . . Electric toothbrush . . .
Regular in-flight movies (TWA) . . . Intra-uterine contraceptive
devices . . . Live telecast of a Presidential news conference (JFK) . . .
Powdered coffee creamer (Coffee-Mate) . . . Cheap (19¢) ballpoint pens
(BiC) . . . Disposable diapers (Pampers) . . .

ANNIVERSARIES OF FIRST PUBLIC OFFERINGS OF NEW PRODUCTS

75th: Coca-Cola . . . Dinner jacket . . . Postum . . . *100th*: Bicycles
(France) . . . Postcards . . .

1962

First: American astronaut to orbit the Earth (John Glenn) . . . U.S.
satellite to reach the Moon . . . Nuclear warhead fired from sub . . . Tab-
opening aluminum cans for soft drinks and beer . . . Sugar-free soft drink
sold nationwide: Diet-Rite Cola . . . Communications satellite, Telstar,
relays live radio and TV to Europe . . . Long-distance xerography . . .
Fillet o' Fish added to McDonald's hamburger outlets . . . Dry soup
mixes . . .

ANNIVERSARIES OF FIRST PUBLIC OFFERINGS OF NEW PRODUCTS

50th: Cellophane (Switzerland) . . . Nationwide public opinion poll . . .
Radio broadcast station . . . Supermarket . . . *75th*: Appendix operation
. . . Illustrated advertisement (Britain) . . . Log Cabin Syrup . . .
Mimeograph machine . . . Sears Roebuck catalog . . .

1963

First: Effective measles vaccine licensed for U.S. manufacture . . .Cas-
sette tape recorders . . . Use of artificial heart . . . Instamatic cameras . . .
Introduction of Tab by Coca-Cola . . . Woman astronaut . . . Weight

Watchers club . . . Successful optical hologram . . . Instant color film (Polaroid) . . . Sloping rear windows on cars: "Fastbacks" . . . Push button telephones . . . TV pictures from space sent back by astronaut Gordon Cooper . . . Trans-Pacific telecast via satellite previews live coverage of 1964 Tokyo Olympics . . .

ANNIVERSARIES OF FIRST PUBLIC OFFERINGS OF NEW PRODUCTS

50th: Crossword puzzle . . . Electric refrigerators . . . Player pianos . . . *75th*: Chewing gum vending machines . . . Motor cars on sale (Germany) . . . *100th*: Baking Powder (Royal) . . . Four-wheeled roller skates . . . Railroad dining car . . .

1964

First: ZIP codes adopted by U.S. Post Office . . . Freeze-dried instant coffee . . . Seatbelts in new cars without extra charge . . . Topless dancers —in San Francisco bar . . . True permanent press slacks from Levi Strauss under its Sta-Prest label . . . Close-up pictures of Moon sent back by Ranger 7 . . .

ANNIVERSARIES OF FIRST PUBLIC OFFERINGS OF NEW PRODUCTS

50th: Airline . . . *75th*: Camera roll film . . . Electric heaters . . . Juke box . . . Pay phones . . .

1965

First: Early Bird I satellite establishes regular telephone and TV communication with Europe . . . Diet Pepsi . . . Transistor microphone (Sony) . . . Home videotape recorders . . . Soft margarine . . . Freeze-dried fruits packaged with breakfast cereals . . . Carnation Instant Breakfast . . . Rechargeable flashlights . . . Tear strip vacuum coffee cans . . . Tear-top peanut cans . . . Plane to fly over 2,000 miles per hour (at Edwards Air Force Base) . . .

ANNIVERSARIES OF FIRST PUBLIC OFFERINGS OF NEW PRODUCTS

50th: Aspirin tablets . . . Hallmark cards . . . *75th*: Commercial (cylinder) phonograph records . . . Data-processing computer . . . Frozen food . . .

1966

First: Moog Synthesizers . . . Flash cubes . . . Mastercharge cards . . . Order for 747 jets (25 for Pan Am) . . . Plastic heart keeps patient alive several days . . . Hillbilly soft drinks: Mountain Dew (Pepsi-Cola);

Kickapoo Joy Juice (National Nu-Grape); White Lightning and Kick (Royal Crown). All fail to catch on . . . Ready-prepared seasoned coating mix in which to shake chicken . . . Meatloaf mix to combine with ground beef . . . Home laundries include added cycles for washing and drying permanent press fabrics . . . Integrated circuits (using silicon chips) in RCA TV sets—first mass consumer product to contain them . . . Almost-completely integrated clock radio (GE) . . . $1 wear-and-throw-away paper dress (Scott Paper) . . . Throwaway academic caps and gowns for graduation ceremonies . . .

ANNIVERSARIES OF FIRST PUBLIC OFFERINGS OF NEW PRODUCTS

50th: Natural color cartoon movies . . . Windshield wipers . . . *75th*: Electric ovens . . . *100th*: Plastic (Britain) . . . Radio telegraph . . .

1967

First: Laser surgery operating theater (in Cincinnati) . . . Heart transplant operation . . . Superbowl game . . . Compact microwave oven for home use . . . Liberalized model penal code abortion statute adopted, by Colorado . . .UHF television programs (join VHF) nationally . . . Combined electric can opener and knife sharpener . . . Toaster-grill ovens . . . Front seat belts as regular equipment in all new cars . . .

ANNIVERSARIES OF FIRST PUBLIC OFFERINGS OF NEW PRODUCTS

75th: Toothpaste tubes . . . Wrigley's chewing gum . . .

1968

First: Flight to Moon (command service module only) with views of lunar surface televised to Earth . . . Over-500,000 net kilowatt nuclear plant—Nine-Mile Point, Oswego, N.Y. . . . TVP (textured vegetable protein) for meat substitutes . . . 911 emergency telephone number (in New York) . . . UHT milk (ultra heat treated) with six-month shelf life . . .

ANNIVERSARIES OF FIRST PUBLIC OFFERINGS OF NEW PRODUCTS

50th: Full-length cartoon movie . . . *75th*: Breakfast cereal . . . Drivers' licenses (France) . . . License plates (France) . . . Movie studio . . . Newspaper color supplement . . . Striptease (France) . . . Tractors . . . Zip fasteners . . . *100th*: Traffic lights (Britain) . . .

1969

First: Commercial 747 jet service . . . Concorde flight . . . Man to set foot on Moon—Neil Armstrong . . . Hurricane "seeded" with silver iodide, reducing intensity . . . Color pictures of the Moon and Earth from the Moon on TV . . .

ANNIVERSARIES OF FIRST PUBLIC OFFERINGS OF NEW PRODUCTS

75th: Commercially-produced motorcycles (Germany) . . . Disc record players (electric) . . . *100th*: A&P . . .

1970

First: Portable electronic calculator . . . Phosphate-free detergents . . . Quadrophonic discs and tapes . . . Use of nuclear-powered heart "pacemakers" . . . Goodyear "Crazy Wheel" colored bicycle tire . . . Unit pricing in supermarkets . . . Digital watches . . . Chunky ready-to-serve soups (Campbell) . . .

ANNIVERSARIES OF FIRST PUBLIC OFFERINGS OF NEW PRODUCTS

50th: Kotex . . . News broadcast . . . Ready-made home radio sets . . . *75th*: Movie actors . . . X-rays . . . *100th*: Typewriters (Denmark) . . .

1971

First: Space probe to orbit another planet—Mariner 9 circles Mars . . . U.S. experiments with acupuncture as anesthetic, pain reliever and cure after doctors return from Mainland China with glowing reports . . . Pocket Instamatic cameras (Kodak) . . . Pay TV via cable (commercial-free) . . .

ANNIVERSARIES OF FIRST PUBLIC OFFERINGS OF NEW PRODUCTS

50th: Bathing beauty contest . . . Betty Crocker mixes . . . Hershey Bars . . . Sports broadcast . . . *75th*: Book matches . . . Electric iron . . . Escalators . . . Ice cream cones . . . IQ tests (France) . . . Outboard motors . . . Taxicabs (Germany) . . . *100th*: Margarine (Holland) . . .

1972

First: Major name brand "100% natural" cereal (Quaker) . . . McDonald's Quarter Pounder . . . Video games for home TV sets (Magnavox "Odyssey") . . . Coin-operated video games (Atari "Pong") . . .

ANNIVERSARIES OF FIRST PUBLIC OFFERINGS OF NEW PRODUCTS

50th: Commercial radio program . . . *Reader's Digest* . . . *75th*: Comic strips . . . Condensed soup (Campbell's) . . . Grape Nuts cereal . . . Recording studio . . . Second-hand car dealer (Britain) . . . *100th*: Chewing gum (Chicle) . . .

1973

First: Space station (Skylab) into orbit . . .

ANNIVERSARIES OF FIRST PUBLIC OFFERINGS OF NEW PRODUCTS

50th: 16 mm home movie cameras and projectors . . . *75th*: Corn Flakes
. . . Flashlights . . . *100th*: Commercially-produced typewriters (Reming-
ton) . . .

1974

First: Sextuplets to survive (Capetown, South Africa) . . . Satellite
owned and operated by U.S. business—resulting from FCC "open skies"
policy, established in 1972—Westar I . . .

ANNIVERSARIES OF FIRST PUBLIC OFFERINGS OF NEW PRODUCTS

50th: Cylinder vacuum cleaners (Electrolux) . . . *75th*: Juvenile
court . . . Public garage (Britain) . . .

1975

First: U.S.-USSR joint flight crews linked up in space . . . Videocassette
recorder (VCR) for consumers—Sony Betamax . . . Computerized supermarket checkout . . . Non-stick chewing gum from Wrigley for denture
wearers . . . Home Box Office cable program service by satellite . . . Tam-
pons advertised on TV (Playtex) . . .

ANNIVERSARIES OF FIRST PUBLIC OFFERINGS OF NEW PRODUCTS

50th: All-electric phonograph . . . *75th*: Paper labels on phonograph
records . . . *100th*: Canned baked beans . . . Milk chocolate (Switzerland)
. . .

1976

First: Successful space craft landing on Mars . . . Home computers
(Apple) . . .

ANNIVERSARIES OF FIRST PUBLIC OFFERINGS OF NEW PRODUCTS

50th: Radio network (NBC) . . . *75th*: Electric typewriters . . . Electric
vacuum cleaners . . . Quaker Oats . . . *100th*: Heinz bottled pickles . . .
Telephones . . .

1977

First: Free flights by space shuttle . . . Male birth control pill devised by
University of Washington Medical School . . . Water detected outside

Earth's galaxy, indicating possibility of life in outer space . . . Instant motion picture system by Polaroid (Polavision) . . . Videocassette recorder with two-hour recording time (VHS) . . . "No name" (generic or unbranded) products in retail markets (Chicago) . . .

ANNIVERSARIES OF FIRST PUBLIC OFFERINGS OF NEW PRODUCTS

50th: Canned baby foods (Gerber) . . . Commercially-produced car radios . . . *75th*: Jell-O (General Foods) . . . *100th*: Bell Telephone Company . . . Jars of toothpaste (Colgate) . . .

1978

First: Fusion nuclear reactor—using seawater and leaving very little atomic waste. But it won't be ready for use till 21st century . . . Legalized gambling in Atlantic City . . . Transatlantic balloon trip . . . Test tube baby born in England from egg fertilized outside womb . . . Scented ballpoint pens (to match particular hue) . . . Volkswagen manufactured in U.S. . . . Home (micro) computers . . . 45 r.p.m. picture disc records on market . . .

ANNIVERSARIES OF FIRST PUBLIC OFFERINGS OF NEW PRODUCTS

50th: Bubblegum . . . Kool-Aid (General Foods) . . . Penicillin . . . *75th*: Aeroplane flight . . . Four-wheel motor cars . . . Magnetic (wire) recorders . . . Pepsi-Cola . . . Police cars . . . Safety razors . . . Western movies . . . *100th*: Phonographs . . . Telephone exchange (Hartford, Conn.) . . .

1979

First: Spine replacement by surgery . . . Land vehicle breaks sound barrier at 739.666 m.p.h., using 6,000 lbs. of thrust from rocket engine of Sidewinder missile . . . Close photos of Saturn from Pioneer 11 . . . Erasable ink pens . . . Nitrite-free hot dogs . . . Double-vision TV set, showing inset of a second program in black and white in corner of color program being viewed . . . Voyagers 1 and 2 send back 33,000 pictures of Jupiter . . . Artificial bones from demineralized bone powder for implants (developed by Harvard researchers) . . . Cracker Jack ice cream bars . . . Video recorders (VHS) with two, four and six-hour modes and Betamax 4½-5 hour modes . . . "Space Invaders" coin-operated video game . . .

ANNIVERSARIES OF FIRST PUBLIC OFFERINGS OF NEW PRODUCTS

50th: Academy Awards . . . Talking picture . . . *100th*: Canned roasted coffee . . . Ivory soap (P&G) . . . Milk bottles . . . Woolworth's (5¢ store) . . .

1980

First: "Asteroids" coin-operated video game . . . Pocket-sized stereo cassette players with lightweight earphones (Sony Walkman) . . . Acoustic microscope . . . Balloon trip across U.S.—3,100 miles . . . California skate brake that attaches to heel of skates . . . Fifty-speed bicycles . . . Invisible braces attached to the back of teeth . . . Chocolate-flavored bubble gum . . . Strawberry Shortcake doll and four scented companions (she smells like strawberries) . . . Long-distance solar-powered flight covering six miles in 22 minutes . . . Magnavox optical laser videodisc system and MCA videodiscs . . . Liquid soap (Soft Soap from Minnetonka) . . .

ANNIVERSARIES OF FIRST PUBLIC OFFERINGS OF NEW PRODUCTS

50th: Air stewardess . . . Birds Eye individually packaged frozen foods . . . 16 mm sound film projectors for amateur use . . . *100th*: Electric light bulbs . . . Electric street lighting for entire towns, replacing gas . . . Newspaper photographs . . .

1981

First: Manned space shuttle—Columbia . . . ZIP plus four adopted— adding four digits to ZIP codes (will save $600 million a year) . . . Soft bathtubs made of polyurethane foam . . . Solar-powered radios . . . RCA videodiscs . . . Talking dashboard system which gives voice warnings through car radio when low on fuel, seat belts unfastened, dangerous oil pressure, and other hazards . . . Direct Broadcast Satellite (DBS) systems approved by FCC. Eliminating middle men, TV networks and cable, DBS enables consumer to pick up certain satellite transmissions with small dish antennae . . . Test tube baby born in U.S. . . . Non-metallic organic battery (may eventually have potential for use in electric cars) . . . Contact lenses that can be worn continuously for up to two weeks (Hydrocube II) approved for general use by FDA . . . Artificial skin for burn victims, made from cowhide, shark cartilage and plastic . . . Cloning of a mammal (mouse) by Swiss scientists . . . Acupuncture successful in treatment of drug (heroin) abuse at Haight-Ashbury free medical clinic . . . "Cable ready" TV sets capable of receiving almost 60 cable channels plus over 120 VHF and UHF direct telecasts . . . Tubeless color TV camera—using metal-oxide semiconductor (Hitachi) . . . Electric wet or dry shaver (Matsushita) . . . Stereo videodiscs and players (RCA) for 1982 delivery . . . Cameras using flat, round discs as film for 15 pictures (Kodak) . . . Pocketsized TV sets with two-inch screens measuring 8 in. long, 3.4 in. wide and 1.4 in. thick, weighing 18.6 oz. (Sony) . . . Home satellite receivers (concave discs hooked into TV sets) called "earth stations," picking up cable programs as well as live telecasts from as far off as Russia. Kits sell for $2,000 and finished systems for $3,000-$5000 . . . Camera which records images on videodiscs (Sony) . . . Dick Tracy-style TV wristwatch with headphones (Seiko) . . .

ANNIVERSARIES OF FIRST PUBLIC OFFERINGS OF NEW PRODUCTS

50th: Alka-Seltzer . . . Electric razor . . .

Winners Relevant to the Rock Era _____

	Rose Bowl	Orange Bowl	Sugar Bowl	Cotton Bowl
1954	Michigan State	Oklahoma	Georgia Tech.	Rice
1955	Ohio State	Duke	Navy	Georgia Tech.
1956	Michigan State	Oklahoma	Georgia Tech.	Mississippi
1957	Iowa	Colorado	Baylor	TCU
1958	Ohio State	Oklahoma	Mississippi	Navy
1959	Iowa	Oklahoma	LSU	TCU
1960	Washington	Georgia	Mississippi	Syracuse
1961	Washington	Missouri	Mississippi	Duke
1962	Minnesota	LSU	Alabama	Texas
1963	Southern California	Alabama	Mississippi	LSU
1964	Illinois	Nebraska	Alabama	Texas
1965	Michigan	Texas	LSU	Arkansas
1966	UCLA	Alabama	Missouri	LSU
1967	Purdue	Florida	Alabama	Georgia Tech.
1968	Southern California	Oklahoma	LSU	Texas A&M
1969	Ohio State	Penn State	Arkansas	Texas
1970	Southern California	Penn State	Mississippi	Texas
1971	Stanford	Nebraska	Tennessee	Notre Dame
1972	Stanford	Nebraska	Oklahoma*	Penn State
1973	Southern California	Nebraska	Notre Dame	Texas
1974	Ohio State	Penn State	Nebraska	Nebraska
1975	Southern California	Notre Dame	Alabama	Penn State
1976	UCLA	Oklahoma	—	Arkansas
1977	Southern California	Ohio State	Pittsburgh	Houston
1978	Washington	Arkansas	Alabama	Notre Dame
1979	Southern California	Oklahoma	Alabama	Notre Dame
1980	Southern California	Oklahoma	Alabama	Houston
1981	Michigan	Oklahoma	Georgia	Alabama
1982	Washington	Clemson	Pittsburgh	Texas

*Penn. State awarded game by default.

	NCAA Basketball Championships	National Invitation Basketball Championship	NCAA College Football*	Pro Football: Super Bowl
1954	La Salle	Holy Cross	Ohio State, UCLA	—
1955	San Francisco	Duquesne	Oklahoma	—
1956	San Francisco	Louisville	Oklahoma	—
1957	North Carolina	Bradley	Auburn, Ohio State	—
1958	Kentucky	Xavier (Ohio)	Louisiana State	—
1959	California	St. John's	Syracuse	—
1960	Ohio State	Bradley	Minnesota	—
1961	Cincinnati	Providence	Alabama	—
1962	Cincinnati	Dayton	Southern California	—
1963	Loyola (Chicago)	Providence	Texas	—
1964	UCLA	Bradley	Alabama	—
1965	UCLA	St. John's	Alabama, Mich. State	—
1966	UCLA	Brigham Young	Notre Dame	—
1967	UCLA	Southern Illinois	Southern California	Green Bay Packers
1968	UCLA	Dayton	Ohio State	Green Bay Packers
1969	UCLA	Temple	Texas	New York Jets
1970	UCLA	Marquette	Nebraska, Texas	Kansas City Chiefs
1971	UCLA	North Carolina	Nebraska	Baltimore Colts
1972	UCLA	Maryland	Southern California	Dallas Cowboys
1973	UCLA	Virginia Tech.	Notre Dame, Alabama	Miami Dolphins
1974	No. Carolina State	Purdue	Oklahoma, Southern Cal.	Miami Dolphins
1975	UCLA	Princeton	Oklahoma	Pittsburgh Steelers
1976	Indiana	Kentucky	Pittsburgh	Pittsburgh Steelers
1977	Marquette	St. Bonaventure	Notre Dame	Oakland Raiders
1978	Kentucky	Texas	Alabama, Southern Cal.	Dallas Cowboys
1979	Michigan State	Indiana	Southern California	Pittsburgh Steelers
1980	Louisville	Virginia	Georgia	Pittsburgh Steelers
1981	Indiana	Tulsa	Clemson	Oakland Raiders
1982	North Carolina	Bradley	Penn State	San Francisco 49ers

*Unofficial national champion selected by AP poll of writers and UPI poll of coaches.

	World Series	Academy Award: Best Actor	Academy Award: Best Actress
1954	New York Giants	Marlon Brando	Grace Kelly
1955	Brooklyn Dodgers	Ernest Borgnine	Anna Magnani
1956	New York Yankees	Yul Brynner	Ingrid Bergman
1957	Milwaukee Brewers	Alec Guinness	Joanne Woodward
1958	New York Yankees	David Niven	Susan Hayward
1959	Los Angeles Dodgers	Charlton Heston	Simone Signoret
1960	Pittsburgh Pirates	Burt Lancaster	Elizabeth Taylor
1961	New York Yankees	Maximilian Schell	Sophia Loren
1962	New York Yankees	Gregory Peck	Anne Bancroft
1963	Los Angeles Dodgers	Sidney Poitier	Patricia Neal
1964	St. Louis Cardinals	Rex Harrison	Julie Andrews
1965	Los Angeles Dodgers	Lee Marvin	Julie Christie
1966	Baltimore Orioles	Paul Schofield	Elizabeth Taylor
1967	St. Louis Cardinals	Rod Steiger	Katharine Hepburn
1968	Detroit Tigers	Cliff Robertson	Katharine Hepburn
1969	New York Mets	John Wayne	Maggie Smith
1970	Baltimore Orioles	George C. Scott	Glenda Jackson
1971	Pittsburgh Pirates	Gene Hackman	Jane Fonda
1972	Oakland As	Marlon Brando	Liza Minelli
1973	Oakland As	Jack Lemmon	Glenda Jackson
1974	Oakland As	Art Carney	Ellen Burstyn
1975	Cincinnati Reds	Jack Nicholson	Louise Fletcher
1976	Cincinnati Reds	Peter Finch	Faye Dunaway
1977	New York Yankees	Richard Dreyfuss	Diane Keaton
1978	New York Yankees	Jon Voight	Jane Fonda
1979	Pittsburgh Pirates	Dustin Hoffman	Sally Field
1980	Philadelphia Phillies	Robert De Niro	Sissy Spacek
1981	Los Angeles Dodgers	Henry Fonda	Katharine Hepburn
1982	St. Louis Cardinals	Ben Kingsley	Meryl Streep

	Miss America	*Time* Magazine Man of the Year
1954	Miss Pennsylvania, Evelyn Ay	John Foster Dulles
1955	Miss California, Lee Meriwether	Harlow Curtice
1956	Miss Colorado, Sharon Ritchie	Hungarian Freedom Fighter
1957	Miss South Carolina, Marian McKnight	Nikita Khrushchev
1958	Miss Colorado, Marilyn Van Derbur	Charles de Gaulle
1959	Miss Mississippi, Mary Ann Mobley	Dwight D. Eisenhower
1960	Miss Mississippi, Lynda Lee Mead	U.S. Scientists
1961	Miss Michigan, Nancy Fleming	John F. Kennedy
1962	Miss North Carolina, Maria Fletcher	Pope John XXIII
1963	Miss Ohio, Jacquelyn Mayer	Martin Luther King, Jr.
1964	Miss Arkansas, Donna Axum	Lyndon B. Johnson
1965	Miss Arizona, Vonda Kay Van Dyke	General William C. Westmoreland
1966	Miss Kansas, Deborah Bryant	The 25 and Under Generation
1967	Miss Oklahoma, Jane Jayroe	Lyndon B. Johnson
1968	Miss Kansas, Debra Dene Barnes	Astronauts Anders, Borman and Lovell
1969	Miss Illinois, Judith Ford	The Middle Americans
1970	Miss Michigan, Pamela Eldred	Willy Brandt
1971	Miss Texas, Phyllis George	Richard M. Nixon
1972	Miss Ohio, Laurie Lea Schaefer	Kissinger and Nixon
1973	Miss Wisconsin, Terry Meeuwsen	John J. Sirica
1974	Miss Colorado, Rebecca King	King Faisal
1975	Miss Texas, Shirley Cothran	Women of the Year
1976	Miss New York, Tawny Godin	Jimmy Carter
1977	Miss Minnesota, Dorothy Benham	Anwar Sadat
1978	Miss Ohio, Susan Perkins	Teng Hsiao-P'ing
1979	Miss Virginia, Kylene Barker	Ayatollah Khomeini
1980	Miss Mississippi, Cheryl Prewitt	Ronald Reagan
1981	Miss Oklahoma, Susan Powell	Lech Walesa
1982	Miss Arkansas, Elizabeth Ward	The Computer (Machine of the Year)

Important Films in the Rock Era _____

Academy Award winners are marked with an asterisk (*).

YOUTH-ORIENTED FILMS

1955

The Blackboard Jungle
East of Eden
Rebel Without a Cause

1956

Don't Knock the Rock
The Girl Can't Help It
Love Me Tender
Rock Around the Clock
Rock, Rock, Rock
Shake, Rattle and Roll

1957

The Big Beat
Jailhouse Rock
Jamboree
Mister Rock and Roll
Tammy and the Bachelor

1958

High School Confidential
King Creole

1959

A Summer Place
Expresso Bongo
Gidget

1960

Because They're Young
G.I. Blues

1961

Blue Hawaii
Hey, Let's Twist
Parrish
Twist Around the Clock
*West Side Story**
Where the Boys Are

1962

Don't Knock the Twist
Follow the Boys
Girls! Girls! Girls!
Kid Galahad

1963

Beach Party
Bye Bye Birdie
Fun in Acapulco

1964

A Hard Day's Night
Bikini Beach
Get Yourself a College Girl
The Girl with Green Eyes

Muscle Beach Party
The T.A.M.I. (Teen Age Music
    International) Show

1965

Beach Ball
Beach Blanket Bingo
Ferry Cross the Mersey
The Girls on the Beach
Go Go Mania
Help!
How to Stuff a Wild Bikini
The Knack
When the Boys Meet
    the Girls

1966

The Big T.N.T. Show
The Endless Summer
Georgy Girl
How I Won the War
You're a Big Boy Now

1967

Blow Up
Don't Look Back
Festival
Good Times
The Graduate
The Hippie Revolt
Magical Mystery Tour
Privilege

1968

Candy
Cream's Last Concert
Head
I Love You, Alice B. Toklas
Mrs. Brown, You've Got a
    Lovely Daughter
Petulia
Revolution
Sympathy for the Devil
2001: A Space Odyssey

Yellow Submarine
You Are What You Eat
Zeffirelli's Romeo and Juliet

1969

Alice's Restaurant
Easy Rider
Goodbye Columbus
If
Last Summer
Medium Cool
Midnight Cowboy
Monterey Pop
Revolution
Take the Money and Run

1970

Brewster McCloud
Catch 22
Elvis—That's the Way It Is
Five Easy Pieces
Gas-s-s-s- or, It May Be
    Necessary to Destroy the
    World in Order to Save It
Gimme Shelter
Groupies
Jimi Hendrix Plays Berkeley
Let It Be
Love Story
The Magic Garden of
    Stanley Sweetheart
Performance
The Strawberry Statement
Woodstock
Zabriskie Point

1971

A Clockwork Orange
Celebration at Big Sur
Mad Dogs and Englishmen
Pink Floyd at Pompeii
Summer of '42
Taking Off
2000 Motels
Two Lane Blacktop

1972

The Concert for Bangladesh
Elvis on Tour
Fillmore

1973

American Graffiti
Class of '44
Godspell
Jesus Christ Superstar
Jimi Hendrix
Let the Good Times Roll
O Lucky Man
That'll Be the Day
Wattstax

1974

Catch My Soul
The Groove Tube
Janis
Ladies and Gentlemen,
   The Rolling Stones
Lenny
Monty Python and the Holy Grail
Pink Floyd Live at Pompeii
Stardust

1975

Cooley High
Nashville
One Flew Over the Cuckoo's Nest*
The Rocky Horror Picture Show
Tommy

1976

All This and World War II
Welcome to L.A.

1977

Between the Lines
Genesis in Concert
Saturday Night Fever
The Song Remains the Same

1978

Almost Summer

American Hot Wax
Big Wednesday
The Buddy Holly Story
FM
Grease
I Want to Hold Your Hand
The Last Waltz
National Lampoon's Animal
   House
Reynaldo and Clara
Sgt. Pepper's Lonely Hearts
   Club Band
Up in Smoke

1979

Americathon
Elvis
Hair
The Kids Are Alright
Meatballs
More American Graffiti
Quadrophenia
The Rose
Rust Never Sleeps

1980

The Blue Lagoon
The Blues Brothers
Caveman
Cheech and Chong's Next Movie
Coal Miner's Daughter
Fame
No Nukes
One-Trick Pony
Roadie

1981

American Pop
Beatlemania
Breaking Glass
Cheech and Chong's Nice Dreams
Endless Love
Heavy Metal
This Is Elvis

HORROR FILMS

1955

Godzilla

1958

The Fly

1960

Psycho

1962

The Day of the Triffids
Kiss of the Vampire

1963

The Birds
The Man with the X-Ray Eyes
The Haunting

1964

The Last Man on Earth

1965

Repulsion

1968

Rosemary's Baby
Night of the Living Dead

1970

Mark of the Devil

1971

The Abominable Dr. Phibes
The Omega Man

1972

Frenzy

1973

The Exorcist

1974

Frankenstein

1975

Young Frankenstein

1976

King Kong
Obsession
The Omen
Carrie

1977

Exorcist II: The Heretic
It's Alive

1978

Coma
The Fury
Hallowe'en
Omen II

1979

Alien
The Amityville Horror
Dracula
Love at First Bite

1980

The Changeling
The Fog
Friday the 13th
Prom Night
The Shining

1981

An American Werewolf in London
Fear No Evil
The Final Conflict
Friday the 13th Part 2
The Funhouse
Hallowe'en II
The Hand
Happy Birthday to Me
The Howling
My Bloody Valentine
Scanners

FANTASY AND SCIENCE FICTION

1955

The Quartermass Experiments

1956

Invasion of the Body Snatchers

1957

The Incredible Shrinking Man

1959

Journey to the Centre of the Earth

1963

Wild in the Streets

1965

Fahrenheit 451

1967

Barbarella

1968

Planet of the Apes
2001: A Space Odyssey

1970

Beneath the Planet of the Apes

1971

The Andromeda Strain
*Escape from the Planet of
   the Apes*

1972

*Conquest of the Planet of
   the Apes*

1973

Battle for the Planet of the Apes
Westworld
Woody Allen's *Sleeper*

1975

Rollerball
Death Race 2000

1976

Forbidden Planet
Futureworld
Logan's Run
The Man Who Fell to Earth

1977

*Close Encounters of
   the Third Kind*
Star Wars

1978

Battlestar Galactica
*Invasion of the Body
   Snatchers* (remake)
The Late Great Planet Earth
The Lord of the Rings
Superman

1979

*Buck Rogers in the Twenty-First
   Century*
Star Trek

1980

The Empire Strikes Back
Xanadu

1981

Altered States
Escape from New York
Flash Gordon
The Incredible Shrinking Woman
Time Bandits

ADULT FILMS WITH YOUTH APPEAL

1954

A Star Is Born
Dragnet
The Glenn Miller Story
Going My Way
The High and the Mighty
On the Waterfront
Seven Brides for Seven Brothers
Three Coins in the Fountain
White Christmas

1955

Guys and Dolls
Love Is a Many Splendored Thing
Marty
Mister Roberts
Oklahoma!
Picnic
The Seven Year Itch
20,000 Leagues Under the Sea

1956

*Around the World in 80 Days**
Bus Stop
Giant
The King and I
Picnic
The Ten Commandments

1957

*The Bridge on the River Kwai**
Peyton Place

1958

*Gigi**
No Time for Sergeants
South Pacific

1959

*Ben Hur**
North By Northwest
Some Like It Hot

1960

*The Apartment**
Exodus

1961

Breakfast at Tiffany's
La Dolce Vita

1962

Days of Wine and Roses
Gypsy
*Lawrence of Arabia**
The Music Man
To Kill a Mockingbird

1963

Charade
It's a Mad, Mad, Mad, Mad World
*Tom Jones**

1964

The Carpetbaggers
Dr. Strangelove
From Russia with Love
Goldfinger
Mary Poppins
*My Fair Lady**
The Pink Panther

1965

Cat Ballou
Doctor Zhivago
*The Sound of Music**
What's New Pussycat?

1966

Alfie
A Man and a Woman
*A Man for All Seasons**
The Chelsea Girls
Hawaii
The Russians Are Coming

Thunderball
Who's Afraid of Virginia Woolf

1967

Bonnie and Clyde
The Dirty Dozen
The Good, the Bad and the Ugly
In the Heat of the Night*
To Sir with Love
Valley of the Dolls
You Only Live Twice

1968

Funny Girl
Guess Who's Coming to Dinner
The Lion in Winter
Oliver*
The Thomas Crown Affair

1969

Bob and Carol and Ted and Alice
Butch Cassidy and the
   Sundance Kid
On Her Majesty's Secret Service
The Sterile Cuckoo
They Shoot Horses, Don't They
Z

1970

Airport
Diary of a Mad Housewife
Hello Dolly
Little Big Man
M*A*S*H
Patton*
Ryan's Daughter

1971

Billy Jack
Carnal Knowledge
Diamonds Are Forever
Dirty Harry
The French Connection*
Klute
Shaft

1972

Cabaret
The Godfather*
The Last Picture Show
The Poseidon Adventure
What's Up Doc?

1973

A Touch of Class
The Day of the Jackal
Enter the Dragon
Five Fingers of Death
Last Tango in Paris
Live and Let Die
Paper Moon
Papillon
Sleeper
The Sting*
The Way We Were

1974

Blazing Saddles
California Split
Earthquake
Freebie and the Bean
The Godfather, Part II*
The Man with the Golden Gun
That's Entertainment

1975

Alice Doesn't Live Here Anymore
Jaws
Return of the Pink Panther
Shampoo
The Towering Inferno
W.W. and the Dixie Dancekings

1976

A Star Is Born
Car Wash
Nickelodeon
The Pink Panther Strikes Again
Rocky*
Taxi Driver
Two Minute Warning

1977

Airport '77
Annie Hall*
New York, New York
Smokey and the Bandit
The Spy Who Loved Me

1978

Coming Home
The Deer Hunter*
Every Which Way But Loose
Hooper
Jaws II
The Lord of the Rings
Midnight Express
Revenge of the Pink Panther

1979

All That Jazz
Apocalypse Now
The Jerk
Kramer vs. Kramer*
Manhattan
Moonraker
The Muppet Movie
1941
North Dallas 40
Rocky II
10

1980

Airplane
Any Which Way You Can
Gilda Live
The Jazz Singer
9 to 5
Ordinary People*
Popeye
Private Benjamin
Stir Crazy
Tess

1981

Arthur
The Cannonball Run
Chariots of Fire*
Excalibur
The French Lieutenant's Woman
For Your Eyes Only
Raiders of the Lost Ark
Reds
Stripes
Tarzan, the Ape Man

Growing Up with TV in the Rock Era

1954

STARTUPS WINNING YOUTH FAVOR	TOP 6*
"Davy Crockett"	1. "I Love Lucy"
"Disneyland"	2. "Dragnet"
"Father Knows Best"	3. Arthur Godfrey's "Talent Scouts"
"George Gobel"	
"Lassie"	4. "You Bet Your Life"
"Rin-Tin-Tin"	5. The Chevy Show (Bob Hope)
	6. "Milton Berle"

Korean war death toll topped by killings in TV drama this year . . . First commercial color television sets marketed . . . Army-McCarthy hearings biggest television show during five-week run . . . NBC and CBS each telecast over 22 hours of color a week . . .

1955

STARTUPS WINNING YOUTH FAVOR	TOP 6
"Captain Kangaroo"	1. "I Love Lucy"
"Cheyenne"	2. "Jackie Gleason"
"Gunsmoke"	3. "Dragnet"
"Mickey Mouse Club"	4. "You Bet Your Life"
"Sergeant Bilko"	5. "Ed Sullivan"
"$64,000 Question"	6. "Disneyland"
"Wyatt Earp"	
"Alfred Hitchcock Presents"	

*Top-rated half dozen (season beginning September of previous year, to April of current year).

Jackie Gleason decides to concentrate on "Honeymooners" . . . Annette joins Mickey Mouse Club . . . Beginning of TV Western era . . . National survey of 1,500 children aged 8-15 finds: (1) They prefer adult programming to children's shows; (2) TV has little effect on reading of comics, club membership or movie attendance . . . U.S. Census Bureau reports that 67% of all U.S. households have TV . . . Broadcasting survey finds that nearly 50% of all TV broadcasting time consists of movies . . .

1956

STARTUPS WINNING YOUTH FAVOR	TOP 6
"$64,000 Challenge"	1. "The $64,000 Question"
"Steve Allen Show"	2. "I Love Lucy"
"Twenty One"	3. "Ed Sullivan Show"
	4. "Disneyland"
	5. "Jack Benny"
	6. "December Bride"

"Ed Sullivan Show" pays Elvis $50,000 to sing "Hound Dog" on TV. Camera above Presley's waist when he gyrates pelvis . . . "$64,000 Question" prize total hits $1 million after giving away $750,000 and ten Cadillacs last year . . . Milton Berle retires after eight years on TV . . . CBS cuts back to seven hours of color a week; NBC to 16 . . .

1957

STARTUPS WINNING YOUTH FAVOR	TOP 6
"American Bandstand"	1. "I Love Lucy"
"Bachelor Father"	2. "Ed Sullivan Show"
"Have Gun Will Travel"	3. "General Electric Theater"
"Leave It to Beaver"	4. "$64,000 Question"
"Maverick"	5. "December Bride"
"Perry Mason"	6. "Alfred Hitchcock"
"Woody Woodpecker Show"	
"Zorro"	

Hanna-Barbera start own firm with "Ruff and Ready" success opening way for their TV cartoon films: "Huckleberry Hound," "Yogi Bear" and "The Flintstones" . . . Former New York Police Commissioner, Arthur W. Wallender, says crime programs glorify criminals and private eyes who put it over on the cops—thereby making kids and parents lose respect for police . . . Tommy Sands's "Teenage Crush" becomes overnight hit after he appears on NBC TV's "Kraft Theatre" . . . Jack Parr replaces Steve

Allen on "Tonight" show . . . Charles Van Doren wins $129,000 on "Twenty One" . . . "American Bandstand" goes network from Philadelphia . . . "Howdy Doody" celebrates its tenth anniversary . . . "I Love Lucy" and "The Lone Ranger" end long runs . . . Nikita Khrushchev interviewed on CBS TV . . .

1958

STARTUPS WINNING YOUTH FAVOR	TOP 6
"Steve Canyon"	1. "Gunsmoke"
"Huckleberry Hound"	2. "Danny Thomas"
"Peter Gunn"	3. "Wells Fargo"
"77 Sunset Strip"	4. "Have Gun Will Travel"
"Yogi Bear Show"	5. "I've Got a Secret"
	6. "Wyatt Earp"

Quiz shows cancelled in major scandal. Prior to cancellations, Teddy Nadler wins record $264,000 . . . Seven out of ten top TV programs are Westerns . . . 11-year-old wins $224,000 on TV quiz show . . . Scare over subliminal messages passes as Government threatens ban and tests question its efficiency . . . Live TV shows disappearing as videotape becomes the less expensive re-usable standard for most programs . . .

1959

STARTUPS WINNING YOUTH FAVOR	TOP 6
"Bonanza"	1. "Gunsmoke"
"Dennis the Menace"	2. "Wagon Train"
"Dobie Gillis"	3. "Have Gun Will Travel"
"Hawaiian Eye"	4. "The Rifleman"
"Rawhide"	5. "Danny Thomas"
"The Twilight Zone"	6. "Maverick"
"The Untouchables"	

"Hit Parade" expires as rock music takes over the hit charts . . . TV quiz show rigging inspires Congressional investigation . . . "Mickey Mouse Club" ends . . .

1960

STARTUPS WINNING YOUTH FAVOR	TOP 6
"Andy Griffith Show"	1. "Gunsmoke"
"The Flintstones"	2. "Wagon Train"

"The Roaring Twenties"   3. "Have Gun Will Travel"
"Surfside Six"   4. "Danny Thomas"
                                5. "Red Skelton"
                                6. "Father Knows Best"

Presidential candidates Kennedy and Nixon debate on TV . . . Year of the Western on TV—11 on ABC, 9 on NBC and 8 on CBS . . . During General Election runup, Kennedy and Nixon forces broadcast 9,000 TV commercials and 29,000 on radio . . . Advertisers spent $10.03 per family on TV spots—ranging from $12.76 in Chicago to $2.73 in Evansville, Indiana and Henderson, Kentucky . . . Presidential election returns most-viewed TV of the year . . .

1961

STARTUPS WINNING YOUTH FAVOR   **TOP 6**

"Ben Casey"   1. "Gunsmoke"
"Dick Van Dyke Show"   2. "Wagon Train"
"Dr. Kildare"   3. "Have Gun Will Travel"
                                4. "Andy Griffith"
                                5. "The Real McCoys"
                                6. "Rawhide"

Chubby Checker popularizes the Twist on Ed Sullivan's show . . . FCC Chairman says TV is a "vast wasteland" . . . Doctors take over from the cowboys on TV . . . National Football League signs $9.3 million two-year contract with CBS . . . President Kennedy orders Federal Space Council to study ways to develop a communications satellite system . . . Strictly controlled game shows offering smaller prizes come back strongly on network TV . . . Kennedy inaugural gets biggest TV audience of year . . .

1962

STARTUPS WINNING YOUTH FAVOR   **TOP 6**

"The Beverly Hillbillies"   1. "Wagon Train"
"McHale's Navy"   2. "Bonanza"
"Tonight Show" starring   3. "Gunsmoke"
    Johnny Carson   4. "Hazel"
                                5. "Perry Mason"
                                6. "Red Skelton"

NBC programming 68% of prime time in color. ABC begins with 3½ hours a week, but CBS still all black and white . . . 1,000 hours of children's TV shows each month are 78.1% cartoons, magic acts and other straight entertainment; 13.1% straight drama or adventure; 8.8% news, science or other information . . . Public now has higher opinion of TV than it had two years ago, according to Roper survey . . . John Glenn's orbital space flight seen by 135 million TV viewers . . . American Cancer Society seeks to stop tobacco company sponsorship of college sports on TV . . . Pay TV starts in Hartford, Connecticut . . .

1963

STARTUPS WINNING YOUTH FAVOR

"Hootenanny"
"My Favorite Martian"
"The Fugitive"
"Mr. Novak"

TOP 6

1. "Beverly Hillbillies"
2. "Candid Camera"
3. "Red Skelton"
4. "Bonanza"
5. "The Lucy Show"
6. "Andy Griffith"

Jack Ruby murders Lee Harvey Oswald in full view of TV audience . . . Superman appears on live TV . . . First instant-replay sports coverage . . . Only NBC telecasting regular color programs; CBS doing little, and ABC nil . . . Dick Clark's "American Bandstand," on the ABC network, cut back to Saturday edition only from afternoon daily plus Saturday evening version . . . NBC reveals plans for made-for-TV movies . . .

1964

STARTUPS WINNING YOUTH FAVOR

"The Addams Family"
"Daniel Boone"
"Gilligan's Island"
"The Man From U.N.C.L.E."
"The Munsters"
"Peyton Place"
"Shindig"

TOP 6

1. "Beverly Hillbillies"
2. "Bonanza"
3. "Dick Van Dyke"
4. "Petticoat Junction"
5. "Andy Griffith"
6. "Lucy"

Vietnam war first in history brought directly into homes via TV . . . Not one police or detective drama on network TV . . . Record 78 million people watch first Beatles appearance with Ed Sullivan . . . A single performance of "Hamlet" on network TV reaches more people than all performances in theaters from Shakespeare's day until now . . . Presidential election battle blankets TV with 29,300 commercials, with another 63,000 on radio—following effective marketing of JFK four years ago . . . Lower prices increase color TV set sales . . . In landmark decision, Supreme Court rules that razor blade manufacturer can't shave fake sandpaper in a TV ad—even for a laugh . . . The Beatles on the "Ed Sullivan Show" tied with election returns for year's top viewing audiences . . .

1965

STARTUPS WINNING YOUTH FAVOR	TOP 6
"Get Smart"	1. "Bonanza"
"Gomer Pyle"	2. "Bewitched"
"Hogan's Heroes	3. "Gomer Pyle U.S.M.C."
"Hullabaloo"	4. "Andy Griffith"
"I Dream of Jeannie"	5. "The Fugitive"
	6. "Red Skelton"

"Spy spoofs" new programming vogue—comedies with bumbling secret agent as the hero . . . TV Westerns down to five shows, from peak 15 in 1960 . . . Radio learns to live with TV as profits rise over $77 million after dropping to $32 million four years ago from $61 million in 1952 . . . "Amos 'n Andy" withdrawn from TV syndication following protests against its stereotyped images of blacks . . . "The Man from U.N.C.L.E." and this year's "Get Smart" score big at colleges . . . Black man plays equally important role with white for first time in "Spy" . . . All but 1½ hours of NBC primetime TV in color as boom finally begins . . . First advertiser to mention competitor by name, Renault starts trend by using Volkswagen in TV commercial . . .

1966

STARTUPS WINNING YOUTH FAVOR	TOP 6
"The Avengers"	1. "Bonanza"
"Batman"	2. "Gomer Pyle"
"Mission Impossible"	3. "Lucy"
"Monkees"	4. "Red Skelton"
"Star Trek"	5. "Batman"
	6. "Andy Griffith"

One out of every three viewers watch "Batman" as it shoots into top six . . . "Green Hornet" adapted to TV, with Bruce Lee in role of Kato . . . "The Honeymooners" returns . . . All three networks offer color TV . . . Situation comedies, Westerns, suspense and mystery programs continue to dominate network schedules, but presentation of full-length movies expanded to five nights a week—with plans to go to sixth night next year . . . Average U.S. home spending 5.21 hours a day watching TV . . . Largest audience for any movie ever shown on TV for "The Bridge on the River Kwai" on ABC . . .

1967

STARTUPS WINNING YOUTH FAVOR

"Smothers Brothers Comedy
  Hour"

TOP 6

1. "Bonanza"
2. "Red Skelton"
3. "Andy Griffith"
4. "Lucy"
5. "Jackie Gleason"
6. "Green Acres"

Procter & Gamble spends $200 million on advertising—mostly television
—eight times the amount paid by Thomas Jefferson for the entire Louisiana
Purchase . . . Johnny Carson reputedly earning $25,000 a week . . . All
network shows now telecast in color . . . "What's My Line?" ends during
its eighteenth year . . . Average 18-year-old, the child of TV's first
generation, has now viewed approximately 17,000 hours of TV, vs. 12,000
hours spent in the classroom . . . More comedy shows on U.S. TV during
first 20 years than on all stages in all history . . . Trendex survey for NBC
reports that more people listen to radio during course of average week than
watch TV . . . "Dragnet" returns . . . Networks begin own feature film
production . . . Both NBC and CBS telecast the Super Bowl game . . .
Final episode of "The Fugitive" ties with President Johnson's "State of the
Union" address for top viewing audience of year . . .

1968

STARTUPS WINNING YOUTH FAVOR

"The Archie Show"
"Hawaii Five-O"
"Here's Lucy"
"Mannix"
"The Mod Squad"
Rowan and Martin's "Laugh-In"

TOP 6

1. "Andy Griffith"
2. "Lucy"
2. "Gomer Pyle"
4. "Gunsmoke"
5. "Family Affair"
6. "Bonanza"

TV viewers see Bobby Kennedy assassinated . . . Nielsen survey reports
average U.S. home watched TV 6.75 hours per day in January . . . 71
murders, killings and suicides, and 254 incidents of violence on TV during
74½ hours of evening time during first week of new season, vs. 81 killings
and 210 violent incidents in 78½ hours during a week in July, says *Christian
Science Monitor* . . . Survey reveals that average adult will spend 10-15
years of his life watching television . . . Average home has TV set on 55-60
hours a week . . . 95% of U.S. homes have TV, 25% more than one
set . . . FCC authorizes pay TV . . . *Journal of Broadcasting* publishes
survey which reveals parents poor at predicting their teenagers' program
preferences, with the reverse being true for the kids—leading to indication

that young adults watch programs parents select but that parents may well avoid teenage choices . . . Chicago Mayor, Richard J. Daley, demands an hour to present "Chicago's Side" (of the police attacks on street demonstrators, so vividly covered by TV). Turned down by the networks; but more than 100 local TV stations and several hundred radio outlets broadcast the Daley program . . . National Association of Broadcasters adopts new rule limiting consecutive commercial announcements to four in any program interruption, and a maximum of three in any station break . . . NBC begins "Heidi" movie telecast on schedule, and loses Oakland Raiders' two-touchdowns-in-nine-seconds defeat of New York Jets . . . Sales of U.S.-made color TV sets top black and white for first time . . .

1969

STARTUPS WINNING YOUTH FAVOR	TOP 6
"The Dick Cavett Show"	1. "Laugh-In"
"The Doctors"	2. "Gomer Pyle"
Glen Campbell's "Good Time Hour"	3. "Bonanza"
"Marcus Welby, M.D."	4. "Mayberry R.F.D."
"Medical Center"	5. "Family Affair"
"The Pink Panther Show"	6. "Gunsmoke"
"Sesame Street"	

Doctors take over again . . . TV shows man's first walk on the Moon . . . Federal Communications Commission reports average child of five sees no less than 13,000 persons violently destroyed on TV screen by the time he reaches age 14 . . . National Commission on the Causes and Prevention of Violence finds TV violence occurring at the rate of seven times an hour, or 600 separated acts of violence a week. Young adult characters accounted for nine out of every ten killers and eight out of ten fatal victims . . . "Dick Cavett" TV show makes quick impression on the young and becomes campus favorite . . . $65,000 now top price for one-minute TV commercial in prime time, for "Laugh-In," "Mission Impossible" and "Mayberry R.F.D." shows . . . CBS fires the Smothers Brothers for failing to comply with program standards . . .

1970

STARTUPS WINNING YOUTH FAVOR	TOP 6
"The Mary Tyler Moore Show"	1. "Laugh-In"
"The Partridge Family"	2. "Gunsmoke"
	3. "Bonanza"
	4. "Mayberry R.F.D."
	5. "Family Affair"
	6. "Here's Lucy"

Threatened with Congressional legislation spearheaded by Senator John Pastore, TV networks try to curb tube violence . . . PBS (Public Broadcasting Service) founded, giving U.S. first-class non-commercial TV . . . Highest cost for one-minute TV commercial now $69,000—up $4,000 in a year . . . "Bob Hope Christmas Show" most-viewed program of year . . .

1971

STARTUPS WINNING YOUTH FAVOR	TOP 6
"Cannon"	1. "Marcus Welby, M.D."
"Columbo"	2. "Flip Wilson"
"Sonny and Cher Hour"	3. "Here's Lucy"
	4. "Ironside"
	5. "Gunsmoke"
	6. "ABC Movie of the Week"

Cigarette ads banned from TV . . . Private eyes return to television . . . "Ed Sullivan Show" ends after 23 years . . . "Lassie" quits after 17 years . . . "Lawrence Welk Show" departs after 16 years . . . Estimated 1.35 million fight fans in U.S. and Canada pay to see simulcast of Muhammad Ali-Joe Frazier fight on closed-circuit TV . . . A. C. Nielsen reports that 7.5% of all U.S. TV homes now on cable . . . Bob Hope tops viewer ratings again . . .

1972

STARTUPS WINNING YOUTH FAVOR	TOP 6
"M*A*S*H"	1. "All in the Family"
"Sanford and Son"	2. "Flip Wilson"
"Streets of San Francisco"	3. "Marcus Welby, M.D."
"The Waltons"	4. "Gunsmoke"
	5. "ABC Movie of the Week"
	6. "Sanford and Son"

Surgeon-General's Advisory Committee on Television and Social Behavior reports: (1) A negative correlation between an early level of aggression and later violence viewing; (2) Parental punishment patterns did not have major effect on adolescent exposure to violent television programming; (3) Color TV presentations seem to effect greater recall for peripheral vs. central material, with high violence color having the strongest effect . . . Super Bowl VI has largest TV audience of the year . . .

1973

STARTUPS WINNING YOUTH FAVOR	TOP 6
ABC's "In Concert"	1. "All in the Family"
"Kojak"	2. "Sanford and Son"
NBC's "Midnight Special"	3. "Hawaii Five-O"
	4. "Maude"
	5. "Bridget Loves Bernie"
	6. "Sunday Mystery Movie"

Watergate hearings hypnotize TV audiences . . . "Star Trek" re-runs attract the mass audience it missed during its first round (1966-69) and cultists form societies to collect mementoes, books, etc. . . . "Shazam" comic book adapted for live TV . . . "Laugh-In" ends its spectacular run . . . The child who watches a moderate amount of TV in the U.S. has seen 80,000 commercials by the age of 16; and over 50% of TV's revenue comes from the grocery industry, according to Robert Choate, at an international symposium: Nutrition, National Development and Planning . . . Final totals for Watergate hearings show commercial networks providing 300 hours of coverage costing them $7-$10 million; while public non-commercial TV collects $1 million in contributions from viewers . . . Super Bowl VII and Nixon Vietnam truce address gain largest TV audiences of year . . .

1974

STARTUPS WINNING YOUTH FAVOR	TOP 6
"Happy Days"	1. "All in the Family"
"The Rockford Files"	2. "The Waltons"
"Six Million Dollar Man"	3. "Sanford and Son"
	4. "M*A*S*H"
	5. "Hawaii Five-O"
	6. "Maude"

"Perry Mason" ends 17-year run without having ever lost a case . . . NBC-TV pays record $10 million for broadcasting rights to *The Godfather* film, topping their previous high of $5 million to MGM for one showing of *Gone With the Wind* two years from now. ABC TV's 3.3 million to 20th Century-Fox for one showing of *The Poseidon Adventure* was previous high . . . NBC plans to charge $225,000 per minute for commercials when they show *The Godfather* . . . Nixon resignation address wins most TV viewers of year . . .

1975

STARTUPS WINNING YOUTH FAVOR   **TOP 6**

"Barney Miller"   1. "All in the Family"
NBC's "Saturday Night Live"   2. "Sanford and Son"
"Starsky and Hutch"   3. "Chico and the Man"
"Welcome Back, Kotter"   4. "The Jeffersons"
                                             5. "M*A*S*H"
                                             6. "Rhoda"

TV pays $60 million for college and pro football, vs. $41 million in 1966, and only $13.9 million just 12 years ago. This year's Super Bowl alone cost $2.5 million . . . "Gunsmoke" clears out after 19 years . . . None of the ten most violent TV shows in Top 10 Nielsen TV show ratings when *McCall's* magazine conducts survey . . . Roper study finds that almost two out of three parents of youngsters under 12 feel that children's programming has improved . . .

1976

STARTUPS WINNING YOUTH FAVOR   **TOP 6**

"The Bionic Woman"   1. "All in the Family"
"Charlie's Angels"   2. "Rich Man, Poor Man"
"The Muppet Show"   3. "Laverne and Shirley"
"Laverne and Shirley"   4. "Maude"
                                             5. "The Bionic Woman"
                                             6. "Phyllis"

Television forces all but opening game of baseball World Series to be played at night—to attract larger viewing audience . . . Over 20 police-private eye shows on network TV—up from seven in 1969 and zero in 1964 . . . "Happy Days," "Charlie's Angels," and "Starsky and Hutch" number among the TV show favorites of 2,000 teenagers polled by the Encyclopaedia Britannica. Fewer than 10% of those polled find TV violence objectionable . . . Both the American Medical Association and the Parents-Teachers Association begin campaigns against TV violence . . .

1977

STARTUPS WINNING YOUTH FAVOR   **TOP 6**

"Three's Company   1. "Happy Days"
"Eight Is Enough"   2. "Laverne and Shirley"
"Soap"   3. "ABC Monday Night Movie"
                                             4. "M*A*S*H"
                                             5. "Charlie's Angels"
                                             6. "The Big Event"

"Roots" watched by over 36 million—top program of year . . . Cheryl Ladd replaces Farrah Fawcett-Majors on "Charlie's Angels" . . . NBC network agrees to pay the USSR $85 million for broadcast rights to the 1980 Summer Olympics . . . Harris survey finds 71% of those polled feel there is too much violence on TV—up 12% from nine years ago . . .

1978

STARTUPS WINNING YOUTH FAVOR	TOP 6
"Battlestar Galactica"	1. "Laverne and Shirley"
"Dallas"	2. "Happy Days"
"The Incredible Hulk"	3. "Three's Company"
"Mork and Mindy"	4. "60 Minutes"
	5. "Charlie's Angels"
	6. "All in the Family"

New time compression device creates a normal-sounding voice when recording of a TV commercial is speeded up by as much as 40%. Tests indicate listeners find faster-than-normal sound messages more interesting; and that there is a higher recall rate . . . Top favorite TV program in junior high school poll is "Mork and Mindy" by wide margin . . .

1979

STARTUPS WINNING YOUTH FAVOR	TOP 6
"The Dukes of Hazzard"	1. "60 Minutes"
"The Ropers"	2. "Three's Company"
"WKRP in Cincinnati"	3. "Alice"
	4. "M*A*S*H"
	5. "The Jeffersons"
	6. "Dallas"

L.A. Superior Court orders TV "Lone Ranger" Clayton Moore to stop wearing black mask, as company owning copyright plans newer films with younger man . . . Twelve pay TV stations operating—with applications for 40 more before the FCC . . . Average daily hours of household TV usage highest yet—up 25 minutes from 1971, and 13 minutes more than last year . . . TV advertising gross breaks $4 billion barrier . . . All three networks relying heavily on ENG (electronic news gathering), with camera crews now bringing news from remote locations in the U.S. and abroad . . . Four years ago, television was named as single greatest influence on the lives of high school seniors—dropping 20% in 1978, and not even mentioned this year, in a poll conducted by Encyclopaedia Britannica Educational Corporation . . . "Heroes of Rock 'n' Roll" special on ABC TV gets enthusiastic reception and reviews . . .

1980

STARTUPS WINNING YOUTH FAVOR	TOP 6
"Hill Street Blues"	1. "60 Minutes"
"Knots Landing"	2. "Three's Company"
"Magnum P.I."	3. "M*A*S*H"
	4. "Alice"
	5. "Dallas"
	6. "The Jeffersons" / "Dukes of Hazzard" } equal

"Dallas" November 21 telecast has record 83 million viewing audience watching to see who shot J.R. . . . NBC drops Olympic telecasts . . . Nielsen estimates average person is now watching TV 32 hours a week—up 41 minutes from 1979 and 95 minutes from 1978. Teenage boys now watch 25 hours, 28 minutes weekly, while girl teenagers view 60 minutes less. Kids 6-11 watch much more—averaging 28 hours, 14 minutes—but women 18-24 top that with 31½ hours, while men 18-35 watch 8 hours less than women . . . Ron Ely replaces Bert Parks as "Miss America Pageant" emcee . . . Navy jet pilot, Thom McKee, wins $312,700 in cash on "Tic Tac Dough," topping Teddy Nayler's $264,000 on "The $64,000 Challenge" in 1958 . . . 102 million watch Super Bowl on TV; with advertising time costing $450,000 a minute . . . Allstate and Hertz reported to be running broadcast message at 20% above normal speed, as problem of keeping video picture and speeded-up voice (obviously getting more words in) is being resolved . . . New estimate has children seeing average 20,000 TV commercials a year—as they've now become $100 billion consumers . . . Johnny Carson's new contract with NBC said to be worth $50 million . . . NBC drops "The Wonderful World of Disney" . . . Average daily hours of TV usage per household now 6 hours and 35 minutes, vs. over an hour less 15 years ago: 5 hours and 30 minutes per day in the 1965-66 season, according to the Nielsen survey . . . All nights of the week from 8-11 P.M., 65.6% of U.S. homes are using TV, with 1,945 viewers per 1,000 homes—of which 44% are women, 36% men, 9% teenagers and 11% children, according to National Audience Demographics report . . . Now 63.4 million homes with color TV (83%). vs. 48.5 million in 1975 (70.8%) and 23.4 million in 1970 (39.2%) . . . Total TV homes now 76.3 million . . .

1981

STARTUPS WINNING YOUTH FAVOR   **TOP 6**

"Flamingo Road"   1. "Dallas"
"The Fall Guy"   2. "60 Minutes"
                                       3. "Dukes of Hazzard"
                                       4. "The Love Boat"
                                       5. "Private Benjamin"
                                       6. "M*A*S*H"

Longest-running shows at start of new season are: ABC Sunday Movies (17 years), NFL Football (11 years), "All in the Family" and "Archie Bunker's Place" (11), "M*A*S*H" (9), "Happy Days" (8), "Barney Miller" (7), "The Jeffersons" (7), "Little House on the Prairie" (7) . . . "Mean Joe Greene" commercial, where the Pittsburgh Steelers lineman gets a Coke from a little boy, becomes so popular that NBC makes full-length movie titled *The Steeler and the Pittsburgh Kid* . . . Supreme Court rules that the various states are free to permit the televising of criminal trials . . . Over 98% of all homes have at least one TV set and 85% have two or more . . . NBC sets "Fame" TV series (based on movie) for next year—a weekly drama series incorporating song and dance numbers. Network hopes it will take over where the "Monkees" and "Partridge Family" shows left off . . . "The Paper Chase," TV series based on Harvard Law School, canceled by CBS, returns to Preppy choice, PBS (Public Broadcast) TV . . . 98% of all U.S. homes (77.8 million—excluding Alaska and Hawaii) have TV sets, and 85% are color, according to A. C. Nielsen Company estimates . . . Videocassette recorder sales up 72% over last year— now estimated 34 million units in use domestically. Average Hollywood film on cassette selling 10,000-15,000 copies, but it only takes 18,000-20,000 in sales to gross $1 million at current prices . . . Industry estimates three counterfeit videocassettes to every legitimate one on market . . . Film companies mount big videocassette rental campaigns . . . In first year of major sales, 250,000 videodisc players are bought. Several hundred disc titles available in RCA (CED) and MCA (laser) formats . . . Rolling Stones Christmas concert on pay TV attracts 146,000 subscribers at $10 a household for gross receipts of $1,460,000 in just five cities—Los Angeles, Phoenix, Chicago, Fort Lauderdale/Miami and Dallas/Fort Worth . . . List of long-run TV series ending during the 1980-81 season includes "The Waltons," "Charlie's Angels," "Eight Is Enough" and "Soap" . . . Failures at attempts to reprise stars and series of yesteryear include: a new version of "Sanford," an effort to revive "The Brady Bunch" as "The Brady Brides," "The Flintstones," and new series shows for Marie Osmond as well as Steve Allen . . . Former "Six Million Dollar Man" Lee Majors has another TV hit in "The Fall Guy" . . . Other name stars trying to make TV comebacks with varying degrees of success are Robert Stack in "Strike Force," Mike Connors in "Today's FBI," Tony Randall in "Love Sydney," Jim Garner in "Bret Maverick," Lorne Greene in "Code Red," and Jim Arness in "McClain's Law" . . . Six Paramount films on RCA videodiscs score from 30% to 40% penetration into homes with videodisc players, vs. only 1% for hit titles on videocassettes . . . TV "General Hospital" soap opera actor Rick Springfield scores as pop singer . . . Sports total 1,300 hours of network TV programming for year. Surveys report that fans want still more coverage . . . Nielsen survey reports that cable TV had 27.3 penetration and 21,930,000 homes in July, vs. 16.7 penetration in about 12 million homes four years ago . . . Of six new TV shows which made last season's Top 30, only three are still there: "Too Close for Comfort," "Magnum, P.I." and Dynasty." These were joined by the late-starting "Hill Street Blues" . . . Teens 12-17 like "Three's Company," "Laverne and Shirley," "Happy Days," "Too Close for Comfort" and "Greatest American Hero" best (in that order), according to Nielsen November rankings. Children 2-11 opt for "Dukes of Hazzard," "Greatest American Hero," "Walt Disney," "Smurfs II," "Mork and Mindy" and "The Incredible Hulk"—with a much higher viewing audience . . .

Books and Magazines Relevant to Youth and the Rock Era _____.

Bestselling Books-*Fiction*	**Bestselling Books-***Nonfiction*
1954 *Not As A Stranger* Morton Thompson	*The Holy Bible* Revised Standard Version
1955 *Marjorie Morningstar* Herman Wouk	*Gift from the Sea* Anne Morrow Lindbergh
1956 *Don't Go Near the Water* William Brinkley	*Arthritis and Common Sense* Revised Edition, Dan Dale Alexander
1957 *By Love Possessed* James Gould Cozzens	*Kids Say the Darndest Things!* Art Linkletter
1958 *Doctor Zhivago* Boris Pasternak	*Kids Say the Darndest Things!* Art Linkletter
1959 *Exodus* Leon Uris	*'Twixt Twelve and Twenty* Pat Boone
1960 *Advise and Consent* Allen Drury	*Folk Medicine* D. C. Jarvis
1961 *The Agony and the Ecstasy* Irving Stone	*The New English Bible: The New Testament*
1962 *Ship of Fools* Katherine Anne Porter	*Calories Don't Count* Dr. Herman Taller
1963 *The Shoes of the Fisherman* Morris West	*Happiness Is A Warm Puppy* Charles M. Schulz
1964 *The Spy Who Came in from the Cold* John Le Carré	*Four Days* American Heritage and U.P.I.
1965 *The Source* James A. Michener	*How to Be A Jewish Mother* Don Greenburg
1966 *Valley of the Dolls* Jacqueline Susann	*How to Avoid Probate* Norman F. Dacey
1967 *The Arrangement* Elia Kazan	*Death of a President* William Manchester

1968 *Airport* Arthur Hailey	*Better Homes and Gardens New Cook Book*
1969 *Portnoy's Complaint* Philip Roth	*American Heritage Dictionary of the English Language*
1970 *Love Story* Erich Segal	*Everything You Wanted to Know About Sex But Were Afraid to Ask* David Reuben, M.D.
1971 *Wheels* Arthur Hailey	*The Sensuous Man* "M"
1972 *The Winds of War* Herman Wouk	*Eleanor and Franklin* Joseph P. Lash
1973 *Jonathan Livingston Seagull* Richard Bach	*The Living Bible* Kenneth Taylor
1974 *Centennial* James A. Michener	*The Total Woman* Marabel Morgan
1975 *Ragtime* E. L. Doctorow	*Angels: God's Secret Agents* Billy Graham
1976 *Trinity* Leon Uris	*The Final Days* Bob Woodward & Carl Bernstein
1977 *The Silmarillion* J. R. R. Tolkien	*Roots* Alex Haley
1978 *Chesapeake* James A. Michener	*If Life Is a Bowl of Cherries What Am I Doing in the Pits?* Erma Bombeck
1979 *The Matarese Circle* Robert Ludlum	*Aunt Erma's Cope Book* Erma Bombeck
1980 *The Covenant* James A. Michener	*Crisis Investing* Douglas R. Casey
1981 *Firestarter* Stephen King	*Cosmos* Carl Sagan

BOOKS POPULAR AMONG THE YOUNG (First Published after 1953)
(Number to left indicates ranking as bestseller that year;
NF = nonfiction)

1954

The Lord of the Rings, J. R. R. Tolkien
Animal Farm, George Orwell
Lord of the Flies, William Golding

1955

(1) *Marjorie Morningstar*, Herman Wouk
(4) *Bonjour Tristesse*, Françoise Sagan
The Guinness Book of World Records

1956

Allen Ginsberg's poem "Howl"
(3) *Peyton Place*, Grace Metalious
(5) *Eloise*, Kay Thompson
The Art of Loving, Erich Fromm

1957

Parkinson's Law, C. Northcote Parkinson
On the Road, Jack Kerouac

1958

(3) *Lolita*, Vladimir Nabokov
The Martian Chronicles, Ray Bradbury
The Dharma Bums, Jack Kerouac
The Subterraneans, Jack Kerouac

1959

(1 NF) *'Twixt Twelve and Twenty*, Pat Boone
(8) *Lolita*, Vladimir Nabokov
Goodbye Columbus, Philip Roth

1960

(10) *Between You, Me and the Gatepost*, Pat Boone
Catch 22, Joseph Heller
To Kill a Mockingbird, Harper Lee
A Separate Peace, John Knowles

1961

(2) *Franny and Zooey*, J. D. Salinger
Stranger in a Strange Land, Robert A. Heinlein

1962

One Flew over the Cuckoo's Nest, Ken Kesey
Silent Spring, Rachel Louise Carson
(5) *Franny and Zooey*, J. D. Salinger
(5) *Happiness Is a Warm Puppy*, Charles M. Schulz
Sex and the Single Girl, Helen Gurley Brown
The Naked Lunch, William Burroughs

1963

(1 NF) *Happiness Is a Warm Puppy*, Charles M. Schulz
(2) *Security Is a Thumb and a Blanket*, Charles M. Schulz
The Feminine Mystique, Betty Friedan
Steppenwolf, Hermann Hesse

1964

(2) *Candy*, Terry Southern & Mason Hoffenberg
(8) *You Only Live Twice*, Ian Fleming
(3 NF) *I Need All the Friends I Can Get*, Charles M. Schulz
(4) *In His Own Write*, John Lennon
(5) *Christmas Is Together Time*, Charles M. Schulz
Up the Down Staircase, Bel Kaufman

1965

(7) *The Man with the Golden Gun*, Ian Fleming
Unsafe At Any Speed, Ralph Nader
The Psychedelic Reader, Timothy Leary
Boys and Girls Together, William Goldman
Demain, Hermann Hesse
Dune, Frank Herbert
How to Talk Dirty and Influence People, Lenny Bruce
The Kandy-Kolored Tangerine-Flake Streamline Baby, Tom Wolfe
A Spaniard in the Works, John Lennon
The Psychedelic Experience, Timothy Leary, Ralph Metzner and
   G. M. Weil, Eds.

1966

Been Down So Long It Looks Like Up to Me, Richard Farina
Human Sexual Response, William H. Masters and Virginia E. Johnson
Diamonds Are Forever, Ian Fleming
The Fantastic Voyage, Isaac Asimov

1967

The Medium Is the Message, Marshall McLuhan
Peanuts cartoon books, Charles M. Schulz
(4 NF) *Stanyan Street and Other Sorrows*, Rod McKuen
The Outsiders, S. E. Hinton
The Harrad Experiment, Robert Rimmer

1968

(3NF) *Listen to the Warm*, Rod McKuen
(5 NF) *Lonesome Cities*, Rod McKuen
(8 NF) *Stanyan Street and Other Sorrows*, Rod McKuen
The Whole Earth Catalog
The Pigman, Paul Zindel

1969

(1) *Portnoy's Complaint*, Philip Roth
(2 NF) *In Someone's Shadow*, Rod McKuen

(4 NF) *Between Parent and Teenager*, Dr. Haim G. Ginott
(9 NF) *Sun Signs*, Linda Goodman
(10 NF) *Twelve Years of Christmas*, Rod McKuen
Slaughterhouse Five, Kurt Vonnegut, Jr.
Unabashed Career Guide, Peter Sandman & Dan Goldenson
My Darling, My Hamburger, Paul Zindel

1970

(1) *Love Story*, Erich Segal
(10 NF) *Caught in the Quiet*, Rod McKuen
Future Shock, Alvin Toffler
The Greening of America, Charles Reich
Sex: Telling It Straight, Eric W. Johnson
Jonathan Livingston Seagull, Richard Bach
Star Trek, James Blish

1971

(10 NF) *Fields of Wonder*, Rod McKuen
This Was Then, This Is Now, S. E. Hinton
Never Jam Today, Carole Bolton
The Female Eunuch, Germaine Greer

1972

The Teenager and Smoking, Gail Gleason Milgram
Ask Beth: You Can't Ask Your Mother, Elizabeth Winship
Go Ask Alice, Anonymous
The Sterile Cuckoo, John Nichols

1973

Fear of Flying, Erica Jong
Breakfast of Champions, Kurt Vonnegut, Jr.

1974

Whole Earth Epilog
Mind Drugs, Margaret O. Hyde, Ed.

1975

(2) *Watership Down*, Richard Adams
Hotline, Margaret O. Hyde
Sex and Birth Control: A Guide for the Young, James E. Lieberman and
    Ellen Peck
Teenage Fitness, Bonnie Prudden
Nontraditional College Routes to Careers, Sarah Splaver
Do Black Patent Leather Shoes Really Reflect Up?, John R. Powers
Growing Up Rich, Ann Bernays

1976

The T-Shirt Book, Laura Torbet
*Why Am I So Miserable If These Are the Best Years of My Life? A
    Survival Guide for the Young Woman*, Andrea Boroff Eagen
Free to Choose, Joyce Slaton Mitchell
Eighteen: The Teen-age Catalog, Jonathan Webster and Harriet Webster
(7) *Slapstick or Lonesome No More,* Kurt Vonnegut, Jr.

1977

The Silmarillion, J. R. R. Tolkien; Christopher Tolkien, Ed.
Confessions of a Teenage Baboon, Paul Zindel
How to Get Together When Your Parents Are Coming Apart, Arlene
    Richards and Irene Willis
What the Ads Don't Tell You About Cosmetics, Ann Carol Rinzler
The Rights of Young People, Alan N. Sussman
It's OK If You Don't Love Me, Norma Klein

1978

You Are Somebody Special, Charles W. Sheed
I Can Be Anything, Joyce S. Mitchell
Heart Songs, Laurel Holliday
(3 NF) *The Complete Book of Running*, James Fixx
Love Signs, Linda Goodman

1979

The College Survival Kit, Irv Brechner
The Cathy Chronicles, Cartoon strips by Cathy Guisewhite
Doonesbury's Greatest Hits, G. B. Trudeau
The Borribles, Michael De Larrabeitis
Roller Fever, Linda Konner
Gilda Radner Cut-Out Doll Book
Jailbird, Kurt Vonnegut, Jr.

1980

(11 NF) *Side Effects,* Woody Allen
(12) *Fanny, Being the True History of Fanny Hackabout-Jones,* Erica
    Jong
(12 NF) *Second Book of Running*, James Fixx
Garfield at Large, Jim Davis
The Official Preppy Handbook, Lisa Birnbach, Ed.
How to Survive a Roommate, James Comer

1981

Mastering Pac-Man, Ken Uston
How to Master the Video Games, Tom Hirshfeld
(7) *Miss Peggy's Guide to Life*, Henry Beard

Jane Fonda's Workout Book, Jane Fonda
The Simple Solution to Rubik's Cube, James G. Nourse
Mastering Rubik's Cube, Don Taylor
Solving the Cube, Cyril Ostrop
101 Uses of a Dead Cat, Simon Bond

NEWS ABOUT BOOKS AND MASS-CIRCULATION MAGAZINES

1954

Twenty million 10¢ horror comics being sold each month . . . *Revised Standard Version Bible* top nonfiction bestseller for third straight year, outselling any other title (including fiction) by 200,000 with 710,359. Three-year total: 3,141,670 . . . During its first year, *Playboy* able to exist on sales alone—no advertising . . .

1955

JFK's *Profiles in Courage* wins Pulitzer Prize . . . National survey of 1,500 selected 8-15-year-olds reports that for middle-class children, "Reading of books remained the preference even above TV viewing" . . .

1956

James Dean Returns by Joan Collins, allegedly dictated by dead star, saying he isn't dead, sells 500,000 . . . *Peyton Place* published. Sells 9.5 million copies over next 12 years—outselling combined output of Hemingway, Fitzgerald, Faulkner, Melville and Dreiser. Fourth most popular book ever published in U.S. . . .

1957

On the grounds that enforcement of such a law would leave nothing for adults to read except that suitable for children, Supreme Court voids Michigan law against selling publications that might corrupt children . . .

1958

Paperback of *Lolita* sells 3 million . . .

1959

Dell pays record $265,000 for paperback rights to *Return to Peyton Place* . . . Court declares 31-year ban on *Lady Chatterley's Lover* unconstitutional and allows new publication. Also rules novel not obscene—lifting ban on mails by Postmaster General . . . Pat Boone's *'Twixt Twelve and Twenty* sells 260,000 copies . . .

1960

25¢ paperback books long past, as 60¢ and 95¢ become the usual prices . . . 85 different book clubs sell 80 million copies . . . During the

1960s, reversing most past history, the ten nonfiction bestsellers outsold the overall total of top ten fiction . . .

1961

Three most popular novels with high school and working youth: *Gone with the Wind*, *Exodus* and *Hawaii* . . . Sale of books more than doubled in past nine years, since 1952 . . . Harold Robbins makes first appearance on bestseller list with *The Carpetbaggers* . . . Tenth grade girls prefer heroines, while twelfth grade girls prefer heroes—with boys at all levels wanting the lead character to be male, in survey of high school reading tastes . . . Long-banned *Tropic of Cancer* by Henry Miller published in U.S.—although censored in many localities . . .

1962

Rachel Carson's *Silent Spring* predicts deterioration of planet—and argues that pesticides upsetting the balance of nature . . . Now 16 hot rod magazines on stands, with total monthly circulation of 3 million . . .

1963

New York court allows publication of banned-as-obscene book, *Fanny Hill* . . . Forty new cookbooks published during first six months . . .

1964

Tremendous expansion of school market in book publishing . . . College bookstores list *The Art of Loving* by Erich Fromm as steady bestseller . . . 250 million paperback books sold . . . *Journalism Quarterly* report on study of reading habits in high school discloses: (1) Adult magazines much more popular than teen periodicals, (2) Seventh grade girls read the most magazines, twelfth grade girls the least, and (3) *Seventeen* and *Ingenue* most popular among the girls, with the boys favoring *MAD* and *Boys Life* . . .

1965

I Ching in . . . Bestseller in college bookshops is *Candy*. Paperback sales: 1.5 million . . . Over 25,000 different paperback books in print, selling almost a million copies a day . . . Sixty new magazines appear—from *Arts and Antiques* to *Penthouse* . . . Average price of hardcover books now $7.65—from $5.29 in 1957-59 . . . Total sales of books now $2 billion, vs. $750 million for 1954 . . .

1966

Tolkien's "Hobbits" in . . . Chicago Public Library says James Bond books big teen craze . . . Average life of bestselling book past four years is 15.7 weeks, vs. 18.8 weeks on list 1953-56 . . . About 28,000 different books published, vs. 12,589 in 1955 . . .

1967

28,762 new book titles published . . . UPI poll of teens names Hermann Hesse top author with *Siddhartha*, along with Tolkien's Hobbits . . . 319 original science fiction books and 20 collections published—vs. 127 new and 91 reprinted Westerns . . . *Playboy* has sales in excess of $50 million . . .

1968

Rod McKuen has record-breaking three books of poetry in year end Top 10 bestsellers. *Listen to the Warm* sold 310,157, *Lonesome Cities*, 267,063 and *Stanyan Street*, from 1967, another 229,985 in 1968 . . . Underground bestseller *The Whole Earth Catalog* first printing only 2,000 copies . . . *I Ching* sells 50,000 copies . . . *Reader's Digest* (circ. almost 18 million) and *TV Guide* (almost 14 million) top magazines. *Playboy* and *Good Housekeeping* neck and neck, each selling 5 million—just under *National Geographic* . . .

1969

Rod McKuen's *In Someone's Shadow* sells 235,000 in three-month period; and *Twelve Years of Christmas* 108,000 in about a month . . . Kurt Vonnegut joins J. D. Salinger as student favorite. Required reading at Harvard, Wisconsin and Washington universities . . . Total sales to date of 36 million makes Charles "Peanuts" Schulz fourth most popular 20th century author . . . Bookstores report tenfold increase in sci-fi sales a week after Apollo flight . . . After 148 years, *Saturday Evening Post* stops publication . . . Harold Robbins's books hit 28 million total sales . . . Chelsea House sells 140 copies of 1897 Sears catalogue at $14.95 . . . Hermann Hesse's works big campus sellers . . . *American Manners and Morals* notes that now "even mother-hen *Reader's Digest* scarcely lets a month go by without an article in which the word sex appears in the title," while *Cosmopolitan* appears to be aimed at the female counterpart of the *Playboy* reader . . .

1970

Everything You Wanted to Know About Sex But Were Afraid to Ask sells over a million hardcover copies in first year out . . . Khalil Gibran's *The Prophet* hits sales of 3 million . . . Sex references in *Reader's Digest*, *McCall's*, *Life*, *Look*, *Time*, and *Newsweek* increased 111% since 1950, after 82% increase from 1950 to 1960 . . . *Whole Earth Catalog* sells 160,000 copies in 1½ years . . . 1960-70 analysis of *Time*, *Newsweek* and *U.S. News* coverage of issues shows: Vietnam War (861 articles), Race relations and urban riots (687), Campus unrest (267), Inflation (234), TV and mass media (218), Crime (203), Drugs (173), Environment and pollution (109), Smoking (99), Poverty (74), Sex/declining morality (62),

Women's rights (47) . . . Three-year investigation of high school reading habits shows student tendency to enjoy books made into movies more than books that were not—with novels the most popular genre . . . First literary appearance of term "preppy" in *Love Story*, spelled "preppie" . . . *National Lampoon* begins publication and becomes almost immediate campus favorite . . . Occult resurgence featured in special issues of *Esquire*, *McCall's* and *Harper's Bazaar*, as well as lengthy articles in *Wall Street Journal* and *Newsweek* . . .

1971

1902 Sears catalogue sells 400,000 as publishers reprint 1903, 1908 and 1927 to satisfy wave of price nostalgia . . . *MAD* magazine circulation reaches 2.15 million—almost double the 1.4 million it hit in its fifth year, 1960 . . . *Look* magazine folds . . . *Horoscope* and *American Astrology* magazines now have circulations of about a half million each; and *Fate*, a general occult periodical, sells around 115,000 copies of each issue . . .

1972

Two-year-old *Jonathan Livingston Seagull* has sold 815,000 hardcover copies in word-of-mouth build . . . Solzhenitsyn expelled from USSR . . . *Life* magazine suspends weekly publication . . . Mystic Arts Book Club (Lyle Stuart) and Universe Book Club (Doubleday) thriving on current occult craze . . .

1973

2,623,953 copies of *The Living Bible* sold—adding to over 5,700,600 already published . . . 81-year-old Tolkien dies in Oxford . . .

1974

Leisure time reading down to 14% from 21% in 1938, according to Gallup poll . . .

1975

New record set as Bantam pays $1,850,000 for paperback rights to *Ragtime* . . . On all-time bestsellers list:
10. *Peyton Place* (10,672,302)
12. *Love Story* (9,905,627)
38. *Catch 22* (6,113,000)
26. *The Prophet* (6,000,000)
24. *Catcher in the Rye* (5,985,626)
42. *Fear of Flying* (5,072,800) . . . 35,608 new books published, of which 8,361 are reprints and new editions, and 4,198 are works of fiction, including 1,809 reprints and new editions . . .

1976

Avon pays $1,550,000 for paperback rights to Woodward and Bernstein's *The Final Days* . . . Original *Baby and Child Care* by Dr. Spock in 30th year with 28 million copies sold . . . *Huckleberry Finn* banned in Chicago suburb for using word "nigger," although Dick Gregory able to title book with same word . . . Jimmy Carter speaks of "sexual lust" in *Playboy* interview . . .

1977

New record for fastest-selling work of fiction probably set by Tolkien's *Silmarillion*, with 1,056,696 copies sold from September 15 publication date to December 31 . . . Avon pays $1.9 million for paperback rights to Colleen McCullough's *The Thorn Birds* . . .

1978

Average price of hardcover fiction book: $11.07. Average price of softcover fiction book: $1.89 . . . China announces end of ten-year ban on Shakespeare, Aristotle, Dickens and Mark Twain . . . 31,802 new hardbound and paperback books published: Fiction only 2,455; Sociology and Economics tops with 5,259; Juveniles 2,617; Medicine 2,177; Science 2,155; Religion 1,454; History 1,361; Literature 1,254; Art 1,229; Other leaders 222 . . . Bestselling college textbook *Accounting Principles* by C. Rollin Niswonger and Philip C. Ness has sold about 2 million copies in over 45 years and earned the authors roughly $2.6 million to date. 3.7 million copies of *Economics* has earned author Paul Samuelson and various assistant editors over $6 million; and college favorite *History of Art* by H. W. Jansen has earned him approximately $3 million on sales over 2 million . . . Reissue of *The Godfather* brings Mario Puzo another $2.25 million in advance for paperback rights; and William Safire's first novel *Full Disclosure* garners $1.35 million . . . *The Amityville Horror* paperback has earned author and publisher about $1.9 million in royalties, on a sale of about 5.7 million. *The Complete Book of Running* has earned author James Fixx about $930,000 on a sale of over 620,000 . . . Total of 41,216 new books published—31,802 for first time and 9,414 new editions. In those totals, fiction accounted for 2,455 new books and 1,238 new editions . . .

1979

Valley of the Dolls' worldwide sales reach 21,472,000 . . . *TV Guide* top magazine (19.5 million), over *Reader's Digest* (18 million) and *National Geographic* (10 million); *National Enquirer* (5 million) tops *Time* (4.3 million) and *Newsweek* (2.9 million) . . . Hardcover book prices up 9.7% in year . . . Rutgers University library and information official points out that Paul Zindel's *The Pigman* and S. E. Hinton's *The Outsider* remain the two all-time favorites among teen readers . . . Judith Krantz gets $3.2 million advance for paperback rights to *Princess Daisy*, and Marilyn French gets $1.91 million for *The Bleeding Heart* . . . Two out of three of about 35,000 books published this year actually lost money . . .

1980

Book sales reach $8.2 billion—12.5% over 1969. Number of books sold increases 3% to 1.7 billion units, vs. upturn of only 1.7% last year. Children's paperbacks up 53.7% in dollars and 32.2% in units—continuing fantastic rise since first introduced 12 years ago . . . Woody Allen has No. 11 fiction bestseller with 190,000 sale of *Side Effects,* his most successful collection of humor pieces to date. His previous *Without Feathers* sold 94,300 in 1975 . . . James Fixx's *Second Book of Running* made No. 12 nonfiction bestseller with 171,900 sales, vs. over 600,000 for his 1978 *Complete Book of Running,* which reached No. 3 on the list . . .Writing as career choice finds new inspiration in $1.5 million Bantam pays for paperback rights to William Styron's *Sophie's Choice*, while Warner Books pays Norman Mailer $500,000 for their softcover version of *The Executioner's Song,* and Avon deals out $525,000 for William Wharton's *Birdy* and $275,000 for Scott Spencer's *Endless Love* . . . Ken Kesey's *One Flew over the Cuckoo's Nest,* which brought him a mere $20,000 in 1963, has now sold over 6.5 million paperbacks. E. L. Doctorow's *Ragtime* cost Bantam $1.85 million in 1977 and has sold over 3 million copies for them. John Irving's *The World According to Garp* is also over 3 million in paperback, but it only cost Pocket Books $100,000 in 1979 . . .

1981

Official Preppy Handbook sells over 2 million copies in first year; and *The I Hate Preppies Handbook* is already nearing 200,000 . . . *The Simple Solution to Rubik's Cube* now has over 4 million copies in print; *Mastering Rubik's Cube* over 1.8 million, and the youngest bestselling author in history, a 13-year-old English schoolboy, tops 450,000 in the U.S. with *You Can Do the Cube* . . . Cats thrive in bookstores, with *Garfield At Large* (750,000), *Garfield Gains Weight* (675,000), and *Garfield Bigger than Life* (650,000). There are 700,000 copies of *101 Uses of a Dead Cat* in print, and *The Second Official I Hate Cats Book* is at 200,000 . . . Video game code books give arcade players hours of playing time for just one quarter. *Mastering Pac-Man,* by blackjack expert Ken Uston, has original paperback press run of 500,000 but store orders prior to printing require another 250,000 before release. A 19-year-old, Tom Hirschfeld, wrote *How to Master Video Games,* which has sold over 650,000 copies. Other paperback titles, selling from $1.95 to $3.95, include: *How to Win at Pac-Man, How to Beat the Video Games,* and *Scoring Big at Pac-Man* . . . Author S. E. Hinton, who writes for the 12-20-year-old age group, sells all four of her novels to film companies. Francis Coppola is directing her *The Outsiders* for Warner Bros., and the Disney studio is filming *Tex*. Coppola is dickering for the rights to her *Rumble Fish*, and her *That Was Then, This Is Now* has also been optioned. She says she doesn't write about the "student council types," but rather, "the ones who are sleeping in other people's garages and scrounging around" . . . Magazines now third highest earner in passive leisure time activities—reaching $10 billion, up ten-fold from 1950. Boom years, beginning in 1976-77, followed long static period . . .

AMERICAN BOOKS ABOUT ARTISTS AND MUSIC IN THE ROCK ERA

1958

Who's Who in Rock 'n Roll, Vic Fredericks, Ed.

1961

Tops in Pops, Steve Kahn

1964

Anything Goes: The World of Popular Music, David Dachs
A Cellarful of Noise, Brian Epstein
Hootennanny Tonight, James F. Leisy
The True Story of the Beatles, Billy Shepherd

1965

The Beatles, Hunter Davies
Encyclopedia of Popular Music, Irwin Stambler

1966

Murray the K Tells It Like It Is, Baby, Murray Kaufman
Folk Rock—The Bob Dylan Story, Sy & Barbara Ribakove

1967

David Bowie, Vivian Claire
The American Folk Scene, David A. DeTurk & A. Poulin, Jr.
Bob Dylan, Daniel Kramer
Popular Music, John Rublowsky
Professional Rock and Roll, Herbert H. Wise, Ed.

1968

The Beatles: The Real Story, Julius Fast
The Beatles: Words Without Music, Rick Friedman
The World of Rock, John Gabree
The Beatles, Anthony Scaduto

1969

Rock from the Beginning, Nik Cohn
American Pop, David Dachs
The Age of Rock, Jonathan Eisen, Ed.
The Sound of Soul, Phyl. Garland
The Jefferson Airplane and the San Francisco Sound, Ralph J. Gleason
Jim Morrison and the Doors, Mike Jahn
Rock and Roll Will Stand, Greil Marcus
Rock Encyclopedia, Lillian Roxon
The Rock Revolution, Arnold Shaw
The Story of Rock, Carl Belz
"Hair": The American Tribal Love-Rock Musical, Gerome Ragni &
   James Rado
The Poetry of Rock, Richard Goldstein
Encyclopedia of Folk, Country and Western Music, Irwin Stambler &
   Grelon Landon

1970

Encyclopedia of Rock and Roll, Len Brown & Gary Friedrich
The Johnny Cash Story, George Carpozi, Jr.
The Age of Rock, 2, Jonathan Eisen, Ed.
Goldstein's Greatest Hits, Richard Goldstein
Rock: A World Bold As Love, Douglas K. Paul & Sue C. Clark
The Rock Story, Jerry Hopkins
Fillmore East and West, James A. Hudson
Tom Jones, Peter Jones
The Glen Campbell Story, Freda Kramer
The Sound of Our Time, Dave Laing
Soul Music, Rochelle Larkin
The Gold of Rock and Roll: 1955-1967, H. Kandy Rohde
Guitar Years: Pop Music from Country and Western to Hard Rock,
   Irwin Stambler
New Sound: Yes, Ira Peck
Rock Giants, Jazz And Pop Magazine Editors
Favorite Pop-Rock Lyrics, Jerry Walker
Rock Is Beautiful, Stephanie Spinner, Ed.

1971

Janis, David Dalton
The Freakshow, Albert H. Goldman
Inside Creedence, John Hallowell
Festival, Jerry Hopkins
Elvis: A Biography, Jerry Hopkins
Johnny Cash Close-Up, James A. Hudson

Buddy Holly, Dave Laing
Rock Folk: Portraits from Rock 'n Roll, Michael Lydon
The Dee Jays, Arnold Passman
The Rock Giants, Pauline Rivelli & Robert Levin
The Rock Scene, Richard Robinson & Andy Zwerling
The Rolling Stone Interviews, *Rolling Stone*
The World of Soul, Arnold Shaw
Positively Main Street: An Unorthodox View of Bob Dylan,
    Toby Thompson

1972

Rock, Bach & Superschlock, Harold Myra & Dean Merrill
And the Beat Goes On: A Survey of Pop Music in America, Charles
    Boeckman
Encyclopedia of Pop/Rock, David Dachs
*Rolling Stones: An Unauthorized Biography in Words, Pictures and
    Music*, David Dalton
The Longest Cocktail Party: A Personal History of Apple, Richard
    Dilello
Rock Raps of the 70s, Walli Elmlark & Timothy G. Beckley
The Sound of the City: The Rise of Rock 'n Roll, Charlie Gillett
It's Too Late to Stop Now: A Rock 'n Roll Journal, Jon Landau
Apple to the Core, Peter McCabe & D. R. Schonfeld
Bob Dylan: A Retrospective, Craig McGregor
The Drifters: The Rise and Fall of the Black Vocal Group, Bill Millar
Motown and the Arrival of Black Music, David Morse
American Music: From Storyville to Woodstock, Charles Nanry, Ed.
Pop, Rock and Soul, Richard Robinson
The Osmond Brothers and the New Pop Scene, Richard Robinson
Bob Dylan: An Intimate Biography, Anthony Scaduto
*No Commercial Potential: The Saga of Frank Zappa and the Mothers of
    Invention*, David Walley
Out of His Head: The Sound of Phil Spector, Richard Williams
Photography of Rock, Abby Hirsch
Rock Music: Where It's Been, What It Means, Where It's Going,
    William J. Schafer
The Sounds of Social Change, R. Serge Denisoff & Richard A. Peterson

1973

Any Old Way You Choose It: Rock and Other Pop Music, Robert
    Christgau
Buried Alive: The Biography of Janis Joplin, Myra Friedman
Making Tracks: The Story of Atlantic Records, Charlie Gillett
Mick Jagger, J. Marks

Those Oldies But Goodies: A Guide to 50s Record Collecting, Steve
   Propes
The Rolling Stone Interviews, Volume 2, Rolling Stone
Trips: Rock Life in the Sixties, Ellen Sanders
Rock: From Elvis Presley to the Rolling Stones, Mike Jahn
The Who, Jeff Stein & Chris Johnston
As Time Goes By, Derek Taylor
Rock Music, Brian Van Der Horst
Hendrix, Chris Welch

1974

Alice Cooper, Steve Demorest
The Rolling Stone Rock 'n Roll Reader, Ben Fong-Torres
S.T.P.: A Journey Through America with the Rolling Stones
Jimi, Curtis Knight
*Rock On: The Illustrated Encyclopedia of Rock 'n Roll for the Solid
   Gold Years*, Norm N. Nite
Golden Oldies: A Guide to 60s Record Collecting, Steve Propes
Rock Is Rhythm and Blues: The Impact of Mass Media, Lawrence N.
   Redd
The Rolling Stone Reader, Rolling Stone
Knockin' on Dylan's Door: On the Road in '74, Michael Dempsey
*Turn It Up! (I Can't Hear the Words): The Best of the New Singer/
   Songwriters*, Bob Sarlin
Mick Jagger: Everybody's Lucifer, Anthony Scaduto
A Revolution in Sound: A Biography of the Recording Industry,
   C. A. Schicke
The Rockin' 50s: The Decade That Transformed the Pop Music Scene,
   Arnold Shaw
The Rolling Stones, George Tremlett
Diary of a Rock 'n' Roll Star, Ian Hunter
Rock Dreams, Nik Cohn
Rock 'n' Roll Woman, Katherine Orloff
The Rolling Stone Record Review No. 2, Editors of *Rolling Stone*
Encyclopedia of Pop, Rock & Soul, Irwin Stambler

1975

The Beatles Illustrated Record, Roy Carr & Tony Tyler
The Sound of Philadelphia, Tony Cummings
Inside the Record Business, Clive Davis
Solid Gold: The Record Business, Its Friends and Enemies, R. Serge
   Denisoff
Presenting David Bowie, Dirk Douglas
The Osmonds, Paul H. Dunn

On the Flip Side, Lloyd Dunn
The Illustrated History of British Pop, Paul Flattery
A Conversation with Elton John and Bernie Taupin, Paul Gambaccini
Who's Who in Rock 'n Roll, Steve Gaines
Buddy Holly: His Life and Music, John Goldrosen
The Compleat Beatles Quiz Book, Ehwin Goodgold & Dan Carlinsky
Billion Dollar Baby, Bob Greene
Jim Croce: His Life and Music, Richard Kasak, Ed.
Nothing Personal: Reliving Rock in the Sixties, Al Kooper & Ben
    Edmonds
Mystery Train: Images of America in Rock 'n Roll Music, Greil Marcus
The Rock Book, Jim O'Donnell
Bob Dylan Approximately, Stephen Pickering
*Golden Goodies: A Guide to 50s and 60s Popular Rock and Roll Record
    Collecting*, Steve Propes
Linda's Pictures, Linda & Paul McCartney
The Bachman, Turner Overdrive Biography, Martin Melhvish
In Their Own Words: Lyrics and Lyricists 1955-74, Bruce Pollack
The Led Zeppelin Biography, Ritchie Yorke
Led Zeppelin, Michael Gross & Robert Plant
Chicago, Mary J. O'Shea
Top 10s and Trivia and R&B 1950-1975, Joseph Edwards

1976

Rod Stewart, Richard Cromelin
John Lennon: One Day At A Time, Anthony Fawcett
Paul McCartney in His Own Words, Paul Gambaccini
Rock Almanac, Charlie Gillett & Stephen Nugent
The Story of Stevie Wonder, James Haskins
Rolling Stone Illustrated History of Rock & Roll, Jim Miller, Ed.
Encyclopedia of Rock, Lee Vinson
The Rock Generation, Dennis C. Benson
Rock, Arlo Blocher
Stevie Wonder: Sunshine in the Shadows, Linda Jacobs
The Allman Brothers Band: A Biography in Words & Pictures, Tom
    Nolan
Rock Revolution, Creem Magazine Editorial Staff, Richard Robinson, Ed.
Elton John, Greg Shaw
The Jacksons, Steve Manning
A Social History of Rock Music, Loyd Grossman
Rock, Roll & Remember, Dick Clark
Electric Children, Jacques Vassal, Trans. & Adapted by Paul Barnett

1977

Rock 'n Roll Is Here to Pay, Steve Chapple & Reebee Garofalo
Rock 100, David Dutton & Lenny Kaye
Stevie Wonder, Constance Elsner
Elvis, Peter Jones
The Illustrated Encyclopedia of Rock, Nick Logan & Bob Woffinden
The Illustrated Rock Almanac, Pearce Marchbank & Miles
Rock Gold 1955-1976, Charles Miron
Rock Art, Dennis Salek, Ed.
The Beatles Forever, Nicholas Schaffner
Rolling Thunder Logbook, Sam Shepard
The Picture Life of Stevie Wonder, Audrey Edwards & Gary Wohl
Oldies But Goodies, Stewart Goldstein & Alan Jacobson
The Improbable Rise of Redneck Rock, Jan Reid
Star-Making Machinery: Inside the Business of Rock & Roll, Geoffrey
  Stokes
Elvis: What Happened, Steve Dunleavy
The Beatles Again, Harry Castleman & Walter Podrazik
West Coast Story, Rob Burt & Patsy North
The History of Rock 'n Roll, Ritchie Yorke
The Facts About a Rock Group: Featuring Wings, David Gelly
Backstage Passes: Rock 'n Roll Life in the Sixties, Al Kooper &
  Ben Edmonds

1978

A Decade of "The Who," Peter Townsend
Rock, Mike Bygrave
Fleetwood Mac: Rumours 'n Fax, Roy Carr & Steve Clarke
Linda Ronstadt, Vivian Claire
The Gold Record, Lucy Emerson
Rock Critics Choice: The Top 200 Albums, Paul Gambaccini
Fleetwood Mac: The Authorized History, Samuel Graham
Rock Almanac, Stephen Nugent & Charles Gillett
Peter Frampton, Marsha Paly
Bob Dylan: An Illustrated History, Michael Gross
Superwomen of Rock, Susan Katz
The Beach Boys and the California Myth, David Leaf
Beatles in Their Own Words, Miles (Compiler)
The Linda Ronstadt Scrapbook, Maury Ellen Moore
Rock On, Volume II: The Modern Years, 1954-Present, Norm N. Nite
Bob Dylan, Alan Rinzler
The Beatles Trivia Quiz Book, Halen Rosenbaum
Honkers and Shouters, Arnold Shaw

On the Road with Bob Dylan, Larry Sloman
Kiss, John Swenson
The Face of Rock & Roll: Images of a Generation, Bruce Pollock &
    John Wagman
The Rock and Roll Trivia Quiz, Michael Uslan & Soloman Bruce
Punk, Dike Blair & Elizabeth Anscombe
Punk Rock, Virginia Boston
Rock, Roll & Remember, Dick Clark & Richard Robinson
Jazz Rock Fusion, Julie Coryell & Lara Friedman
Rock 'n' Roll Circus, Mick Farren & George Snow
The Book of Rock Quotes, Jonathon Green
Frampton!, Susan Katz
Lillian Roxon's Rock Encyclopedia, Rev. Ed., Compiled by Ed Naha
Baby, That Was Rock & Roll: The Legendary Leiber & Stoller, Robert
    Palmer
*The Making of Superstars: The Artists and Executives of the Rock Music
    World*, Robert Stephen Spitz

1979

The Rolling Stone Record Guide, Dave Marsh, Ed., with John Swenson
The Beach Boys, Byron Preiss
Elvis in Concert, John Reggero
Rolling Stones Trivia Quiz Book, Halen Rosenbaum
Woodstock Festival Remembered, Jean Young & Michael Lang
It's Rock 'n' Roll, Eugene Busmar
Rock Album Art, Angie Errigo
What Rock Is All About, Peter Lane
The Concerts, Photos by Laurie Lewis
Stranded: Rock & Roll for a Desert Island, Greil Marcus
Where Have They Gone: Rock n Roll, Doug Payne & Bruce McColm
San Francisco Rock Experience, Debora Hill
The Bee Gees, Kim Stevens
Peter Frampton, Irene Adler
Bruce Springsteen, Paul Gambaccini
Born to Run: The Bruce Springsteen Story, Dave Marsh
Yesterdays: Popular Song in America, Charles Hamm
Bee Gees: The Biography, David Leaf, Ed.
Woodstock Census, Rex Weiner
Barefoot in Babylon: The Creation of the Woodstock Music Festival, 1969,
    Robert Stephen Spitz

1980

Contemporary Music Almanac 1980, Ronald Zalkind, Ed.
Breaking the Sound Barrier: A Critical Anthology of the New Music,
    Gregory Battock

Things We Said Today: The Complete Lyrics & A Concordance to the Beatles' Songs, Colin Campbell & Alan R. Murphy

The Rock 'n' Roll Bible, Roy Carr & Nick Logan

Rock Voices, Matt Damsker

Official Price Guide to Collectable Rock Records, 2nd Ed., Randell C. Hill

Boogie Lightning: How Music Became Electric, Michael Lydon & Ellen Mandel

The Rock Music Source Book, Bob Macken

The Poetry of Rock: The Golden Years, David R. Pichaske

The Rolling Stone Illustrated History of Rock & Roll 1950-1980, Rev. & Updated, Jim Miller, Ed.

Thirty Years of Rock & Roll Trivia, Fred Worth

Blondie, Ann Bardach

Bee Gees—The Authorized Biography, Maurice, Barry & Robin Gibb

The Superstars of Rock: Their Lives and Their Music, Gene Busmar

Good Vibrations: The Beach Boys on Record 1961-79, Brad Elliot

Whatever Happened to . . . ? The Great Pop & Rock Music Nostalgia Book, Steve Faber

David Bowie: The Discography of a Generalist, David J. Fletcher

No One Here Gets Out Alive, Jerry Hopkins & Daniel Sugarman

Mott the Hoople, Willard Manus

The New York Times Great Songs of Abba, Milton Okun, Ed.

Rock Group Family Trees, Pete Frame

The Rolling Stone Book of Days: 1980, Rolling Stone

Grace Slick: The Biography, Barbara Rowes

Rock & Roll Puzzles, Pat Fortunato

Kenny Rogers: Gideon, Milton Okun, Ed.

1981

The Supergroups, Cynthia Dagnal

Elvis, Albert Goldman

The Day the Music Died, Joseph C. Smith

All You Needed Was Love: The Beatles After the Beatles, John Blake

The Book of Rock Lists, Dave Marsh and Kevin Stein

Rock Hardware, Tony Bacon

The New Music, Glenn A. Baker & Stuart Cope

Who's Who in Rock, Michael Bane

Rock-N-Roll Rip-off, Emmett Barnard

Breaking the Sound Barrier: A Critical Anthology of the New Music, Gregory Battcock & Cyril I. Nelson

Who's Who in New Wave in Music, 1976 to 1980: A Catalog & Directory, Compiled by David Bianco

The Boy Looked at Johnny: The Obituary of Rock & Roll, Julie Burchill & Tony Parsons

Christgau's Record Guide: Rock Albums of the Seventies, Robert Christgau
American Premium Record Guide: Identification & Values—78's, 45's, & LP's, 2nd ed., L. R. Docks
Sound Effects: Youth, Leisure, & the Politics of Rock 'n' Roll, Simon Frith
Are the Kids All Right?, John Fuller
The Rock Yearbook, Michael Gross & Maxim Jakubowski, Eds.
Rock Album Art, Gary Herman
The Literature of Rock, Nineteen Fifty-Four to Nineteen Seventy-Eight, Frank Hoffmann
David Bowie: An Illustrated Discography, Stuart Hoggard
Rock Record, Terry Hounsome & Tim Chambre
Whatever Happened to . . .? The Great Pop & Rock Music Nostalgia Book, Spencer Howard & John Brunton
Rock Reconsidered: A Christian Looks at Contemporary Music, Steve Lawhead
Pink Floyd: An Illustrated Discography, Miles
New Wave Explosion: How Punk Became New Wave Became the '80s, Myles Palmer
The Poetry of Rock: The Golden Years, David R. Pichaske
Rock & Roll Babylon, John Pidgeon
When Rock Was Young: A Nostalgic Review of the Top Forty Era, Bruce Pollock
Spotlight Heroes, J. Rowlands
Five Hundred & Five Rock & Roll Questions Your Friends Can't Answer, Nicholas and Elizabeth Schaffner
Rock Bottom: The Best of the Worst in the History of Rock, John Tobler
The Electric Light Orchestra Story, Bev Bevan
Visions of Rock, Mal Burns, Ed.
Whole Lotta Shakin' Goin' on: Jerry Lee Lewis, Robert Cain
David Bowie: An Illustrated Record, Roy Carr & Charles Shaar Murray
The Beatles: An Illustrated Record, Rev. 3rd Ed., Roy Carr & Tony Tyler
One Hundred Pop-Rock Stars, David Dachs
Queen: An Illustrated Biography, Judith Davis
Chuck Berry: Rock'n'Roll Music, Howard A. Dewitt
Good Vibrations: The Beach Boys on Record, 1961-1981, Brad Elliott
The Superstuds, Howard Elson
Musical Houses: Homes & Secret Retreats of Music Stars, Environmental Communications
Feel Like Going Home: Portraits in Blues & Rock 'n' Roll, Peter Guralnick
I Me Mine, George Harrison
Cuts from a San Francisco Rock Journal, Debora Hill
San Francisco Rock Experience, Debora Hill
The Wild Eyed Boy: A Press Account—the Factual & Sometimes Fictional Biography of David Bowie, Thomas R. Kamp

Led Zeppelin, Howard Mylett
Rod Stewart, Paul Nelson & Lester Bangs
Chase the Fade, Anne Nightingale
The Police Released, Proteus Pub.
The Bee Gees, Larry Pryce
Elvis Costello, Krista Reese
Giants of Rock Music, Pauline Rivelli & Robert Levin
A Day in the Life, Tom Schultheiss
The Police: Portrait of a Rock Band, Phil Sutcliffe & Hugh Fielder

Comics and Comic Strips in the Rock Era _____

1954

Peanuts comic strip begins . . . Comic books reach peak popularity with 650 titles available—selling over a billion copies a year . . . Senate Subcommittee hearings investigate charges that comic books are responsible for juvenile delinquency . . . *Marmaduke* begins long career in comics . . . Comics Code Authority formed. Authorized by Congressional legislation. Some of the self-regulating code taboos are: (A-2) No comics shall explicitly present the unique details and methods of crime; (A-5) Criminals shall not be presented as to be rendered glamorous; (A-6) In every instance good shall triumph over evil; (A-7) Scenes of excessive violence shall be prohibited; (A-8) No unique . . . methods of concealing weapons shall be shown; (A-11) The letters of the word "crime" . . . shall never be appreciably greater . . . than the other words contained in the title; (B-1) No comic magazine shall use the word "horror" or "terror" in its title; (B-5) Scenes dealing with or instruments associated with walking dead, torture, vampires and vampirism, ghouls, cannibalism and werewolfism are prohibited; (C-4) Females shall be drawn realistically without exaggeration of any physical qualities . . . 26 publishers agree to eliminate obscene, vulgar and horror comics from their lists . . . In his book, *Seduction of the Innocent,* Dr. Wertham begins a long-standing controversy by seeing a direct link with homosexual fancies in Batman and Robin; while maintaining that comic books were the roots of much juvenile delinquency . . . As "The Lone Ranger" departs from the radio airwaves, he leaves behind his 160th comic book, along with books, films and a multitude of paraphernalia . . . Artist Robert Rauschenberg gains notoriety using comic strip pages from newspapers as background to his abstract "paintings" . . . Comic books now have greater circulation than *Reader's Digest, Life, Ladies' Home Journal, McCall's* and *Better Homes and Gardens* combined . . .

1955

Comics Code Authority seal of approval appears on okayed comic books . . . *MAD Comics* becomes *MAD* magazine, as Comics Code makes approach difficult in original form . . . Many comic book publishers suspend publication as golden age ends . . . Thirteen states enact laws to control comic books' content . . . $100 million—four times the expenditure for public libraries—-paid out for comic books . . . Regularly issued comic books drop from 650 to 400 . . . University of California report estimates a billion comic books being sold annually . . . In his first 24 years as a detective, *Dick Tracy* has been blinded and shot and wounded 27 times, while collecting about 50 bullet-holed hats to show the extent of the near misses . . . New York State makes it illegal to sell obscene, objectionable comics to minors or to carry words like "crime," "sex," "horror" or "terror" in any title—with a dozen states soon following in similar fashion . . . Mort Walker's *Beetle Bailey* banned from *Stars and Stripes* for past year as being bad for soldiers' morale . . . During Davy Crockett craze, even *Charlie Brown* wears Crockett headgear . . .

1956

Jules Feiffer's cartoons debut in New York *Village Voice,* introducing psychoanalysis to comic strips . . . *L'il Abner* stars in Broadway musical . . . Success of *Archie* comic books serves as springboard for its launch as newspaper comic strip . . .

1957

Comic books in print drop from 400 to 250 . . . *Have Gun Will Travel* and *Tales of Wells Fargo* highlight wave of TV crossovers to comic books . . . *Captain America* comic books discontinued because of lack of reader interest . . .

1958

Comic hero *Kerry Drake* takes a wife . . . *Little Orphan Annie's* creator, Harold Gray, not amused by appearance of *Lulu Arfin' Nanny* in *Pogo* . . . In past 15 years, 64.2% of Sunday comic strips humorous vs. 35.8% adventure or melodrama, according to Francis E. Barcus research. Also, 73.8% of all strips set in America showed city life while 80.9% of foreign sites were portrayed as rural; and 72% of comic population was male, with most married men ruled by wives . . . Pop art pioneer, Jasper Johns, paints over *Alley Oop* . . . *Lois Lane* No. 1 comic book hits stands . . . *Steve Canyon* begins a second career on TV—while continuing into his 12th year in the comics . . .

1959

Eighth grade boys averaging 4.5 comic books a month. Twelfth graders average less than one . . . Two great comic strips of yesteryear, *Tillie the Toiler* and *The Gumps*, discontinued . . .

1960

Of the 39 new comic strips issued in past four years, 32 are of a humorous nature ("funnies") . . . *MAD* magazine receiving over 2,000 letters a week . . . Andy Warhol, who began using comic strip figures as models for his paintings last year, scores with *Dick Tracy* . . . *Ponytail* comic strip begins . . .

1961

Marvel Comic Books introduces *Amazing Adventures* and *The Fantastic Four*, starting new era of fantasy superheroes. The "four" are: scientist Reed Richards, who changes into rubberlike Mr. Fantastic; Benjamin Grimm, who becomes an orange-colored colossus, The Thing; Sue Storm, who transforms into the Invisible Girl, and her brother Johnny, the Human Torch . . .

1962

New boom in comics begins, but new superheroes—unlike those past—have a variety of neuroses and foibles . . . *Spider-Man* begins in *Amazing Fantasy Comics* No. 15 . . . Opinion Research survey of comic strip audience reports 100 million read Sunday comics, and daily audience just slightly smaller . . . Marvel Comics publishes first issue of *The Incredible Hulk* . . . Opinion Research survey of comic strip popularity places: (1) *Blondie*, (2) *Dick Tracy*, (3) *Little Orphan Annie*, (4) *Peanuts*, (5) *Rex Morgan, M.D.*, (6) *Dennis The Menace*, (7) *L'il Abner*, (8) *Mary Worth*, (9) *Nancy*, and (10) *Snuffy Smith* . . . *Little Annie Fanny* debuts in *Playboy* magazine as super-Playmate who is always threatened by a sex-obsessed world—thereby mocking its foibles . . . *Dr. Kildare* moves from TV to a comic strip . . .

1963

First issue of *Fantastic Four Annual* costs 25¢ . . . First publication of Marvel's *The Amazing Spider-Man* . . . Marvel's *Incredible Hulk* folds due to lack of support, but they find a new home for him in *The Avengers* . . . Pop art celebrity, Roy Lichtenstein, uses comic strip approach—including the screen of dots—to create some of the year's most important contributions to the art world . . .

1964

Marshall McLuhan claims that the ten-year-old's love of *MAD* magazine tells us what the 18-year-old beatniks first tried saying ten years ago—that the iconic age has replaced the Pictorial Consumer Age (the genteel art of "square" society) . . . Chester Gould introduces a comic strip called *Sawdust* as a subplot in *Dick Tracy*—commenting on the world of comics while poking fun at himself . . . *Captain America* returns as a "living legend" of World War II . . .

1965

East Village Other publishes one of first underground comix strips: *Captain High* . . . *Esquire* magazine notes that *Spider-Man* is as popular in the collegiate radical sector as Che Guevara . . . Hippies groove with Marvel's *Doctor Strange*, who lives in Greenwich Village . . . With "camp" at a peak, old film serial of *Batman* is revived, with all 15 episodes in a 4½-hour program—leading to his restored fame in print, TV and films . . . Marvel Comics' Merry Marvel Marching Society promises little for $1, and gets rush for membership . . . Ray Bradbury writes foreword for *The Collected Works of Buck Rogers in the 25th Century*, saying of the 12 adventures dating from 1929 to 1946: "Beaten down by dull reality, dying for romance, we waded out into a sea of space and happily drowned" . . . *Eerie* and *Creepy* magazines debut—telling stories in form of comic strips as journals rather than comic books . . . Negro girl removed from group of teenagers in *Brenda Starr*, as syndicate fears offending readers in Southern states . . . Syndicate censors turn down *Peanuts* sequence which has Linus's blanket coming to life and jumping at Lucy—on basis that such violence unacceptable to readership . . . Attempt to revive *The Shadow* in comic books fails—though reprints of novels starring him succeed at later date . . . *Tarzan* novels adapted to comic books in new series . . .

1966

Uninhibited underground comix take off in leading underground newspapers *Berkeley Barb*, *Los Angeles Free Press* and *Detroit Fifth Estate*, as Robert Crumb's *Captain High* hits in the *East Village Other* . . . A rare copy of Action Comic No. 1 sells for $2,000 . . . *The Spirit* brought out of retirement by Harvey Comics . . . Jules Feiffer calls *Li'l Abner* cartoonist Al Capp's praise of him in a *Playboy* interview a doubtful compliment, in view of Capp's opinions on social matters . . . Syndicate's censor fears that calling woman in *Kerry Drake* Jet Black might offend black readership, since the girl wasn't black. Name change to Sable Black okayed . . . Musical about *Superman* presented on Broadway stage . . . University of Texas magazine, *Texas Ranger*, carries one of first big underground comix, Gilbert Shelton's *Wonder Wart-Hog* . . .

1967

Peanuts reaches New York stage via the show *You're A Good Man, Charlie Brown . . . Star Trek* comic book published . . . *Peanuts* offshoots called a $15 million business by *Life* magazine . . .

1968

Captain America revived by Marvel Comics . . . First underground comic book, *Zap*, appears. Robert Crumb produces it under private imprint and gets big reception from hippies and their peers when it's hawked on street corners in San Francisco. In book, R. Crumb is joined by Rick Griffin, Victor Moscoso, and S. A. Wilson—soon to be recognized as leading underground comic cartoonists . . . With *Feds 'n' Heads* comic book, Gilbert Shelton becomes second only to R. Crumb in the ranks of radical cartoonists . . . *Doonesbury* debut set on Yale campus with cast of characters who would be recognizable in Haight Ashbury or Greenwich Village . . . *Wonder Woman* ends 17 Amazonian years by opening a fashion boutique and enjoying the sorrows of love, after doffing her star-spangled uniform . . . Close to 300 million comic books sold—with an estimated 100 million reading comic strips daily . . . Robert Crumb's *Fritz the Cat* first appears in men's magazine *Cavalier* . . .

1969

Top underground comix artist Robert Crumb's works exhibited at New York's Whitney Museum . . . *Spider-Man* almost overtakes *Superman* in sales . . . *Doonesbury*, by 20-year-old Garry Trudeau, is syndicated to first 25 of 300 newspapers which will carry it . . . Marvel pioneers love comic book field with *Our Love Story*—designed strictly for girls—and *My Love*, for a mixed audience—full of, as they call them, "groovy chicks" for the pin-up trade . . . Robert Crumb's *Fritz the Cat* appears in a small pamphlet, *R. Crumb's Comics and Stories* . . . *Batman* temporarily closes Bat-Cave and sends young assistant Dick Grayson (who aged only about four years since his first appearance in 1940) to college . . . Comics Magazines Association of America (CMAA) applied Code test to 18,125 comic books in past 5 years. This year 309 out of 1,000 books failed to satisfy the Authority, but most lapses minor . . . Bridgeport, Connecticut, Federal Court decision allows tax exemption on Mort Walker gift of $1,055 original *Beetle Bailey* drawings to Syracuse University, thereby setting a precedent in defining comics as works of art . . .

1970

Playboy article attacks underground comix as "obscene, anarchistic, sophomoric, subversive and apocalyptic" . . . *Steve Canyon* marries

Summer Olsen . . . *It Ain't Me Babe* is first comic book devoted exclusively to women's liberation . . . Competition to name koala bear in *Bower's Ark* in just a few papers draws 49,329 entries, with "Cubcake" winning out . . . Spiro Agnew immortalized in *Pogo* . . . Although *Li'l Abner's* creator, staunch conservative Al Capp, has had a big go at longhaired hippies and students, while criticizing police inability to enforce law and order, L'il Abner's hairstyle is trimmed in modern fashion . . . Torn by self-doubt, *Captain America* searches for a new image (a sort of "Easy Rider"), having traveled a full circle from his brief life as a "commie-smasher" during the McCarthy inquisition . . . *Captain America* joined by *The Falcon*, a black hero trained by him . . . Black comic strip heroine, *Friday Foster*, debuts . . . Modern-day superhero American Indian *Red Wolf* brought into focus in Marvel comic books . . . Comic books medium continues to grow (especially with 5-14 age group). Six publishers producing 170 titles a year with total circulation of 4.5 million copies. Three out of four purchasers read 5-25 books in average month . . .

1971

Comics Code policy eased to permit comic book stories dealing with drugs—as a menace. Strict dress codes are also liberalized, and the suggestion of seduction is now a possibility . . . Bantam Books and Dell publish collections of underground comix . . . Thirty new humorous comic strips made it in past 10 years, vs. 15 adventure strips . . . Currently 60-80% can be considered "funnies" . . . *Dennis the Menace* in 20th year is thriving daily in 700 newspapers around the world . . . *Skeezix* celebrates his 50th birthday on St. Valentine's Day . . . *Newsweek* reports that the *Peanuts* industry has grossed $150 million—including revenues from films, TV, dolls, books, toys, souvenirs, etc. . . . *Peanuts* children have only been made to age two to three years in the past 20 . . . Romance comic books make big comeback. Charlton alone publishes: *I Love You, Sweethearts, Love Diary, Time for Love, Teen Confessions*, and six more similar titles . . . In *The Amazing New Adventures of Superman*, after confrontation with a double, the superhero is humanized and is no longer the untiring machine who can give help anywhere at any time—making him more credible to newer generations . . . May issue of *Spider-Man* first comic book published by member of CMAA to appear without their approval: as seal of approval on the covers of many comic books becomes so small it is hardly missed, and liberalization of many Code points indicates gradual phase-out similar to what happened to Hollywood Hays code . . . *Superman* comic books issued in 1938 selling for $400 . . .

1972

Li'l Abner comic strip, now in its 38th year, has 80 million daily readers worldwide . . . *Archie* comic books averaging 50 million copies a year—

although he still drives an ancient car, and wears his hair short (post-World War II style), he now dresses differently—following the latest fashions . . . Number of main characters in *Pogo* comic strip passes 150 mark . . . Paperback reprint editions of *Peanuts* now over 60 million—ranking cartoonist Charles Schulz with bestselling authors like Erle Stanley Gardner and Mickey Spillane . . . *Classics Illustrated* sold over a billion copies in first 30 years, including translations in over 30 foreign languages—combining great literature with the comic book approach to awaken young reader interest in good books, never meant as a substitute. Each booklet says, "Don't miss the enjoyment of reading the original, obtainable at your school or public library" . . .

1973

Captain Marvel revived in *Shazam* comic book . . .

1975

President Ford says: "There are only three major vehicles to keep us informed as to what is going on in Washington: the electronic media, the print media and *Doonesbury* . . . not necessarily in that order" in speech to Radio and Television Correspondent Association . . . *Doonesbury* first comic strip ever to receive the Pulitzer Prize . . .

1976

Superman vs. the Amazing Spider-Man comic book published . . .

1977

Mickey Mouse celebrates his 50th birthday . . . *Spider-Woman* makes comic book appearance . . . Marvel Comic No. 1 sells for $7,000 . . .

1978

Superman comic strip becomes source of one of the top ten money-making films of all time . . . *Garfield* the cat makes his first newspaper appearance and becomes an instant hit with young people—with adults soon following . . .

1979

Drabble, by Kevin Fagan, currently the youngest syndicated cartoonist in the U.S. (135 newspapers), debuts in *Seventeen* . . . "The Amazing Spider-Man" and "The New Adventures of Wonder Woman," featuring Lynda

Carter, debut on CBS TV . . . Pre-*Superman* space hero goes Hollywood as success of Clark Kent's alter image on film inspires film of *Buck Rogers in the Twenty-First Century* . . . Now 50.3 million Sunday comics sections being distributed and read by over 100 million people . . . Another copy of *Marvel Comics* No. 1 sells for $13,000. The seller bought it two years ago for $5,500 from its owner, who bought the book for 10¢ in the fall of 1939 . . .

1980

Blondie comic strip 50 years old—in 1,200 newspapers worldwide . . . Garry "Doonesbury" Trudeau marries "Today" show hostess Jane Pauley, and mushrooming Preppy movement welcomes the match as the news media-Prep couple of the '80s . . . Movie version of comic strip *Popeye* one of top grossing films of the year . . .

1981

Dick Tracy into 50th year of crime fighting . . . Comics hero *Flash Gordon* featured in major film, as *Superman II* follows giant success of 1978 original . . . "Buck Rogers" revived on TV in a new series . . . Nearly 30 million U.S. comic book collectors purchase 138 million new comic books from estimated 5,000 dealers . . . Comic Book Price Guide, now in 12th edition, requires 400 double-column pages to list nearly all comic books printed from 1900 to date. Full run of mint condition Action Comics, the book that introduced *Superman,* is listed at $37,440 for the 500 books. The same run was priced at $2,354 ten years ago . . . *Comic Vendor* publisher says fewer than 300 of the 17,000 comic book titles published to date have any real investment value . . . Los Angeles book dealer thinks reason a pulp comic book can sell for from $13,000 to $17,000, vs. $950 for an "exeptionally clean, bright" first edition of Mark Twain's *Huckleberry Finn,* is that "comic books were never saved" as books being undervalued and relatively cheap relative to other collectibles . . . Expert on collectibles at the famous Sotheby's auction house in New York feels comic books may be a passing craze among collectors . . . Now seven *Garfield* books in print, plus 1.25 million *Garfield* calendars—as well as dolls, notepaper, pencil boxes, coffee mugs and other gift items . . .

Bibliography

Allen, Margaret. *Selling Dreams* (London: J. M. Dent & Sons Ltd., 1981).

American Chamber of Commerce Researchers Association (ACCRA). *Price Report: Inter-City Cost of Living Indicators—205 Cities.*

American Film Institute Catalog: Feature Films 1961-70 (New York: R. R. Bowker, 1976).

Bacon, Tony, ed. *Rock Hardware* (Poole, Dorset, U.K.: Blandford Press, 1981).

Baker, R. *New and Improved* (London: The British Library Board, 1976).

Basic Petroleum Data Book (American Petroleum Institute, 1978).

Bassett, Michael. *The American Deal* (London: Heinemann, 1975).

Batterberry, Michael, and Batterberry, Ariane. *Mirror Mirror* (New York: Holt, Reinhart & Winston, 1977).

Belz, Carl. *The Story of Rock* (New York: Harper & Row, 1969).

Berger, Arthur Asa. *Pop Culture* (Dayton, Ohio: Pflaum/Standard, 1973).

Bernard, Barbara. *Fashion in the 60's* (New York: St. Martin's Press, 1978).

Birnbach, Lisa, ed. *The Official Preppy Desk Diary 1982* (New York: Workman Publishing, 1981).

Birnbach, Lisa, ed. *The Official Preppy Handbook* (New York: Workman Publishing, 1980).

Black, J. Anderson, and Garland, Madge. *A History of Fashion* (London: William Morrow, 1975).

Black, J. Anderson, and Garland, Madge. *In Fashion.* Revised by Kennett, Frances (London: Orbis Publishing, 1980).

Blair, Walter, and Hill, Hamlin. *America's Humor* (New York: Oxford University Press, 1978).

Books in Print (New York: Bowker, 1960-81 editions).

The Bowker Annual of Library and Book Trade Information 1980. Simora, Filomena, ed. (New York: R. R. Bowker, 1980).

Bozzell, Robert D., Cox, Donald F., and Brown, Rex V. *Marketing Research and Information Systems* (New York: McGraw-Hill, 1969).

Brooke, Tim, and Marsh, Earle. *The Complete Directory to Prime Time Network TV Shows, 1945-Present* (New York: Ballantine Books, 1979).

Brooks, John. *The Fate of the Edsel and Other Business Ventures* (London: Victor Gollancz, 1963).

Brooks, John. *The Great Leap: The Past Twenty-Five Years in America* (London: Victor Gollancz, 1967).

Brown, Joe David, and the Correspondents of *Time*. *The Hippies* (Chicago: Time Inc., 1967).

Brown, Les. *The New York Times Encyclopedia of TV* (New York: Times Books, 1977).

Browne, Ray B., Landrum, Larry, and Bottorff, William. *Challenges in American Culture* (Bowling Green, Ohio: Bowling Green University Press, 1970).

Bureau of the Census. *Historical Statistics of the United States—to 1957* (Washington, D.C.: U.S. Department of Commerce).

Burke, John D. *Advertising in the Marketplace* (New York: McGraw-Hill, 1980).

Burt, Rob, and North, Patsy. *The West Coast Story* (Secaucus, N.J.: Chartwell Books, 1977).

Butler, Albert. *Encyclopedia of Social Dance* (New York: Albert Butler Ballroom Dance Service, 1979).

Butler, Ivan. *The Horror Film* (New York: Thomas Yosloff, A. S. Barnes, 1979).

Cable, Mary, and Editors of *American Heritage*. *American Manners and Morals* (New York: American Heritage Publishing Co., 1969).

Calasibetta, Charlotte. *Fairchild's Dictionary of Fashion* (New York: Fairchild Publishing, 1975).

Cantor, Norman F. *The Age of Protest* (New York: Hawthorn Books, 1969).

Cantor, Norman F., and Werthman, Michael S. *The History of Popular Culture* (New York: Macmillan, 1968).

Cardew, Maren Lockwood. *The New Feminist Movement* (New York: Russell Sage Foundation, 1974).

Carlsen, G. Robert. *Books and the Teenage Reader* (New York: Harper & Row, 1980).

Carruth, Gorton. *The Encyclopedia of American Facts and Dates* (New York: Thomas Y. Crowell, 1959).

Carson, Rachel. *Silent Spring* (Boston: Houghton Mifflin, 1962).

Carter, Ernestine. *The Changing World of Fashion* (London: Weidenfeld & Nicolson, 1977.

Carter, Ernestine. *20th Century Fashion* (London: Eyre Methuen, 1975).

Castleman, Harry, and Podrazik, Walter. *The Beatles Again* (Ann Arbor: The Pierian Press, 1977).

Cavan, Sherri. *Hippies of the Haight* (St. Louis: New Critics Press, 1972).

Chafe, William Henry. *The American Woman* (New York: Oxford University Press, 1962).

Chapple, Steve, and Garofalo, Reebee. *Rock 'n' Roll is Here to Pay* (Chicago: Nelson-Hall, 1977).

Clark, Al, ed. *The Rock Yearbook 1982* (London: Virgin Books, 1981).

Clark, Dick. *Rock, Roll and Remember* (New York: Popular Library, 1976).

Clawson, Marion, and Knetsch, Jack L. *Economics of Outdoor Recreation* (Baltimore, Md.: Johns Hopkins Press, 1966).

Clements, John. *Chronology of the United States* (New York: McGraw-Hill, 1975).

Cohn, Nik. *Pop from the Beginning* (London: Granada Publishing, 1969).

Coleman, James. *The Adolescent Society* (New York: The Free Press/Macmillan, 1961).

Collis, John. *The Rock Primer* (London: Penguin Books, 1980).

Cooke, Alistair. *The Americans* (London: The Bodley Head, 1979).

Corson, Richard. *Fashions in Eyeglasses* (London: Peter Owen, 1967).

Corson, Richard. *Fashions in Hair* (London: Peter Owen, 1971).

Corson, Richard. *Fashions in Makeup* (London: Peter Owen, 1972).

Crawford, Hubert H. *Crawford's Encyclopedia of Comic Books* (Middle Village, New York: Jonathan David Publishers, 1978).

Cray, Ed. *Levi's* (Boston: Houghton Mifflin, 1978).

Cross, Jennifer. *The Supermarket Trap* (Bloomington: Indiana University Press, 1976).

Cummings, Tony. *The Sound of Philadelphia* (London: Methuen, 1975).

Daniels, Les. *Comix: A History of Comic Books in America* (London: Wildwood House, 1973).

David, Nina. *TV Season '76-'77* (Phoenix, Arizona: Oryx Press, 1978).

De Bono, Edward, ed. *Eureka!* (London: Thames & Hudson, 1974).

Deford, Frank. *There She Is* (New York: Penguin, 1978).

De Grazia, Sebastian. *Of Time, Work and Leisure* (New York: The Twentieth Century Fund, 1962).

Dellar, Fred. *NME Guide to Rock Cinema* (London: Hamlyn, 1981).

Dempsey, Michael. *Knockin' on Dylan's Door* (San Francisco: Straight Arrow Publications, 1974).

Denisoff, R. Serge. *Solid Gold* (New Brunswick, N.J.: Transaction Books, 1975).

Denisoff, R. Serge, and Peterson, Richard A. *The Sounds of Social Change* (Skokie, Ill.: Rand McNally, 1972).

Dethloff, Henry C. *Americans and Free Enterprises* (Englewood Cliffs, N.J: Prentice-Hall, 1979).

Dickson, Paul. *The Great American Ice Cream Book* (New York: Atheneum, 1972).

Direnzo, Gordon J., ed. *We, the People: American Character and Social Change* (Westport, Conn.: Greenwood Press, 1977).

Dodds, John W. *Everyday Life in Twentieth Century America* (New York: G. P. Putnam's Sons, 1960).

Dollar, Charles M., ed. *America: Changing Times* (New York: John Wiley & Sons, 1979).

Dorner, Jane. *Fashion* (London: Octopus, 1974).

Dorner, Jane. *Fashions in the Forties and Fifties* (Westport, Conn.: Arlington House, 1975).

Dufour, Barry. *The World of Pop and Rock* (London: Macdonald Educational, 1977).

Edwards, John. *The Seventies* (London: Macdonald Educational, 1980).

Edwards, Joseph. *Top 10s and Trivia and R&B, 1950-1975* (St. Louis: Blueberry Hill Publishing Co., 1976).

Ehrenreich, Barbara, and Ehrenreich, John. *The American Health Empire* (New York: Vintage Books, 1971).

Ehrenreich, Barbara, and Ehrenreich, John. *Long March, Short Spring* (New York: Monthly Review Press, 1969).

Eisen, Jonathan, ed. *The Age of Rock 2* (New York: Vintage Books/Random House, 1970).

Encyclopaedia Britannica "Book of the Year" (Chicago: Encyclopaedia Britannica, annual).

Encyclopedia Americana (New York: Americana Corporation, 1977).

Erikson, Erich, ed. *Youth: Change and Challenge* (New York: Basic Books, 1963).

Erickson, Robert S., Luttberg, Norman T., and Tedin, Kent L. *American Public Opinion* (New York: John Wiley & Sons, 1980).

Ewing, Elizabeth. *Dress and Undress* (New York: Drama Books Specialists, 1978).

Ewing, Elizabeth. *Fashion in Underwear* (London: B. T. Batsford, 1971).

Ewing, Elizabeth. *History of 20th Century Fashion* (London: B. T. Batsford, 1977).

Facts on File. (New York: Facts on File, weekly).

Fairlie, Henry. *The Spoiled Child of the Western World* (New York: Doubleday, 1975).

Farren, Mick, and Snow, George. *Rock 'n Roll Circus* (London: Pierrot Publishing, 1978).

Fawcett, Anthony. *John Lennon: One Day at a Time* (New York: Grove Press, 1976).

Felton, Bruce, and Bowler, Mark. *Best, Worst and Most Unusual* (New York: Thomas Y. Crowell, 1975).

Fireman, Judy. *TV Book* (New York: Workman Publishing, 1977).

Fishwick, Marshall. *Parameters of Popular Culture* (Bowling Green, Ohio: Bowling Green University Popular Press, 1974).

Flattery, Paul. *The Illustrated History of British Pop* (New York: Drake Publishers, 1973).

Flexner, Stuart Berg. *I Hear America Talking* (New York: Van Nostrand Reinhold, 1976).

Fortune Editors. *Consumerism* (New York: Harper & Row, 1972).

Fox, Jack, ed. *Youthquake* (New York: Look/UPI/Cowles Educational Books, 1967).

Frame, Pete. *Rock Family Trees* (London: Omnibus Press, 1980).

Freedland, Nat. *The Occult Explosion* (London: Michael Joseph, 1972).

Frith, Simon. *The Sociology of Rock* (London: Constable, 1978).

Fullerton, Timothy T. *Trivia: A Compendium of Useless Information* (New York: Hart Publishing, 1975).

Garland, Phyl. *The Sound of Soul* (Chicago: Henry Regency, 1969).

Garraty, John A. *The American Nation: A History of the U.S.* (New York: Harper & Row, 1979).

Gertner, Richard, ed. *International Motion Picture Almanac* (New York: Quigley Publishing Co., annual).

Gertner, Richard, ed. *International Television Almanac* (New York: Quigley Publishing Co., annual).

Gies, Joseph. *Wonders of the Modern World* (New York: Thomas Y. Crowell Co., 1966).

Gilbert, Eugene. *Advertising and Marketing to Young People* (New York: Printers Ink Books, 1957).

Gilder, George. *Sexual Suicide* (London: Millington, 1974).

Gillett, Charlie. *The Sound of the City: The Rise of Rock and Roll* (London: Outerbridge & Dienstfrey, 1970).

Gillett, Charlie, and Frith, Simon. *Rock File 4* (London: Granada Publishing, 1976).

Gleason, Ralph J. *The Jefferson Airplane and the San Francisco Sound* (New York: Ballantine Books, 1967).

Glessing, Robert J. *The Underground Press in America* (Bloomington, Ind.: Indiana University Press, 1970).

Glynn, Prudence. *In Fashion* (London: George Allen & Unwin, 1978).

Gold, Annalee. *75 Years of Fashion* (New York: Fairchild Publishing, 1975).

Goldman, Eric F. *The Crucial Decade—and After: America 1945-60* (New York: Vintage Books/Random House, 1960).

Goldstein, Stewart, and Jacobson, Alan. *Oldies But Goodies* (New York: Mason/Charter, 1977).

Goodman, Paul. *Growing Up Absurd* (New York: Vintage Books, 1960).

Gorey, Hays. *Nader* (New York: Grossett & Dunlap, 1975).

Gray, Andy. *Great Pop Stars* (London: Hamlyn, 1974).

Greer, Thomas V. *Cases in Marketing* (New York: Macmillan, 1979).

Grenville, G. S. P. Freeman. *Chronology of World History (to 1973)* (London: Rex Collings, 1975).

Grinder, Robert E. *Adolescence* (New York: John Wiley & Sons, 1978).

Gross, Michael., *Bob Dylan: An Illustrated History* (New York: Grossett & Dunlap, 1978).

Gross, Michael, and Jakubowski, Maxim. *The Rock Year Book 1981* (London: Virgin Books, 1980).

Grossman, Loyd. *A Social History of Rock Music* (New York: David McKay Co., 1976).

Grun, Bernard. *The Timetables of History* (New York: Simon & Schuster, 1975).

Gunderson, Gerald. *A New Economic History of America* (New York: McGraw-Hill, 1976).

Hackett, Alice Payne, and Burke, James Henry. *80 Years of Best Sellers, 1895-1975* (New York: R. R. Bowker, 1977).

Hague, John A., ed. *American Character and Culture in a Changing World* (Westport, Conn.: Greenwood Press, 1979).

Hamm, Charles. *Yesterdays: Popular Song in America* (New York: W. W. Norton, 1979).

The Hammond Almanac 1980 (Maplewood, N.J.: Hammond Almanac Inc., 1979).

Hardy, Phil, and Laing, Dave. *Encyclopedia of Rock 1955-75* (London: Aquarius Books, 1977).

Hargreaves, Robert. *Superpower: America in the 1970s* (London: Hodder & Stoughton, 1974).

Harrop, David. *America's Paychecks: Who Makes What* (New York: Facts on File Publications, 1980).

Harte, Barbara, and Riley, Carolyn, eds. *Contemporary Authors* (Detroit: Gale Research, 1963).

Hechinger, Grace, and Hechinger, Fred M. *Teen-Age Tyranny* (New York: Morrow, 1962).

Helitzer, Melvin, and Heyer, Carl. *The Youth Market* (New York: Media Books, 1970).

Heron, House, ed. *The Book of Numbers* (New York: A&W Publishers, 1978).

Hess, John L., and Hess, Karen. *The Taste of America* (New York: Grossman Publishers, 1977).

Hill, Gladwin. *Madman in a Lifeboat: Issues of the Environmental Crisis* (New York: New York Times Book Company, 1973).

Hoare, Ian. *The Soul Book* (London: Eyre Methuen, 1975).

Hochman, Stanley. *Yesterday and Today: A Dictionary of Recent American History* (New York: McGraw-Hill, 1979).

Hodson, H. V., ed. *The Annual Register* (New York: Longman).

Holdstock, Robert, ed. *Encyclopedia of Science Fiction* (London: Octopus Books, 1978).

Hopkins, Jerry. *Festival!* (New York: Macmillan, 1970).

Horn, Marilyn J. *The Second Skin* (Boston: Houghton Mifflin, 1975).

Horsley, Edith. *The 1950s* (London: Bison Books, 1979).

Hougan, Jim. *Decadence (Radical Nostalgia, Narcissism and Decline in the Seventies)* (New York: William Morrow, 1975).

Howell, Georgina. *In Vogue* (New York: Schocken Books, 1976).

Information Please Almanac. (New York: Simon & Schuster, annual).

Inge, M. Thomas, ed. *Handbook of American Popular Culture*, 3 Vols. (Westport, Conn.: Greenwood Press, 1979, 1980, 1981).

Jahn, Mike. *Rock* (New York: Quadrangle-The New York Times Book Co., 1973).

Janowitz, Morris. *The Last Half Century: Societal Changes and Politics in America* (Chicago: University of Chicago Press, 1978).

Jasper, Tony. *The 70's Book of Records* (London: Macdonald Futura, 1981).

Jenkinson, Philip, and Warner, Alan. *Celluloid Rock* (Farncombe, Surrey, U.K.: Lorrimer Publishing, 1974).

Jensen, Malcolm C. *America in Time* (Boston: Houghton Mifflin, 1977).

Kahn, Herman. *The Next 200 Years* (London: Associated Business Programmes, 1977).

Kahn, Herman, and Wiener, Anthony J. *The Year 2000* (New York: Macmillan, 1969).

Kane, Joseph Nathan. *Famous First Facts* (New York: H. W. Wilson, 1964).

Katona, George. *The Mass Consumption Society* (New York: McGraw-Hill, 1964).

Katona, George. *The Powerful Consumer* (New York: McGraw-Hill, 1960).

Keenan, Brigid. *The Women We Wanted to Look Like* (London: Macmillan, 1977).

Keesing's Contemporary Archives (London: Keesing's Publications-Longman, annual).

Keyes, Jean. *A History of Women's Hairstyles, 1500-1965* (London: Methuen, 1967).

Klapp, Orrin E. *Collective Search for Identity* (New York: Holt, Reinhart & Winston, 1969).

Klapp, Orrin E. *Heroes, Villains and Fools* (Englewood Cliffs, N.J.: Prentice-Hall, 1962).

Knowles, Ruth Sheldon. *America's Oil Famine* (New York: Coward, McCann & Geoghegan, 1975).

Kraus, Richard. *Recreation and Leisure in Modern Society* (New York: Appleton-Century-Crofts, 1971).

Kursch, Harry. *The Franchise Boom* (Englewood Cliffs, N.J.: Prentice-Hall, 1969).

LaFeber, Walter, and Polenberg, Richard. *The American Century* (New York: Wiley, 1979).

Laing, Dave, Dallas, Karl, Denselow, Robin, and Shelton, Robert. *The Electric Muse* (London: Eyre Methuen, 1975).

Landau, Jon. *It's Too Late to Stop Now* (San Francisco: Straight Arrow Books, 1972).

Landy, Eugene F. *The Underground Dictionary* (London: MacGibbon & Kee, 1971).

Langer, William L. *An Encyclopedia of World History* (Boston: Houghton Mifflin, 1972).

Leech, Kenneth. *Youthquake* (London: Sheldon Press, 1973).

Leerburger, Benedict A., Jr., managing ed. *Cowles Encyclopedia of Science, Industry and Technology* (New York: Cowles Education Corporation, 1967).

Leuchtenburg, Wiliam E. *A Troubled Feast: American Society Since 1945* (Boston: Little, Brown, 1973).

Leuchtenburg, William E., ed. *The Unfinished Century: America Since 1900* (Boston: Little, Brown, 1963).

Lewis, Peter. *The 50s* (London: Heinemann, 1978).

Lichty, Lawrence W., and Topping, Malachi C. *American Broadcasting* (New York: Hastings House, 1976).

Lincoln Center Library, New York: Dance Division clipping files.

Lindof, Edmond. *An Album of the Fifties* (New York: Franklin Watts, 1978).

Linton, Calvin D., and Payne, Wayne A. *The American Almanac* (New York: Thomas Nelson, 1977).

Lipset, Seymour Martin. *Rebellion in the University* (London: Routledge & Keegan Paul, 1972).

Lipton, Lawrence. *The Erotic Revolution* (Nashville, Tenn.: Sherbourne Press, 1965).

Lipton, Lawrence. *The Holy Barbarians* (New York: Julian Messner, 1957).

Logan, Nick, and Woffinden, Bob. *The Illustrated New Musical Express Encyclopedia of Rock* (London: Salamander Books, 1977).

Los Angeles Chamber of Commerce Research Committee. *The Dynamics of the Youth Explosion* (Los Angeles Chamber of Commerce, 1967).

Lukenbill, W. Bernard, ed. *Media and the Young Adult* (Chicago: American Library Association, 1977).

Macken, Bob, Fornatale, Peter, and Ayres, Bill. *The Rock Music Source Book* (New York: Doubleday, 1980).

MacNeil, Robert. *The People Machine* (London: Eyre & Spottiswoode, 1970).

Maltin, Leonard, ed. *TV Movies: 1981-82 Edition* (New York: New American Library, 1980).

Manchester, William. *The Glory and the Dream (1932-72)* (Boston: Little Brown, 1974).

Manning, Peter K., and Truzzi, Marcello. *Youth and Sociology* (Englewood Cliffs, N.J.: Prentice-Hall, 1972).

Marchbank, Pearce, and Miles. *The Illustrated Rock Almanac* (London: Paddington Press, 1977).

Marcus, Greil, ed. *Stranded: Rock and Roll for a Desert Island* (New York: Alfred A. Knopf, 1979).

Marsh, Dave, and Stein, Kevin. *The Book of Rock Lists* (New York: Dell, 1981).

Mattfeld, Julius. *Variety Music Cavalcade* (New York: Prentice-Hall, 1962).

McCabe, Peter, and Shonfeld, Robert B. *Apple to the Core* (London: Sphere Books, 1973).

McCarthy, Joseph F. *Record of America: A Reference History of the United States* (New York: Charles Scribner's Sons, 1974).

McCormick, Donald. *Approaching 1984* (Newton Abbott, U.K.: David & Charles, 1980).

McLuhan, Marshall. *Culture Is Our Business* (New York: McGraw-Hill, 1970).

McLuhan, Marshall. *Understanding Media* (London: Routledge & Keegan Paul, 1964).

McWhirter, Norris, ed. *The Guinness Book of World Records* (New York: Sterling Publishing Co., 1980).

Mehnert, Klaus. *The Twilight of the Young* (London: Secker & Warburg, 1978).

Merriam, Eve. *Figleaf: The Business of Being in Fashion* (Philadelphia: J. B. Lippincott Co., 1960).

Mezzrow, Milton "Mezz," and Wolfe, Bernard. *Really the Blues* (New York: Random House, 1946).

Michener, James A. *Michener on Sport* (New York: McGraw-Hill, 1976).

Milinaire, Caterine, and Troy, Carol. *Cheap Chic* (New York: Harmony Books/ Crown Publishers, 1975).

Miller, Douglas, and Nowak, Marian. *The Fifties* (New York: Doubleday, 1977).

Miller, Jim, ed. *Rolling Stone Illustrated History of Rock & Roll* (New York: Random House, 1980).

Mintz, Morton, and Cohen, Jerry S. *America Inc.* (New York: Dial Press, 1971).

Mirkin, Stanford H. *What Happened When* (New York: Ives Washburn, 1966).

Miron, Charles. *Rock Gold (All the Hit Charts from 1955-76)* (New York: Drake, 1977).

Moore, Truman. *Nouveaumania* (New York: Random House, 1975).

Morris, Richard B. *Encyclopedia of American History* (New York: Harper & Row, 1976).

Morris, Richard B., and Irwin, Graham W. *An Encyclopaedia of the Modern World* (New York: Harper & Row, 1970).

Moskowitz, Milton, Katz, Michael, and Levering, Robert, eds. *Everybody's Business* (New York: Harper & Row, 1980).

Murrells, Joseph. *The Book of Golden Discs* (London: Barrie & Jenkins, 1978).

Myra, Harold, and Merrill, Dean. *Rock, Bach and Superschlock* (Nashville, Tenn.: A. J. Holman, 1972).

Nanry, Charles, ed. *American Music from Storyville to Woodstock* (Brunswick, N.J.: Transaction Books, 1972).

National Automobile Dealers Used Car Guide Co. *N.A.D.A. Official Used Car Guide January 1980—Eastern Edition*. McLean, Virginia.

National Center for Education Statistics, 1980. *The American High School—A Statistical Overview*. Washington, D.C.

Neville, Richard. *Playpower* (London: Jonathan Cape, 1970).

New York Times Directory of the Theater (New York: New York Times Book Co., 1972).

Nite, Norm N. *Rock On* (New York: Thomas Y. Crowell, 1974).

Norback, Craig T., and Norback, Peter G. *TV Guide Almanac* (New York: Ballantine Books, 1980).

Nord Media Inc. *The Video Business Guide* (New York: Nord Media, 1980).

Nugent, Stephen, and Gillett, Charles. *Rock Almanac* (New York: Anchor Books, 1978).

Nye, Russel. *The Unembarrassed Muse: The Popular Arts in America* (New York: Dial Press, 1970).

O'Neill, William L. *Coming Apart: An Informal History of the 60s* (1971).

Packard, Vance. *The Hidden Persuaders* (New York: David McKay Co., 1957).

Packard, Vance. *A Nation of Strangers* (New York: David McKay Co., 1972).

Packard, Vance. *The Sexual Wilderness* (New York: Longmans, 1968).

Packard, Vance. *The Waste Makers* (New York: Longmans, Green & Co., 1961).

Partridge, William L. *The Hippie Ghetto* (New York: Holt, Reinhart and Winston, 1973).

Pascall, Jeremy. *The Illustrated History of Rock Music* (London: Hamlyn, 1978).

Pascoe, L. C., ed. *Encyclopaedia of Dates and Events* (London: English Universities Press, 1974).

Passell, Peter. *The Best, Encore* (New York: Kimble Mead, 1977).

Passman, Arnold. *The Deejays* (New York: Macmillan, 1971).

Patterson, James T. *America in the Twentieth Century* (New York: Harcourt Brace Jovanovich, 1976).

Peellaert, Guy. *Rock Dreams* (Leyikont Discographie, 1973).

Perry, George, and Aldridge, Alan. *The Penguin Book of Comics* (New York: Penguin Books, 1967).

Peterson, Deena. *A Practical Guide to the Women's Movement* (New York: Women's Action Alliance, 1975).

Pichaske, David. *A Generation in Motion* (New York: Schirmer Books, Macmillan, 1979).

Polakoff, Keith, Rosenberg, N., Bolton, G., Story, R., and Schwarz, J. *Generation of Americans* (New York: St. Martin's Press, 1976).

Propes, Steve. *Golden Goodies* (Radnor, Pa.: Chilton Book Co., 1975).

Propes, Steve. *Those Oldies But Goodies* (New York: Collier Books, Macmillan, 1973).

Queensbury Group. *The Book of Key Facts* (London: Paddington Press, 1978).

Ramo, Simon. *America's Technology Slip* (New York: John Wiley & Sons, 1980).

Reader's Digest. *Almanac.* (Pleasantville, N.Y.: Reader's Digest Association, annual).

Reader's Digest. *Great Events of the 20th Century* (Pleasantville, N.Y.: Reader's Digest Association, 1977).

The Readers Guide to Periodical Literature (New York: H. W. Wilson, annual).

Reich, Charles A. *The Greening of America* (New York: Random House, 1970).

Reitberger, Reinhold, and Fuchs, Wolfgang. *Comics: Anatomy of a Mass Medium* (London: Studio Vista, 1972).

Robertson, Patrick. *The Book of Firsts* (New York: Clarkson N. Potter, 1974).

Robinson, Jerry. *The Comics* (New York: G. P. Putnam's Sons, 1974).

Robinson, Lilian S. *Sex, Class and Culture* (Bloomington, Ind.: Indiana University Press, 1978).

Rolling Stone Editors. *The Age of Paranoia* (San Francisco: Straight Arrow Publishers, 1972).

Root, Waverly, and De Rochemont, Richard. *Eating in America* (New York: William Morrow, 1976).

Rosen, Stephen. *Future Facts* (New York: Simon & Schuster, 1976).

Rosenberg, Bernard, and White, David Manning, eds. *Mass Culture Revisited* (New York: Van Nostrand Reinhold Co., 1971).

Rosencranz, Mary Lou. *Clothing Concepts* (New York: Macmillan, 1972).

Roxon, Lillian. *Rock Encyclopedia* (New York: Grossett & Dunlap, 1969, 1971, 1978).

Ryan, Mary P. *Womanhood in America: New Viewpoints* (New York: Franklin Watts, 1974).

Ryan, Mary Shaw. *Clothing* (New York: Holt, Reinhart & Winston, 1960).

Sann, Paul. *The Angry Decade: The Sixties* (New York: Crown, 1979).

Sann, Paul. *Fads, Follies and Delusions of the American People* (New York: Crown, 1967).

Scheiber, Harry N., Vatter, Harold G., and Faulkner, Harold U. *American Economic History* (New York: Harper & Row, 1976).

Schever, Steven H. *The Television Annual 1978-79* (New York: Macmillan, 1979).

Schramm, Wilbur, Lyle, Jack, and Parker, Edwin B. *Television in the Lives of Our Children* (Palo Alto, Calif.: Stanford University Press, 1968).

Scott Publishing Co., ed. *Scott Specialized Catalogue of U.S. Stamps* (New York: Scott Stamp and Coin, annual).

Selbie, Robert. *The Anatomy of Costume* (London: Mills & Boon, 1977).

Shaw, Arnold. *The Rockin' 50's* (New York: Hawthorn Books, 1974).

Shaw, Arnold. *The Rock Revolution* (New York: Crowell Collier, 1969).

Sichel, Marion. *Costume Reference 10, 1950 to the Present Day* (London: B. T. Batsford, 1979).

Sigel, Efrem, Schubin, Mark, and Merrill, Paul. *Video Discs* (White Plains, N.Y.: Knowledge Industries Publications, 1980).

Simmons, J. L., and Winograd, Barny. *It's Happening* (Santa Barbara, Calif.: McNally & Loftin, 1967).

Skolnik, Peter L., Torbet, Laura, and Smith, Nikki. *Fads (from the 1890s to the 1970s)* (New York: Thomas Y. Crowell, 1972, 1978).

Snowman, Daniel. *Kissing Cousins: An Interpretation of British and American Culture, 1945-75* (London: Temple Smith, 1977).

Sontag, Susan. *Against Interpretation* (New York: Farrar, Straus & Giroux, 1967).

Stambler, Irwin. *Encyclopedia of Pop, Rock and Soul* (New York: St. Martin's Press, 1974).

Stambler, Irwin, and Landon, Grelun. *Encyclopedia of Folk, Country and Western Music* (New York: St. Martin's Press, 1969).

Star, Steven H., Davis, Nancy J., Lovelock, Christopher H., and Shapiro, Benson P. *Problems in Marketing* (New York: McGraw-Hill, 1977).

Stearns, Marshall, and Stearns, Jean. *Let's Dance* (New York: Macmillan, 1968).

Stein, Peter J. *Single* (New York: Prentice-Hall, 1976).

Story of Pop (London: Phoebus Publishing Co., Octopus Books, 1974).

Taishoff, Sol, ed. *Broadcasting Cable Yearbook* (Washington, D.C.: Broadcasting Publications, 1981).

Talarzyk, W. Wayne. *Contemporary Cases in Marketing* (New York: The Dryden Press, 1979).

Taylor, Derek. *As Time Goes By* (San Francisco: Straight Arrow Books, 1973).

Tobler, John, and Frame, Pete. *25 Years of Rock* (London: Hamlyn, 1980).

Toffler, Alvin. *Future Shock* (London: The Bodley Head, 1970).

Trager, James. *The People's Chronology* (London: Heinemann, 1980).

Trapunski, Edward. *Special When Lit: A Visual and Anecdotal History of Pinball* (New York: Doubleday, 1979).

U.S. Bureau of the Census. *The Statistical Abstract of the United States* (Washington, D.C., annual).

U.S. Department of Agriculture. *National Food Review* (Washington, D.C., quarterly).

U.S. Department of Labor, Bureau of Labor Statistics. *Estimated Retail Food Prices* (Washington, D.C., monthly).

Van Doren, Charles, and McHenry, Robert, eds. *Webster's Guide to American History* (Springfield, Mass.: G. & C. Merriam, 1971).

Vassal, Jacques. *Electric Children*. Translated and adapted by Barnett, Paul. (New York: Taplinger Publishing Co., 1976).

Von Hoffman, Nicholas. *We Are the People Our Parents Warned Us Against* (New York: Quadrangle, 1968).

Wallechinsky, David, and Wallace, Irving. *The Book of Lists* (New York: William Morrow, 1977).

Wallechinsky, David, and Wallace, Irving. *The People's Almanac* (New York: Doubleday, 1975).

Wallechinsky, David, and Wallace, Irving. *The People's Almanac No. 2* (New York: Bantam, 1978).

Wentworth, Harold, and Flexner, Stuart. *Dictionary of American Slang*, 2nd ed. (New York: Thomas Y. Crowell, 1975).

White, David Manning, and Abel, Robert H. *The Funnies* (New York: The Free Press of Glencoe/Macmillan, 1963).

White, David Manning, ed. *Pop Culture in America* (New York: Quadrangle/New York Times, 1970).

Wilcox, Ruth Turner. *The Dictionary of Costume* (New York: Charles Scribner's Sons, 1969).

Wilcox, Ruth Turner. *The Mode in Costume* (New York: Charles Scribner's Sons, 1958).

Williams, Neville. *Chronology of the Modern World, 1763-1965* (London: Penguin Books, 1975).

Williams, William Appleman. *Americans in a Changing World* (New York: Harper & Row, 1978).

Wills, Gordon, and Midgley, David. *Fashion Marketing: An Anthology* (London: George Allen & Unwin, 1973).

Wolfe, Tom. *The Electric Kool-Aid Acid Test* (London: Weidenfeld & Nicolson, 1968).

Wolfe, Tom. *The Kandy-Kolored Tangerine-Flake Streamline Baby* (London: Jonathan Cape, 1966).

Wolfe, Tom. *Mauve Gloves and Madmen, Clutter and Vine* (New York: Bantam Books, 1977).

Women's Bureau, Office of the Secretary, U.S. Department of Labor. *Conference Report: Young Women and Employment, 1978* (Washington, D.C.: U.S. Department of Labor, 1978).

World Almanac (New York: Newspaper Association Enterprises, 1954-1981).

Worth, Fred L. *The Trivia Encyclopedia* (Los Angeles: Brooke House, 1974).

Wuthnow, Robert. *The Consciousness Reformation* (Berkeley, Calif.: University of California Press, 1976).

Yablonsky, Lewis. *The Hippie Trip* (Racine, Wis.: Western Publishing Company, 1968).

Yarwood, Doreen. *The Encyclopedia of World Costume* (New York: Charles Scribner's Sons, 1978).

Year (New York: Year/News Front, annual).

Year/News Front Editors. *Historic Decade 1950-60* (1960 Edition of *Year*). (New York: Year/News Front, 1960).

York, Ritchie. *The History of Rock and Roll* (London: Methuen, 1976).

Zalkind, Ronald Z. *Contemporary Music Almanac 1980/81* (New York: Schirmer Books, 1980).

PERIODICALS

Advertising Age

American Heritage

The American Scholar

American Sociological Review

American Speech

ASCAP in Action

Billboard

Business Week

Current

Esquire

Fast Food

Forbes

Fortune

Good Housekeeping

Harpers

Harpers Bazaar

Journal of Popular Culture

Ladies' Home Journal

Life

Look

Mademoiselle

McCall's

Newsweek

New York

New York Review of Books

New York Times

Parents

People

Popular Music and Society

The Public Opinion Quarterly

Rolling Stone

Saturday Evening Post

Saturday Review of Literature

Senior Scholastic

Seventeen

Teen

Time

U.S. News and World Report

Variety

Woman's Home Companion

About the Author

Herb Hendler is an author and playwright. As vice-president and head of Capitol Records' Beechwood Music in the 1960s, he was associated with over a dozen Top 40 hits, including "Ode to Billy Joe" and Associations' "Cherish." Hendler was a part of the rock scene from its beginning until 1973 when he founded The Franklin School of Contemporary Studies in London. He resides in London currently.